EXPLORING SOCIAL CHANGE

Charles L. Harper
Creighton University

 PRENTICE HALL, Englewood Cliffs, New Jersey 07632

Library of Congress Cataloging-in-Publication Data

Harper, Charles L.
    Exploring social change.

    Bibliography: p.
    Includes index.
    1. Social change.   2. United States—Social
conditions—1945–   .   3. Social movements.   I. Title.
HM101.H285   1989   303.4   88-9843
ISBN 0-13-295973-9

Editorial/production supervision: Linda B. Pawelchak
Cover design: Ben Santora
Manufacturing buyer: Ray Keating/Peter Havens

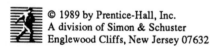 © 1989 by Prentice-Hall, Inc.
A division of Simon & Schuster
Englewood Cliffs, New Jersey 07632

Printed in the United States of America
10 9 8 7 6 5 4 3 2 1

ISBN   0-13-295973-9

Prentice-Hall International (UK) Limited, *London*
Prentice-Hall of Australia Pty. Limited, *Sydney*
Prentice-Hall Canada Inc., *Toronto*
Prentice-Hall Hispanoamericana, S.A., *Mexico*
Prentice-Hall of India Private Limited, *New Delhi*
Prentice-Hall of Japan, Inc., *Tokyo*
Simon & Schuster Asia Pte. Ltd., *Singapore*
Editora Prentice-Hall do Brasil, Ltda., *Rio de Janeiro*

For

Robert A. Harper (1899-1986)
Alma Hagy Harper (1901-1987)

...who gave me a world,

Anne

...who makes my world beautiful,

and

Russell and Stan

...who will inherit my world.

CONTENTS

3 ECONOMICS, POLITICS, AND THE MEANING OF CHANGE IN RECENT DECADES   33

Part Two
Explaining Change

4 THEORIES ABOUT THE CAUSES AND PATTERNS OF CHANGE   53

5 CONTEMPORARY SOCIOLOGICAL THEORY AND CHANGE   76

Part Three
Processes of Social Change

6 INNOVATIONS AND HOW THEY SPREAD   98

PREFACE

This is a book for all those who are curious about social change. It is also about how sociologists study change. It is thus about the substance of social change in the modern world and about major sociological ideas, concepts, and methods of inquiry that have been applied to the understanding of social change. I think the topic of social change is of intrinsic interest to everyone, since its pervasive impact is felt by all and is often the cause of considerable perplexity. Sociological perspectives are uniquely suited to illuminate social change because of their holistic treatment of the different aspects of social life that other disciplines (politics, law, economics) address in a more partial way. Sociology is also a lively and contentious discipline, and I have not ignored sociological controversies or omitted complex ideas that defy oversimplification. Yet I have tried to write a book for relative newcomers to sociology, avoiding the most arcane jargon and professional idiom for what I hope are clear language and fertile examples.

The contents of this book are based on what I think is important to communicate, based on years of teaching courses about social change. As with many books, it was born out of frustration with existing text materials. The book begins with a synoptic overview of recent change in American society. The middle chapters deal with selected change processes and with sociological theories of change. The later chapters are about global change processes in the modern world. A more descriptive overview of the chapter topics and organization of the book occurs at the end of Chapter 1, so I won't elaborate more here.

Many minds other than the author's are involved in writing a book. I would like to acknowledge my indebtedness to five teachers who have been particularly influential in my own intellectual development: Ray Cuzzort, Ernest Manheim, Oscar Eggers, Jerry Cloyd, and Jack Siegman. I would also like to thank my students and colleagues at Creighton University who suffered through critical reading of numerous (very) rough drafts and Dean William H. Cunningham of the College of Arts and Sciences of Creighton University, who provided a sabbatical leave that enabled me to write most of the book. I also owe a special debt of gratitude to the editorial staff of Prentice Hall, particularly to Bill Webber and Kathleen Dorman, for their continual encouragement and assistance.

A NOTE TO INSTRUCTORS

This is a compact but flexibly organized core text that can be used with a wide variety of supplements. Chapters are connected and developmental, but some may be omitted or treated in a different sequence with minimal loss of continuity. Here are a few suggestions for some optional ways of organizing the course.

For those desiring a more purely descriptive course about change in America and the world, Parts II and III dealing with theory, models, and change processes could be omitted entirely, though you may have to "decode" for students some references in Part IV about the material covered in the middle sections. Another alternative, more consistent with comparative and anthropological interests, would be to omit the American materials in Part I; begin with the materials on innovation and diffusion (in Chapter 6); and follow it with the materials on modernization, development, and world issues in Part IV. You can, of course, rearrange the sequence by having students read the theory and change process chapters first, but based on my teaching experience I don't recommend it. I deliberately placed the materials on change in American society first as a means of engaging students before addressing more conceptually demanding issues about theory, models, and processes.

There are, of course, a wide variety of supplementary materials that one could use to supplement and expand any chapter in the book, many available in soft cover. I have a list of such works that I would be happy to share with you if you write me either directly or through the publisher.

Charles L. Harper
Omaha, Nebraska

CHAPTER ONE
BY WAY OF
INTRODUCTION

It is impossible to live in the United States today without being bombarded with the reality and pervasiveness of change. The mass media are full of reports of new or continuing crises of grave international import in some little-known part of the world. It is also full of reports about changes in family life, health, and prospects for economic prosperity or decline. And then there are the fascinating and worrisome reports about the dazzling array of technological innovations, such as biotechnology and "computerization of everything," that have the potential to "revolutionize" our lives. While we live in a world that is pregnant with possibilities, it is also at times a frightening and hazardous world. The pace of change in general, and particularly the rate at which the world is becoming a single though highly disordered system, gives a kind of urgency to the notion that crisis is the ordinary state of social life. While it would be false to say social change is historically new, it is probably correct to say that people in modern societies are more likely to perceive change as the normal state of the world. Even though we are frightened and fascinated by change, we have come to expect it. Particularly in modern society, life is a journey, not a home.

We are bombarded by the big events of major world transformations, but social change is also the story of individuals and of differences between generations in families. Let me introduce the topic of social change by telling you a personal story about the world of my father and the world of my sons—and how they differ.

One day in January about ten years ago when my parents had come to visit I walked into the kitchen and observed my father just standing with the refrigerator door open looking into it. When I asked him what he was doing he said, "Well, I was just thinking that we didn't have all these different kinds of food when I was growing up."

My first impulse was to think, Here it comes, another story about the good/bad old days. But instead I asked him to explain. He was thinking particularly about the variety of fresh food (grapefruit, oranges, apples, lettuce, etc.) that was unavailable to him as a child, particularly in January. From that began a series of conversations in which I made a serious attempt to try to understand the world he lived in as a child.

My father was born in 1899 on a small farm in southeastern Missouri. His life, as far as I can tell, was typical of at least half of the American population at that time. Like most farmers of the late nineteenth century, the family farm was tied to a market economy. His father borrowed money from a bank to buy land, and corn and hogs were sold to make payment to the bank and to purchase seed for next year's crop. To me the most striking thing about his early life was the extent to which the family farm was a *subsistence* operation and not a money household economy. The family lived—almost literally—on what they could grow, produce, and store. His diet (to return to how I got into this) was mainly what could be made from corn, wheat, and salt pork. At the right time of the year there were fresh vegetables from the garden (some of which were canned for the winter), and in the fall there were a few apples from the tree. They did buy some household goods: kerosene for lamps, cloth, overalls and shoes (one pair a year), coffee, and sugar. There were "special" purchases from the mail order catalogue. Much of the money for these extras came from what his mother could produce in the vegetable garden and sell to the town grocer.

As you can see, his mother made a substantial contribution to the household economy, as did each child as he or she was old enough to help with the variety of farm and household chores. But though the family was a cooperative affair, his father was the unquestioned dictator of the family. Women and children in those times had no legal rights whatsoever, and only such privileges as were granted by the male head of the household. As in most American families of the time, *patriarchy* ruled supreme.

The social life of my father's family may seem dull by today's standards. It centered mainly around visiting with the neighbors, going to the country church—"when the weather was good,"—and a trip into town on Saturday (an all-day trip). Even though each farm was privately owned and managed, it was embedded in a community life that was strikingly different from that most of us experience today. During planting and harvest times the neighbors gathered in rotation at each other's farms to cooperatively share the labor. Women spent all day cooking for a grand feast after the day's labor. My father described these as exciting social events in an otherwise routine existence.

As a teenager—the term was not used then—my father was interested in the opposite sex (some things *don't* change!). Formal contacts between young men and women were different then. They did not date, but courted. Courtship was understood as a prelude to possible marriage and was under the strict control of parents. At one time my father said that he was courting two different girls, whereupon his mother sat him down and told him to "get serious and quit foolin' around." "Foolin' around" applied to seriousness of intent, not—as it would today—to premarital sexuality, which was strictly taboo in any case.

There were five children born into the family. One died during childbirth, one died as a teenager from tuberculosis, and one survived into adulthood as an invalid with what was called "spastic paralysis"—probably what today would be called polio. Only my father and a sister survived to become fully functional adults. This survival rate was not at all unusual for the time.

The thing that distinguished my father and his sister from their peers was that they finished high school (in 1910 only about one out of ten persons did). Not only did they finish high school, they both borrowed money from a bank and went to the regional teacher's college and were certified to teach. When I asked my father why he went into teaching (I expected an inspiring answer) he said that he had decided that there must be a better way to make a living than "walking behind a plow and the ass end of two mules," and that becoming a teacher was one of the only things you could do without having some money to start with. His first job was as the teacher in a nearby one-room country schoolhouse. Thus, he left the family farm in his early 20s and entered a very different world, one that was being born in the twentieth century. It was a world not of self-sufficient farms, but of cities, automobiles, salaries, and bureaucratic organizations. Today he remembers the farm life as a "hard one," but, like most older people, he is nostalgic about the lost world of his youth.

The world of my sons is very different, and since it is a more familiar one I will contrast it only briefly with that of my father.[1] My two sons have lived all their lives in a city of half a million people, a much more complex environment than that of my father. Because of improvements in diet and health care, their physical survival was never in question as it was for my father and his four siblings. The household in which my sons live is a *cash* economy, and unlike my father's household, all their material needs are purchased in local stores after being produced in remote parts of the nation—and the world. The only remnant of the family farm is the tomato patch which (in some years) provides seasonal condiment to the incredible variety of fresh and prepared foods available without regard to season at the local supermarket. While my father was able to observe his parents working on the farm and recognize the significance of their work—it showed up on the table—my son's parents (both of us) work for cash in large organizations remote from everyday family life. It was some years before my sons were able to understand where I went every day and what it meant to be a professor.

The social life and entertainments available to my sons seem varied and exciting when compared to those available during my father's youth. They have traveled to distant parts of the country: At their age, my father had never left the county of his birth. They grew up with the rich electronic fantasy world of television, Darth Vader, and video games, as well as the world of summer camps, soccer, softball leagues, and "Dungeons and Dragons." Unlike my father, they spend a great amount of time hanging around with their peers in settings that are only loosely monitored by adults. They are interested in the opposite sex (although only vaguely so, and not as much as many of their peers). They don't go courting, neither do they date (as I did in high school). They do hang around in amorphous heterosexual flocks at school events and parties. Like most children in middle class families they are urged not to get too serious too soon (but I'm sure there is some tentative "foolin' around" in the modern meaning of that phrase!).

The family life of my sons is different from that of their grandfather. While their parents have much authority, neither is a dictator, as was my father's father. There is much negotiation between them and their parents about duties, rights, and privileges. The most important difference, however, is that their mother and I are now divorced, which makes them like many—but not most—of their contemporaries.

They will not complete high school as a matter of choice, as did my father, but because it is the minimal education expected. And like most of their middle class contemporaries, they will also go to college (or some kind of higher education) both because it is expected and for career reasons. In striving for independence as a young man my father had few options. My sons will have a much greater range of career choices, but at some point even they will have to contend with an economy in which opportunity is, in fact, not open-ended.

This is briefly the story of change in the lives of the males in two generations of my family. Their story is not representative of change in the lives of all American families. You might find it interesting to compare their story with stories about change between generations in your own family. Imagine a far-fetched situation. Suppose you are an investigator from another planet researching human life on earth and have just read the story of change in the two generations of my family. You might ask, "Well—you have told me about the life of your father's generation and that of your sons' generation and how they are different. But how did they get to be so different?"

I would say that to understand why the lives of individuals change as they do, you must understand some things about the broader contexts of societal change, such as changes in the economy, urbanization, and technological change, which shape individual and family life in various ways. It is always interesting for us to think about how our individual lives are changing, but to understand this more fully we must examine the forces of change in the structure of society. That is what this book is about.

WHAT IS SOCIAL CHANGE?

People have always been fascinated and agitated by the problem of understanding permanence and change. Among the ancient Greek philosophers Heraclitus of Ephesus argued that the world was a process in constant flux and development, while his counterpart, Parmeniedes of Elea, maintained that the world was an indestructible, motionless continuum of matter and space, and that change is illusory. This ancient polarization of thought is also found in sociological thinking. While the founding fathers of sociology in the late nineteenth century were all concerned with a general understanding of change, American sociology in the 1950s became more preoccupied with understanding stability and persistence. Robert Nisbet, for instance, wrote that

> Nothing is more obvious than the *conservative* bent of human behavior, the manifest desire to preserve, hold, fix and keep stable....given the immense sway of habit in individual behavior and of custom, tradition, and the sacred in collective behavior, change could hardly be a constant. (1969:271)

This view argues that societies are basically stability-seeking structures, and change is, at best, a series of historically specific events. Since no general understanding of change was possible, the study of social change was often neglected. During the 1960s there was a reawakening of interest in change and models of society that could account for change in a systematic way. I won't spend more time here with this abstract controversy, but only argue that we should not deny the reality of either general processes of stability or change. Both are real, and we recognize one in relation to the other. To deny the reality of either persistence or change does violence to the way the people experience the world.

Here is a working definition that I will expand later: *Social change* is the significant alteration of social structure through time. This definition begs two questions: What is "significant"? And what is "social structure"?

Significance, I must admit, is largely in the eye of the beholder. When you assert that "nothing important has really changed," or that "things have really changed," those are judgments about significance. At its root, *social structure* means a persistent network of social relationships in which interaction has become routine and repetitive. At increasingly abstract levels social structure can be understood as persistent social roles, groups, organizations, institutions, and societies.

There are different types of alterations of structure. First, there are *changes in personnel*, in which new people and role incumbents with different life histories and experiences are continually entering and leaving established structures. These may produce only minimal or gradual changes in the structures that they enter and leave, however. Second, there are changes in *the way parts of structures relate*. These may include changed role relationships—such as differences between family roles in my father's and my sons' families that I mentioned earlier. They can also include changes in the structure of power, authority, and communication within a structure. They can mean the proliferation of new substructures (such as new departments in organizations) or the consolidation or realignment of existing substructures. Third, there are changes in *the functions of structures*, that is, changes in what they do and how they operate. For example, a drug rehabilitation organization can become a religious cult (as happened with

Synanon); a club of hobbyists can become a political lobby; or a religious organization can come to function as a family counseling and social service agency, or an advocate of political change. Fourth, there are changes in *the relationships between different structures.* For example, since 1900 in America labor-management relations have evolved from what were often uncivil and violent confrontations to today's ritualized and highly routinized negotiations. Fifth, there is *the emergence of new structures.* Since medieval times corporations and nation-states have emerged as new structural forms, which incorporated and partly replaced existing forms. And some contemporary observers claim to see an emerging world system in which there is such a degree of political and economic integration that the separateness and independence of nation-states and their economies is being severely curtailed.

Besides considering the different types of alterations of structure that can occur, there are five other brief orienting comments about change that I would like to make here. They are related to (1) levels of change, (2) different time frames, (3) causes of change, (4) how change relates to human intentions (or "agency"), and (5) some other terms often associated with change.These orienting comments and distinctions specify the general notion of change in various ways, and most (but not all) are discussed in more depth later in the book. It is important to note that in what follows I am broadening my earlier straightforward (but narrow) definition of social change (as transformations in structure) to include a broader range of social and cultural phenomena.

First, change happens on *many levels.* It is important to try to be clear about exactly what is changing, that is, the units within which change is taking place. The study of change can focus on *aggregate individual characteristics,* such as changes in attitudes and demographic characteristics like age, sex, and life span. It can focus on changes in aspects of *culture,* such as values, norms, knowledge, and technology. It can focus on changes in *structural units* (and this level is more consistent with my earlier working definition) from small systems to large, inclusive ones. Here are some of the different structural levels that one could focus on, and some examples of what one might study at each level.

Structural Level	Changes
Small group	in roles, communication structure, influence, cliques
Organizations	in structure, hierarchy, authority, productivity
Institutions	in economy, religion, family, education
Society	in stratification, demography, power
Global	in evolution, international relationships, modernization and development

Second, it is important to distinguish between *long-term and short-term change.* Short-term changes in our lives are often more apparent, but longer-term changes may be more significant, if harder to perceive. Focusing only on short-term changes is also deceptive, because there are repetitive cycles that operate in the sort term, such as yearly business cycles and family developmental stages, that may not be changes at all from the standpoint of the longer time span. To take the latter example, individuals may experience dramatic and often traumatic change as they go from being newlyweds to having young children, to a family with teenagers, to an empty-nest family where the children have left. But these short-term changes that are most apparent to individuals do not necessarily imply any long-term change in American families. American families are of course changing, but our personal experience is not a very good gauge of that. To some extent whether we focus on the long term or the short term is a function of our interest. It is legitimate to focus on short-term change, but we need to be aware of how this is embedded in longer-term change.

Third, we are interested in distinguishing between *causes and consequences of change,* though this is not always easy. In the social sciences, causes are always inferences, not things that are self-evident from any given bits of data. Furthermore, whether we treat something as a cause or a consequence is often arbitrary and a matter of our interest. If there is a causal sequence between A→B→C, then B is both a consequence of A and a cause of C.

There is an important distinction between *exogenous* and *endogenous* causes of change. Exogenous changes are those that result from bringing in things from the outside, such as new technologies, ideas, styles, diseases, and so on. Although they vary a great deal, all social systems are in the final analysis open systems, subject to the penetration of new elements from other systems. Historically, traders, immigrants, and occupying armies have been important carriers of exogenous change. Polar Eskimos, for instance, now zoom around the Arctic in snowmobiles with repeating rifles, imported innovations which have irrevocably altered their way of life—and have nearly caused the decimation of their traditional sources of food. Eskimo people now die of diseases unknown before contact with others from the outside.

Even if a group were perfectly insulated from exogenous change, there still would be change from internal sources. These are termed endogenous causes of change. This is a subtle but important point. Social systems are not only open systems as described above, they are *morphogenetic,* that is, they generate change in their own structure.[2] What are some of the internal features of social systems that would generate change, even if a group were perfectly isolated from the influence of other groups? They include the inevitable gap between shared ideals and actual practices, individual differences and uncertainties in the socialization process (how and what individuals learn about the social world), and flexibilities and variations in the way social roles are defined and enacted (Moore, 1974:12-22). Undoubtedly there are others, such as the competition for control of power and scarce resources that is likely to exist within any social system. An endogenous source of change in American society, for instance, is the commitment to an equality and nondiscrimination and the common institutional practices of racism and sexism (a kind of gap between shared ideals and actual practices).

A fourth basic distinction is *the way social change relates to human intentions and "agency."* There are those changes that I call *autonomous trends,* which are unintended—meaning that nobody is trying to bring them about. Examples of such trends include shifts in fertility and mortality rates, the composition of a population, the growth of metropolitan communities, and so forth. Then there are those changes that are *planned and intentional,* such as changes in laws; allocation of scarce resources; the dissemination of new technologies; changes in tariffs, taxation, social policy; and so on, that are deliberately induced by legislators and planners of all sorts. Finally, there are those changes that are *intentionally sought by broad groups within a population,* but are not planned in the bureaucratic sense by elites. This is the province of social movements, whereby people seek a wide variety of changes, such as the improvement of conditions for minorities, environmental improvements, and so forth. In other words there are three broad varieties of change in relation to human agency: trends, intentional planned changes that relate to an elite decision-making process, and intentional changes that relate to social movements that involve broad segments of the population. I will have more to say about these types of change in subsequent chapters.

Finally, I would like to distinguish change from some similar terms, specifically the terms *process, progress, evolution,* and *development.* Any aspect of human behavior can be seen as a *process,* which focuses our attention on the active and dynamic aspect of behavior (the opposite of process is structure). But there are behavioral processes that maintain stability as well as processes of change. Change is a process, but not all processes are change. *Progress* implies qualitative improvement: Things get better. The notion of progress is inherently value-laden (better by whose values?). It is an important normative concept, but not a scientific one. We can argue about whether particular changes represent progress or not. *Evolution* is most often used "to describe some kind of more or less orderly progression from a simple to a more complex entity" (Vago, 1980:5). Evolution is an important type of change and has a central place in some classical theories of change. But not all change is evolution. Change is often described as *development.* We can talk about developmental change in organizations, but among scholars, the notion of development is often used to describe economic and political change in third world countries, or as a rough synonym for modernization. All of these concepts have been associated with change in different ways, but *change* is the broad, generic, neutral term.

SOCIOLOGY AND SOCIAL CHANGE

Sociology began in the late nineteenth century as an attempt to understand the emergence of the modern world. The earliest sociologists—Auguste Comte, Herbert Spencer, Karl Marx, Emile Durkheim, Max Weber—all attempted to understand the transition from the medieval to urban, industrial, and capitalist societies. Although they did not share a common view of this process, they did share the vision that the study of human societies and change could be understood in a general way, rather than as only the accumulation of the accidents of history. They were fascinated by the idea that the study of society and change could be done scientifically, although then—as now—there was not complete agreement about exactly what this means.

Sociology is certainly not the only intellectual discipline that is concerned with change. Political scientists and economists are also concerned with understanding change in specific spheres of human life. By contrast, sociologists, and perhaps anthropologists, are more concerned with understanding change in human life and societies in a global and holistic manner. Historians are also vitally concerned with the study of change, which is the basic stuff of history. Historians differ among themselves in interests, methods, and focus. But compared to sociologists, historians are more likely to be interested in particular events, persons, and occurrences. As sociologist Wilbert Moore has said, "Although we cannot meet the challenge of history, if by that we mean accounting for unique events, we must attempt to *identify recurrent combinations of antecedents and consequences*" (1974:73). The interests of sociologists and historians in understanding change are different but complementary in many ways. Sociologists are more likely to search for general and recurring patterns in change processes. In sum, sociologists have a unique interest in studying change because of a commitment to holism and scientific methods. *Scientific methods,* as I am using the term here, merely means that sociologists are likely to seek generalizations governing the operation of social change and to examine those generalizations using the best evidence possible.

WHAT YOU CAN EXPECT FROM THIS BOOK
AND HOW IT IS ORGANIZED[3]

Since change is everywhere, a book about it could be about anything and everything. Studying change is like viewing a scene: It can be done from different distances, altitudes, and angles. With the mind-boggling diversity of possible topics and approaches, any single book about social change is necessarily selective. I have deliberately entitled this book *Exploring Social Change* to indicate that it explores selected aspects of change and does not pretend to be a comprehensive treatment of change in all its possible manifestations. Others would have written the book differently, or emphasized different things. It is about social change in a general way, and each topic could be examined in much more detail and depth than I have been able to do in a single short book. While each part of the book can be read separately, I have tried to show connections between the main topics in the book, which treat change from different "altitudes and angles." It is not a book written around a single theme or idea, and I want to warn you that it will not all come together at the end in a neat, tidy picture. Social reality is too complex and complicated for that. What you can expect from this book is a number of useful ways of understanding change processes that are going on in the social world.

Here is a brief preview of the topics explored in the book. The first part of the book deals descriptively with what I think are some of the important changes going on in contemporary American society. The last part of the book focuses on similar important aspects of social change on an international or global basis. In between these descriptive parts are several chapters that deal with sociological explanations and perspectives about change and some particular social change processes. Let me be more concrete.

Part I examines change in American society since the mid 1940s. Chapter 2 focuses on general trends in American society and culture, as well as change in three important aspects of everyday life: population characteristics, families, and work. Chapter 3 focuses on change in the American economic and political systems in recent decades.

Part II focuses on theory—how we explain change. Chapter 4 examines theories about the causes and patterns of change, while Chapter 5 describes three major contemporary sociological theories (functionalist, conflict, and interactionist) in terms of how each would explain change (using some of the material from Chapter 2).

Part III examines processes of change by focusing on two different perspectives for understanding change: innovations and their diffusion and social movements. It is perhaps the most technically demanding part of the book because it surveys two large bodies of sociological research related to different approaches to understanding change processes. Chapter 6 examines the literature about innovations and how they spread. Chapters 7 and 8 are about social movements and social change. Chapter 9 is about the planning of change and explores a variety of strategies for creating change. It draws heavily on the other chapters in Part III.

Part IV is about change at the international and global level. Chapter 10 focuses on development, or modernization, in the third world countries of Asia, Africa, and Latin America. Chapter 11 looks at development from a different perspective and examines some issues in development policy. Chapter 12 continues the focus on global change by exploring the emergence of a world system and some trends having to do with population and resources. The last chapter looks at some projections and models for understanding the future.

There are two other things I think you need to know about the book. I have tried to write an objective, scientific book about how social scientists analyze and understand social change. But it is also a book that in places exhibits my own values, hopes, and fears about the human condition. It is impossible (and I think undesirable) to eliminate one's own opinions and values from scholarly work. But they should be labeled as such, so I have put "I think..." statements in front of those places where I am particularly aware that not all would agree with what I have written. Finally, as should be obvious to you by now, the book is written in an informal and I hope unpretentious style. I tried to write as if I were carrying on an imaginary conversation with you as an individual, rather than communicating with an anonymous group of people. It is the way I like to communicate, and I hope it makes the book more engaging for you to read.

NOTES

1. As I write this they are both in high school.

2. The opposite of morphogenetic is *homeostatic,* which means that a system is self-regulating to maintain stability. Homeostatic systems are familiar: for instance a home thermostat that maintains constant upper and lower temperature level, or your body, which attempts to maintain constant levels of chemicals and hormones. By contrast, in morphogenetic systems such as social systems the capacity for change is built into the very nature of the system itself.

3. Many writers put information like this in the preface to a book, but since some readers—including me—are likely to skip lightly over a preface, I decided to put this material here, because it is important that you get an idea of what kind of book you are going to be reading and a preview of its contents.

CHAPTER TWO
AMERICAN TRENDS AND THE SETTINGS OF EVERYDAY LIFE

There are basically three ways of describing social change. One is to discuss change in terms of *significant events,* for instance, World War II, the assassination of President Kennedy, the Vietnam War, the Watergate episode, or the OPEC oil boycott. Each of these events can be shown to have had a significant impact on the development of contemporary America. Even so, these are unpredictable and nonrecurrent events that cannot be the heart of a systematic attempt to undertand *patterns* of change. At the other extreme you can talk about change in terms of *generalized trends.* These are social processes that make it possible to describe compactly what are assumed to be the underlying patterns or directions of change. Trends are useful tools to get a broader perspective on concrete aspects of change. But it is not enough to think only in terms of abstract trends. We ordinarily think of such trends as endless linear processes: They don't tell us about nonlinear variations or about upper limits to such trends, and they certainly don't tell us how such trends are modified by the significant events mentioned above. A third way of discussing change is to examine *macroscopic change in institutions, structures, and populations.* I think this is a very informative way of studying social change, but it does have the disadvantage of focusing on change in separate realms, such as change in the family, politics, or the economy, so that it may be difficult to perceive the connections between change in these (artificially) separated realms.

In the two chapters that follow, I will describe change in American society from all three of these different vantage points. This chapter begins by examining change from the highest and lowest "altitudes": I describe some of the broadest structural and cultural trends in American social life, and then focus on change in those settings closer to the everyday life of individuals—in population characteristics, family, and work. While mainly descriptive, I have used this discussion to highlight several longstanding sociological controversies about the nature of life in modern societies. Chapter 3 refocuses our approach by exploring change in two large-scale institutional realms that together shape much of the character of American social life: politics and the economy. It ends with the significant events perspective, through a discussion of both the reality and perceptions of the human meaning of political and economic change in the postwar decades. As above, my intent is primarily descriptive, but Chapter 3 also explores what I think are some problems and structural contradictions that are important for the future of American society.

A word about the time frame: I have chosen to focus on the recent past because I want to emphasize a time period that is familiar to you. But many of these changes—particularly the structural trends—are not unique to American society and have been operative in industrial societies at least since the 1600s. You can see them as the most recent (but peculiarly American) manifestations of the social processes that have been a part and parcel of the process of industrialization itself. The time span is from 1945 (the end of World War II) to the mid 1980s. I should warn you that as we come close to the present, the data about change becomes less clear-cut and its meaning more controversial.

The most basic conceptual distinction in social science is the distinction between *social structure* and *culture*. As I defined it in the introductory chapter, social structure means the persistent relationships between people, from the smallest and most intimate to the largest and most abstract. Culture—which was not explicitly defined in the introduction—is the blueprint for living that people share. It includes symbols, knowledge and beliefs, values (what is good and bad), norms (how people are expected to behave), and technologies (the techniques by which people deal with the material world). The distinction between social structure and culture is an artificial one, but it is a convenient way of talking about different aspects of social life. I will discuss social change in America in terms of (1) structural trends, related to changes in the nature of relationships in American society, and (2) cultural trends, related to changes in technology and values and beliefs about social life.[1]

STRUCTURAL TRENDS

A first important trend in American society is the *centralization and growth in scale* of social life. Growth in scale means the increasing absorption and integration of small isolated social units into larger networks of relationships, while centralization means the growing power of a few or single social units to control and coordinate relationships between other previously more autonomous units. These processes can be seen clearly in the process of urbanization. Around 1900 about half of Americans lived in scattered small towns and rural areas. Now at least 70 percent are concentrated in a handful of large urban areas that dominate the social, political, and economic life of the nation. Such centralization and growth in scale can also be seen in the growth and dominance of large-scale organizations and a decline in the autonomy of small-scale, local facilities. In the economy this has meant the increasing dominance of huge corporate entities, and a decline in the proportion of economic assets controlled by small-scale entrepreneurs (more about this later). Such trends toward centralization are also evident in education, the media, government, and even recreational facilities.

Second, while centralization and growth in scale have meant the development of mass markets, mass media, and a mass electorate, there have also been increasing *differentiation and specialization* of social life. Thus we have not only the mass media, which assumes an undifferentiated mass of information consumers, but also highly specialized media, which addresses those with highly specialized and exotic tastes and interests. Consider, from the time that the printed matter available to most Americans was a local newspaper, a farmer's almanac, and perhaps a Sears catalogue, the range of publications that are available today at the local urban bookstore or newsstand: There are publications for sky divers, joggers, weight lifters, vegetarians, occult religionists, survivalists, soldiers of fortune, gourmet cooks, as well as for those with an impressive variety of sexual appetites. Indeed, the variety of tastes and interests addressed by the highly differentiated mass media is seemingly endless. The same argument can be made with regard to the availability of highly differentiated social, religious, and recreational groups catering to specialized interests. One can also see this increasing differentiation in the realm of occupations: There used to be "generalized" doctors, elementary school teachers, and engineers; now, increasingly one has to know what *kind* of doctor, teacher, or engineer one is talking about.

Such differentiation has meant that more social roles in everyday life are segmented and limited in scope: There has been a decline in the availability of more general, diffuse, and multifaceted roles, and probably a decline in generalized knowledge and skills. Perhaps such roles remain mainly in the realms of friendship, the family, and household do-it-yourselfers. Indeed, the joint trends of growth in scale and increasing differentiation probably mean that as persons we occupy increasingly narrow niches in an ever larger and more complex social system.

A third trend is *bureaucratization*. Bureaucracy means social systems with formal structure and roles which are "designed" for special purposes. Bureaucratic organizations, whether in the economy, education, religion, social welfare, or government, have become the organizational framework for the society. In terms of the individual this means that we spend more time in formal roles (the behavioral specifications for which are defined in some organizational rule book) and in formal contractual relationships with others. Bureaucratic modes of organization are coming to permeate areas of social life formerly organized on an informal or traditional basis. These trends can be seen, for instance, in the evolution of the one-room country schoolhouse, where things were run on a traditional and informal (if autocratic!) basis, to the large contemporary high school, where students and subjects are separated into different categories and everyone's behavior, including the teacher's, is regulated by the rules. Similar trends toward bureaucratization can be found in economic life, in social welfare activities, and in recreation. Indeed, families remain perhaps the last bastion of nonbureaucratic settings in contemporary America, and even here the extent to which bureaucratic organizations impinge upon and shape life in American families has probably increased.

This discussion of basic structural trends in American society raises a number of questions posed by some of the earlier and more recent sociological critics of modern industrial societies. Thus Max Weber (1921) asked whether the pervasive bureaucratization of social life would ultimately erode the quality and character of informal relations.He thought so. Similarly others (Simmel, 1921; Wirth, 1957; and Korhauser, 1959) developed what has come to be known as the *mass society thesis,* which argues that these trends have produced not only the erosion of informal and traditional social relations but also a kind of homogenization of social life in which the richness of social differences has declined as we all become a part of the masses. As such, being creatures of mass markets, media, and electorates, modern man becomes increasingly rootless, anomic, and subject to manipulation. This is in fact a newer form of an older kind of social criticism going back at least as far as de Tocqueville and Edmund Burke, conservative critics of the French enlightenment, who decried the "leveling" aspects of democracy.

In such polemical form the mass society thesis is difficult to evaluate, yet in some respects it is clearly a flawed argument. There is, for instance, a large volume of contemporary research which conclusively demonstrates the continuing vitality of informal group participation and continuing attachments to neighborhoods and local communities among most Americans—even in a highly urbanized and bureaucratized world. Modern students of bureaucracies have demonstrated that, within bureaucracies there normally exists a rich informal life and culture among stable work groups. Segmental, formal bureaucratic relations apparently have not eroded or replaced informal or traditional relations but rather have been grafted onto them, so to speak. Similarly, there is little evidence that significant social homogenization, or leveling of social distinctions has occurred. There is little evidence that regional, ethnic, or social class distinctions, are disappearing (Glenn and Simmons, 1967) and as suggested above, there is little evidence that participation in a mass market decreases the diversity of goods, services, or culture available to Americans. Yet this is a slippery argument, and there is a germ of truth to the mass society thesis. Underneath the apparent diversity there *is* homogenization and standardization. Mass markets increasingly provide the same incredible diversity of goods and services on a national scale, without regard to region and locale. Given, for example, the diversity of restaurants in the typical urban area, it is increasingly hard to order French fried potatoes that are not precut, frozen, and distributed in a highly standardized way.

I think the important questions are not whether diversity continues to exist (it does), or whether nonbureaucratic ties and roots continue (they do), but rather whether or not the informal and traditional life of Americans is integrated in any meaningful way with the larger structures of the society, or whether the power and initiative to shape the character of social life has passed decisively into the realm of the large-scale organizations. One observer (Coleman, 1982) has termed contemporary America an "asymmetrical society," in which individuals become less and less able to give direction to their lives as "corporate actors" increasingly gather resources and power, which they devote to their own care and feeding. These are clearly more difficult questions to answer satisfactorily than other questions posed by the mass society thesis.

CULTURAL TRENDS

Technology defines how humans relate to and cope with their environment, and this is an important aspect of any culture. When Americans think about change they are likely to think first in technological terms. So the first cultural trend I will discuss is the continual *increase in technical complexity and sophistication.* This has produced an increasing ability to convert environmental resources into a usable form, whether in terms of agricultural production, industry, or the production of energy. It means a growth in economic productive capacity. In terms of contemporary society it not only means increasing control over the environment but also an enhanced ability to store and control information. This is particularly evident in the advent of computers, which increasingly form the information matrix of society. That such a process of increasing technical efficiency has been operative in American society needs no documentation: It is well known. The increase in sophisticated technology is strongly connected with the structural trends mentioned earlier (especially growth in scale and differentiation), although you can endlessly debate which is the cause and which is the effect.

The efficiency of modern technology is a complicated issue, however, and often only apparent when efficiency is defined in narrow terms that do not include the larger economic, ecological, and social costs of production. American agriculture, for instance, is marvelously efficient in terms of per acre yield. But if you factor in the costs of diesel fuel, fertilizer, pesticides, water, food processing, and transportation, you find that it "requires more than nine calories of energy input to deliver one calorie of food to the consumer" (Humphrey and Buttel, 1982:150). To take another example, a nuclear power plant is very productive in narrow terms of kilowatt hours of energy that can be produced. But it is not nearly as cost-effective when you consider all the longer-range costs of the years of planning, regulation, and construction of plants, and the costs the disposal of nuclear wastes—not to mention the human, economic, and environmental costs of a possible nuclear accident.

Besides the hidden inefficiencies of complex technologies, there are larger issues about whether in the long run such ever increasing technical efficiency is at some point maladaptive for human beings (Ellul, 1964). An increasingly complex technological environment means that individuals are able to comprehend (and operate) a narrower realm of their material world. And it is an axiom that the more complex the technology, the more susceptible it is to system breakdowns that have large-scale implications. A more obvious long-range problem with complex technologies is their ecological impact. Increasing efficiency has given us increased productivity, but also a decrease in the soil fertility in many areas, industrial pollution, acid rain, the destruction of natural areas, and the near and impending possible exhaustion of many natural resources. I think that it is not increased technical efficiency per se which creates such difficulties, however, but the fact that heretofore such capacity has been harnessed to economic policies of profligate waste, exploitation, and high consumption. Indeed, such technological capability could be hooked up to goals that seek to minimize environmental carnage and use the natural environment in a sustainable way.

The remaining cultural trends I will explore are *changes in values, attitudes, and norms*. They are more difficult to clearly describe than the trends I have discussed so far, but different sociological observers (Williams, 1970; Inkles, 1979) have come to some similar conclusions about them. Furthermore, unlike the structural and technological trends, they are of more recent origin and relate to an American context, rather than being broadly associated with the industrialization process in general.

A second cultural trend is toward *increasing cultural complexity and ambiguity*. While always a culturally pluralistic nation, trends in the past emphasized the assimilation of national and ethnic subcultures into a common American core culture (even though this process was never complete). In the past two decades the trend has been to reemphasize ethnicity and make it legitimate—as a basis of pride and identity. We have also witnessed the evolution of a distinctive Afro-American subculture, as well as occupational, sexual, and age-based subcultures (the youth culture of the sixties, for instance). The progressive evolution of such cultural complexity has produced less coherence and clarity of common cultural norms. There has been an increase in moral relativism and ambiguity, and more emphasis on individual rights and options as opposed to binding traditions. While critics of contemporary culture decry this ambiguity and relativism it can also be said that these trends mean that individuals have a greater range of legitimate options and alternatives regarding work, family matters, sexuality, and lifestyles in general than was true in the past. These trends do not mean that there is no common cultural basis in American life, but rather that such a core of common cultural norms and values have become more ambiguous to perceive and more problematic in their ability to shape behavior. Americans have shifted from a common set of cultural standards in the direction of a plurality of such standards.

If American culture has become more complex and ambiguous, a third and related trend has been an *increase in the tolerance of diversity*. That means that

Americans are more likely to view cultural differences and different moral points of view as being legitimate differences. Thus there is a growing trend toward the tolerance of political, racial, sexual, and religious differences, which is reflected in the concerted effort to extend political rights to those who are disenfranchised and in the concern for civil rights and due process of law. This growing tolerance has meant greater openness to a range of options in acceptable behavior. There is, for instance, greater sanction for premarital sexuality and abortion, for women being involved in the labor force and in the political process, for living as a single person, or for being married without having children (Yankelovich, 1981). Researchers in "Middletown" (Muncie, IN) in 1924 found that 94 percent of the population agreed that Christianity was the one true religion. In a follow-up study in 1977 only 41 percent agreed that this was true (Caplow et al., 1982). The trend toward greater tolerance is widespread and only partly explainable by the increasing average educational level in America. Surveys in the 1950s and the 1970s have shown that not only has political tolerance increased in the country as a whole, but that even at similar levels of education there is now more support for civil liberties than there was two decades ago. Thus 84 percent of the college graduates in 1973 were rated politically "more tolerant," compared to only 65 percent of this group in 1964 (Nunn et al., 1978).

A fourth trend perceived by many is a trend toward *increasing concern with self-gratification.* Pollster Daniel Yankelovich finds, for instance:

> In the 1970s all national surveys showed an increase in preoccupation with the self. By the late 1970s, my firm's studies showed more than 7 out of 10 Americans (72%) spending a great deal of time thinking about themselves and their inner lives—this in a nation once notorious for its impatience with inwardness. The rage for self-ful-fillment, our surveys indicated, had now spread to virtually the entire U.S. population. (1981:5)

For the most part, this trend is viewed positively. It means that "most Americans were involved in a project to prove that life can be more than a grim economic chore [and] eager to give more meaning to their lives, to find fuller self expression and to add a touch of adventure and grace to their lives...where strict norms had prevailed in the fifties and sixties, now all was pluralism and freedom of choice..."(Yankelovich, 1981:5). This is in some sense an intensification of the old and venerable value of individualism, but historically individualism was tempered by other values (humanitarianism, social obligation, and compliance with established norms). The recent mutation of individualism into self-concern has, according to many observers, produced what has been termed the "me decade" and the "culture of narcissism" (Lasch, 1979).

This increasing concern with the gratification of the self has been abetted by the widespread diffusion of the perspectives of humanistic psychology and the human potential movement during the 1960s. On the negative side, this trend has meant that as concern for one's individual happiness and satisfaction became the master criteria for evaluating life situations, Americans are perhaps more easily dissatisfied and harder to please than in the past. They have higher expectations for such self-gratifications, and these become important—as we shall see—in explaining some recent trends in family life and work.

A fifth cultural trend, exhaustively documented by Lipset and Schneider (1983) and by the Institute for Social Research of the University of Michigan (Institute for Social Research Newsletter, 1979b), is a *decreasing trust in national leaders and social institutions.* This trend was particularly dramatic in the 1970s, during which Americans became increasingly cynical about the credibility, competence, and honesty of the leaders of government, industry, and institutions in general. While this may relate to specific events of the seventies (the unpopular Vietnam War, Watergate, mismanagement of the economy) it also is related to an increase in critical reporting in the mass media and perhaps an increasingly sophisticated knowledge about how the American system actually works. The cynicism which was always a property of elites has somehow become possessed by the masses. In any case, the trend is general: It applies not just to specific leaders (Richard Nixon, for instance) but to leaders in general and pervades all institutional sectors—religion, the media, and education as well as government and corporations. While some have viewed this growing public cynicism as a full-blown legitimacy crisis, that is, a complete loss of faith in the validity and credibility of the social system, Lipset and Schneider, who are perhaps closest to the hard evidence of the trend, argue otherwise. "What bothers the public is the apparent growth of the concentration of power and the cynical, self-interested abuse of power by government, business, and labor leaders...but problems [are seen] as aberations and not structural problems...Americans still believe in the legitimacy and vitality of the American system" (1983:409).

In sum, I think these are some basic recent trends in American society and culture. *Structural trends* include centralization and growth in scale, differentiation and specialization, and bureaucratization. *Cultural trends* include increasing technological complexity, cultural complexity and ambiguity, tolerance, concern with self-development, and mistrust of leaders and institutions.

STABILITY AND COUNTERTRENDS

In discussing change, it is important to point out that not everything changes. I will briefly indicate some things that seem to me not to have changed, as well as some countertrends that run contrary to the trends suggested above. Most observers (e.g., Inkles, 1979) argue that there has been great continuity in American cultural patterns, for instance in the American emphasis on self-reliance, autonomy, and achievement. Individualism also continues to be a strong focus of American culture, although, as discussed above, its form and manifestation was considerably transmuted during the recent decades. There is also, I would argue, a continued emphasis on innovativeness and openness to new experience in American life which remains strongly imbedded in American cultural life. Turning to structural stability, one of the most stable features of American society over the postwar years has been the pattern of social stratification and inequality. Looking, for instance, at changes in the distribution of income shows them to be very minor, almost negligible (Table 2-1). Looking at total wealth, which is more concentrated than income, would produce much the same pattern of overall stability. Most redistribution of income (toward greater equality) took place in the decades between 1920 and 1940; in the postwar period there was a remarkable stability of the distribution of material resources. This stability regarding the pattern of social inequality can be seen by using a very "big lens," so to speak. When one takes a close look there have, in fact, been some small shifts in the distribution of resources that are significant for various segments of the population. I will return to this issue later.

At the beginning of this discussion, general trends were described as linear patterns of change. But are there upper limits? Is there, for instance, an upper limit to the process of urbanization? Surely so, when most people in a given society live in urban settings. Although it is not possible to predict how long this process will continue in America, it is difficult to envision much further urbanization in Japan, which is today almost completely urbanized. One could ask a similar question about the process of bureaucratization. Is further bureaucratization possible when almost everything—perhaps excluding family life—is bureaucratized already?

Certainly in the long run these trends are not in fact completely linear. But other than the notion that a society may become saturated by a certain trend, there are other reasons to think that trends will not continue unabated: *For each of the trends discussed there is a visible countertrend in American society.* Along with the pervasive rationality that characterizes a highly bureaucratic and technological society there has been a revival of interest in the nonrational, as evidenced by the popular interest in the occult, in mysticism, and in the dramatic popularity of non-Western religious cults in recent years. The growth of interest in meditation and other forms of nonrational inner experiences has been a trend of enormous proportion. Contrary to the trends of centralization and specialization has been the visible growth of the countercultural movements of the sixties and seventies, emphasizing the virtues of smallness, self-sufficiency, and voluntary simplicity. Indeed, there is today a rather well-articulated "New Age" consciousness movement, with its own networks and media, involving such things as holistic health, organic food, and integral lifestyles. Such a movement represents a vivid counterpoint to the trend toward more specialized roles and instrumental relationships. Also, the shift in power and social initiative toward large-scale bureaucratic system has been accompanied by, or perhaps has produced, a countertrend for individuals to band together into activist groups,

TABLE 2-1   Percentage Distribution of Aggregate Income: 1947 and 1981

	Lowest Fifth	Highest Fifth	Highest 5%
1981	5.0%	41.9%	15.4%
1947	5.0	43.0	17.5

Source: U.S. Bureau of the Census, *Statistical Abstract of the United States,* 1983:47.

voluntary associations, and social movement organizations which articulate their grievances and concerns. Thus minorities, women, the handicapped, the aged, and a whole spectrum of others have been involved in grass-roots organizing for empowerment, and such structures have formed a significant counterbalance to the forces of the centralization of power. Finally, the trend toward cultural ambiguity, relativism, and lifestyle options was vigorously challenged in the late seventies by the revival of evangelical Christianity (in the guise of the Moral Majority) which sought, among other things, to restore moral coherence and certitude and to reinforce the traditional form of the American family and sexual mores.

None of this means that the predominant trends have been stopped or reversed by these countertrends. The recent revival of interest in the occult and mysticism has not, for instance, reversed the trends toward rationality and instrumentalism in American culture, and as yet cultural movements toward voluntary simplicity and "New Age" consciousness are only dimly visible counterpoints to the dominant trends of increasing specialization and interdependence. Nor, it would seem, has the new evangelicalism been able to undo the growth of tolerance and the sanction for lifestyle alternatives that are strongly present in American culture today. But the existence of these significant countertrends does mean that the pace of the dominant trends has been considerably modulated and that their continuation into the future should not be taken for granted.

CHANGE IN THE SETTINGS OF EVERYDAY LIFE: POPULATION, FAMILIES, AND WORK

I will now shift "altitudes" and move away from the large-scale abstract trends to explore changes in those settings closer to the everyday life of individuals. I will discuss trends in the changing characteristics of the American population (demographic change). While demography focuses on the concrete characteristics of individuals, it still does so in aggregate terms, so you might personalize this discussion by thinking about your individual situation in the context of demographic change. After exploring the changing nature of the population, I will focus on two of the most important areas of change for individuals: their families and work settings.

Demographic Change

The most important demographic trend in America is that *we are becoming an older population*. This change is caused by the joint effects of a long-term decline in the birth rate and the gradual extension of longevity (see Tables 2-2 and 2-3).

TABLE 2-2   Demographic Trends, 1960-1984 (in millions)

Population	1960	1970	1980	1984
Under 18 yrs	64.2	69.7	63.5	62.7
18-64 yrs	98.6	113.5	137.2	145.4
65+ yrs	16.6	20.0	25.6	28.0
Median age	29.5	28.0	30.0	31.3
Persons/household	3.33	3.14	2.76	2.71
Birth rate/1000	23.7	18.4	15.9	15.7
Death rate/100,000	955	945	878	867
Life expectancy males	66.6	67.1	70.0	71.1
Females	73.1	74.8	77.4	78.3

Source: U.S. Bureau of the Census, Statistical Abstract of the United States, 1984: xviii-xix; 1986: xviii-xix.

TABLE 2-3   Demographic and Family Trends, Truncated Tables, 1900-1980

	1910	1940	1970	1981
Birth rate/1,000	30.1	20.4	17.8	15.9
Divorce rate/1,000	.9	2.0	3.3	5.3

	1920	1950	1970	1979
Life expectancy, males	53.6	65.6	67.1	69.9
Life expectancy, females	54.6	71.1	74.8	77.6

	1910	1940	1970	1981
Marriage rate/1,000	10.3	12.1	10.6	10.6

	1800	1900	1976
Mean number of children per family	6	4.7	1.8

Source: U.S. Bureau of the Census, Statistical Abstact of the United States, 1983: 60,71.

This change is characteristic of all industrial societies: It is the product of many factors, for instance, changes in norms about the desired number of children, the universal availability of contraception, the control of epidemic disease, and improvements in the health and nutrition of individuals.

A second demographic change in America is not a long-term trend but is more properly understood as a unique event—that is not likely to recur. That is the "baby boom" after World War II, which represented a temporary interruption of the long-term trend toward a declining birth rate. While this was a one time event, its consequences are so profound that one can not really comprehend many changes in American society without taking it into account. The baby boom lasted from 1945 to roughly the end of the sixties as illustrated in Table 2-4. The baby boom can be described as a large population bulge squeezed be-

TABLE 2-4   The Baby Boom

Year	Births (in millions)
1945	2.8
1950	3.6
1957	4.3
1964	4.0
1967	3.6

Source: U.S. Bureau of the Census, Statistical Abstact of the United States, 1987:59.

tween two "bust" generations. As the boom generation has moved through society like a pig in a python, it has caused dislocations and adjustments, a process that will continue until the year 2000 or so, when the "boomers" begin to die. What have some of these changes been?

Postwar families with lots of babies were partly responsible for the increased demand for new houses during the 1950s. Such growth in the demand for new housing, combined with federally subsidized housing loans and the construction of urban freeways, created the mushrooming growth of suburbs. Suburbanization, of course, was not new, but it greatly accelerated in the postwar years and was substantially fueled by the baby boom. During the 1950s, the increased demand for teachers and new elementary schools seemed almost insatiable, and by the 1960s the expansion of colleges and universities began. Indeed, during that decade one new college every week was opening. The sixties represented the peak of the expansion of higher education. Now, of course, as the boomers have largely graduated, higher education is in a period of declining enrollments and retrenchment. During the seventies the boomers began to move into job markets; 3.5 million did so *each year* during that decade, 700,000 more per year than in the sixties (Eitzen, 1974:534). They faced stiff competition, for during the 1970s American women were also entering the job market in record numbers and the robust economic growth of the sixties slowed. The slower growth in the demand for labor was particularly apparent in professional and service occupations, a fact that affected the boomers with a special vengeance, since an unprecedented 25 percent of them had graduated from college and sought such jobs. Thus the boomers faced stiffer competition for jobs than the smaller generation that preceded them. They will occupy many job positions for several decades, making job markets more crowded for the generation that follows them. By the year 2010 the boomers will retire and qualify for retirement and social security benefits, and this will create enormous strains on public budgets, as well as booming markets for geriatric services of all sorts.

But if the boomers have affected society by causing continual dislocations and adjustments, they have also left a decisive stamp on the nature of American society and culture. They are the generation that spawned the cultural transformations of the sixties, with the sexual revolution, the revitalized feminist movement, and the antiwar movement. As college-aged young adults, the counterculture they created changed the nature of America. More than any other group of Americans, they are responsible for the growing tolerance of diversity in American life. Now, faced with a stiffly competitive adult world and uncertain careers, the heady radicalism and optimism of the sixties has been modified. They have, I think, become liberated conservatives, that is, more conservative on economic and political matters, but still culturally tolerant and egalitarian.

The direction of these trends bring us to a fundamental social-demographic dilemma, in which social policy and demographic trends seem to be on a collision course. We have an increasingly aging population while our policies about compulsory retirement have meant that a decreasing proportion of the elderly are in the labor force. Of the adult male population over 65, 55 percent worked in 1920, 32.2 percent in 1960, 20.8 percent in 1975, and projections are that by 1990 only 16 percent will be in the labor force (Bureau of the Census, 1970:132). Now a smaller population of the employed is being asked to support a larger dependent aging population. Certainly, large numbers of the over-65 population could be productive in the labor force (witness the age of President Reagan and the members of the Supreme Court). As older Americans grow in numbers, a move to roll back mandatory retirement policies has developed which has broad social support, not only among the elderly. The dilemma is that keeping large numbers of the over-65 population in the labor force may block occupational mobility—clog the channels so to speak—for younger cohorts. But keeping older workers out of the labor market requires larger, perhaps unbearable, tax burdens on the younger generation. This is not, however, an insolvable dilemma, for it must be remembered that the cohort of workers just behind the boomers is much smaller, so that allowing those who are over 65 and wish to continue to work to do so may produce only a modest mobility clog. At any rate, there is a trade-off down the road that Americans will have to make between maximizing job mobility for the young working cohort and minimizing the extent to which they will have to finance the old-age security of their elders.

In sum, America's demographic composition is changing in ways that will have profound effects on the nature of American society. There are now more people over 65 than there are teenagers—a historically unprecedented condition. "By the late 1980s, one-half of our households will be headed by baby boomers...[and]...one-fourth of the population will be elderly. These two groups will define our society for a very long time" (Zinmeister, 1985:16). Yet not so long ago America was characterized as a youth-oriented society.

Changing Families

The trend toward a lower birth rate has produced one obvious change in American families: *a decline in the size of the average family.* Mean household size has declined from 3.33 persons per household in 1960 to 2.71 in 1984 (see Table 2-2). But perhaps the change in American families most often noted and much discussed is the *trend toward a higher divorce rate.* While this trend is almost universally condemned, I argue that its implications are at least ambiguous. The often-quoted statistic, that about 4 out of 10 marriages now end in divorce is usually cited as a preface to an argument that American families are in the process of disintegration. But it seems to me that this is an arguable conclusion, for when the divorce rate is considered in the context of the number of *families* at any given time (versus the number of marriages in a given year), the rate is about 52 divorces per 1,000 marriages, or 5.3 percent (see Table 2-3). Looked at this way the imminent decline of the American family looks less likely.

Other things also suggest to me that the American family is not in such a state of decline as is commonly supposed. The remarriage rate among divorced persons is very high (suggesting that their disillusionment is not with the state of being married, but with a particular partner). Historically the rate of family breakup for all reasons has remained virtually constant since colonial times—but in earlier times most marriages were terminated by the death of a spouse rather than divorce. And in fact, the rise in the rate of divorce has been leveling off in the latter part of the 1970s and declined about 4 percent between 1981 and 1982. Whether this is a halt to the long-term trend or a temporary pause remains to be seen. Part of the explanation is probably that the large boomer cohort is now passing through the tenuous early years of marriage (the highest divorce-prone years) into mid-life. It has also been suggested that the slowdown in the divorce rate in the late seventies is a function of a sluggish economy, since it has long been established that economic recessions produce—at least temporarily—a decline in the frequency of divorce. Others (Reiss, 1981; Yankelovich, 1981) argue that the decline in the divorce rate is related to changes in cultural values: that there have been shifts toward valuing more enduring relationships as opposed to transitory experience. I should add that while marriage *is* still the preferred way to live for most adults, there is an increase in the proportion of households composed of nonmarried people (both divorced and the never married). Marriage remains popular, but singlehood is becoming a viable option.

Another trend in American family life is a *shift toward a divergence of family types.* For years the "typical family" referred to by Americans has been the mom-dad-and-kids arrangement. Today, less than half of the families in America resemble this historical image of the family. In 1980, only 20.9 percent of American families were composed of two parents, a nonworking wife, and children. Another 21.9 percent had two parents, a working wife, and children. About a fifth (20.8 percent) had a nonworking wife and no children, 18.8 percent had a working wife and no children, 14.6 percent were unmarried female-headed families with children, and 3 percent were unmarried male-headed families with children (U.S. Bureau of Labor Statistics, cited in *Omaha World Herald,* 1980:1-B). These structural variations are not radical departures from the notion of the traditional family. The axes of variation have to do with (1) the number of parents, (2) the presence of children, and (3) the number of wage earners in the family. More radical departures (communal households, group marriages, homosexual families) exist but represent a tiny proportion of American families. Nonetheless these modestly divergent family types have significantly different needs and characteristics that are not often addressed by the social institutions that have the greatest connection to family life (schools, churches, the legal system).

In addition to this trend toward a plurality of types of families, no discussion of families and households would be complete without at least mention of the *trend toward nonmarital cohabitation*. It is estimated that 25 percent of the college-age population has cohabited, at least briefly. And since 1960 the number of unmarried cohabitants residing together has more than doubled—rising from 439,000 couples to 957,000 in 1977 (Glick and Norton, 1977; cited in Blake, 1979). These informal living arrangements have become so common that the census bureau needs a new category to describe them (POSSLQ: person-of-the opposite-sex-sharing-living quarters)! Some cohabitation arrangements are permanent alternatives to marriage, but most are what Reiss (1980) calls "courtship cohabitation," which is viewed by the participants as a prelude to marriage. Such arrangements may become an increasingly common part of the engagement process of Americans. At least, there seems to be no trend for cohabitation to replace the popularity of legal marriage.

Americans continue to rate family life as the overwhelming source of life's satisfactions. In one survey, respondents were asked "What's the most important thing in your life?" Sixty-one percent responded family, 9 percent responded work, and 29 percent gave other answers (American Enterprise Institute, 1981:26). And this at a time when the viability of American families is so widely questioned! The family remains, it seems, a vital center for most Americans. Few Americans choose to live alone as a permanent condition, and those who live together overwhelmingly choose to be legally married. In fact, one could argue that in spite of the increased instability and diversity of contemporary families, the quality of family life is on the whole better today than it was previously. Longitudinal evidence about the quality of family life is hard to come by, but one study supports this assertion. A classic sociological community study of "Middletown" (Muncie, IN) in the 1920s described much family life, especially among blue collar workers, as "bleak, dreary, and devitalized." The study found surprisingly little husband-wife communication and a restricted sexual life. A restudy of the same community in 1982 found much higher levels of marital satisfaction, more husband-wife communication, and more time spent with children than previously (Caplow et al., 1982).

That there has been an increase in the typical quality of familial satisfaction seems plausible for several reasons. Ironically, the increase in the divorce rate may mean that unhappy relationships are more likely to be terminated today, leaving a larger proportion of intact marriages with higher average levels of satisfaction. Second, the decrease in average family size may have had an impact. The literature on the effects of family size suggests that in smaller families there is less role segregation, more husband-wife interaction, and more time spent with children. Smaller families also tend to be less paternalistic and more equalitarian, both with respect to husband-wife and parent-child relationships. Small family size has also been found to be related to improved physical and mental health (especially among mothers!) and to increased mental ability in children (Eitzen, 1974). Finally, cultural value changes may have had an impact on increasing the quality of family life. These would include an increasing emphasis on equalitarian relationships generally, and, within the family, a shift from fixed "role scripts" toward negotiable ones. Patriarchal authority still exists, but patriarchy is no longer an absolute tyranny in younger and smaller American families.

Demographer Judith Blake (1979) has proposed an interesting thesis about change in the contemporary American family. She begins by refering to an old and somewhat shopworn sociological argument that the industrial revolution so severed connections between work and family life that families in industrial societies have evolved into isolated units. As economic, protective, recreational, and educational functions of the family came to be assumed by other institutions, and families became increasingly differentiated from the larger social environment, it became plausible to speak of "isolated nuclear families" as typifying those in the industrial world (Parsons and Bales, 1955). The loss of more general family functions produced a family with more specialized functions: the provision of emotional gratification for adults and the early socialization of children. And as the family became more isolated from broader community life, it came to have the character of a "private sphere" providing a haven from the rough and tumble worlds of the workplace and the political community.

Blake's thesis is that this trend has reversed in recent years, that there has been *a decline in the structural differentiation, isolation, and functional specialization of families*. Her argument is that American families are coming to have less distinct boundaries and a greater degree of articulation with the larger community. As evidence for her thesis, she suggests that today there is a "diminishing set of distinctions" that differentiate family from nonfamily matters. First, there is a declining distinction between marriage and nonmarriage. Nonmarital cohabitation arrangements are increasingly treated as if they were marriages, as, for instance, in recent celebrated "palimony" court judgments. Such nonmarital arrangements are increasingly sanctioned, or at least not stigmatized in any serious way. Second, there is a declining distinction (and less stigma) between having children and childlessness in marriage. Having children used to be a cultural imperative for a complete family whereas now it is increasingly viewed as an option. The significance of this for Blake's thesis is that the option of childlessness, in combination with a lower birth rate generally, means that more people are living a larger proportion of their married lives without children. And, if one of the things that distinguishes families from other social units is that families are places where children are reared, this distinction is becoming less meaningful. A third declining distinction has to do with the legitimacy/illegitimacy of children. While legitimacy may well be a principle that is universally understood (if anthropologists are correct), the distinction is virtually without significance for most children in the United States today. Children born "out of wedlock" are simply not as stigmatized as they were in the past. States are becoming reluctant to include legitimacy status on birth certificates and the distinction is of virtually no legal significance. Increasingly, mothers of illegitimate children decide to keep and rear them rather than place them for adoption. Fourth, and perhaps most important, is the declining distinction between family roles and work-force roles. Wives are increasingly not only wives and mothers but workers as well. And as women enter the labor force men are at least somewhat more likely to play an active role in family affairs—especially child nurturance. Fifth, Blake argues that "privatization" is declining and the articulation between family and the rest of society is increasing. If it is true that it is increasingly difficult to keep the rest of society out of the family (by virtue of the intrusive aspects of the mass media if nothing else), it is also true that what used to be private family matters are increasingly matters of public concern. Child abuse, for instance, was an unheard-of social problem two decades ago, and then it would have been unthinkable for wives to bring (successful) suits against husbands for rape, as has been done recently.

Blake offers all of these "declining distinctions" as evidence that families are becoming less clearly differentiated and more connected to the rest of society. Such "streamlined" families have some positive consequences for individuals.

> People are in a far more discretionary and flexible position regarding family statuses, and are far less penalized for not being squarely a part of traditional family life. Alternatives are available....For individuals, this means that the trade-off for losing the idealized and romanticized solidarity of the traditional family is not only a more adaptable set of familial statuses, but a more satisfying set of nonfamilial ones. One can deny the importance of this to individuals only by overlooking centuries of negative instances—of people pressed into marriage and parenthood whose talents and spirits were mutilated by domesticity; or of those who, in spite of personal desire to participate, were not absorbed into the mainstream of familial life and left, without options, to languish and suffer in the shadows. (Quotation from Judith Blake, "Structural Differentiation and the Family: A Quiet Revolution," reprinted with permission of The Free Press, A Division of Macmillan, Inc., from *Societal Growth: Process and Implications*, edited by Amos H. Hawley. Copyright © by The Free Press.)

In sum, American families are smaller, more diverse structures, and—according to Blake—likely be less privatized and less segmented from other parts of the social world. Most Americans still want to be married and have children at some stage in their adult life. I think it is more correct to say that the American family system is in a state of disorderly change, rather than a state of decline.

Transforming Work

Trends in the nature of work in America seem paradoxical. First, there is a *continuing high commitment to the work ethic*, which emphasizes the centrality and social usefulness of hard work, even above other pleasures of life. In spite of the talk of the growth of a "consumption ethic," which has supposedly eroded the work ethic, opinion polls show otherwise. One poll, for example, found that when asked whether people should "place more emphasis on working hard and doing a good job rather than on what gives them personal satisfaction" 64 percent of the respondents agreed, 20 percent disagreed, and 24 percent were uncertain (American Enterprise Institute, 1981:25). Second, *there has been a significant decline in work satisfaction since about 1970.* This decline is reported independently in research by the University of Michigan Institute for Social Research, the Gallop organization, and NORC (National Opinion Research Corporation); and estimates of the magnitude of the decline vary from 10 to 25 percent. While the decline is more severe among unskilled occupations it is also noted among all occupational groups, including highly skilled laborers, managers, and professionals. The evidence suggests that when people are asked "global questions" about job satisfaction they report that they are fairly well satisfied, but they report much higher levels of dissatisfaction when they are asked about specific aspects of their job, or whether they would enter the same occupation again (Tausky, 1984:100-103). There is not an open revolt of the workers but a significant increase in grumbling about the conditions of work among the labor force at all levels. Thus the paradox: a continuing high commitment to the virtue of work in the abstract coupled with a pervasive decline in the satisfaction with the work that people themselves are doing.

A significant shift in job satisfaction is not a trivial issue, for not only does work represent a major aspect of one's investment of time, but there are well-documented spillover effects into one's nonwork life. Job dissatisfaction is significantly related to mental health: to lower self-esteem; higher levels of anger, anxiety, and tension; and trouble in getting along with others. It is also related to poorer physical health: to increases in migraine headaches, heart disease, ulcers, and arthritis (Institute for Social Research Newsletter, 1979a). Perhaps most significantly, job satisfaction is related to life span. One longitudinal study (Palmore, 1969) found job satisfaction to be one of the best predictors of longevity. There are, in addition, social consequences of lower work satisfaction. It has been found to be related to reduced participation in voluntary associations, less trust in others and in government, increased pessimism regarding the future, and feelings of political powerlessness. Thus a widespread decline in work satisfaction suggests that we may be moving toward a society characterized by widespread alienation, mistrust, and lower social participation.

Why has this decline in work satisfaction occurred? Only partial answers are possible. One factor may be related to shifts in the occupation structure itself. The most celebrated change is the trend toward a *service economy*—that is, a shift from an economy based on the production of goods to one based on the production of services. This trend has been pervasive. In 1948, 46 percent of the gross national product (GNP) was accounted for by the production of goods and 54 percent by services. By 1978 goods accounted for only 34 percent and services 66 percent (Ginsberg and Vojta, 1981). It is more common to document this trend by examining shifts in employment. In 1940, 21 percent of the work force was employed in agriculture, 40 percent in the production of goods, and 43 percent in services. By 1980, 3 percent were employed in agriculture, 30 percent in goods, and 67 percent in service occupations (American Enterprise Institute, 1981:22).

Some have seen this shift toward a service economy as a wholly benevolent trend. Thus Daniel Bell (1969) and many others argued that in a "postindustrial society" jobs are increasingly upgraded; dirty and low-skilled jobs are being replaced by sophisticated jobs requiring training and decision making. In this view dull work will increasingly be done by machines and human labor will become less routine and more interesting. "Theoretical knowledge" will come to compete even with capital in shaping the production of abundance. My own view of the shift to a service economy is less benign than that of Bell and the celebrants of "postindustrialism."

Certainly, the service economy produced jobs like those that Bell and others described as characterizing a postindustrial economy: doctors, social workers, systems analysts, chemists, managers, and so forth, who do interesting nonroutine work requiring advanced and specialized training. But most jobs in the service economy are of another kind. Three of every five new jobs between 1950 and 1976, and 70 percent between 1973 and 1978 were in just two industries: retail trades and "services" (a census category that excludes professional, technical, and managerial workers). The kinds of jobs we are discussing are jobs in retail sales, eating and drinking establishments (especially fast food restaurants), photocopying, data processing, janitorial services, and health care workers—mainly lower-level hospital employees. What these jobs have in common are low pay, poor working conditions, little job security, and little opportunity for advancement. They are not jobs requiring high skills or much in the way of the autonomous decision making described by Bell and his colleagues. Ginsberg (1977) has calculated that during the period from 1950 to 1976, there were 2.5 times as many new jobs created below the mean salary level as there were above the mean. Currie and Skolnick argue that the "typical workplace of the service society is not to be found in the doctor's office or that of the computer analyst, but rather in the fast-food franchise, the hospital kitchen, or the convenience store" (1984:309).

The controversy about the effects of automation and computerization, which has been with us in one form or another at least since the 1950s, is relevant here. As with the shift toward the service economy, there are those who argue that increasing automation and computerization have effects that are benign. Shepard (1981), for instance, argues that these trends mean that an increased proportion of workers will be in work environments permitting greater freedom, control, and autonomy. Again, I am suspicious of this view. While it is undoubtedly true that computerization (for example) has enhanced some jobs—research workers, librarians, mathematicians, accountants, and so forth—it has adversely affected others. You have to be aware of the *kind* of work most workers do with computers. The most common connection between computers and employees is not the researcher analyzing data but the office worker sitting at a video display terminal routinely entering and processing masses of information. In an early study of work in a computerized office system, Ida Hoos (1961) reported that many office machine operators found their jobs more interesting prior to computerization because they had performed a wider variety of tasks, such as filing, checking, posting, and typing. Their new jobs were more simplified and required both accuracy and speed. Deprived of freedom of movement about the office and interaction with other employees or customers, many office workers felt chained to their machines. Similar observations can be made about other high-tech jobs.

Even in the exemplary postindustrial industry—telecommunications—the effect of the increasingly technological level of work is not wholly benign. At a 1979 conference sponsored by the Communication Workers of America on the effects of new communications technology on work, it was suggested that the increasingly technological level of work in the communications industry has not only made traditional work skills obsolete but has fragmented and downgraded jobs to lower pay levels, rigidly centralized work, and made workers subject to automatic pacing, monitoring, and oversupervision. It has eroded workers' self-control over work life and lowered their sense of accomplishment, freedom, and prestige.

This seems a severe indictment of the increasingly technological level of work. While I don't view such high-tech work as a wholly undesirable force, I suspect that its "liberating" effects, described by the celebrants of postindustrialism, have been greatly overstated. While automation and computerization may have enhanced work for some, it has also contributed to the growing routinization of work and a decline in skill levels required for perhaps a greater number of workers (see Braverman, 1974, for an elaboration of this argument).

There is another piece to the puzzle of the current decline in work satisfaction. At the same time that much work may be becoming narrowed and segmented by technological upgrading and trivialized by the proliferation of less challenging and less remunerative jobs in the service economy, the American work force is becoming more highly educated. By 1980 one out of every four American workers had a college degree, and by 1990 this figure will be higher as the boomers who went to college in unprecedented proportions come to dominate the work force. Along with more education comes not only more skills, but higher *expectations* for jobs that are highly paid, secure, and have opportunities for advancement, creativity, and self-actualization.

The rub is that the American economy has not been able to produce jobs commensurate with the abilities and expectations of a highly educated work force in sufficient numbers. In fact, trends seem to point in the other direction. In 1960 the Bureau of Labor Statistics estimated that almost 90 percent of college graduates entering the labor force obtained professional, technical, managerial, or administrative jobs, while during the 1970s, one-third with like education had to settle for lesser positions (Levitan, 1984). This raises the specter of underemployment, that is, working for a job at which one is overqualified. According to a 1975 Department of Labor survey, fully 35 percent of American workers felt overqualified for the work they were doing. Such feelings are undoubtedly related to the negative consequences of low morale, high levels of dissatisfaction, and status frustration combined with an unprecedented ability to articulate grievances.

Given these trends it is easy to explain the job dissatisfaction of the recent college graduate who works as a routine data processor or fast food handler, but what of the decline in satisfaction of those employed in the traditional professions (the "good jobs")? Part of the answer is that the work of doctors, lawyers, engineers, and architects has been bureaucratized and routinized in organization-al settings, as has the work of everyone else. Another part of the answer is that professionals have probably been as much infected with the cultural trends of the sixties and seventies as everyone else. One of these trends, which I think is connected to problems of work dissatisfaction in contemporary society, was mentioned above: an increased interest in and belief in the legitimacy of the un-qualified search for personal gratification and autonomy. In short, Americans, just as they expect more from marriages, expect more from their jobs. I argue that this increase in expectations affects a broad spectrum of American workers—from blue collar workers to lawyers and physicians. These raised ex-pectations are particularly damaging in conjunction with the increasing routinization, fragmentation, and trivialization of work in a high-tech service economy.

NOTES

1. In a sense, culture can be understood as the *content* of social structure. When people interact in relationships they must talk about *something,* and this is often about how ex-isting knowledge, values, norms, technologies, etc. relate to their present focus of atten-tion.

CHAPTER THREE
ECONOMICS, POLITICS, AND THE MEANING OF CHANGE IN RECENT DECADES

It is always easier for us to see changes in our everyday life. But, as the discussion in the last chapter about changing work settings and the development of the service economy makes clear, you can't go very far in understanding personal life changes without understanding how these are embedded in large-scale institutional change. Two of these institutional arenas are the economy and the political system, which jointly shape the social circumstances in which the lives of individuals and families take place. Economic and political changes are complex and difficult but important to understand. They define the winners and losers of change by affecting the changing distribution of resources; wages; the availability of credit; and the growth and decline of jobs, industries, and communities. Politics and economics are so intertwined and interpenetrating that they are separated only artificially. However, I will have to do so because one can't talk about everything at once. After first describing change in the economic and political systems, this chapter will explore some perceptions about the meaning of political-economic change in recent decades. At the end of the chapter I will describe briefly some of the problems and contradictions in the American system that have important consequences for the future.

CHANGE IN THE ECONOMY

Centralization and Growth in Scale

Nowhere are the trends toward centralization and growth in scale mentioned earlier more in evidence than in the economy. Look, for example, at the growth in concentration of manufacturing assets as shown in Table 3-1. Concentration can be illustrated in another way, by examining the proportion of the production of particular products accounted for by the four largest firms (see Table 3-2).

Trends toward concentration have been more pronounced in manufacturing than in other economic activities, but trends toward more concentration are noticeable in other economic realms also. Multiunit organizational chains and franchises have grown more rapidly than single unit organizations in retailing and banking. In 1970 such multiunit organizations accounted for 31.8 percent of

TABLE 3-1   Manufacturing Assets, Percentage Shares of Large Corporations

Corporate rank	1950	1960	1970	1980
100 largest	39.7	46.4	48.5	46.7
200 largest	47.7	56.3	60.4	59.7

Source: U.S. Bureau of the Census, *Statistical Abstract of the United States.*, 1983:535

TABLE 3-2   Percentages of Selected Products by the Four Largest Producers

Product	1953—1958	1977
Passenger cars	98	99+
Chewing gum	81	93
Light bulbs	90	89
Cigarette	80	88
Watches and clocks	82	84
Refrigerators	65	82
Tractors	72	80
Cotton fabrics	40	78
Sanitary tissue	37	70
Television sets	55	70
Mens's underwear	31	66
Roasted coffee	46	62

Source: Adapted from U.S. Bureau of the Census, "Concentration Ratios in Manufacturing, 1977," in *Census of Manufacturers*, May 1981, Table 9.

all retail sales. By 1981, they accounted for 35.8 percent (U.S. Bureau of the Census, 1983b). In some areas of retailing, tendencies toward concentration are very pronounced. In spite of the apparent diversity in food brands, for instance, most food processing in the United States is accounted for by one half dozen or so giant food processors (Beatrice, United Brands, General Mills, etc.). Franchises and firms owned by conglomerates are slowly coming to invade many of those niches in the economy habitually dominated by small-scale, freestanding firms (wineries, day care centers, hairdressers, restaurants, and hospitals, for example). But what of stock ownership? In one sense it is widely diffused. In 1980 over 31 million Americans owned some corporate stock. But the bulk of stock ownership is concentrated in a few hands. In 1982 the wealthiest 1 percent of the American population owned 44 percent of all corporate stock and 31 percent of all bonds (U.S. Congress, Economic Report to the President, 1982:204). The conclusion is inescapable that economic assets and trade are increasingly in the hands of large-scale businesses, some of which possess larger assets than the gross national products of medium-sized nation. Along with the growing concentration of the economy have been changes that are not merely quantitative. The way the economy operates has been transformed as well.

The Bimodal Economy

Galbraith (1973) argued that the contemporary economy has become "bimodal," that is, composed of two broad sectors which he termed the *market sector* and the *planning sector*. The market sector is the subordinate sector which consists of thousands of small independent firms that control roughly half of the nation's total economic assets. These firms are in areas difficult to organize on a large-scale basis: They are likely to deal in services that remain very labor-intensive. They exist in a classical free market setting which is very responsive to changes in consumer demands. Wages tend to be low and labor nonunionized. Such markets are highly unstable, and profits fluctuate greatly from year to year, depending on market conditions. There are few government supports and regulations for such firms. The planning sector, by contrast, consists of firms that are bureaucratically organized on a massive scale, and these firms tend to be technological rather than labor-intensive. These firms, according to Galbraith, increasingly form the dominant sector of the economy, in which 500 to 600 firms control the other half of the economy. In this sector wages tend to be high and labor strongly unionized. Thus between the two modes of the economy, jobs are distributed in a bimodal fashion also, in what some have called a "dual labor market." Profits tend to be higher than in the market sector. The large firms exist in a setting of extensive government support, subsidy, and regulation and have a symbiotic relationship with government regulatory agencies. From the standpoint of the operation of the economy the most important feature of the planning sector is its tendency toward oligarchic control of markets (by planning, advertising, collusion, vertical integration, and government subsidies and support). All of this means that these giant firms tend to dominate their respective markets, rather than vice versa: They are minimally subject to the fluctuations of consumer demand or current economic conditions.

Some Consequences of the Bi-modal Economy

There are important consequences deriving from the evolution of this bimodal economy, with a powerful oligopolistic sector.[1] As Berle and Means (1934) demonstrated in their now classic study of oligopolistic firms during the great depression, prices in concentrated industries are far more inflexible and decrease slowly—if at all—when consumer demand decreases. What one gets are not market-determined prices and wages but administered prices and wages (hence, Galbraith's term, *planning sector*). In other words, the free competitive market envisioned by Adam Smith, in which supply and demand are the main-springs of economic regulation, is considerably constricted in the contemporary economy. We have increasingly controlled markets with minimal competition. The ability of large concentrated industries to weather decreases in demand without lowering prices was partly responsible for the phenomenon of "stagfla-tion" during the 1970s, in which demand decreased, unemployment increased, but prices remained high or increased. The economy is increasingly no longer self-regulating. Needless to say the consequences for individuals during periods of high unemployment and high prices are devastating.

The social consequences of such a transformation of the economy are per-haps more subtle than the economic ones but pervasive none the less. Accord-ing to one observer:

> Giant corporations become private governments, in the sense that their actions govern the alternatives open to millions of people and thousands of communities. Prices, investment policy, product development, location of plants, wage and employment policies—the whole range of corporate policy—are decisions of na-tional importance because of the size and significance of the organizations that make them. In that sense much of our life is governed by the decisions made by a small group of men who are responsible only to themselves, who select their successors, and whose organizations continue for an indefinite period. A pattern of economic decision-making has emerged that is only imperfectly controlled by market forces and which has questionable legitimacy and limited accountability. (Fusfield, 1972:3)

As you can see, then, the structure of the modern economy is implicated in politi-cal changes and controversies and is not economic only in a narrow sense.

CHANGE IN THE POLITICAL SYSTEM

Growth in the Scale and Scope of Government

In the American political system, one of the most obvious trends is—again—a dramatic growth in the scale and the scope of government activity. Prior to 1929, America had a limited government, limited mainly to providing for national defense, police and fire protection, and guaranteeing legal contracts. Since that time the functions of government have mushroomed, both during the period of the great depression and in the postwar period. In addition to the above limited functions, government also seeks to regulate and stabilize the economy and to provide for the general welfare of the population through a vast array of welfare-state programs (social security, unemployment assistance, aid to the disabled, aid to education, subsidies for research—to name only a few). During the postwar period, the federal government also became a prime sponsor of social reform efforts, aimed at extending civil rights and equal opportunity to the disenfranchised and the disadvantaged. With this expansion of governmental functions has come a growth in government spending. Table 3-3 documents growth in government spending from 1950 to 1980: from 70 to 959 billion dollars, from 17.2 percent of the gross national product to 36.5 percent. Note that the most significant increases have been in the later years (since 1970), and also that welfare spending has tended to increase relative to defense spending, which has declined as a percentage of government spending during the postwar period. Federal government outlays have declined relative to the proportion of government expenses by state and local governments. This latter trend is particularly significant, as will become clear.

Thus, government has grown in the scope of its activity and in terms of dollar outlays. But the growth of government has been unlike the growth of the economy. By comparison with the economy, the growth of government has been relatively *decentralized*. Much of the popular concern with the growth of big government (with its image of faceless bureaucrats immune to local conditions and concerns) seems misplaced. The greatest growth, both in dollars spent and the number of employees, has been at the state and local level. Government has grown most closest to home, in literally thousands of unconnected state, county, and municipal agencies. Indeed the growth in the number of federal employ-

TABLE 3-3   Growth In Government Spending, 1950-1984

Year	$\$^a$ (billions)	$ (per capita)	Federal (%)	Welfare[b] %GNP	Welfare[b] %all $	Defense %GNP	Defense % all $	Fed. %GNP	All %GNP
1950	70	464	60.3	8.9	37.6	4.8	29.1	16.1	17.2
1955	111	670	63.5	8.6	32.7	10.6	58.1	18.0	19.0
1960	151	841	59.7	5.5	38.0	9.1	49.0	18.5	22.0
1965	206	1061	57.9	5.5	42.4	7.7	40.1	18.0	24.4
1970	333	1638	55.5	7.8	47.8	8.4	41.8	20.2	29.2
1975	560	2263	52.1	11.7	55.8	5.8	26.4	21.9	36.5
1980	959	4232	54.8	12.2	56.8	5.2	22.7	22.4	____
1982	1233	5445	57.6	12.8	55.7	6.1	24.9	24.0	____
1983	1351	5772	58.2	13.2	____	6.5	26.0	25.1	____
1984	1451	____	____	12.1	____	6.4	26.7	23.8	____

[a] Current dollars.
[b] Welfare includes social insurance, public assistance, health and medical programs, veterans programs, education, and housing.

Sources: U.S. Bureau of the Census, *Statistical Abstract of the United States*, 1983:273,350; 1985:315; 1986:xiii, 262,301,356,331. U.S. Congress, Joint Economic Committee, Economic Report to the President, 1983:265,328.

ees was very modest during the late sixties (averaging 2.2 percent per year) and actually declined slightly from 1970 to 1981. By contrast, the number of state and local government employees grew relentlessly (in 1950 they comprised 67 percent of all government workers, by 1970 77.9 percent, and by 1980 82.2 percent). The *kind* of work done is also interesting. In spite of the growth of welfare spending relative to defense spending, the largest category of federal workers are civilian Department of Defense employees. In 1981 they numbered more than a million, making up one third of the 2.9 million federal workers. Following civilian defense workers, the second and third most common categories were postal workers (665,000) and workers in health care (225,000). Considering both the rapid growth in expenditures and the modest growth in employment, one could even make the argument—unpopular as it may be—of a growth in governmental efficiency! The largest category of state and local government workers are in education (half are teachers), followed by health care workers as the second largest category (Currie and Skolnick, 1984). In sum, the growth of government has been structurally decentralized—in contrast with the economy, which has become vastly centralized as it has grown.

The expansion of the scope of government activity has also been relatively decentralized: With the exception of the social security system and veterans benefits, most expansion of welfare programs and aid to education has been at the state and local levels. Not only has governmental growth been decentralized, but that growth has been fairly modest in absolute terms when compared with other comparable industrialized societies. Thus the United States has the lowest taxes and expenditures relative to the gross domestic product of most of our trading partners, except Japan. Taxes and expenditures as a proportion of the gross domestic product were lower in the United States than in Australia, Austria, Denmark, Norway, Sweden, West Germany, United Kingdom, and Canada (Currie and Skolnick, 1984:43; U.S. Bureau of the Census, 1983:870).

Changes in the Structural Basis of Politics

In talking about politics it is necessary to distinguish between *government,* which passes laws, creates formal decisions, and allocates budgets and *political parties,* which aggregate and balance (conflicting) political demands. Parties have the functions of converting diffuse political sentiments into specific political programs, developing policy, and grooming leadership. American political parties are not so much ideological groups (as are European parties) as they are loose coalitions defined by common economic interests as well as social and cultural characteristics.

Decline in the Effectiveness of Political Parties One of the best-documented trends in American political parties in the postwar years is the progressive weakening of the power and influence of parties themselves (Schattsneider, 1960; Eldersveld, 1964; Ladd and Hadley, 1975; Pomper, 1984a). This has been documented in several ways. There has been a decline in the dependability of party support and an increase in "volatility," that is, shifts in votes between elections. Shifts between parties averaged 5.9 percent from 1920 to 1948 and 17.1 percent from 1948 to 1972. There has been a growth in ticket splitting. Voting a straight ticket declined from 72 percent in 1948 to 50 percent in 1966. And there has been a growth in the proportion of the electorate that identified themselves as independents, from 20 percent in 1940 to 34 percent in 1974 (Janowitz, 1978). This decline in dependable support for the two American political parties does not represent a decline in political interest or involvement, at least as measured by electoral participation. In 1940 52.7 percent of the electorate voted, and in 1980 this proportion had declined only a few percentage points, to 47.4 percent. Although there has been no significant decline in electoral participation, there *has* been a decline in the perceived efficacy of that participation. In answer to the question "Does it make any difference who wins?" 53 percent said no in 1952 and 66 percent said no in 1964 (Janowitz, 1978:111). Increasingly, American political parties command less secure loyalties of their various constituent groups.

A major cause of the weakening of mass party loyalty is the growth of what William Schneider (1987) has called "anti-establishment populism," meaning the growing popular mistrust of government and its efficiency at all levels. The confidence of Americans to trust the federal government to do what is right fell from 76 percent in 1964 to 54 percent in 1970 to 25 percent in 1980. And the proportion of American who feel that the government is run "by a few big interests looking out for themselves" grew from 29 percent in 1964 to 69 percent in 1980 (University of Michigan, cited in Schneider, 1987). The political establishment of neither major American party has been exempt from the pervasive growth of this popular mood. President Carter and President Reagan were both elected as popular antiestablishment candidates not strongly identified with the established Democratic or Republican Party elites.

I think this decline in the stable bases of support for political parties is part of a broader trend of the growth of distrust in public institutions (see Chapter 2). But there are other causes more specific to the political process itself. It is in part due to electoral reforms that have been established over the last fifty years. The oldest of these is the universal use of the secret (or "Australian") ballot, which weakened poll workers' ability to influence voters. Perhaps more significant was the shift from selecting candidates by party caucuses, which could be manipulated by party regulars, to the widespread adoption of direct primary elections, which opened up the candidate selection process theoretically to everyone. Also, the institution of personal registration requirements have made it less possible for parties to control the composition of the electorate in any given election. These reforms, all applauded because they reduced the likelihood of the more obvious forms of electoral fraud, ironically reduced the ability of the political parties to control the outcome of elections. There are more ironies. The rise of the independent voter and increased ticket splitting are very consistent with an individualistic conception of the desirability of informed and sophisticated voters. All of these changes have supposedly increased the ability of individuals to participate in and shape the outcome of the electoral process, and are generally viewed positively as a decrease in the political cronyism of the past, in which political decisions and candidate selection took place in smoke-filled rooms. The unanticipated consequence of these trends has been to decrease the effectiveness of political parties as organizations.

This consequence is exacerbated by the corrosive effects of the mass media on the political process. While the media have been effective in disseminating political information, they have also helped to create a situation in which a candidate's looks, style, and stage presence are perhaps as important as his political policy. We have moved away from party politics in the direction of personal candidate politics. The result of these changes is that "the presidential contests have long since ceased to be party affairs. A contender described as a Republican or Democrat wins, but it is not primarily a party victory (Ladd, cited in Lipset, 1981:174). This has produced a situation in which we have presidents with perhaps personal mandates, but weak mandates for a political party: Platforms and policy statements become perfunctory and the executive regime exists without a significant organizational power base.

In these emerging circumstances, the party's central function of the aggregation and conversion of political demands is greatly diminished. Parties increasingly have less control over (1) the selection of candidates, (2) the grooming of political leadership, and (3) the formulation of policy. If, for instance, the party leaders had been in tight control of the nomination process, it is doubtful that either Jimmy Carter or Ronald Reagan would have ever obtained the presidential nomination. Ironically, as parties themselves became weaker, they became more susceptible to manipulation and control by their most activist and ideologically extreme constituencies (Schneider, 1987). Thus the New Right (including religious fundamentalists) have steadily gained control of parts of the Republican Party machinery, alienating not only the older, moderate wing of the Republican Party, but many traditional convervatives as well. Similarly the New Politics that emerged from the 1960s continued to gain momentum in the Democratic Party. The party has moved significantly to the left as a narrow coalition of liberal purists and various minority factions has progressively alienated Democratic Party moderates and particularly older, more conservative Southern Democrats. Thus as they have become more distant from the loyalties of the masses of American voters, both parties have become more ideologically polarized, ideologically purist (as a liberal and a conservative party), and less pragmatic and issue oriented. They have also are threatened with political irrelevance as the real political action has increasingly moved outside the arena of party politics.

The Rise of Political Action Committees While political parties have declined as the structural basis of political power in the American system, the importance of single-issue political groups has increased. Single-issue interest groups are not new, by any means, but they have proliferated in recent decades and have come to have a new significance as the power of political parties has declined. The 1971 Federal Election Campaign Act legitimated the existence of such groups and created a mechanism for any group or corporation to establish a segregated separate fund for political purposes. Such political action committees (PACs, as they are called) have become a major force in American politics. Currently there are a vast array of such single interest groups representing business, the professions, ethnic groups, ecological interests, and religious groups. There are groups organized around the issues of gun control, abortion, motorcycle helmet laws, and almost every conceivable cultural issue. There are groups organized to promote the interest of those previously marginal to the political process (e.g., homosexuals, prostitutes). Horowitz claims that in 1978 there were 500 such groups representing corporate interests, 53 representing minorities, 34 representing social welfare interest groups, 33 representing females, 15 representing agricultural interests, and 6 representing population and environmental interests (1979). Certainly his listing is not exhaustive, but it serves to illustrate the diversity of groups that currently exist.

Yet while the diversity of groups and interests represented by PACs is astonishing it should be noted that the ones with the greatest financial resources are those representing the interests of corporations and organized labor. Between 1974 and 1982, 33 percent of the contributions to congressional campaigns came from corporate PACs, 24 percent from unions, 26 percent from trade and professional groups, and 17 percent from all others. These "others" represent primarily ideological interest groups (Malbin, 1984:42). PACs have become far more important as a source of campaign money than political parties, outstripping them in the mid-1980s by margins of five to one (Pomper, 1984a:63).

Horowitz (1979) argues that these special-interest groups may over time replace parties as the structural basis of electoral politics, and he views the development of such groups in a positive way. According to this line of thinking, PACs represent the ability of individuals to organize freely about issues that are important to them. Certainly, as Horowitz argues, life without the ability of individuals to so organize themselves would be less democratic. Yet there are questions. First, I would underline what has just been noted: that in a political system based on single-issue groups, those representing corporate and trade groups are likely to have the greatest resources for shaping the political process. Perhaps, as some may argue, this has always been so, but in such a system the ability of corporate interest groups to dominate the political process is undoubtedly enhanced. Second, even if this were not true, it is still true that PACs, unlike political parties, are *special*-interest groups which make no pretense of representing more general interests and are perhaps incapable of performing the aggregation and conversion functions of political parties. That is, it is doubtful whether PACs can truly balance and seek to reconcile divergent interests or create a widespread consensus about broader societal interests. Pomper (1984a) argues that as the electoral process declines as an effective form of political participation newer forms of popular participation have emerged, including not only PACs but also the proliferation of mass demonstrations and protest activities— once considered appropriate only for those on the fringes of the political system. By now we are accustomed to tractors being driven around Washington, truckers clogging the highways, and mass rallies occurring for almost every issue. And at the local level neighborhood associations have grown which have assumed many of the tasks previously undertaken by parties, including voter registration and community welfare. Pomper suggests that the newer forms of participation

> are all legitimate expressions of democratic opinion. Yet most lack the virtue of political party activity: interchange of opinion, mutual learning and compromise, and the achievement of a community through involvement in a common cause. Worse still are the obstacles they create for policy-makers. They operate differently from parties which emphasize accommodation and recognize divergent interests. Protesters emphasize the "nonnegotiable demand," single-interest groups suffer from tunnel vision, and neighborhood groups are inherently parochial. (Quotation published by permission of Transaction, Inc., from "Party Politics," by Gerald Pomper, *Society*, Vol. 21, no. 6, 1984. Copyright © 1984 by Transaction, Inc.)

We may be witnessing the shift from pluralism to the "massification of self-interest" and an increasing fragmentation of the American political system.

The Consequences of Economic and Political Change

Consideration of these trends in the economy and the polity in tandem does not lead to very sanguine conclusions about the immediate future of democracy in America. Major economic trends included the enormous growth and centralization of economic assets by large corporate entities, which now control at least half of the economic assets in the economy. Political trends included the decentralized growth of government, the decline in power of political parties, and the proliferation of fragmented single-issue groups. It is reasonable to conclude that the political system is becoming less effective in representing the truly general interests and is more likely to reflect narrower economic interests of large corporations. As Walter Burnam put it in 1969,

> It seems evident enough that if this long-term trend toward a politics without parties continues, the policy consequences must be profound. One can put the matter with the utmost simplicity: political parties, with all their well-known human and structural shortcomings, are the only devices thus far invented by the wit of Western man that can, with some effectiveness, generate countervailing collective power on behalf of the many individually powerless against the relatively few who are individually or organizationally powerful. Their disappearance as active intermediaries, if not as preliminary screening devices, would only entail the unchallenged ascendancy of the already powerful....[The decline of parties]would after all, reflect the ultimate sociopolitical consequences of the persistence of Lockeian individualism into an era of Big Organization: oligarchy at the top, inertia and spasms of self defence in the middle, and fragmentation at the base. (Cited in Etzkowitz, 1974:435-37)

Burnam's observations are probably more true now than when he wrote them. And while America is unquestionably among the more democratic nations in the world—both in terms of the pervasiveness of democratic values and established legal procedures for the orderly resolution of political conflict—his conclusions are indeed gloomy for anyone concerned about changes in the structural bases of effective democracy in America.

THE MEANING OF RECENT POLITICAL-ECONOMIC CHANGE: PERCEPTIONS AND REALITIES

Let me turn in the rest of this chapter to a broader look at the meaning of political and economic trends in recent decades. I will talk not about decades of equal years, but about periods in which social change is widely perceived to have taken significantly different directions. *I caution you* that the remainder of this chapter is interpretive; it deals with the meaning of change, which is always contentious in nature. Moreover, it is interpretive because I attempt to come close to the present. It is more difficult to write about change in the present than that in the past, perhaps because we see the complexities of the present more clearly. And in interpreting what is going on today one is more affected by one's own values—personal, political, and scholarly.

Recent Change in the United States: Popular Perceptions

It is a widely held popular perception that recent social change in the United States can be understood in terms of three time periods: (1) a period of *growth and expansion* from 1945 to about 1970, (2) a period of economic *stagnation and limits* during the 1970s, and (3) the beginnings of *recovery* in the early 1980s.

Growth and Expansion: 1945 to 1970　The period immediately after World War II (1945-1970) was a period of rather continuous economic expansion. The GNP grew continuously (from 213 billion dollars in 1945 to 554 billion dollars in 1962), there were trade surpluses averaging 6.3 billion per year, a modest inflation rate (usually between 3 and 4% per year), and low unemployment rates (between 2 and 5% per year). Throughout this period the material quality of life improved for many American families. There was a growth in real per capita income, and the proportion of affluent American families grew significantly (U.S. Bureau of the Census, 1984). Ownership of homes grew at an unprecedented rate. The aspirations of most middle-class Americans included a ranch-style suburban house chock full of such labor-saving devices as dishwashers and washing machines, air conditioners, two cars, home freezers, and a vast potpourri of exotic appurtenances that would utterly astound the masses of people in most other nations.

While there were those who were systematically excluded from the American dream of universal affluence during the 1950s and 1960s, popular movements and the federal government instigated reform efforts aimed at eradicating racial injustice and ending poverty. While in the long run the efforts did not succeed, their failure was never as complete as critics alleged. Between

1959 and 1970, for instance, those officially living in poverty declined from 22.4 percent to 12.6 percent of the American population (U.S. Bureau of the Census, 1983b:3). These efforts must be understood in terms of the general expansion of the welfare state since the great depression of the 1930s, through the efforts of both Democratic and Republican political administrations. The developing welfare state social policy had two broad commitments: (1) at least a minimal level of intervention by the government in managing the economy itself to avert another severe depression and (2) a system of public services and benefits that would provide a basic cushion for those most at risk in the private profit economy—the old, the sick, and the involuntarily unemployed (Currie and Skolnick, 1984:7). Other government initiatives during this period sought to protect civil liberties, extend political franchise more broadly, and reverse environmental degradation. In sum, most would argue that the story of change in America during the fifties and sixties is a remarkable success story: an ever-expanding economy, growing affluence and security of a sizable part of the population, and significant gains in social justice and equity.

Stagnation and Limits: The 1970s   Change took a dramatically different direction during the 1970s. It was a period of economic stagnation and limits: of very slow rates of economic growth, skyrocketing inflation, two dramatic recessions, and increasing trade deficits. There was much talk toward the end of the seventies of the deindustrialization of America, as the sluggish performance of the American economy was compared unfavorably with that of our Japanese and Western European trading partners. It was a time of "stagflation"—high unemployment combined with high inflation. Wages grew during this period in current dollars, but not in constant dollars (those that factor out the effects of inflation). *Real* wages were stagnant and even declined. In constant (1977) dollars the average gross weekly earnings was 187 dollars in 1970 and 173 dollars in 1980 (U.S. Bureau of the Census, 1986:xxi). Meanwhile the consumer price index doubled and came close to tripling by 1981, and the costs of necessities (e.g., food, medical services, housing) rose faster than other costs. This penalized those in lower income brackets more than others. The proportion of Americans living below the official poverty rate began to grow again, from 11.1 percent in 1973 to 15.3 percent in 1983 (U.S. Bureau of the Census, 1986:457), and living standards for many "middle Americans" began to deteriorate. Savings declined, as did home ownership, and indebtedness grew. Attempts to maintain family living standards, which barely kept up with rising prices, explains much of the dramatic entry of women into the labor force. Sociologists have termed this phenomenon "the shrinking middle," or, more abstractly, "restratification" (Rose, 1986).

   In this context of frustrated expectations and economic stagnation, much of the popular support for social justice and reform efforts diminished. In the expansionary sixties society was perceived to be a "variable sum game" in which all could benefit. During the seventies decade of scarcity, limits, and economic stagnation, society came more to be perceived as a "zero sum game" in which one person's gain was another person's loss (Thurow, 1980). The deeply embedded American value of individualism came increasingly to mean the privatization of interests, without the moderating influence of concern for the larger community. Hence the seventies were dubbed the "age of narcissism" and the "me decade." Politically, a prominent characteristic of public opinion during the seventies was

> ...widespread disillusionment with government. The public did not reverse its position on the legitimacy of most government functions, such as helping the poor and regulating business. But the feeling grew that the federal government had become excessively wasteful and ineffective in carrying out those functions. Something had to be done. (Schneider, 1987:52)

This antigovernment revolt, which became manifest in a tax revolt in 1978 and the election of a conservative president, Ronald Reagan, in 1980, had in fact been brewing for many years.

Beginnings of Recovery? The 1980s   The new direction stimulated by the difficulties of the seventiess was understandably shaped by a critique of the social policies of previous decades. The conventional political wisdom of the late seventies and early eighties was that many of the problems of the seventies were caused by (1) excessive government spending (which drained investment capital from the private economy), (2) excessive welfare state programs (which stifled the work ethic, lowered productivity, and caused unproductive dependency on public services), and (3) too much government regulation of the free market economy (which stifled the ability of the private enterprise system to produce profits and growth). A new conservative Republican administration, elected in 1980, had a radically different program for producing an economic recovery and a revitalization of the American spirit.

It rejected the whole idea of extensive government intervention in the economy and social life. In terms of social policy the Reagan administration advocated *reprivatizing* the U.S. economy by tax cuts, reducing government budgets deficits, reduced spending on social programs, and eliminating some social programs. Responsibility for social welfare and education was shifted back to state and local governments, and, increasingly, to private and charitable organizations. Enforcement was weakened for all sorts of federal regulations that were held to interfere with the normal operation of the private economy (e.g., equal opportunity in hiring, environmental regulations). The new conservative philosophy of the eighties sought to roll back the burdensome and inefficient welfare state and let the free enterprise system work.

There is little doubt that in terms of certain macroeconomic indicators the recovery was working by the mid-1980s. The GNP (in constant dollar terms) grew at an average of 6.8 percent per year between 1983 and 1984, compared with an annual average increase of 3.1 percent between 1970 and 1980. The value of common stocks increased dramatically compared to the 1970s: The average annual increase in the value of common stocks on the New York Stock Exchange was 10.8 percent for 1980 and 1983, compared with 4.1 between 1970 and 1980.

The rate of increase in personal income remained virtually unchanged, but price increases for goods and services moderated considerably: from an average annual increase in the consumer price index of 7.8 percent between 1970 and 1980 to 4.3 percent for 1983 to 1984. Corporate profits (before taxes) increased annually at a rate of 16 percent during 1983 and 1984, compared with 12 percent during the 1970s (U.S. Bureau of the Census, 1986:xxiv-xxv). The value of the dollar soared in relation to other national currencies, and while the balance of trade problems were not substantially altered, international investment began to flow to the United States.

The recovery was working for a variety of complex reasons. It worked partly because the election of a conservative, Republican, probusiness administration itself boosted the confidence and morale of the business and investment community, and partly because businesses were given tax breaks and more freedom to operate with fewer restrictions (in the areas, for examples, of environmental and labor regulations). But it worked also because the Federal Reserve System clamped a tight lid on interest rates and regulated the money supply to flatten the spiraling price hikes of the 1970s. It also worked because energy prices fell sharply during the early 1980s.

Recent Change in the United States: Complex Realities

The above analysis represents a fairly widespread perception of periods of recent economic and political change in America. It is also a highly selective picture. Reality is more complex, and I would like to deal below with some of these complexities. No one seriously questions—descriptively at least—the phenomenal economic growth and social progress of the early postwar period. It is the decades of the seventies and eighties that are more complicated.

How Stagnant Were the 1970s?   As a matter of fact the real GNP (after adjusting for inflation) grew during the seventies at an annual rate of 3.7 percent, a rate comparable to the 3.5 percent yearly growth rate of the 1950s (U.S. Congress, Economic Report to the President, 1981:234, Table B-2). Manufacturing productivity did not decline in the 1970s. "With the exception of the brief and wholly abnormal period of 1960 to 1965, productivity increases during the 1970s in American manufacturing were as vigorous as...they had been at any time from 1950 onward" (Schwartz, 1983:110). In spite of the allegations about government spending drying up investment, rates of investment in relation to the size of the GNP did not decline during the 1970s.[2] Government spending increased in dollar figures during the 1970s, but as a percentage of incomes, individual rates of taxation increased only modestly over earlier periods.[3] As a percentage of profit, corporate taxes declined slightly during the 1970s (Schwartz, 1983:85-86). The federal deficit grew in absolute dollar terms, but—a little-recognized fact—as a proportion of the GNP the national debt has been declining steadily since 1945—*until* the beginning of the recovery of the 1980s.[4] Excluding military spending, government spending in 1978 amounted to 26 percent of the GDP[5] (Magaziner and Reich, 1982:43). This is a large proportion of the GDP, but a smaller one than most other industrial nations were spending on domestic programs at the time, when the American economy was alleged to be doing worse.[6] If the 1970s was a decade in which many Americans struggled to maintain their standard of living, it was also a decade that continued the growth of home ownership and availability of consumer amenities of the earlier period.

> From 1965 through 1979, the proportion of American families owning air conditioners rose by 30 percent; those owning clothes dryers rose by 34 percent; color TVs, 66 percent; food waste disposals, 26 percent...and a 50 percent increase took place in the number of automobiles on the road....By the end of the 1970s two-thirds of all American families had their own homes, the highest percentage of the 20th century. (Schwartz, 1983:112)

Between half and three quarters of the growth in ownership of various products took place after 1970 (U.S. Bureau of the Census, 1981:763).

What can you conclude from these facts about the 1970s? First, in spite of difficulties and frustrations, in some ways the economic growth of the early postwar period continued during the seventies. What remains to be explained are the higher prices, slow growth of individual real wages, higher rates of unemployment, and "the shrinking middle," all of which were very real. Second, it is too simple to argue that the growth of government spending on social programs or the national debt were the singular causes of the difficulties of the 1970s. Since I have argued that the decade is widely misunderstood, let me describe some of these other causes of the problems of the seventies.

First, one of the major causes of the difficulties of the 1970s was *demographic change*. The workers of the early postwar period were the relatively small cohorts born during the great depression and World War II. In the late 1960s the large baby boom cohort (see Chapter 2) entered the labor force suddenly and in *huge* numbers. "From 1965 to 1980 the nation's work force grew by 40 percent, swelling by almost 30 million the number of workers seeking jobs" (Schwartz, 1983:124). No other industrial nation had to cope with such an influx of new workers. The result was that even though the economy continued to grow and produce jobs, the number of jobs were divided among more job seekers, which depressed wages and opportunity and increased unemployment. The problems of this crowded generation were compounded because many of the boomers were highly educated and expected better jobs than they got. The problem was also compounded because growing divorce rates and changed attitudes about working women further added to the growing number of job seekers during the seventies. Under these demographic circumstances, *any* economy would have had difficulties maintaining employment and wages, and perhaps *any* political administration would have been blamed for mismanagement.

A second category of causes of the difficulties of the seventies was international in origin. In the early postwar period Americans dominated world trade and the world economy. But by the late sixties the economies torn by World War II had rebuilt to become not only trading partners of America, but significant competitors. Not only did they rebuild, but they often did so with state-of-the-art technologies that challenged the superiority of American industry. By Western European and Japanese standards, the American steel industry operated with antiquated production equipment. Another international factor that dramatically affected the state of the economy in the seventies was the increase in the cost of petroleum. The boom and prosperity of the early postwar years was partly based on cheap energy prices from America's large and readily available domestic sources. During the 1960s imported oil grew as a component of America's energy budget. During the 1970s the world price of oil tripled, beginning in 1973 with the Arab oil boycott and continuing in the late seventies with the Iranian revolution. Such increases in the cost of energy supplies increased the costs and prices of all goods and services. These increases affected every other nation, particularly third world nations, but because Americans were the most profligate consumers of energy in the industrial world, the shocks to the American economy were dramatic.

A third source of the difficulties of the seventies was the way that the American business management and investment were practiced. American managers became more likely than their European or Japanese counterparts to manage and invest for secure short-run profits rather than for long-run productivity, efficiency, or competitiveness (see Hays and Abernathy, 1980, for a comparative study). SOCAL oil company, for example, when it was swimming in profits in the late seventies, did not invest in increased or more efficient energy production. It invested instead in commercial bonds (with an 18.5% return) and simple bank certificates of deposit (with a 14 to 18% return rate). "Those were safe, guaranteed returns...when compared to the uncertainties of investing in a refinery, a coal mine, or a savings association" (Gartner, 1981). This is not an isolated example. The trend to invest in something other than an increased productive capacity has become quite general (Bluestone and Harrison, 1982). A related problem is that corporate growth increasingly involved the buying of other existing corporations. Profits and the growth of a particular corporation is maintained, but such mergers do not create jobs or add productive capacity. In macroeconomic terms the slices of the economic pie are simply rearranged. American corporations spend more buying and selling each other (and preventing hostile takeovers) than in expanding markets and plant modernization. It is investment, but not the sort that produces aggregate economic growth. What is a good short-term investment for an individual firm does not necessarily add up to a good long-term investment policy for the economy and the nation.

To summarize the argument I have been making, government welfare state spending may have contributed to the problems of the 1970s, but I think there were other important causes that have not been a part of the common political rhetoric of the times. These were (1) the dramatic entry of the crowded generation into the labor force, (2) increases in energy prices and international competition, and (3) short-sighted investment practices directed at secure profits rather than growth.

The Reality of the Recovery of the Eighties   In comparison to the 1970s, real growth occurred in the eighties. Inflation and the rise of prices moderated.

Yet it was in some ways a strange recovery, and the conservative program has not gone completely according to plan: Government spending and deficits have continued to increase. In 1980 the federal government spent 591 billion dollars, and by 1984 this had increased to 852 billion dollars. And while the level of federal deficit grew at an average annual rate of 9.1 percent between 1970 and 1980, it grew by 14.1 percent during 1983 and 1984 (U.S. Bureau of the Census: 1986:xxiii). The budget cuts for social programs were more than compensated for by increases in defense and military spending. The major change was not a cut in government spending, but a change in what the government spent money for. The reprivatization strategy of the recovery did not signal "a return to a presumed golden age of small-scale, genuinely competitive capitalism with government a distinctly minor character in the drama of social and economic life" (Currie and Skolnick, 1984:496). The large, highly centralized oligopolistic firms that have been evolving for many years continued to dominate American economic life—with fewer restrictions and less public accountability.

Unemployment continued to be high by the standards of the 1960s. It is true that between 1979 and 1985 six million jobs were created, mostly in the low-paying service categories. But in the same time period 1,834,000 jobs were lost in the "skill-and-brawn" base of production, where Americans make things (White, 1985:40). The fact is that in a mature industrial or service economy that is so capital and technology intensive, economic growth can occur that leaves whole segments of the population untouched (see Chapter 2). No longer can it be said that a "rising tide lifts all boats."

The recovery benefited some segments of America more than others. In the mid-eighties, for example, the farm economy was in the deepest state of depression and experiencing the highest rate of farm foreclosures since the great depression of the 1930s. The economic recovery was accompanied by a decline in pay increases, job security, and eroding medical and private pension benefits for many Americans. The "shrinking of the middle" in America continues. For those on the lower margins of society, cuts in social programs continue to produce higher rates of poverty. In 1979, for example, 79 percent of the children from poor families received some support through the welfare system (AFDC). By 1982 only 53 percent received help (VanderZanden, 1986:179). Homelessness and actual physical hunger increased in America during the 1980s. Thus for many American individuals, the eighties was still a "decade of limits." The recovery looked better in terms of macroeconomic indicators and for the corporate economy than it did for many individuals and families.

By the mid-1980s the buoyant economic growth of the earlier years of the decade showed signs of considerable weakening. In other words, the recovery showed signs of being a typical business cycle rather than a manifestation of long-term change. For instance, compared with the phenomenal rise in the value of stocks between 1980 and 1983, the Dow Jones industrial stock index declined by 1 percent between 1983 and 1984 (U.S. Bureau of the Census, 1986:xxv). That the economic growth of the mid-1980's was mainly a cyclical fluctuation was dramatically demonstrated by the most severe stock market crash since the Great Depression in October 1987. As Thurow argued in 1984, "A cyclical recovery from a recession is not a cure for long-run structural problems" (1984:19).

Retrospect: The Meaning of Change in Recent Decades   Let me summarize the argument I have been making about the meaning of change in the postwar American decades. The first postwar period from 1945 to 1970 was indeed a period of economic growth and social progress. The 1970s were worse, but not as bad as they were popularly portrayed, and some of the causes of the difficulties were widely misunderstood. The early 1980s was a period of economic growth and recovery for some, but for many Americans standards of security, income, opportunity, and welfare deteriorated. These problems cannot be addressed by a cyclical economic recovery but require a fundamental redirection of social and economic policy. I believe it is clear that social justice (which most Americans still value) cannot be automatically achieved through the operation of the private economy alone, and that Americans are going to have to come to terms, one way or another, with their own version of the welfare state. That has at least been the experience of every other Western industrialized nation. I also think economic success requires a more "corporatist" form of capitalism in which the government is actively involved in stimulating (1) real economic growth that goes beyond reshuffling ownership and (2) competitiveness in the international marketplace. This also has, in a variety of forms, been the experience of other Western industrialized nations.[7] The American challenge, I think, is to preserve the economic improvements of the 1980s with the vision of a humane society that treats with care those disadvantaged by social and economic change. Obviously, there is not a simple political formula for addressing these issues, at least not one that is acceptable to the diverse interest groups in American society.

THE AMERICAN PROSPECT: LOOKING AT THE FUTURE

Let me end this discussion by shifting the focus to briefly examine the important social consequences of some of these trends for the American future. Among the more important of these is the continuing trend of *restratification*, or the shrinking middle. This is a pervasive but fairly recent development: Between 1945 and the early 1970s the distribution of income remained remarkably stable, with a modest trend toward a growing middle and shrinkage at the extreme bottom and the extreme top of the American socioeconomic hierarchy. But between 1978 and 1986 those families in the American middle (defined as being between the government's high and low family budget lines) shrank from 52.3 percent to 44.3 percent. And at the top end of the stratification system, the number of millionaires grew from 180,000 in 1976 to 410,000 in 1982 (VanderZanden, 1986:156). By one estimate, two-thirds of those leaving the middle fell in income status and one-third rose (Rose, 1986:9). The shrinking middle does not have a single cause: It is caused by (1) occupational changes in the dual labor market that tend to create mainly low-wage service jobs, (2) by the influx of the boomers into the labor force at entry-level positions, (3) by the increasing divorce rates that create larger proportions of low-income female-headed families, and (4) by the aging of the American population. It was also significantly amplified by the conservative social policies of the 1980s which tended to give significant advantages to those well connected to banking, finance, and the corporate economy while cutting social programs for the middle income and the poor. Contrary to much of our recent history, America seems to be evolving toward a *two class society,* with a significant top and a very large base at the bottom but a much slimmer middle connecting the two extremes.

America is becoming restratified regionally as well. The economic problems of the nation are becoming much more noticeable in the broad heartland of America in comparison to both the eastern and western coastal regions. Prior to 1981, according to a congressional study, growth in family incomes was about the same between the coastal states and the heartland states. Since 1981 California and fifteen east coast states enjoyed an average annual personal income growth of 4 percent, while the rest of the nation had only a 1.4 percent growth rate (Associated Press, 1986, cited in the *Omaha World Herald,* July 10, 1986:1). Much of the problem stems from hard times in the agriculture, petroleum, mining, timber, and heavy-manufacturing sectors, all of which are concentrated in the country's midsection. Growth has come largely in service areas like the financial information and convenience food industries, which are heavily concentrated in the coastal areas. The future continuation of this trend would be to produce income and economic disparities between regions which roughly parallel those that existed between the northern and the southern states during the first half of the twentieth century. Given the equalitarian themes in American culture, a continuation of these trends is likely to produce significant increase in personal frustration among those excluded from the top. Such an increase in mass frustration is likely to manifest itself in more intense social conflict—between regions, economic groups, ethnic groups, and age generations. In a nutshell the twenty-first century may be a period of intense social struggle that will test the cohesiveness of American society. Having said this, I should hasten to say that it is not inevitable that either of these trends will continue unabated.

At a more abstract level, I think there is a long-developing contradiction in American society that will continue to be a source of tension and social change. There is, I believe, a growing contradiction between American *culture* and the *structural organization* of American society as a developed industrial nation. The trends of American culture are to continue, deepen, and expand the values of freedom, individualism, and opportunity. The American cultural dream not only means these, but it substantially means more—more things, more entitlements, more democracy, and more opportunity. At the same time the social organization of community, political, and economic life has exhibited linear trends toward large-scale, bureaucratized, and highly centralized organizations which—in combination with seemingly stubborn limits to economic expansion—have severely limited the range of individual freedom, opportunity, and expectations for improvement. The continuing American dilemma will be, I think, to find a way to reconcile the culture of individualism and freedom with the hierarchical and highly structured institutional framework of society in an age of limits.

This will undoubtedly be a difficult task, but I think that struggling with these dilemmas is not only a chronic source of tension and conflict but also of social innovation and creativity. There are two outlooks on the American prospect that I think are inherently unproductive. One is to be captured by the vision of prophets of gloom and doom who argue that the decline-and-fall-of-everything is just around the corner. The other is to naively try by some magic to resurrect the booming expansionary good times of the fifties and sixties with their visions of limitless affluence and American domination of the world market. Some things are unalterably different than they were then. The American dream requires reshaping.

NOTES

1. *Oligopoly* is the technical economic term for markets that are controlled by a few large producers.

2. Nonresidential investment as a percentage of the GNP was 9.8 percent in 1950, 9.5 percent in 1960, 10.2 percent in 1970 and 10.8 percent in 1979 (U.S. Bureau of the Census, 1980:562).

3. Combined state and federal income taxes amounted to 10.8 percent of Americans' personal incomes in 1960 and rose to 12.9 percent in 1970 (U.S. Bureau of the Census, 1965:420; 1981:280).

4. In 1945 (at the end of World War II) the national debt was 120 percent of the GNP, in 1960 it was 58 percent, in 1970 it was 40 percent, and in 1980 it was 35 percent (U.S. Bureau of the Census, 1983:246).

5. Gross domestic product, a measure that excludes overseas earning.

6. In 1978 government expenditures as a proportion of the GDP was 28 percent for Japan, 40 percent for France, 42.1 percent for West Germany, 51.4 percent for the Netherlands, and 56.8 percent for Sweden (Magaziner and Reich, 1982:43).

7. It is reasonable to fear that this kind of "state-guided" capitalism is connected with political authoritarianism. That was certainly the case in the fascist regimes of Germany and Italy before World War II and is the case in Korea and Singapore in the 1980s. Yet the experiences of the Japanese and the West Europeans suggest that it need not be incompatible with western democratic political forms. Needless to say, a more corporatist form of capitalism is exactly opposite the direction that the conservative political policies of the 1980s have taken the United States.

CHAPTER FOUR
THEORIES
ABOUT THE CAUSES
AND PATTERNS
OF CHANGE

In Part I we explored social change in America mainly in a descriptive way with little attempt to explain why such changes occurred except by referring to specific events and their possible meaning. Such descriptive and concrete understanding is important, but we also need to ask in a more general way why such changes have occurred. There are more general explanations—theories—about how societies work and how change comes about. Put quite simply, theory merely means how we explain things. Theories are general explanations that enable us to make sense out of particular facts and events. They answer our questions about how and why things happen or develop the way that they do. The word *theory* usually has a negative meaning for American students. Indeed, in popular American usage, the word has negative connotations: If something is described as "theoretical," it usually means that it is overly abstract, impractical, too idealistic, unclear, or removed from any everyday-life significance. But in fact, theories are essential to everyday-life, as well as any scholarly or scientific enterprise. Without being aware of it, we theorize about things all the time.

Science involves not only the collection of facts and data, but also attempts to provide coherent explanations about why the facts are arranged as they are. Research as an empirical enterprise, therefore, is not the ultimate goal of science, but is important as a means of verifying or disconfirming theory. Verified theory, which provides us with more comprehensive ways of understanding and comprehending why the world is the way it is, is the *ultimate* goal of science, even though this goal is very elusive in short-run practical terms. The facts do not, unfortunately, speak for themselves, but have to be interpreted. More formally, a *scientific theory* is an abstract explanatory scheme that is potentially open to disconfirmation by evidence. Being abstract means that it is composed of generalizations not tied to particular events.

Theory in Sociology

Social science, like all science, assumes that such events are not entirely random and that, in spite of the complexity and apparent unpredictability of the social world, there is at least a degree of order and predictability that underlies these appearances. Any scientific attempt to understand social change must be centrally concerned with theories about change. Given such complexities of the social world, social scientists often use *models*, which are simplified theories shorn of much elaboration and detail. While we usually assume that a theory asserts something that is true about the world, a model may be used as a heuristic or an "as if" device. That is, a model may be used as a useful metaphor or analogy to facilitate our understanding of something, without the model itself being true in any real sense. For instance, we might use a computer model to understand the way in which the human brain processes information, or a biological organism as a model to understand something about human groups. But in a literal sense the human brain is not a computer and groups are not biological systems. Such use of models is useful but obviously very slippery. Theories can rarely be tested empirically as totalities. Hence we usually try to extract from theories statements of relationships that *can* be examined empirically. When translated into the concrete language of research, these become *hypotheses*.

Having discussed theories in general, scientific theories, models, and hypotheses, we come to another distinction that is important here. It is conventional in sociology to distinguish between theories of large-scale structures and processes (macro theories) and theories of small-scale structures and processes (micro theories). In between these, in terms of scope and abstractness are what are called middle-range theories. For instance, macro theories deal with societies, institutions, or general processes, such as conflict. Middle-range theories would include general theories of organizations, revolutions, and so forth, while micro theories would deal with face-to-face interpersonal behavior or the dynamics of small groups.

Discussing Theories of Change: An Overiew of Part II

I want to focus here primarily on different types of explanations of change, that is, on the *theories* of change, rather than on *theorists*. Therefore, while I have mentioned some of the classic thinkers of the late nineteenth and early twentieth centuries, all of whom were concerned with understanding the transformation to the modern world, I have not attempted to discuss their individual works in great depth. I have used the works of Marx and Weber to illustrate different types of explanations of change. Others are mentioned only in passing.[1] Since sociology as a discipline was originally concerned with understanding the development of industrial societies, many of the macro theories of change focus on the emergence of societies from a preindustrial form. While the time frame of previous chapters focused on the recent American past, the time frame of Chapter 4 reaches further into the past, and many illustrations have to do with understanding the two great transformations in human history: from hunting and gathering to agricultural societies, and from agricultural to industrial societies.

I will focus here mainly on macro theories of change. Some middle-range theories are discussed in later chapters (e.g., theories of social movements and modernization processes as they relate to change). This chapter describes theories that relate to understanding (1) the causes of change and (2) the patterns or directions of change. In the next chapter we will examine the three dominant theoretical perspectives in contemporary sociology (functionalism, conflict theory, and symbolic interactionism) in terms of their implications for understanding change.

THE CAUSES AND PATTERNS OF CHANGE

What are the most important general causes of change? And when we look at change from a broad perspective, can general patterns or directions of social change be seen? These are two basic questions about social change that are explored in this chapter. First I will address the issue of the causes of change. Explanations fall into two general categories: those that emphasize *materialistic factors* (such as economic production and technology) and those that emphasize *idealistic factors* (such as values, ideologies, and beliefs). Second, I will discuss the issue of general patterns or directions of change from several perspectives. One suggests that change takes place in a *linear* and nonrepetitive pattern. Another emphasizes that change is often *cyclical* and repetitive. A third presents a *dialectical* model, which in some ways combines the ideas of linear and cyclical change. Finally, I will briefly discuss another interesting idea about the pattern of change that is called the *center-periphery* model.

MATERIALISTIC PERSPECTIVES

Many have speculated that material factors are the primary causes of social and cultural change. Material factors in this context usually mean economic factors, or technologies related to economic production. In general, it is argued that new technologies or modes of economic production produce changes in social interaction, social organization and, ultimately, cultural values, beliefs, and norms. The most influential classic thinker to adopt this argument was Karl Marx.

The Marxist Perspective

In an often-quoted statement which illustrates his general argument, Marx stated that "the windmill gives you a society with the feudal lord, the steam-mill the society with the industrial capitalist" (1920:119). Marx argued that the forces of production are central in shaping society and social change. By "forces of production," Marx meant primarily production technologies (e.g., windmills) which, in his view, lead to the creation of certain "social relations of production" (e.g., relations between the feudal lord who owns the windmill and his serfs). These relations of production are structured relationships that relate to the methods by which goods and services are produced. Thus, in this perspective economic classes form the basic anatomy of society, and other things (ideas, ideologies, values, political structures, etc.) arise in relation to them. Changes in the forces of production (technologies) erode the basis of the old system of economic relationships and classes and open new possibilities.

To illustrate this way of explaining change, consider the transition from feudalism to industrial capitalism in Europe between 1600 and the late 1800s. This transition was made possible by a number of inventions (e.g., steam power, the power loom, the making of coke from coal and its use in blast furnaces to produce steel) that led to economic production in factories (rather than hand manufactures). These developments made possible increases in productivity and ultimately produced (1) new opportunities for work in urban factories and (2) new economic classes (industrialists and workers), both changes for which the feudal system had no place in its culture, political forms, or categories of people. Gradually the predominant basis for wealth shifted from agricultural production on the landed estates of the aristocracy to industrial production in the urban factories.

As the economic and structural basis of society changed, new political forms emerged (parliamentary democracy) as did new cultural values and ideologies which were consistent with the emerging system (e.g., political freedom, the "virtues" of free enterprise). This social transformation took the forms of bloody revolution in France, attempts at revolution in Germany, and piecemeal reforms in England (also punctuated by violence).

Turning to the analysis of change in industrial capitalism (his real goal), Marx similarly argued that change would occur because of the dislocations (or "contradictions") between productive forces and the social relations of production. Capitalists need profits and compete intensely among themselves. This would lead them to upgrade productive technologies, and attempt to minimize the costs of labor. Thus workers became increasingly exploited while the economy becomes more productive, leading to a series of increasingly intense "crises of overproduction" (periodic economic collapses due to the accumulation of inventories that can't be sold). As these tensions intensified, workers, both as workers and consumers, would become increasingly "immiserated" (in relative terms). Marx argued that workers would take over the economy and reorganize it in their own interests, thus ending the domination of the capitalists and the capitalist system. While he did not make revolution inevitable in the short run, he thought that it was quite probable in the long run.

This depiction of Marx's theory of change is vastly oversimplified and does not do justice to the detail, subtlety, and complexity of his voluminous writings—nor to the elaboration of his perspective by neo-Marxist scholars. Marx was analyzing industrial capitalism as it existed in the 1880s, and his predictions were wrong in many respects (particularly in his expectations about the transformation of society by the workers). Yet for all its flaws, Marxian theory remains an insightful explanation of the technological and economic forces that generate tensions and change in capitalist societies.

Other Materialistic Perspectives

Other thinkers have emphasized material factors as causes of change. For instance, William Ogburn in the 1930s wrote extensively about the technological causes of social change in America. He argued that the advent of the automobile had changed American society in many ways: by increasing geographic mobility, by accelerating the growth of suburbs, and by changing courtship customs (by removing them from the direct supervision of adults). In general, Ogburn's argument is that material culture (technology) changes more rapidly than nonmaterial aspects of culture (ideas, values, norms, ideologies). As a generalization I think it is debatable, but it is true that humans are often more willing to adopt new techniques and tools than to change their cultural values and traditions. He argued that there is often a "cultural lag" between the nonmaterial culture and the material culture, which is a source of tension.

Speculation about the social effects of various technological innovations is a popular activity in America, which says something, I think, about the centrality of technology in American culture. There is, for example, much speculation about the effects of computers. Some speculate that while the computer has enhanced information storage, it makes possible more repressive forms of social control through the (potential) development of large centralized data banks about the characteristics of individuals. Others speculate that the advent of decentralized computers (home computers) may eventually reintegrate work and the family (after their separation in the last 200 years by steam power and the factory system) in an economy that increasingly depends on the generating and processing of information. Most of such speculation depends upon the assumption that material factors are the primary causes of change.

How Technology Causes Change[2]

Technology can cause change in three different ways. First, technological innovations increase the alternatives available in a society. "New technology may bring previously unattainable ideals within the realm of possibility, and it may alter the relative difficulty or ease of realizing differing values" (Lauer,

1977:162). Second, new technology alters interaction patterns among people. Third, technological innovations create new "problems" to be dealt with.

Consider the introduction of snowmobiles into northern areas of Alaska and Lapland. It vastly changed patterns of reindeer-herding and hunting among the Eskimos and Lapps. It vastly increased the geographic mobility of hunters and the amount of game that could be killed. It shortened the workweek of hunters and trappers dramatically, increased their leisure time, increased their earnings, and established a new basis for stratification in the community (based on who owns and who does not own a snowmobile). It generated a serious ecological imbalance as populations of snowbound game animals were wiped out (Pelto and Muller-Willie, 1972:95). This example illustrates all three ways in which technology can cause change. It is important to emphasize that they are found together; that is, while technology creates new opportunities, it changes the structure of human groups and communities, and it ultimately creates a new set of problems. Planners of deliberate technical innovation often forget about the last two factors.

Finally, it is well to mention some of the limits of considering technology as a cause of change. Significant social change can occur without technical change. And technological change may not produce significant change at all levels of society. For instance, the shift from using coal to using gas for home heating may have produced significant change in the energy industry, but it is doubtful whether it caused other significant changes (e.g., in community stratification or family systems). It certainly did not revolutionize communities as did the introduction of snowmobiles among the Lapps.

IDEALISTIC PERSPECTIVES

There are those who have seen ideas, values, and ideologies as causes of change. These can collectively be termed *ideational* aspects of culture, to distinguish them from the material aspects of culture discussed above. *Ideas* here include both knowledge and beliefs; *values* are assumptions about what is desirable and undesirable; and *ideology* means a more- or less-organized combination of beliefs and values that serves to justify or legitimize forms of human action (e.g., democracy, capitalism, socialism). Perhaps the classic thinker in sociology who argued most persuasively that ideational culture can have a causative role in change was Max Weber (1864-1920).

Weber's Perspective

Weber (1905) argued, contrary to Marx, that the development of industrial capitalism can't be understood only in terms of material and technical causes, although he did not deny their importance. Weber observed that the technical conditions for the development of industrialism have existed in many societies (e.g., in classical China and India, in postmedieval Europe). He argued that certain value systems in western society produced the development, in interaction with material causes.

Weber observed that the regions of Europe in which industrial capitalism was most developed at the earliest dates were those regions with the heaviest concentrations of Protestants. This, he argued, was not accidental. He argued that the values of Protestantism—more specifically Calvinism and related religious groups—produced a cultural ethic which sanctified work and worldly achievement, encouraged frugality, and discouraged consumption. The *unintended* social consequence of this religious worldview, which he termed "this-worldly asceticism," was to encourage the development of large pools of capital (by encouraging work, savings, and dampening "frivolous" consumption), and to encourage rational reinvestment and economic growth. Weber argued that industrial capitalism would not have developed in Catholic areas, even though the material and technical preconditions were often present. Catholicism, in its medieval forms, had value assumptions inimical to such developments in the economic realm. First, economic activity was not sanctioned by religious values: Work in the economic realm was not a religiously sanctioned calling, as it was for the Calvinist, but merely the mundane activity that kept one alive. Catholicism encouraged, an "otherworldly asceticism" in which the highest forms of human activity was devotion to God. Second, there was not in the Catholic scheme of values any reason to ban consumption. Calvinism, by contrast, was suspicious of material consumption beyond the bare necessities as leading to moral corruption. Finally, Calvinism suggested that each man is a free moral agent, accountable only to God. Catholicism, by contrast, made men accountable to the Church, which sought to regulate the operation of the economy and other secular aspects of the society in terms of their religious values. Thus in medieval Europe religious authorities attempted to establish fair wages and prices, to regulate economic competition, and to prohibiting making a living as a moneylender—an activity identified as parasitical usury. These regulations, though not always successful, tended to retard the development of free market capitalism.

Weber also argued that there were ideational barriers to the development of capitalism in China and India. In China, the dominant religious values were those derived from Confucianism, which emphasized adjustment to the world as it is, rather than working for salvation and bringing about the "kingdom of God" as the Calvinist was enjoined to do. Thus Confucianism tended to "freeze the past." The minority Chinese religion, Taoism, was, according to Weber, so thoroughly mystical and otherworldly that worldly activity was devalued, and the supreme good was seen in psychic states. Similarly in India, salvation was seen in the observance of religious ritual, not in work in the world, which itself was viewed as a part of the world of illusion. The object of Hinduism was not work in the world, but escape from it through reincarnation. While Weber's characterization of the world religions is surely oversimplified and not adequate in terms of today's scholarly understanding of them, the major thrust of his argument remains: Values and beliefs—both religious and secular—can have a decisive impact on shaping social change.

It is important to clarify Weber's position about change. While his argument about the relationship between the values of Calvinism and the development of industrial capitalism is often, and appropriately, used to illustrate the theoretical approach that emphasizes the role of ideas and values as causative agents, Weber was not saying that ideational factors are the only important causes of change. In fact, Weber's position is much closer to that of Marx than I have portrayed it here. It is really an argument with Marx only in so far as Marx devalued the role of ideas and values as causes. Weber felt that social causation was so complex that it was indefensible to single out certain factors as more basic than others. I will return to this issue shortly.

Other Ideational Perspectives

Guenter Lewy (1974) expanded Weber's argument about the role of religion in social change, by documenting historical instances in which religious values have had a decisive influence in shaping the direction of change. He mentions, for instance, the Puritan revolt in England, the Islamic renaissance promoted by followers of the Mahdi in the Sudan in the 1800s, and the Taiping and Boxer Rebellions in China. Like Weber, Lewy does not ignore the material conditions related to change, but asserts that it is impossible to understand the impetus and directions of change without considering the independent role of religious values and religious authority. One could add more contemporary examples to Lewy's historical ones. It would, for instance, be impossible to give a plausible account of the Iranian revolution of the 1970s without considering the impact of Islamic fundamentalism and the charismatic leadership of Khomeini.

One could list some pervasive cultural values that have broadly shaped the directions of change in the modern world. The ideals of freedom and self-determination would be among these, as would the positive value attached to material growth. In addition to these very abstract values, one could mention more specific values and ideological systems that have had an enormous effect on shaping the direction of social change in the contemporary world. Barber has commented on the influence of Marxism and nationalism:

> As an ideology, as an active critic of established "capitalist" values and norms, and as the active propagator of "socialist" values and norms, Marxism may have caused more social change than any other force in the modern world. In both industrial and would-be industrial societies, its consequences have been very great. Only nationalist ideology, which is also a powerful and independent type of ideological system in the modern world and which the universalist values expressed in Marxism have consistently neglected or underrated, might be said to have had an influence on modern social change of the same magnitude as Marxism. (1971:260).

How Ideas and Values Cause Change[3]

It is important to recognize that ideational culture often acts as a barrier to change. As in the above example, Confucianism in China may have been a barrier to the development of free market capitalism. Furthermore, the same set of ideas and values can promote change in one time and place and retard change at others. At its inception in the 1700s, the doctrines of the virtues of free trade, the free market system, and the undesirability of government interference in such markets (propounded by English political economists Adam Smith and David Ricardo, among others) was a very revolutionary doctrine. It was a penetrating critique of the then dominant mercantilist economic philosophy (in which the kings sought to regulate the economy in national interest) and helped to mobilize support for the dismantling of the mercantilist system. In contemporary America, the ideology of the virtues of the free enterprise system has become a conservative ideological system, which serves to defend and justify the existing economic system and deflect attempts to alter it in fundamental ways. Likewise, as Stokes (1975) has observed, Calvinism may have been a religious doctrine potent with implications for change in its original setting, but in its South African context, Afrikaner Calvinism became a conservative force, which justified continued domination by the white minority and the apartheid system. Thus ideas and ideologies bear no determinant relation to change. Rather, we must understand the way that ideas, values, and ideologies are *used* in particular social contexts.

Ideational culture can cause change in a least three different ways. First, it can legitimize a desired direction of change. This should be obvious. Think how difficult it would be in America to promote change that would *deliberately* result in less equality or less democracy! There are more concrete illustrations. John Dewey's philosophies of progressive education shaped the reform of American public education for several decades (particularly between the 1920s and 1950s), producing an educational system that was, among other things, more oriented to the practical and vocational needs of students, and more community centered (see Swift, 1971). In the 1980s the back-to-basics movement again reshaped the goals and priorities of the American educational system.

Second, ideologies can provide the basis for the social solidarity necessary to promote change. They can be, in other words, "integrative mechanisms, neutralizing the conflicting strains that are found in most societies" (Lauer, 1977:195). Ideology can be a powerful mobilizing force in times of war, for instance, justifying and promoting the war as a holy crusade, a defense of democracy, or creating the thousand year Reich. But think, also, in less dramatic circumstances, of how recent American presidents have concocted ideologies to mobilize support for social change. Since the 1920s America has seen the return to normalcy, the new deal, the fair deal, the new frontier, the great society, and the war on poverty. One can write off these constructions as ordinary political sloganeering, but there is more. Each of these ideological constructions not only defined a set of goals and agendas for change, but helped to mobilize support within the population relative to those goals.

A third way that ideational culture can promote change is by highlighting contradictions and problems. In recent times, American values about equality of opportunity have identified racism and sexism as problems and have generated social movements and official policy directed at ameliorating them. Values, in other words, can highlight areas of discrepancy between the ideal and the actual, a source of tension which often generates change.

The Interaction of Causes

If it can be reasonably argued that material and ideational factors are both causes of change, as the foregoing suggests, we are brought to consideration of the interaction of causes and the notion of multiple causation. In fact, those who emphasize either factor also recognize the other as a causal factor. It's a matter of the relative weight and emphasis given to each. Weber, for instance, would give a greater role to the autonomy of ideas as causes than would most Marxians. However, Marxians recognize a certain role of ideational factors in causing change. Many contemporary Marxians have argued, for instance, that once ideas are established they acquire a certain degree of autonomy from the material base that gives rise to them, and that ideas have

> a possibility of reacting...on the functioning of the economic base. Man's creative thought, inventing ever more perfect instruments of production, transforms, gradually and indirectly, the general economic structure, all social relations, and, as a result, the whole of human reality. (Schaff, 1970:82)

The Marxian position in general, then, is that ideas derive from social and economic structures but become themselves factors in social change. Max Weber's writings contain perhaps the most explicit recognition of the interaction of causes and multiple causation. He argued that social change was the joint product of the interaction of systems of cultural values with possibilities present in the material base. In his terms, ideas are the "switchmen" that determine along which tracks material interests will roll. There is at critical historical junctures what Weber termed an "elective affinity" between certain congeries of ideas and material factors which are mutually reinforcing and which, between them, result in certain concrete directions of change.

PATTERNS OF CHANGE

Let us turn now to the question of general patterns and directions of change. Theories can be grouped into three categories in terms of how they view the pattern and direction of change: (1) linear models, (2) cyclical models, and (3) dialectical models. Also, I will discuss here what are termed "center-periphery" models of change, though these are in some ways different from the other theoretical models of the patterns of change.

Linear Models of Change

Linear models assert that change is cumulative, nonrepetitive, and usually permanent. Change never returns to the same point. Linear (or evolutionary) models can depict change in two stages (diachronic) or in terms of a process that has intermediate stages. The classic thinkers in sociology and anthropology propounded many diachronic theories of change, which are essentially like before and after snapshots of large-scale change in society. Examples of such are Redfield's theory about the transition from "folk" to "urban" societies, Durkheim's theory of the transition from "mechanical" to "organic" solidarity, and Tonnies' theory of change from "gemeinschaft" to "gesellschaft." These theories differ in the factors that they emphasize, but all view the broad historical pattern of change in human societies as involving the transition from small, undifferentiated societies with a homogeneous culture to large societies with a high degree of structural differentiation and a heterogeneous culture. Each, in some sense, depicts the evolution from preliterate to modern societies. Here I am going to illustrate linear theories of change by discussing Lenski's contemporary macro linear "stage" theory of change.

Lenski (Lenski and Lenski, 1982) developed a broad evolutionary theory of different types of societies (hunting and gathering, pastoral and horticultural, agricultural, industrial) in which the transitions from one form to the next were caused by innovations in the technology of economic production that produced an ever larger and more certain surplus of food and material resources. At each larger stage, according to Lenski's theory, society came to be able to support a larger population, and it became more complex and internally differentiated.

Hunting and gathering societies are the oldest type of human societies and still exist in a few scattered places. They were essentially subsistence economies, which produce no significant economic surplus. These were small nomadic groups whose daily life was occupied by the hunting of animals and the search for edible foods. The plains Indians of North America, the polar Eskimos, and the Bushmen of the Kalahari desert in southern Africa are near-contemporary hunters and gatherers. They traveled in bands of about fifty people, following the wild game and carrying virtually all their possessions with them. "Society" was coterminous with the family and kinships unit, though hunters and gatherers were aware of related bands and people with whom they shared language, culture, and territory. There were few larger scale social units or statuses not defined by age, sex, or kinship. The division of labor was simple, based on age and sex. Males were typically hunters, while the women and children searched for edible plants. Leadership was informal and situational, and there were no nonsubsistence roles: *Everyone* helped with the search for food. These were very *equalitarian* societies, since everyone had some rights to share in the food, but this equality was more often based on the sharing of scarcity rather than the sharing of wealth, since there was little surplus to hoard in any case. In sum, hunters and gatherers were small, undifferentiated societies which took food from the physical environment as they found it. They required a very large territory to support even small nomadic bands.

Pastoralists and horticulturalists discovered a more efficient way of making a living from the environment, by cultivating crops (yams, corn) and the domesticating of animals (sheep, goats). Examples of horticulturalists were the woodland Indians of eastern North America and the Trobriand islanders in Melanesia (New Guinea). Raising crops and shepherding animals produced a more certain and a larger food supply. While pastoralists continued to be nomadic, the horticulturalists began to live in larger settled residences. The central social unit among horticulturalists was the *village*, which could support populations of several hundred people and incorporate several different family and kinship units. Thus compared to the hunters and gatherers, these groups represented a growth in the scale of human society as well as an increasingly complex division of labor. The food surplus could support people with full-time nonsubsistence roles (leaders, craftworkers, artists, warriors, magicians). Complex and stable social institutions that were separate from the family and kinships began to emerge. Probably the earliest of these was a separate political system, in which villages came to be ruled by "headmen" and hereditary rulers. Thus the level of social inequality increased, with a generalized distinction between rulers, specialists, and ordinary people.

Agricultural societies originated between five and six thousand years ago and included what we normally call the earliest civilizations (e.g., ancient Egypt, Mesopotamia, ancient China, and the Roman Empire). The technical bases of agricultural societies were the plows drawn by draft animals and grain-cereal agriculture—both of which led to increased productivity and levels of surpluses that surpassed those of true horticulturalists. The invention of basic irrigation techniques and metalworking and the development of mathematics, calendars, and literacy were also important technological bases of agricultural societies. As with the horticulturalists, the development of agricultural economies was associated with a vastly increased *scale* of human social life. The basic social unit was now the city-state, with a central city of perhaps 20,000 people surrounded by a much larger area of villages that are within the sphere of control of the city. Although cities were much larger and denser human settlements, probably 90 percent of the population of agricultural societies still lived in rural villages.

If the scale of life was vastly increased in agricultural societies, so was the degree of internal differentiation and complexity. Now there emerged a whole panoply of nonsubsistence occupational specialties (traders, scribes, priests, potters, weavers, metalworkers, warriors, slaves, healers, etc.), and these coalesced into societywide stratified social classes. Such classes, in descending order of dominance, typically included (1) kings and nobles, (2) priests and scribes, (3) merchants and warriors, (4) craftworkers and artisans, and at the bottom (5) peasants and slaves who farmed the land. There was a dramatic increase in trade and communication between city-state systems, as well as an expansionary dynamic: The stronger city-states tended to conquer the smaller ones, ending in vast political empires ruled by hereditary dynasties. The desire for plunder was probably its own justification for such an expansionary dynamic, but some have argued that it was also due to the economic necessity of maintaining control over remote sites for the coordination of irrigation projects. Wittfoegel (1957) has termed these "hydraulic societies."

Industrial societies began about two hundred years ago in Europe. They began to evolve as technological innovations—first in the textile industry in England—began to substitute machine production for human and animal labor. Industrial production depended not only on the invention of new machines, but also on the utilization of new energy sources to power them—water power, steam engines, hydroelectric power, petroleum, and so forth. This new system vastly increased societies' level of productivity and their ability to produce surpluses of both agricultural and industrial products. A phenomenal economic growth began that was driven by intensification of capital investment and technology (and eventually the deemphasizing of labor) as components in economic production.

The social and cultural changes that flowed from the new industrial system of production were profound. Since the new engines and machines were large and expensive, centralized production in factories began to supplant decentralized "cottage" production which had preceded the industrial era. People began to migrate to the cities in unprecedented numbers, not only because the factory jobs were located there, but also because the upgrading of agricultural technology had reduced the demand for laborers in rural areas. Labor became increasingly a cash commodity rather than a subsistence activity, and work became increasingly separated from family life. The long-term consequence of this was that most people in industrial societies came to reside in larger urban centers (beginning the long-term global trend of urbanization). In industrial societies wealth and power began to be connected not so much with control of land—as in all previous types of societies—but with ownership and control of industrial enterprises. A new class system based on industrial wealth rather than the hereditary control of land began to emerge.

The vast increase of productivity required more raw materials and larger markets, hence it stimulated improvements in communication and transportation. This expansion and centralization of markets was supported by nationalistic desires for territorial consolidation and expansion. The consequences of these economic and political trends was another vast increase of the *scale* and *social complexity* of human social life over that of agrarian societies.[4]

Notwithstanding the misery and exploitation of the early industrial "sweatshops," the long-term consequence of industrial societies was a rise in the material living standards of ordinary people. Lenski argues that industrial societies are somewhat more equalitarian than agricultural societies, with regard to both political rights and the distribution of material goods, thus reversing the long-term evolutionary trend toward greater inequality in agricultural societies. But industrial societies are not utopias: with greater mass consumption comes environmental despoliation, pollution, cyclical economic depressions, depersonalization, and a great deal of moral ambiguity. Overt oppression may have been traded for more subtle forms of alienation. Without question, more people eat more regularly than in hunting and gathering bands, but it is questionable whether they are happier or lead more satisfying social lives. Lenski's theory of linear change cannot be simplistically equated with a theory of human progress.

To summarize more abstractly, Lenski argues that at each stage there is an increase in social complexity and an increase in the "adaptive capacity" of society (hunting and gathering → pastoral → horticultural → agricultural → industrial). Each represents a sort of "discontinuous leap" in human history. Lenski argues that at each stage technical productivity and population density must increase if successive stages of evolution are to emerge. But each seemingly discontinuous stage of social evolution is in fact dependent upon more subtle cumulative processes involving the gradual addition of new elements to a continuing base. Each society does not necessarily pass through the same set of fixed stages. The United States, for example, was never a society of hunters and gatherers or pastoralists, though it was once largely a society of agriculturalists—prior to the dominance of the industrial economy in the mid-nineteenth century. Lenski does argue that his scheme depicts the evolution of the "whole of humanity," as an historical abstraction. In a similar vein Steward has proposed thinking about broad linear patterns of change as "multilinear evolution," which means that

> certain basic types of culture may develop in similar ways under similar conditions, but few concrete aspects of culture will appear among all groups of mankind in a regular sequence. (1955:4)

In spite of the complexities and difficulties with linear models of change at the most abstract levels, we often conceptualize change as linear, cumulative, and nonrepetitive.

CYCLICAL MODELS OF CHANGE

One of the oldest conceptions of the long-term pattern or direction of change is that is it cyclical or repetitive. The French have a phrase for it: "plus ça change, plus c'est la même chose" (the more a thing changes, the more it stays the same). This view does not deny change but denies that it is leading anywhere over the long term (Moore, 1974:44). Advocates of cyclical models of change argue that in important ways, history *does* repeat itself.

The classic macro cyclical theories of change were mostly "rise-and-fall" theories of civilizations. In the ancient world a systematic statement of such a rise and fall theory was that of Ibn Khaldun (1332-1405), who attempted to explain the perennial conflict between city dwellers and nomads in the medieval Islamic societies of North Africa, and the resulting political cycles of the rise and fall of dynasties. In the early twentieth century social scientists began to phrase such cyclical theories not in terms of moral cycles of recurring decadence, but in terms of biological models of growth and decay. Societies were thus said to be like organic systems, going though periods of youth, adolescent growth, mature vigor, and senility in old age. The most pessimistic among these was

Oswald Spengler (1880-1936) who argued in the 1930s that Western European civilization was in its twilight years and could be expected to be replaced by newer, more vigorous civilizations. His major statement of this thesis, aptly titled *The Decline of the West*, was published in 1932 and fit well with the post-World War I intellectual pessimism of the times. Similar, but less pessimistic, were the theories of Arnold Toynbee (1962) who at least held out hope of the revitalization of declining civilizations by reinvigorating the creativity of elites. Within sociology, the most influential cyclical theory was that of Pitirim Sorokin (1889-1968) who argued that the master "cycles" of history were oscillations between periods dominated by idealism and those dominated by hedonism and materialism, interspersed by periods of transition that creatively "blended" the two dominant cultural frameworks. In the Western historical context, Sorokin argued that medieval Europe was an epoch dominated by idealism, the Renaissance and Reformation were transition periods, and contemporary Western societies are dominated by materialism and hedonism. He anticipated the ultimate collapse of Western materialism and a return to a more idealistic culture. As you can see, these classic cyclical theories are rather pessimistic: They do not urge us to look for much long-range significant change, much less any improvement in the human condition.

It is important to understand what is going on here. Cyclical theories become plausible if we agree with the analyst that the "important aspects" of change are historically repetitive. What the "important aspects" are, of course, is always arguable. This selectivity—emphasizing some things, deemphasizing others, and using historical evidence in a highly selective way—illustrates what I think is a general problem with purely cyclical macro theories. *All* theories do that to some extent, but I think the problem is particularly pronounced with the purely cyclical ones. In addition to the problem of selectivity, in their pure form they deny the importance of developmental, nonrepetitive change. To assert that there are cycles in history is one thing, but to argue that the singular transformations associated with agricultural change or the Industrial Revolution are without lasting importance is quite another thing, and few would agree. I will not detain us here with a more detailed examination of these classic views, but I will return to the problem of large-scale cyclical theories.

Less Abstract Patterns of Cyclical Change   It is relatively easy, on the other hand, to see some cyclical patterns of change at less abstract levels. Perhaps the most familiar example is the business cycle that tends to exist in free market economies, involving repetitive cycles of economic expansion and contraction. Production tends to increase until overproduction occurs and inventories cannot be sold. At this time businesses begin to cut back on production initiating economic contraction and recession. At the time that such contraction falls below demand, a new wave of expansion of production is initiated. While these business cycles are well documented, all governments in industrialized economies have sought to intervene by various methods (to either stimulate or dampen growth at the appropriate times) to smooth out such cycles.

Social scientists have also identified repetitive cycles of change and development in American nuclear families. It is argued that families have common characteristics and problems at each stage in the family life cycle, which are determined primarily by the presence, number, and ages of children in the family. Thus Duvall and Miller (1985), Rodgers (1973), and many others maintain that family problems and characteristics are different in families consisting of a young couple without children, families with young children, families with older children, and families whose children have left the home. This cycle is not, of course, repeated in any one family, but is, it is argued, an ongoing dynamic that is repeated among millions of American families. The same dynamic is not observed in extended family systems, which are likely to have a variety of people of different ages at different phases throughout their existence.

I have often thought that the typical college semester has a repetitive dynamic about it in the way that it is experienced. Students and faculty begin each new semester with a great deal of enthusiasm and motivation to stay on top of their work. By midsemester enthusiasm and self-discipline lags, and people are catching up or coping with their tasks on a day-to-day basis. Toward the end of each semester there is another spurt of self-discipline and motivation to work, in order to finish the semester as well as possible. But with each semester the cycle seems to be repeated. The question can be raised as to whether these cycles are really change at all, or are they rather ongoing dynamics of the way stable systems function? From the standpoint of the *participants* in the social system, things may seem to change dramatically. But from the standpoint of the *system* itself, there may be no change in the long run. Thus the answer about whether there is significant change going on depends upon the level of analysis and the time frame.

Contemporary Macro Cyclical Theories

Notwithstanding my critical comments above about the older macro cyclical theories of change, we are still fascinated with the possibility of "long cycles" in history. Numerous analysts have noted a periodicity of the outbreak of major wars in Western history over the last two hundred years and wondered about it. And some economists (mainly European) have argued that there are "long wave" cycles of expansion and contraction in the world economy, termed Kondratieff cycles, with peaks between forty-five and sixty years apart. Forrester makes a plausible case for such long wave cycles:

> The economic long wave is the phenomenon responsible for the great depressions of the 1830s, the 1890s, and the 1930s and causes such episodes to occur approximately 50 years apart. Present worldwide economic crosscurrents suggest that we are entering another such downturn of the long wave. Around 1931, as now, there was great concern about foreign debt and the possibility of default. Three to five years later, a number of major Latin American defaults did occur. In the past few years, we have again seen speculative bidding-up of prices of physical assets and land, and the collapse of those prices, as occurred during the 1920s and 1930s. (1985:16)

But even though we continue to be fascinated by the possibility of such long cycles in history, the evidence for such cycles remains controversial, and many American academic economists assert that no such economic cycles exist.

One of the more articulate contemporary advocates of a macroscopic cyclical theory of social change is Daniel Chirot, who argues, "The key to a sensible theoretical approach to change is the recognition that there exist long periods of history in which the essential forces at work remain quite similar" (1986:292). Like most cyclical theorists, he argues that these cycles can be compared with one another, but unlike Sorokin and the classic thinkers, Chirot thinks that such similar cycles are limited to specific historical eras. And even within any specific historical era such cycles are not actually unvarying: Enough permanent changes accumulate to make the general pattern invalid. New eras have different sets of cycles and mainsprings of change and require different models of cycles (1986:292). Chirot argues that repetitive cycles are embedded in longer-range historical eras that are not repetitive and therefore, in fact, combines cyclical and linear models of change. I am here emphasizing its cyclical aspects for purposes of illustration.

To simplify things for the sake of his argument, Chirot depicts human development in two broad historical eras, *premodern* and *modern*, as would an oversimplified linear theory. But he understands the dynamics of change within such eras quite differently from Lenski, who argued that each new technological and economic base produced qualitatively different societies. According to Chirot, societies of the premodern era, that is, the preindustrial agrarian societies of the Near East, Europe, and Asia, were the "great civilizations." They had dense populations, powerful states, and elaborate cultures, and they experienced recurrent cycles of crisis and decline. Because

> populations in that era grew more quickly than technology advanced, societies tended to experience recurrent crises of overpopulation, malnutrition, disease, and social chaos...Proximity to nomads, dependence on fragile irrigation systems, and endemic diseases combined with population cycles to magnify the periodic catastrophes. (1986:292)

Throughout these recurrent cycles of growth, crisis, and decline the state was controlled by elites that competed with each other for the key resource: taxable peasants.

With the development of industrial societies in the modern era, the state commands much greater mass loyalty, develops a nationalist ideology, and seeks to promote the general welfare and to stimulate economic production. But most importantly in industrial societies the old cycles of overpopulation and recurrent disasters have ended to be replaced by cycles with new dynamics. Compared with preindustrial societies, the outstanding feature of modern industrial societies is their technological inventiveness. In modern societies each economic cycle begins with a new technology applied to production, new profits, and economic growth. Eventually markets become saturated by overinvestment in aging industries followed by business failures and an economic crisis. This is accompanied by high levels of unemployment, political stress, and social disruption. This crisis is typically a prelude to the development of new economic technologies and a new dynamic of economic expansion.

More concretely, Chirot sees the cycles of industrial societies as follows. The *first industrial cycle* began in Europe with the Industrial Revolution in textiles from the 1780s to the 1820s. At its stage of overexpansion it produced the unstable political atmosphere of Europe in the 1830s and 1840s. The *second cycle*, based on the development of iron and railroads, lasted until the 1870s. The transition to the *third cycle*, based on steel and the chemical industry was "sufficiently painful to provoke intense imperialistic rivalries among the advanced Western powers" (1986:293-94), and led to the international conflict that resulted in World War I. That war and its aftermaths—the great depression of the 1930s and World War II—made the transition to the fourth cycle very long, painful, and difficult. This *fourth cycle*, based on automobiles and high mass consumption, began to benefit most people in the industrial nations only after 1950. "The great tragedies of the twentieth century can only be explained as the unfortunate conjunction of normal cyclical changes combined with bitter international conflicts that have stemmed from them" (Chirot, 1986:294. All quotes from *Social Change in the Modern Era*. Copyright © 1986 by Harcourt Brace Jovanovich, Inc. Reprinted by permission of the publisher).

After World War II there was an enormous period of worldwide economic expansion involving the development of more extensive trade relationships between the industrial nations, and between the industrial and the less developed nations of the non-Western world (more about this in the last part of this text). By the 1970s there was a worldwide recession and many have seen the stagnation and overexpansion of this fourth industrial cycle. Others have speculated about the development of new postindustrial economic technologies and forms based on computers and the information age (Bell, 1969; Naisbett, 1982). If the world is moving into a new fifth industrial phase, Chirot argues that "the same patterns of sectoral decay in old leading industries, and the rise of new firms, new regions of technological dynamism, international tensions, and pressures on governments to help smooth the transition are being repeated." The really important question is "whether or not the present cyclical change that began in the 1970s will produce a renewed series of traumatic events" (1986:294). It should be obvious to you that this is more than a mere academic question. Chirot's theory of change is intriguing, important, and controversial. It mixes cyclical and linear models of change in a creative and complex fashion. I will return to his theory in the final chapter.

DIALECTICAL MODELS OF CHANGE

Dialectical models are also more complex notions than purely linear or cyclical ones. They assume that change is in the long run cumulative and developmental and is not a smooth and gradual evolutionary process. Dialectical models of change involve conflicts between opposing principles and trends (or "inner contradictions" as Marxians would call them) as well as struggle between groups with contradictory interests within the society. Such contradictions in culture and social structure are viewed as the causative "engines" of change. The long-term outcomes are the "directional vectors" which result from the struggles between opposing tendencies and groups. Although the basic notion of the dialectic derives from the writing of Hegel, the best-known advocate of a dialectical theory of social change was Marx. He argued that change resulted from "class struggles" between those with a vested interest in maintaining existing production systems and those with interests in new and emerging ones.

In some ways, dialectical models of change combine both linear and cyclical theories. How so? Roberta Ash Garner, for instance, argues that

> History "repeats itself" only in the sense that some processes of change persist. The contents of these processes, the specific behaviors that are changing, are never quite the same....Small changes pile up until the system collapses. The old system give way to a new one. The old system drops into the past, never to be revived. However, the new system, already at the moment of its appearance contains stresses that will slowly enlarge, like cracks in the foundation of a building, until the whole collapses. Yet the process is not cyclical. Growth, decay, and collapse never return us to the initial starting point. Change is spiral rather than cyclical. (1977:408)

In this dialectical view, the cycles of the birth and decline of social systems are determined by the unraveling of stresses and contradictions that are inherent in social life. Yet the resultant "vector" of these built-in conflicts produces more than just a "turning of the wheel" of historical cycles—there is real, cumulative change in the longer view of history.

While such dialectical thought is rooted in classical Marxism, contemporary dialectical theories differ from classical Marxism in that they do not accept economically based "class conflict" as the only, or even the most important, source of "contradictions" that produce conflict and change. Let me briefly explore several varieties of contemporary dialectical thinking about social change.

There are those who argue that contradictions result from differential rates of change in various institutional sectors of a society. "For example, technology and the productive system as a whole tend to change more rapidly than the political and ideological superstructure, which changes slowly and contains a large cargo of cultural 'baggage' carried over from the past" (Ash Garner, 1977:311). We have met this view before, in the guise of Ogburn's "cultural lag" theory, and while it does not deny the importance of class conflict as a manifestation of contradictions, it locates the sources of contradictions more broadly in differential rates of change.

Other dialectical theories depart more significantly from the materialist view of the causes of change. Raymond Aron (1968), for instance, uses the notion of contradictions to mean contradictions between structural imperatives and individual aspirations (or at best, cultural themes). He argues that there are three common sources of inner contradictions in contemporary societies. First, modern societies are equalitarian with regard to the aspirations of people but hierarchical with regard to structure and organization. Hence there is a dialectic of equality in modern societies. *Second*, there is a contradiction regarding socialization in modern societies: Individuals desire increasing individuation and uniqueness, while the structures of socialization create increasing "massification" with pressures toward conformity and sameness. Hence, the "dialectic of socialization." Third, in societies around the world, there is a desire for higher levels of affluence and national autonomy at the same time that the world is becoming increasingly interrelated and interdependent. The desire for such autonomy is frustrated by such dependency. Hence, according to Aron, the "dialectic of universality."

Within this dialectical framework (defining contradictions between strucural imperatives and human aspirations and culture), Gorz has depicted more concretely the fundamental contradictions of advanced industrial societies as follows:

> Industry expects the universities to produce swarms of skilled workers, who can be put directly to work in production, applied research and management. However, the monopolies are perfectly well-aware of the danger for the existing order of a general upgrading of educational standards. For once a certain level of culture has been reached, highly skilled workers feel the vital need for professional, intellectual and existential independence....The problem for big management is to harmonize two contradictory necessities: the necessity of developing human capabilities, imposed by modern processes of production and the—political—necessity of insuring that this kind of development of capabilities does not bring in its wake any augmentation of the independence of the individual, provoking him to challenge the present division of social labor and distribution of power....*It is impossible, in the long run, to bottle up independence*....[managers] dream of a particular kind of specialized technician, recognizable by the coexistence in one and the same person of zest for his job and indifference about its purpose, professional enterprise and social submission, power and responsibility over technical questions and impotence and irresponsibility over questions of economic and social management. (Emphasis added. 1972:487, 489)

Others have used the notion of contradictions in a more purely *structural* way, to mean that there are competing principles of social organization which produce conflict and ultimately change. Wallerstein (1974), for instance, has produced a somewhat different dialectical rendition of the transition from feudalism to industrial capitalism than that of Marx. He argues that it was the conflict between (at least) three contradictory modes of political and economic organization that led to the ultimate demise of feudalism. First was the contradiction between the older subsistence agriculture with its serfs and the newer commercialized cash crop agriculture with its wage workers. Second was the contradiction between the older decentralized craft production and the newer centralized factory system. Third, was the contradiction between the small market system of local trade with the vast expansion of markets that attended the colonial expansion into the non-European world. The outcomes of these competing modes of social organization gradually defined the emerging parameters of the industrial world:

1. Nationally and internationally marketed goods came to be more important than those of local craft production, hence the vast growth in scale of industrial economies and societies.
2. Local guild masters of the late feudal system were replaced by the entrepreneurs of the free marketplace as the dominant economic elites.
3. New political and cultural forms emerged which reflected the growing dominance of the commercial entrepreneurs and merchants.
4. Despite repeated revolts, displaced workers and peasants failed to establish control over either town politics or the work process.

To summarize, while dialectical theories of change involve a distinct notion about the pattern of change, the framework has been used not so much to identify temporal patterns or directions of change but rather to identify aspects of social organization likely to generate conflict and change. Its major use is in a broader "conflict theory" of change (discussed in the next chapter).

CENTER-PERIPHERY MODELS OF CHANGE

Center-periphery models describe the manner in which change spreads from one society to another, or from one region to another within a society. Hence they are spatial rather than temporal models, as previous ones have been. The center-periphery model assumes the diffusion of an item of change from a center of innovation to the ultimate adopters of change. In such models the diffusion of change is assumed to be "a centrally managed process of dissemination, training, and the provision of resources and incentives" (Schon, 1971:81). Such dif-

FIGURE 4-1 CENTER-PERIPHERY MODELS OF CHANGE

CENTER-PERIPHERY
MODEL

PROLIFERATION-OF-CENTERS
MODEL

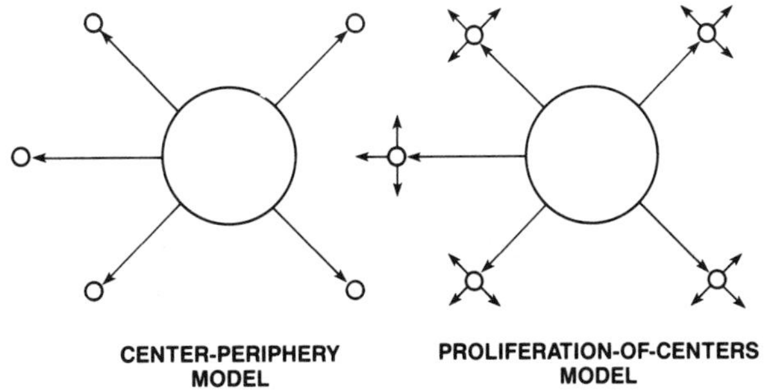

Source: From Donald A. Schon, *Beyond the Stable State: Public and Private Learning in a Changing Society,* copyright 1971 by Donald A. Schon and Random House, Inc. Used with permission of the publisher.

fusion from a cultural center depends on change agents (traders, soldiers, missionaries) who introduce innovative items in remote areas.

There are three variants of center-periphery models. The first has been termed *the Johnny Appleseed model*. In this variant the change agent is a kind of "evangelist" who roams his territory spreading a message. Into this category fall the traveling scholars, saints, and artisans of the Middle Ages; Voltaire and Thomas Paine; and the "bards" of activism of the 1960s in America such as Ralph Nader or Saul Alinsky. The second variant has been termed *the magnet model,* in which bright "provincials" go to the cultural center, learn the innovation, and carry it home. Schon (1971) cites the nineteenth-century German universities, which attracted students from all over the world, as examples of the magnet model. This method of the diffusion of change continues today, as artists and fashion designers continue to study in Paris, or as students from the third world continue to go to the United States, the United Kingdom, or the Soviet Union to study and return home. A third variant of the center-periphery model is what Schon terms the *proliferation of centers* model, in which peripheral sites become subcenters with more remote peripheries of their own. These subcenters become partly autonomous and differentiated from the original center.

The effectiveness of a center-periphery system for the diffusion of change depends upon several factors. First, it depends upon the amount of resources at the center and the "energy" it is able to invest in the process of diffusion. Second, it depends upon the number of peripheral locations being served, and third, it depends upon the length of the spokes, or radii, over which persons, material, and information must flow. Ultimately, the effectiveness of a center-periphery system depends upon the maintenance of an effective logistical system, and such a system may fail because the center lacks resources, overloads the spokes of transmission, or mishandles feedback from the periphery. Thus the ancient world empires often collapsed because they became overextended: Too few resources were used to supply too many remote sites over a far-flung geographical area. The attractiveness of center-periphery models is in their utility to illuminate change in a variety of concrete contexts. They can be used to understand the growth and expansion of political empires, market systems, and a wide variety of cultural frameworks. Center-periphery models can help us understand the growth and diffusion of such diverse things as of Christianity, Coca Cola, and Communism (Vago, 1980).

SUMMARY: CAUSES AND PATTERNS OF CHANGE

We have now discussed theories of the causes of change (material causes, ideational causes, interacting causes), and several models of the directions and patterns of social change (linear, cyclical, dialectical, and center-periphery). Clearly, a case can be made for each of these theoretical approaches. How can they all have some validity?

Part of the answer is that the different approaches focus on different units of analysis and levels of abstraction. For example, linear and cyclical models both focus on changes over time, but linear models concentrate on understanding cumulative and developmental change processes that occur in many concrete social units, whereas cyclical processes focus on repetitive change processes in *particular* structural units (e.g., civilizations, families). Dialectical models assume that in the short term change is repetitive in that it involves the conflict between "contradictory" aspects of society (variously conceived), but they also assume that there *is* a long-term direction to change which is the outcome of these conflicts. With the exception of Marx, dialectical theorists have focused more on identifying the contradictions which cause change rather than the long-range trajectories of change that are the outcomes of the dialectical process. Still different are center-periphery models which focus on the dissemination of a particular innovation within a concretely defined geographic area or social system.

Another part of the answer has to do with the way that we *use* theory. We tend to use theory in practical ways by selecting the theoretical approach most appropriate to explain the particular phenomenon or problem in which we are interested. In terms of this pragmatic approach to theory, there are no true or false explanations (theories), but different approaches are more useful or less useful—depending on what we want to explain. But the question (about reconciling different theories) is still more complex than selective attention to different units/levels of analysis or the analyst's utilitarian choice of the most appropriate theory for his/her work. Theories may be practical tools to explain things, but in terms of the goals of science, they are also "truth statements" about the way the world is. Different theories represent honest and important intellectual disagreements about—in this case—the causes and patterns of social change. While it will never be achieved, I think that social scientists need to work toward the goal of unified, integrated theory. Kenneth Boulding (1970) has suggested that we will have a more complete understanding of social life when we understand the relationship between (1) equilibrium processes, (2) cyclical processes, and (3) cumulative processes. This is a *large order,* which includes not only understanding change processes but the processes that serve to maintain stability and persistence as well.

NOTES

1. If you are interested in pursuing any of these classic views in depth, there are many sources available. See Coser, 1977; Turner and Beeghley, 1981; Ritzer, 1983; Appelbaum, 1970; and especially Schneider, 1976.
2. The following relies heavily on Lauer, 1977.
3. Again, I am indebted to the ideas of Lauer (1977) in the following section.
4. If this is beginning to sound like the description of recent structural trends in the United States presented in previous chapters, it is not accidental.

CHAPTER FIVE
CONTEMPORARY SOCIOLOGICAL THEORY AND CHANGE

There are three established theoretical frameworks in contemporary sociology. These are structural functionalism, conflict theory, and interactionism (there are really many more theories, but these are the most widely recognized). They embody three different images of society and social change and provide different answers to the most basic sociological questions. For our purposes, these questions boil down to, what factors determine the structure of society and the nature of change? One answer is that society and change are shaped by the necessities of survival (the structural functionalist answer). Another is that society and change are shaped by conflict among the parts and groups within society related to authority and the control of scarce resources (the conflict theory answer). A third type of answer is that society and change are shaped by the meanings and definitions that emerge from interaction between the various actors and parts of society (the symbolic interactionist answer). The three theories derive from different historical sources. Structural functionalism originated in organic analogies between biological systems and social systems commonly used in nineteenth century sociology and anthropology. Conflict theory is historically rooted in classical Marxism, although contemporary conflict theory in sociology has considerably modified early Marxist thought. Symbolic interactionism derives most directly from the thinking of American pragmatist philosophers of the early twentieth century: William James, John Dewey, and George Herbert Mead. In this chapter I will discuss these three theoretical perspectives and their implications for explaining social change. After discussing each of these three theory perspectives I will briefly explore how each might be used to understand the changes in American society. The main focus of this application is on the meaning of the changes in recent decades discussed in Chapter 3: the expansionary fifties and sixties, the stagnant and difficult seventies, and efforts at recovery and reform in the eighties. In other words, the application of the three perspectives focuses mainly on changes in the domestic economy and distributional issues (e.g., inequality). You might want to try to apply them to explain other important events effecting change in American society during this period (e.g., the Vietnam war, new developments in reproductive technology).

STRUCTURAL FUNCTIONALIST THEORY

Structural functionalism (functionalism, for short) assumes that a society is a system of interrelated parts and subsystems which function or engage in activities that promote the survival of the whole system. The initial focus of much functional thinking is to define activities that are necessary for the survival of the entire system ("functional requisites" or "imperatives"). Lists of such functional requisites vary in length and abstractness. According to Mack and Bradford (1979) there are five such functional requisites. Every social system must be concerned with

1. The replacement of individuals (by reproduction or recruitment)
2. Socialization (enabling individuals to participate)
3. The production of goods and services (hence, an economy)
4. The provision of social order (hence, a political system)
5. The maintenance of common symbols, values, and motivations (hence, culture)

Parsons (1951) states the functional requisites more abstractly. He argues that there are four basic functions that any society (or any of its subsystems) must be concerned with for its survival.

1. Adaptation (the generation of resources from the environment)
2. Goal attainment (choices about the consumption of resources)
3. Integration (regulation of relationships between the parts of the system)
4. Latency or "pattern maintenance" (providing cultural legitimation for the manner in which other functions are accomplished)

Less abstractly, Parsons is talking about the functions of (1) the economy, (2) the political system, (3) the legal system, and (4) the diverse agencies that perpetuate culture. It is important to note that Parsons emphasizes *culture* as the major force which binds and integrates the various aspects of the social world. He has, in fact, labeled himself as a "cultural determinist" (Parsons, 1966). This assumption, as you will see, has an important impact on how he develops a theory of social change. You can see that the functional requisites depicted by both Mack and Parsons lead to a discussion of social institutions. From this perspective, different functional requisites are viewed as producing differentiated *structures* that "specialize" in accomplishing them (e.g., the family, economy, polity, religions).

Much functionalist thinking (particulary in the 1950s) viewed society as a system that persists by maintaining "equilibrium," that is, the various structures and institutions are viewed as operating in concert in a mutually reinforcing way to maintain stability in the way that each functions and in the relationships between them. Society is thus viewed as a "homeostatic" system, which operates to perpetuate itself. This was a way of explaining persistence and stability but not change. This inability to explain change was criticized by many during the early sixties (Parsons was the focus of much of this criticism), and functional theorists began to be more concerned with the problem of understanding change. How did they do so?

Structural Functionalism and Social Change

Functionalist thinking about change begins by asserting that in the actual world, integration and "balance" in society is always incomplete. To some degree real societies are "out of sync" for a variety of reasons. They develop inconsistencies, contradictions, and institutional practices that do not mesh in an integrated way. There is a constant struggle to maintain order and integration in connection with the realities of such *strains* (a general term for such inconsistencies and lack of integration). Functionalist theory understands social change as the maintenance of a "moving," or dynamic, rather than a static equilibrium between the components of the social system. There are many possible sources of such strains. Most obvious, since social systems are all "open" in varying degrees to their environments, stains can be the result of "exogenous" discrepant culture items that are "imported" from surrounding environments, both natural and social. There may be new ideas, values, and technologies from other groups and societies, carried by immigrants, traders, or missionaries. And changes in the physical environment (e.g., drought, pollution, depletion) may produce strains in maintaining certain levels or kinds of economic activity. But strains can also be of "internal," or "endogenous," origin in this revised functionalist view. They can result, for instance, from inconsistencies between widely shared values and actual behavior. They can result from different values themselves that may have contradictory implications for choices and behavior. They can be strains resulting from innovations that do not "work" within the established institutional practices. They can be strains resulting from differentiated social roles that have different outlooks and responsibilities. Strains may be produced by different rates of change in various institutional realms that may become somewhat isolated and don't "mesh" in an integrated fashion. Consider the following examples of strains in contemporary America: (1) conflicts between the traditional female role and the realities of dual-income families; (2) in the 1980s, the overproduction of college graduates and the underproduction of professional and upper middle class jobs; (3) values about equal opportunity versus the realities of racism and discrimination. Even though functionalists do recognize that strains can originate from within the social system, exactly how this happens within the framework of the theory is not clear, given the equilibrium assumption.

While certain levels of strain can be tolerated, if strains exceed certain limits (and functional theory provides few clues as to what these limits are) they produce change in some aspect of the system—as an attempt to contain or adapt to strain. Thus functional theorists argue that changes in the parts of a system

> may balance each other so that there is no change in the system as a whole; if they do not, the entire system will probably change. Thus while functionalism adopts an equilibrium perspective, it is not necessarily a static point of view. In this moving equilibrium of the social system, those changes that do occur are seen as doing so in an orderly, not a revolutionary way. (Ritzer, 1983:224)

In response to his critics' pointing out that his theory was incapable of explaining change, Parsons (1966) developed an *evolutionary* theory of change that distinguished between several types of change. First, there is *system maintenance* which restores a previous pattern of equilibrium (such as rebuilding a community after a disaster). This is certainly change, but of a limited sort that is implied in the static functional perspective. Second, there is what Parsons calls *structural differentiation*, which means the increasing differentiation of subsystem units into patterns of functional specialization and interdependence. Such newly specialized and separated subunits (or "departments" in organizations) often develop problems in the coordination of their activities and functions.

Thus structural differentiation typically produces "integrative problems," that may require the development of new mechanisms of integration, coordination, and control. In concrete terms this often means the development of new management procedures, roles, and structures. Parsons terms this third type of change (differentiation + new integrative mechanisms) *adaptive upgrading*, in that it means that the social system becomes more effective in generating and distributing resources and enhancing its survival. But all such changes can occur without altering the "key features" of the system (basic cultural values, goals, distribution of power, internal patterns of order, overall organizational unity, etc.).

Parsons reserves the term *structural change* for change in such key features of the system. His argument is that fundamental change of the total system involves changes in the system of cultural values that legitimate and stabilize the system. It may or may not be necessary to redefine, or "generalize," basic and fundamental values and goals to create a more diverse and complex system. For example a university may create new departments and programs (differentiation), and new levels and procedures of administration to coordinate them (adaptive upgrading), without changing the basic goals and values that serve to legitimate the university as a system (perpetuating knowledge, research, service to society). As another illustration at the societal level, Parsons argues that in spite of the enormous growth in size, complexity, and specialization in American society some core values have remained constant (e.g., "instrumental activism," the emphasis on efficiency and getting things done). Indeed, there is often much resistance to the alteration of basic values. Overall structural change (involving the alteration of abstract core values) is less likely than differentiation and adaptive upgrading, even though it does occur in the long run of historical development.

In sum, functionalists suggest that certain types of changes are more or less likely in terms of whether or not they preserve the "key features" of the system or transform them. And in doing so, they suggest what kinds of change will be most and least common. Most common are system maintenance and differentiation, intermediate would be the development of new integrative and coordinative mechanisms, and least common are new abstract values and systems of cultural legitimation.

More recent *neofunctionalist theories* of social change define society not as an "equilibrating system," but as a "tension-management system" (Moore, 1974:11). The difference is subtle but important. Olsen describes this amended functionalist theory of change as an "adjustment perspective":

> Whenever stresses or strains seriously threaten the key features of an organization—whatever they might be—the organization will...initiate compensatory actions to counter these disruptions, in an attempt to preserve its key features. If the compensatory activities successfully defend the threatened key features, then whatever changes do occur will be confined to other, less crucial features....To the extent that the organization successfully practices such adjustive maneuvers, it survives through time as a relatively stable social entity....There are limits, however, beyond which adjustive or counterbalancing activities and changes cannot go if the organization as a whole is to be maintained in its present form. When disruptive stresses and strains or their resulting conflicts are so severe and prolonged that compensatory mechanisms cannot cope with them, the key organizational features being protected will themselves be altered or destroyed. The entire organization then changes; there is a change of the organization rather than just within the organization. (1978:341)

One of the weaknesses of functional theory is that it deals mainly with gradual evolutionary change which enhances the survivability of the system in question. It is less able to deal with rapid or discontinuous change, or change involving fundamental transformations of the system, or the emergence of new values. It understands change as a response to the development of "strains," but the sources of strain are ambiguous, unless they are exogenous in origin. But

FIGURE 5-1 CASUAL IMAGERY: FUNCTIONALIST THEORY OF CHANGE

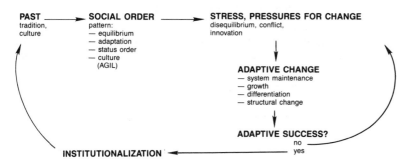

such exogenous strains are outside the theory's frame of reference, and hence, unpredictable. The theory is still a theory of order and stability which has been amended to account for change.

A Functionalist Interpretation of Recent Change in American Society

Functionalists would focus on how changes occurred to keep the American system viable. How did the American system function in the post-World War II period?

In America, as in any society, values act to legitimize how the rest of society works. In the economic realm, important and long-established American values included materialism, growth, affluence, and economic efficiency. Important social values included freedom, individualism, equality, and humanitarianism. In an oversimplified way you can understand America as having two clusters of values—not always consistent—which are (1) economic and instrumental and (2) social and humanitarian. These values served to legitimate an economic system of private ownership, markets, production, and profits (in short—capitalism). They also served to legitimate a political system that was democratic, promoted human social welfare, and stabilized and supported the free enterprise system. Ignoring for the moment other parts of the American system (family life, religion, and education), these cultural values, the free market economy, and the democratic state are the key features that defined how the American system was supposed to work.

The phenomenal postwar expansion of the American economy illustrates not only growth but *structural differentiation*, in the growing diversity of firms, occupations, and products. The growth of large, centralized corporations coupled with increasing technological productivity illustrates *adaptive upgrading* as a form of change. Continual economic growth produced growing affluence of individuals and families in the large American middle; over time the expectation developed that the American way of life would produce continual improvements in individual living standards and welfare. Since the American pie was growing, it was possible—and consistent with American values—to try to distribute rights, opportunity, and security as broadly as possible within the American population. Popular movements for social justice flourished, and by the early sixties the government sponsored a civil rights movement and President Lyndon Johnson's Great Society program seeking to eradicate discrimination and poverty. In the postwar period American society seemed like a well-functioning "growth machine" capable of producing and equitably distributing rights, opportunity, and material well-being.

Strains and stresses appeared in the 1970s in the way the system was able to function. These included increasing international economic competition (so that the United States was no longer the world's dominant economy), vast increases in the cost of energy supplies, mushrooming population (the baby boomers) entering the work force, and an increase in government spending relative to the growth of the GNP, all of which hindered the performance of the economic and social system. These system strains affected individuals in the form of unemployment, decline in real wages, and frustrated expectations for improvement in careers and living conditions. Beyond these economic stresses, social strains began to accumulate as well: There was growing frustration about political and legal intervention in traditionally private areas of social life, for example, in male/female relationships, family patterns, schooling, hiring practices, and civil liberties. The unintended consequence of progressive governmental involvement in domestic and economic life was to limit the ability of both individuals and corporate entities to act in ways that were in their best *private interests*. The massive and diverse frustrations of the seventies eventually produced significant political discontent with the government and the liberal political policies of previous decades.

These strains of the 1970s produced *adaptive changes* in the 1980s directed at restoring the viability of the social system and making it function more effectively. The election in 1980 of a conservative administration with a large electoral majority signaled the beginning of this dramatic political, social, and economic change. A government extensively involved with regulating the economy changed to one less involved, and one that gave more freedom to private market forces and to groups and movements seeking to restore traditional patterns of family and social life. These changes illustrate which clusters of values were more important in American life: Public efforts to produce more opportunity, justice, and welfare for the disadvantaged were given up in order to stimulate economic growth and freedom (opportunity for private gain) for individuals and corporations. The fact that these political changes were widely popular is evidence that they at least addressed some very pervasive stresses in the American system in the 1970s.

Adaptive changes were directed at maintaining the system, but also at adapting the system to new conditions imposed by demographic and international factors. They did not involve the development of new values so much as a *respecification of values*, deemphasizing the idea that the government should provide for the general welfare (except in a minimal way), and emphasizing the free play of private interests as the most efficient and best strategy to provide for the general welfare and address the manifold problems of American society. People were once again responsible for their own fate in a free and competitive arena. At least that was the ideology of the new conservative political movement that spearheaded change. The fact that these changes benefited some more than others is not a theoretical problem for functional explanations, which have often viewed inequality as "functional" for the survival of the system. In the 1980s there was an economic recovery and an increase in cultural cohesion around the values of the new conservative movement. In sum, a functionalist explanation of recent change in American society would emphasize growing differentiation and adaptive upgrading of the system, as well as the accumulation of strains and adaptive changes addressing them. These changes increase the ability of the system to function while modifying but preserving the key features (e.g., values, political and economic institutions) of the system. Change is therefore an evolving modification of the past.

CONFLICT THEORY

Functional theory can be viewed as basically a theory of stability that has been modified to account for change. In contrast, conflict theory has always been centrally concerned with understanding change. In the functionalist perspective strains emerge somewhat mysteriously when there is "malintegration," but such strains are viewed by conflict theory as being *inherent in social structure*. In other words, contemporary conflict theory has *dialectical* assumptions about society and change, and much theoretical effort has gone into identifying the "inevitable" sources of such strains and contradictions. In general, conflict theories of change argue that *inequality* is the inherent source of strains and contradictions in social systems. Such inequality occurs as actors and groups in society struggle to control scarce resources, and such struggles (conflicts) are viewed as the "engines" of change. Exactly *what* is scarce, and *what* is unequally distributed is, as we shall see, a matter of controversy.

For classical Marxist theory, conflict is rooted in economic inequality. Since I have described the basic elements of Marxian theory in Chapter 4, I will not repeat them here, except to mention some limitations of classical Marxism as a theory of change.

Since Marxian theory suggests the inevitability of revolutionary change (which transforms the class system and the economy), Marxism deals more effectively with radical and discontinuous change. Indeed, it is limitation of Marxian theory that it treats change other than total system transformation as less significant. But the most common criticism of classical Marxism is that it too narrowly conceives of the structural basis of conflict, which it views as always related to economic conflict centering on control of the means of production. Other kinds of conflict based on politics, religion, or ethnic and ideological differences are treated as less important or derivative of economic conflict. Thus classical Marxism would have a difficult time dealing adequately with much conflict in the contemporary United States, some of which is only partly economic, and some, not economic at all (e.g., between blacks and whites; between "liberated" feminists and defenders of traditional female roles; between prochoice advocates and antiabortionists; between gays and straights). Or, to take global examples, recent conflicts in Lebanon and Iran are not reducible to purely economic categories. Many have attempted to modify Marxian theory into a more adequate dialectical-conflict theory. [1]

Conflict Theory and Social Change

To illustrate a contemporary conflict perspective on social change, I will focus on the works of perhaps the best known contemporary conflict theorist, Ralph Dahrendorf (1958, 1959, 1968). Even though Dahrendorf has considerably modified classical Marxism, he shares a number of assumptions about society and change with Marx, as follows:

1. Conflict and "malintegration" are viewed by both as pervasive and normal conditions within society (in contrast to the "equilibrium" assumption of functionalists).
2. Such conflict is presumed by both to be caused by opposing "interests" that inevitably occur in the structure of society.
3. Opposing interests are viewed by both as "reflections" of differences in the distribution of power among dominant and subjugated groups.
4. For both, interests tend to polarize into two conflict groups.
5. Both thinkers view conflict as *dialectical* so that the resolution of one conflict creates a new set of opposed interests, which, under certain conditions, will generate further conflict.

Most important for understanding change is the sixth similarity between Dahrendorf and Marx:

6. Social change is seen by both as a pervasive feature of social systems, resulting from the dialectic of conflict between various "interest groupings" within any system (adapted from Turner, 1978:145-46).

But unlike Marx, Dahrendorf (1959) argues that it is not control of the means of production, per se, but social control *in general* which is the broadest basis of conflict in social systems. This shift in a basic assumption has important implications for differentiating his conflict theory from classical Marxism. Specifically, Dahrendorf suggests that any established social system—from small to large scale—is an "imperatively coordinated association," having roles and statuses which embody power relationships. Some clusters of roles have power to extract conformity from others. Furthermore, power relationships in established systems tends to be institutionalized as *authority*, in which power to control becomes invested with "normative rights" to dominate others. Dahrendorf terms such systems "imperatively coordinated associations" (hereafter ICAs). Some have authority to give orders, others are obliged to obey (thus, parents have authority over children, teachers over students, correctional officers over prison inmates, etc.). Those in charge are assumed to have an inherent interest in maintaining control, while subordinates have a similar interest in gaining concessions and control.

Given the latter assumption, any system can be viewed as having two collectivities, which represent (1) those with an interest in maintaining authority and control and (2) those whose interest is in gaining control and redistributing authority. These collectivities are not necessarily organized structures aware of such interests, but they have the potential to become organized. Dahrendorf terms them "quasi-groups" with "latent" interests—-meaning that they have the potential to become aware of their interest in maintaining or gaining control. Such collectivities with latent interests can become organized as "manifest" interest groupings which are organized and aware of their interests relating to the other collectivity. The organization of manifest interest groups from collectivities with latent interests is not automatic but depends upon the presence or absence of several factors. These include: (1) the possibility of open communication about issues relating to authority, (2) the existence political freedom of association, and (3) the availability of material, technical-administrative, and ideological resources.

In most societies and structures the dominant groups control the conditions that enable them to retain authority, but in many systems those without authority live under conditions that do not enable them to increase authority. Thus the organization of manifest from latent interest groups is always problematic. The development of a manifest interest group means that a group has the potential to organize and mobilize for conflict with other groups in the system about the distribution of authority (and the rights, obligations, and resources connected to authority). In sum, Dahrendorf speaks of three types of structures regarding conflict: *latent interest groupings* (or quasi-groups), *manifest interest groups*, and *conflict groups* (where conflict is actually occurring.

When it occurs, conflict can take many forms. It can be *unregulated* and perhaps violent, as in the cases of the creation of civil disorder, terrorism, and sabotage; or it can be *regulated* by social norms, as in the cases of economic boycotts, parliamentary debate, or moral persuasion. *Intense conflict*, according to Dahrendorf, involves a high degree of mobilization, commitment, and emotional involvement and produces a great amount of structural change and reorganization over time. On the other hand, he argues that *violent conflict* may be an unorganized, "random" acting out of frustration, when a conflict group is not effectively mobilized. In any case, Dahrendorf argues that violent conflict is a measure of the "combativeness" of conflict, not its intensity, and produces abrupt change, but not necessarily the greatest amount of change over time.

Finally, Dahrendorf makes an important distinction between *pluralized* and *superimposed* conflict. When conflict is pluralized, there are many directions or "axes" of conflict between diverse ICAs. Thus one can speak in the United States about actual or potential conflicts between the interests of farmers versus food processors, workers versus management, doctors versus patients, blacks versus whites, and so forth, but these conflicts are dyadic and unrelated. They do not "add up" to any general direction or axis of conflict within the system. On the other hand, where conflict is "superimposed," such dyadic conflicts are cumulative and add up to a large cleavage within society. Conflict within the system becomes polarized into an "us" against "them" situation, and all fragmentary grievances are superseded. During the 1970s and 1980s conflict in the Union of South Africa has become relatively superimposed; the main dimension of conflict is the racial conflict between whites and blacks, and other axes of conflict became relatively subsidiary. Where conflict is relatively pluralized, the total system can have much conflict between various ICAs without producing any overall direction of change. Change tends to be piecemeal, that is, between parts of the system without much change in the total system. Such change occurs by gradual "drift" as the parts undergo reorganization. When conflict is superimposed, however, change is dramatic (or "intense," to use Dahrendorf's term) at the total system level. This is not to say that such change is necessarily violent. In systems in which there is a total mobilization along a single cleavage, the costs of civil war *may* be perceived as too high on both sides and lead to bargaining and concessions.

In contrast to notions about the "inevitability" of total change in classical Marxism, Dahrendorf argues that the outcome of conflict is also problematic in producing change. It can result in total or partial system change regarding the redistribution of rights, resources, and authority. Conflict can also result in the defeat of the insurgent group. Conflict *can* produce stability as an ongoing stasis, or stalemate, in which there are no winners between groups that are bound in conflict relationships.

Finally, Dahrendorf argues than any settlement of conflict is temporary. True to its Marxian roots, Dahrendorf's conflict theory is dialectical: each restructured system carries within itself the seeds of its own transformation. That is, each new "resolution" of the problem of rights and authority creates new categories of "those in charge" and "those who are not," and the new categories are likely to become new cleavages along which conflict will emerge. Unlike classical Marxism, conflict theory does not suggest a "final resolution" which will put an end to structured conflict (e.g., the realization of the classless communist society). It is distinctly *antiutopian*.

Dahrendorf's conflict theory can be criticized on a number of grounds. First, it does not deal adequately with change that takes place in the absence of conflict (e.g., technological change). Related to this is a narrow view of change: "Significant" change is viewed only as that involving the redistribution of authority, rights, and resources. In spite of its weaknesses, functional theory defined a variety of types of significant change. Second, societies and groups are viewed as having *dichotomous* authority relations, rather than a continuous gradation of such relationships, which is often the case in large, complex systems. Third, Darendorf's theory speaks more of institutionalized roles and authority than of noninstitutionalized power relationships. Power relationships depend upon the possession of resources rather than legitimized roles and are (also) not dichotomized. They are perhaps as powerful causes of change as authority, and Dahrendorf's theory needs to be recast to account for them to be an adequate theory of conflict (see Turner, 1986, for an interesting attempt to do

FIGURE 5-2 CASUAL IMAGERY: CONFLICT THEORY OF CHANGE

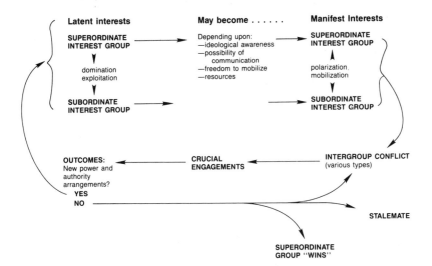

so). Fourth, while Dahrendorf avoids that narrowness of the classical Marxian emphasis on economic roots of change, the Marxian analytic categories (opposed economic interest groups) are conceptually and empirically clearer than are Dahrendorf's "quasi-groups in imperatively coordinated associations" (Turner, 1986:157-58). Finally, it is important to note that in spite of its roots in Marxism, Dahrendorf's theory has much in common with Parsonian functionalism. Both theories deal with institutionalized roles and authority rather than power. Ritzer (1983:234) in fact, argues that Dahrendorf's theory is merely an inverted functional theory. It just deals with different issues (e.g., conflict and change rather than order and persistence). Yet this overstates the similarity. Conflict theory makes dialectical assumptions about the sources and patterns of change that are lacking in the functionalist framework. The work of Collins (1975) who developed the perspective and who treats power more than authority, and who views age, gender, and race as well as economic status as important conflict relevant categories is, I think, more useful than the seminal work of Dahrendorf. In spite of the above criticisms, conflict theory is a pervasive and useful macro theory of society and change in contemporary sociology.

A Conflict Theory Interpretation of Recent Change in American Society

Conflict theorists begin by analyzing the potential for conflict between various parts of a population that compete to control social power and society's valued resources. In terms of such control the dominant population groups in American society are the owners, managers, and beneficiaries of businesses (particularly large ones), and the politicians who represent their interests. The subordinate population groups are the much larger middle and working classes, who are not necessarily poor by global standards, but who nonetheless depend upon the economic elites and their firms for their livelihood. Most subordinate in terms of power and resource shares are the lower classes, who provide cheap labor when needed (though many are elderly and unskilled) and otherwise live a marginal life. Conflict theorists assume that each of these social strata is interested in protecting or increasing its share of power and resources and that, given their overproportionate share of these, the economic elites are usually better able to do so. Historically the Republican Party represented the interests of the corporate and economic elites while the Democratic Party sought to represent the interests of a large and diverse coalition that included some business groups, the middle and working classes, and—occasionally—the poor and marginal.

During the good times of the 1950s and 1960s all strata were able to prosper, and conflict among them was moderated by continual economic growth and expansion. The economic elite flourished as corporations became larger and economic assets more concentrated. Economic growth produced a measure of affluence and the promise of more for the middle and working classes. The lives of many of the poor and deprived gradually improved, although perhaps not in proportion to the improvement in the lives of others. During this period politicians responded to popular movements for social justice by passing civil rights legislation to end racial discrimination and developing social welfare and job training programs to bring the poor and the marginal into the mainstream of American society. Thus the Democratic administrations of Kennedy and Johnson developed civil rights enforcement and the War on Poverty, based not only on a humanitarian vision of society, but also on an attempt to stay in power by creating a solid base of electoral support among minorities and the poor. Because the American pie was expanding it was possible to keep the economy going, support the desires for affluence in the American middle, and create opportunities and benefits for those on the margins of society. At least it was possible to *try* without greatly intensifying conflict about who gets what. While these efforts were instigated by Democratic administrations, Republican administrations of the early and mid-1970s (Nixon and Ford) largely continued them.

But the 1970s ushered in an era of generally bad times, that in one way or another threatened all strata of American society. Corporate stability and earnings weakened, real wages for those in the American middle stagnated, and the boomers entering the job market found themselves with limited opportunities in terms of their education and expectations. This general economic decline increased the potential for conflict between various strata. In addition there was a significant base of discontent with the cultural changes of the 1960s as they affected the family, sexuality, and education, which in the public mind also connected with the liberal administrations of the previous decades. Confidence in government plummeted as did political support for the social welfare programs of the 1960s. Underlying these changing circumstances was the long-developing popular erosion of party loyalty (for both parties) and the rise of political action committees, which had the effect of giving more political power to the wealthiest groups of Americans. The political price was paid by Carter, who was identified with the liberal policies of the past and who lost overwhelmingly in the 1980 election to President Reagan and a conservative administration.

While dissatisfaction with the conditions of the 1970s was widespread, the new administration more narrowly represented the political and economic interests of economic elites, who were the prime beneficiaries of the conservative policies for change. Its programs addressed the alleged problems of capital shortage and declining investment by cutting taxes on business and wealth, dismantling governmental regulation of business, reducing unemployment and educational benefits for the middle classes, and slashing income maintenance programs for the poor. These measures had the effect of redistributing wealth and power *upward* to elite strata and systematically reducing the share of national income going to the middle classes and the poor. They amplified the process of restratification and began what Priven and Cloward (1982) have called the "new class war."

In sum, a conflict theorist would argue that for a time from the late 1950s to the early 1970s those in the middle and bottom levels of American society were able to improve their economic and political lives somewhat relative to those at the top through the combination of a booming economy with effective political representation. In the more recent age of limits, social and economic elites were more firmly in control of the political process, and the system was being shaped more narrowly in their interests and for their gain.

INTERACTIONIST THEORY

While it is a familiar sociological perspective, symbolic interactionism (hereafter, SI) is not as well developed or articulated as the others discussed above, as a theory of either social structure or change. Rooted in the now classic writings of Mead (1934) and Cooley (1902), SI is understood by most American sociologists as a micro theory of the self and interpersonal relations. There *is,* however, a macroscopic image of social order and social change implied by the SI perspective, and I attempt to develop it here.

You should be aware that in doing so I have taken some liberties with the SI perspective. To be more precise, the perspective developed here should be called a "social definition paradigm" (Ritzer, 1983), but I have kept the term SI because it is a more broadly familiar term for the perspective I want to develop.[2]

Basic to the image of society in SI is the assumption that social structure and social order are made possible by, and constituted by, shared symbolic meanings that emerge from interaction between people and groups. Thus in answer to the question "Where does society come from?" the SI perspective argues that the "real basis" of society is not to be found in objectively existing structures external to the activities of humans, but rather emerges from the definitions and meanings that human actors create as they interact.

They become "real" only insofar as actors take them into account and behave as if they *are* real (people usually do). The capacity to share meanings and definitions not only enables individuals to participate but makes joint action itself (and therefore groups and structures) possible. And change in such meanings and definitions is the key to understanding social change in the SI causal imagery.

While such definitions and meanings originate in subjective human consciousness and symbolic capacity, they become externalized and "objective" to the extent that they become widely shared. Such objectivized meanings (for which "culture" is an elliptical way of speaking) become separated from individuals, and individuals are assumed to behave in accordance with these "externalized" definitions and meanings. While it is true that societal actors collectively produce and externalize objective meanings, the reverse is also true: Any given actor also "internalizes" such meanings that are available in the social environment. Thus the real irony of the SI perspective is that out of this "artificial" world of human creation

> the names we affix to things begin to take on a life of their own. We are trapped in the reality of our own words. We become the prisoners of the symbols we create. We are in a position not unlike Victor Frankenstein in Mary Shelley's terrifying novel. The creature has come to rule the creator. (Pfohl, 1985:292)

While illustrating an important assumption of SI theory, Pfohl's statement is also a bit exaggerated. Most theorists in the SI tradition assume that humans are *not* in fact prisoners of the realities they create, but that social life is a process in which actors modify such meanings as they adjust and readjust to each other. At best, in SI imagery, "society" and "culture" are "objects" that people perceive in situations, take account of, and adjust to as they go about defining and mapping appropriate lines of action.

At the macro level, society is viewed as an emergent phenomenon which is "constructed" from symbols created by actors, publics, and reference groups. Society is literally a *social construction* (Berger and Luckmann, 1967) which is the outcome of the historical process of symbolic interaction between social actors, both individual and corporate. In modern societies such constructed social reality is a complex plurality of definitions and meanings which are only partly consensual. Such a diversity of meanings both reflects and reinforces the actual social complexity of modern societies.[3] Shibutani beautifully depicts the diversity and fragmentation of social meanings and definitions in modern societies:

> Modern mass societies, indeed, are made up of a bewildering variety of social worlds. Each is an organized outlook, built up by people in their interaction with one another; hence, each communication channel gives rise to a separate world. Probably the greatest sense of identification and solidarity is to be found in the various communal structures—the underworld, ethnic minorities, the social elite. Such communities are frequently spatially segregated which isolates them further from the outer world, while the "grapevine"....provide(s) internal contact. Another common type of social world consists of the associational structures—the world of medicine, of organized labor, of the theater, of cafe society. These are held together

not only by various voluntary associations within each locality but also by periodicals...[and] specialized journals. Finally, there are the loosely connected universes of special interest—serviced by mass media programs and magazines....Each of these worlds is a unity of order, a universe of regularized mutual response. Each is an arena in which there is some structure which permits reasonable anticipation of the behavior of others, hence, an area in which one may act with a sense of security and confidence. Each social world, then, is a culture area, the boundaries of which are set neither by territory nor by formal group memberships but by the limits of effective communication. (1955:566)

Thus societal structure and coherence exists only within the framework of those outlooks, meanings, and definitions that are broadly established. Within these, there is a shifting melange of groups and structures, based on class, ethnicity, occupation, residence, and so forth, each of which develops its own differentiated and somewhat particularistic subcultural "definition of the situation." Indeed, in highly differentiated societies like the United States, there is a virtual tapestry of contending "points of view," so that at any given time there is only a *partial* consensus about what constitutes "objective social reality." In turn such subcultural definitions of the situation reinforce structural diversity.

Interactionism and Social Change

The SI understanding of social change in complex systems begins with the assumption of a plurality of definitions of social reality reflecting differentiated "reference groups" (to steal a term from role theory). Change begins when such definitions of the situation *become problematic*. If actors perceive problems with accepted lines of action (often through negative responses from others), they begin to reassess situations and often redefine them. At first this position may seem painfully obvious, but it really isn't, since the contention of the SI perspective is that meaningful change does not occur when "external conditions" change, but rather when people redefine situations regarding those conditions, and alter social behavior accordingly.[4] Furthermore, the alteration of definitions of the situation to be congruent with alterations in "external realities" is by no means automatic. For instance

most environmental sociologists readily agree that social systems tend to persist or remain structurally unchanged in spite of "contrary signals" sent from the environment. Societies "ignore" soil erosion, overfishing, and the like. (Humphrey and Buttel, 1982:13)

If the relation between environmental constraints and definitions of the situation is a loose one, the relationship is even more indeterminate where social and political "realities" are involved. To summarize, the essence of meaningful social change for SI theory is when actors redefine situations and act upon such revised meanings and redefinitions. This is a very different emphasis from those of functionalism or conflict theory.

Unlike those theories, SI does not tell us much about the "structural" sources of such redefinitions. Without examining each particular case, all we know is that for whatever reasons, old definitions and meanings (and connected lines of action) become perceived as unsatisfactory. Such problem situations are not, in the SI view, related to any *particular* structural source (e.g., malintegration, inequality in authority). In contrast to functionalism and conflict theory, SI argues that human beings are relatively less constrained by external structural factors. Such macro structural factors are relevant to change only to the extent that they are taken into account in the ongoing reconstruction of the meanings attached to situations and the consequent alterations of social behavior patterns. People are relatively "free," in this view, to ignore or attend to structural "stresses" and define them in various ways. Such stresses are, in the interactionist view, virtually anything that people come to believe that they are, and do not stand in any determinant relationship with "objective reality." At the societal level, "problems" can be understood as the injustice of poverty or racism, as unreasonable demands made by those seeking "entitlements" from society, as the insidious influence of witches or the invasion of flying saucers. Change, in the same highly differentiated society, occurs as these competing claims contend for credibility and attention.

If SI is mute about the relationship between the perception of problems and "objective" realities, neither does it tell us whether actors will seek to reconstruct reality by engaging in cooperative joint action with others or by engaging in conflict with other actors in attempting to establish a more adequate definition of the situation. Thus SI is in principle compatible with either functionalism or conflict theory (the following account leans more toward conflict theory, but this is not implied in SI).

The actual change process begins with *claims-making* by spokespersons for a reference group or subsystem of some sort. Such claims-making activity is the articulation of what is unsatisfactory in the existing situation, along with "better" definitions of the situation and advocacy of "new" lines of action. An important part of this process is to define *other* relevant persons and groups in a manner consistent with the interest and perspectives of the claims-makers. Weinstein and Deutschberger have defined this process as *altercasting* (1963:141). Whether or not such claims are widely accepted depends upon the claims-making agents having the power to disseminate their views to others without significant challenge by other claims-makers. This seems unlikely in a large complex system except for the most powerful and influential claims-making agents. Most claims-making involves not only the articulation of a problem, but also articulating grievances against another group held responsible for the problem. When this is the case, altercasting involves getting someone to represent the role of the villain, and it is unlikely that "villains" accept this role passively. For example, during the 1970s, industrialists and environmentalists often struggled to get each other defined as the respective villains in the environmental controversy.

Finally, successful claims-making involves *access* to important structures and facilities that control the definition of social reality. Concretely, this means

FIGURE 5-3 CASUAL IMAGERY: SYMBOLIC INTERACTIONIST THEORY OF CHANGE

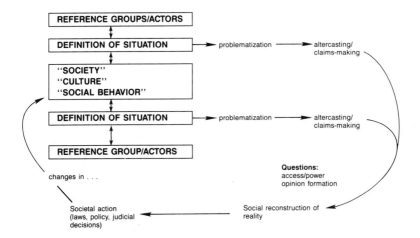

that in the United States successful claims-making agents seek access to the mass media and the judicial system. Access implies power and resources. Hence, other things being equal, higher status groups are likely to have more effective claims-making agents. The role of the American mass media is to "amplify" and disseminate claims (though the media are not neutral regarding all claims!). The role of government and the judicial system is to adjudicate competing claims and promulgate policies and laws regarding them. Government authorities may "decide" in favor of one of several claimant groups on an issue and seek to transform social reality by promulgating laws and policies. Often, however, government may avoid any basic attempt to alter society but rather seek to regulate the behavior of various claims-making groups in order to minimize the disruptiveness of the conflict between them (Harper, 1981).

To summarize, social change in the SI perspective involves the collective reconstruction of social reality. Change inheres in the attempts of various groups to transform social definitions and meanings, along with the action patterns associated with such changes in meaning.

There are many possible criticisms of the SI perspective on change. First, interactionism is ambiguous regarding the perception of unsatisfactory "definitions of the situation." Why do preexisting cultural constructions and their associated lines of action become understood as unsatisfactory and in need of modification? The theory itself is mute about this important issue. Second, SI ignores sources of change that don't lie in the symbolic realm (imposition of change by power, technological innovation, resource limits) but rather asks how people respond to and define things outside the realms of cultural meanings. While this is a useful theoretical question, it does not get us closer to understanding the change-causing conditions underlying human perception. Third, the particular version of SI developed above implies "power" as a relevant factor. (Why do certain groups have greater *access* to the shaping of public opinion than others?) The concept of power is implied in much SI theory, especially "societal reaction theory" regarding deviance, but it is not treated systematically by SI theories. Finally, and perhaps the most telling criticism of SI theory, social change can't be understood apart from the popular redefinition of society.

An Interactionist Interpretation
of Recent American Social Change

An interactionist analysis of change begins with an analysis of the existing images or constructions of reality, how they become problematic (or questioned), and how definitions of problems emerge along with altered constructions of social reality. Social change is the process of altering behavior, structures, and policies, but that cannot be understood apart from examining the changing conceptions of reality that interpret, guide, and legitimize such changes and courses of action.

The national self-image of Americans in the postwar period can be described as "American triumphalism." America was the world's dominant economic, political, and military power, and most Americans viewed the American system as a moral example for how the rest of the world should develop. The dominant conception of the role of government was inherited from the prewar Roosevelt New Deal era: Government should be extensively involved in avoiding economic catastrophe and in providing for the good of society. There was, of course, during this period a more conservative definition of the appropriate role of government, but that was a distinctly minority position. In the early postwar period governments of both Democratic and Republican administrations sought to (1) fight the spread of communism through military preparedness and diplomatic means, (2) support the development of the private economy, viewed as basically sound but in need of regulation and fine tuning, and (3) extend rights and economic security in ways consistent with the free market system and American values of individualism.

In this period many claims-makers interested in social problems articulated concerns about "communist infiltrators" seeking to subvert the American system. What concern there was with American society itself, was largely about those left behind in the expanding affluence system, as well as the possible corrupting influence of universal affluence, rootlessness, and loneliness in bureaucratic "consumerist" society (Riesman, 1961; Whyte, 1957). In the late 1950s and the 1960s poverty and racial discrimination were again discovered by the articulators of social problems. An important book entitled *The Other America* (Harrington, 1962) influenced the thinking of President Kennedy as well as many others. Stimulated by a dramatic civil rights movement, several intellectual spokespersons challenged the popular definition of society and its problems by highlighting the continuing discrimination and poverty affecting a large minority of marginal Americans. Thus, in this self-confident period, the stage was set for the emergence of a new direction in social policy. New politicians had come to power, surrounded by a new coterie of intellectual spokespersons. Change in the definition of American society, its problems, and policy imperatives occurred during the Kennedy-Johnson years. The emergence of the War on Poverty, in which the government attempted to provide support, training, and opportunity for the disadvantaged was in some respects an extension of the New Deal conception of an activist government. The goal was not only affluence, but affluence equitably shared, and the eradication of the evils of racism. Unlike the 1950s, during the 1960s it was not assumed that the Great Society would be the natural result of capitalistic economic expansion without decisive intervention of the federal government. It is fair to say that even in the expansionary sixties many Americans viewed these policy initiatives as illegitimate.

The late sixties and the seventies provided a series of shocks to the mood of American triumphalism and optimism. The America that had triumphed in World War II lost an embarrassingly small war in Vietnam that generated vocal domestic critics of every political persuasion. The Watergate episode demonstrated political corruption at the highest levels. The OPEC oil boycott raised the price of oil and helped stimulate a severe recession in 1975. Profit margins and increases in real wages eroded. Iranian revolutionaries held Americans hostage for months. All of these were "high drama" events vividly portrayed in the mass media. By contrast the growth of foreign economic competition and the entry of the boomers into the job market were low visibility events that only marginally attracted the attention of policymakers, or impacted the public definition of society and its problems. As the decade developed, triumphalism, optimism, and the American dream were increasingly contradicted by events—at least as they appeared in the mass media. The confusion of the seventies became a growing crisis of meaning, which some saw as a full-blown "legitimacy crisis." A pessimistic mood developed: Americans, individually and collectively knew something was wrong. Even President Carter spoke about an American "malaise" as a disease of the spirit. There was little agreement about exactly *what* was wrong, except that it was connected in the public mind with government which was supposed to be managing things.

In the context of this crisis of meaning, in which the older definitions of social reality had become problematic, new claims-makers emerged and began to articulate new definitions of social reality and to propose new directions for change. It was in this context the Reagan and his conservative administration gained political control in 1980. The new conservative movement in politics capitalized on widespread discontent and articulated a radically different view of social reality and problems. This new movement also had its widely read intellectual spokespersons and articulators (e.g., Gilder, 1984; Murray, 1984). The problems of America were the "failed policies of the past" and liberal politicians who had been the engineers of the Great Society programs became *altercast* in the role of villains.

Thus it was that the meanings of political labels shifted. To be conservative became good and to be liberal became bad. The problem was "big government" that overly regulated the private economy and the lives of ordinary individuals and too much public spending. Even Democratic politicians formerly associated with previous policies began to speak in more conservative tones.

Reducing the size of the federal deficit became the domestic problem that determined the feasibility of other political agendas. It was not possible to undo overnight the developments of the previous decades, but the momentum of political change was clearly moving in that direction. Ironically, while the public mood, definitions, and language became transformed, evidence from public opinion polls showed that most people had not shifted their attitudes in a conservative direction. Most thought it was still appropriate for government to try to help the needy, be concerned for the environment, advance civil liberties, and so forth. In fact, by the mid-1980s about half of Americans thought the conservative administration was "going too far" in eliminating social programs (Ferguson and Rogers, 1986). But in the mid-1980s these concerns were overridden by the specter of economic decline that affected paychecks and pocketbooks.

When difficulties appear with the conservative definition of the situation and policy agendas, new spokespersons will articulate altered views of social reality that will reshape the directions of change, insofar as these can be achieved by public policy. What these will be is impossible to predict. They will be a modification of the past, but not a replay of the past. In sum SI theorists would argue that social life is shaped by our collective images and illusions about the social world. When "troubles" become pervasive and widespread, the prevailing view of social reality is called into question. New social definitions that articulate grievances and problems will emerge and shape directions for change.

Summary: Comparing the Three Theories

The three contemporary sociological theories have very different causal imagery about society and change. Functionalism locates the origins of change in "malintegration," which produces strains and innovations that deal with such strains. Change is usually conceived as differentiation and the elaboration of new integrative mechanisms. Conflict theory locates the sources of change in structured inequality which produces a struggle to control scarce resources (authority, power). To the extent that change results from these struggles, it is understood as the redistribution of rights, duties, and obligations. SI theory argues that the sources of change can be found in the perception of "trouble" with the existing situation and in attempts to redefine situations and attendant lines of action and public policies that flow from such altered constructions of reality. The three perspective not only explain things in different ways, but they explain different *things* about social change.

I hope, however, from my illustrations above that you have noticed that although the three perspectives are different in what they emphasize, they are not totally contradictory. They emphasize different factors, and there are very real differences between them, but in some respects they use different terms to describe the same processes. Let me here mention only one of these areas of similarity. All three perspectives argue that at some point cultural and symbolic factors are critical in understanding change. This is so apparent with SI that it requires no comment. But it is also true for functionalism and conflict theory. Functionalists, particularly those influenced by Parsons, argue that consensual cultural values and symbols serve to legitimate the social order, but also act as the "switchmen" (in Weber's metaphor) that determine along which tracks social change will move. Change in such cultural symbols themselves, however, is difficult to explain from the functionalist perspective. Conflict theorists also recognize the stabilizing role of cultural values, although rather than seeing them as representing a "grand consensus" developed in the marketplace of ideas, they view values as ideological systems manipulated by the dominant groups in society. Values and symbols, in this perspective, become instruments for the maintenance of dominance and "cultural hegemony." Conflict theorists recognize that for conflict to emerge from socially structured inequality, there must be a process of erosion of such cultural legitimations which justify the status quo, although conflict theorists provide few clues as to exactly how this process takes place. Thus the role of ideas and culture is important, although differently understood, in all three theoretical orientations. There are undoubtedly other dimensions of the three theories that could provide points of convergence.

NOTES

1. See, for instance, Collins, 1975; also the entire critical theory orientation in Ritzer, 1983.

2. The social definition paradigm includes not only the conventional micro SI perspective, but also a number of related perspectives, including phenomenology (Berger and Luckmann, 1967), ethnomethodology (Garfinkle, 1967), societal reaction theory (Pfohl, 1985; Spector and Kitsuse, 1977). All of these perspectives focus on "the way actors define their social situations and the effect of these definitions on ensuing action and interaction" (Ritzer, 1983:424).

3. This seems like a circular or tautological statement. But SI theory does not assume a logic of causes, but rather a logic of interaction. In the present instance, this means that "objective" social complexity and the plurality of "subjective" definitions of social reality are interacting phenomena. Definitions create social reality. Once created, such "objective" realities shape definitions in an on going way. Neither has causal priority in the SI framework.

4. Note that this is not only an assumption about how change proceeds, but also a *definition* about what aspects of change are socially important.

CHAPTER SIX
INNOVATIONS
AND HOW
THEY SPREAD

Our focus in exploring social change shifts again. Part I was concerned with describing the major trends of change in American society, and Part II examined broad types of explanations of change. In Part III I want to focus on *change processes* themselves, as they occur in various settings. One could examine change processes from a variety of perspectives, but I have chosen to focus here on only two: (1) the creation of innovations and how they diffuse throughout groups and societies and (2) how large groups of people in society advocate change (social movements).[1] For both of these perspectives there are large, established traditions of sociological literature and research. In a few short chapters I will explore each of these frameworks in as much depth as is possible, and I want to warn you that I will not ignore scholarly controversies about them, either theoretical or empirical.

This chapter is about innovations and how they spread. Chapters 7 and 8 are about social movements: why they develop, how they themselves change, and the impact they have on society. At the end of Chapter 8 there is a brief application of the social movements framework to examine the development and impact of the feminist movement in America. Most of this book is concerned with describing and explaining change, but Chapter 9 is different—it is about the creation of change. It is about the implications of the materials on innovation and social movements for the advocacy, planning, and creation of change.

INNOVATION AS A CHANGE PROCESS

One way of conceptualizing change processes is as the discovery or invention of novelty, its communication to others, and its adoption within a population or social system. Yet exactly how innovations occur, how they spread, and why people adopt or reject them is not simple to understand. From the standpoint of those promoting innovation, people often seem irrationally resistant to the simplest change. Consider the following example:

In 1955 the public health service in Peru attempted to persuade villagers in Los Molinos, a village in the coastal region of Peru, to boil water before drinking it or using it in cooking. Although all of the water sources of the village were contaminated, it was not feasible for the village to install a sanitary water system. But the incidence of typhoid and other water-borne diseases could be reduced by boiling water before consumption. From the standpoint of the local hygiene worker, the task was simple: to persuade the housewives of Los Molinos to add waterboiling to their existing pattern of behavior. But even with the aid of a medical doctor and the encouragement of housewives who were already boiling water, the campaign failed. Of the two hundred families of Los Molinos, only eleven were persuaded to boil water. Why did this simple innovation fail? The failure can be traced partly to cultural beliefs of the villagers. Local tradition links hot foods with illness. Boiling water makes it less cold and hence appropriate only for the sick. But if a person is not ill, he is prohibited by cultural norms from drinking boiled water. Because of its association with illness, villagers learn from childhood to dislike boiled water. Most can tolerate cooked water only if flavoring, such a sugar, cinnamon, lemon, or herbs, is added. There are other reasons for the failure. The public health worker was viewed by many of the villagers as an outsider and as a snooping dirt inspector from the government, rather than as a friendly authority. In addition, the public health worker tried to convince housewives that they ought to boil water because there were germs in the water that caused diseases. But the villagers had little comprehension of the germ theory of disease and thought that germs, if they existed, would surely drown in the water. Thus the attempt failed because the innovation (1) contradicted traditional beliefs and values, (2) was viewed as being imposed by hostile outsiders, and (3) was promoted in terms that the recipients could not understand (Rogers and Shoemaker, 1971:2-6).

This chapter begins by examining the innovative process itself in terms of two broad questions: (1) What are innovations and the innovative process? and (2) What are the individual, structural, and cultural circumstances affecting the rate and probability of innovation? Next, some of the questions raised in the foregoing illustration about water boiling are explored: What factors facilitate the spread of innovations? In other words, how and why do people adopt or reject them? This gets us into the rather large body of scientific literature about the diffusion of innovations that has developed over the last several decades.

THE ACT OF INNOVATION

An innovative act involves "a linkage or fusion of two or more elements that have not been previously joined in just this fashion, so that the result is a qualitatively distinct whole....It is a true synthesis in that the product is a unity which has properties entirely different from its individual antecedents" (Barnett, 1953:181). While all innovation involves producing something that is qualitatively different there are different degrees of innovativeness. Ryan (1969) has described degrees of innovativeness as follows: A *variation* is a borderline innovation, which involves the modification of something that already exists, such as changing the shape of a tool or sail or increasing the number of spokes in early wheeled carts. There is no new combination of diverse elements, but rather a creative modification of what exists. More innovative is *substitution*, in which new materials or ideas are used. Examples would include the substitution of metal for stone, Teflon for aluminum, or the use of a computer model to conceptualize the workings of the human brain. More innovative yet are what Ryan calls *mutations*, involving novel combinations and reorganization of elements rather than substituting one for another. An example would be the innovation of printing in fifteenth-century Europe. The printing press involved the creative combination of elements that existed during the thirteenth and fourteenth centuries: block printing, first used to print playing cards and money; oil-base ink created by Flemish artists; metal casting with antimony, which made lead hard enough to use; paper, imported to Europe though the Mongol Empire; and a "press," adapted from the wine and linen industries. The most basic element of all was, of course, the alphabet, requiring the repetition of a few symbols, in contrast to the pictographic written languages of the Orient. A distinction is sometimes made between *basic* (or strategic) and *improving* innovations. This distinction is based on the idea that some innovations are more important than others in that they involve greater novelty, and some are strategic in that they "trigger" other innovations. Thus the basic discovery of the facts about the circulation of the blood triggered other discoveries in medicine and physiology in rapid succession. And the invention of the cathode ray tube was the basic innovation upon which a host of others are based (e.g., the radio, television, radar, electric-eye doors, CRT terminals for computers). Barnett thinks that this is a subjective distinction, in that all innovations involve the same "creative process," and all have cultural antecedents. He argues that if one were to strictly apply the distinction, then primitive man is the basic innovator and modern man is the adapter or improver! I would grant to Barnett that the distinction is a relative one, yet if all that one means is a distinction between the more basic design and subsequent modifications, then the distinction seems useful, especially when applied to a cluster of related innovations.

The Innovative Process

The process of innovation has been variously described. Barnett (1953) describes three stages of the process. First is *identification*, in which one finds areas of similarities and differences, or "locates areas of sameness in apparently dissimilar things" (cited in Ryan, 1969:86). Second is the act of *substitution*, in which new elements are placed in configuration; and third is *discrimination*, in which the new product is evaluated and compared with the old. Usher (1954) describes the process a bit differently, from the perspective of "gestalt" psychology. In his view the first phase of the process is a perception of the problem, stimulated through unfulfilled needs and wants. Second, there is "setting the stage," in which the person assembles all of the elements (data, materials) of the solution. This may or may not be a deliberate process. Third, there is an "act of insight" in which the new configuration of meaning appears. The gestalt perspective emphasizes that this occurs as a "flash of insight," a sort of "aha!" experience, in which previously disparate elements seem to fall into place. Fourth, in Usher's perspective, is the "critical revision," in which the new innovation is made workable in some particular context. Innovations which are not widely adopted may never undergo the last phase. The basic innovation for the generation of electricity from solar energy has been understood for years now, but the critical revision which would adapt such a system to current technical and economic circumstances has yet to be undertaken.

To this scheme, you could add Hadamard's (1954) notion of an "incubation period" prior to the creative insight. Reviewing the self-reports of creative accomplishments of famous mathematicians, Hadamard found that they often described a period in which they were "stuck" in unproductive modes of activity. Typically they engaged in some kind of peripheral activity while the "mind" continued to engage the problem at another (unconscious?) level. After a sufficient "rest period" creative solutions emerged. Like the "act of insight," the reality of an "incubation period" after which problems can suddenly be resolved is a common experience. But the accounts of incubation periods provided by gestalt psychologists are more descriptive without explaining very much about exactly how they happen.

Implicit in these views of the process of innovation is the notion that innovation occurs as a problem-solving mechanism. But is this always so? Is "necessity the mother of invention"? What is meant by "necessity"? What we need is related to physical needs, but also to the values and goals existing in a particular social order. Needs are also situational, thus the circumstances of warfare have always been productive of innovations that were not needed in peaceful times. The notion of needs involves some kind of felt tension, some source of dissatisfaction with the status quo. But there are many examples of innovations and inventions made without such a state being present. And there are many inventions that are looking for a necessity, in a manner of speaking. For example, Teflon was inadvertently discovered by Du Pont chemists in 1938. Teflon was a unique material in that very few substances would stick to it. Between 1939 and 1964 Du Pont spent 100 million dollars in developing the manufacturing process and trying to find a marketable necessity until they came up with using it for frying pans in 1964 (Ryan, 1969:84). Another example can be found in the development of the silicon microchip, now widely used in computers, calculators, watches, and so forth. Such integrated circuit microchips were developed independently by Jack Kilbey and Robert Noyes, in 1958 and 1959, six months apart. The first models were about one quarter inch square and capable of containing six to eight separate circuits. While in theory the uses of such small integrated circuits were obvious, there was no existing market for them and they were terribly expensive to produce. The impetus for their use and development came when NASA, under the urging of the Kennedy Administration in the 1960s, undertook to put a man on the moon. Such microcircuitry had obvious advantages when space and payload were at a premium. Current microchips have undergone so much development (improving innovations) that now upwards of a million separate circuits can be contained in a quarter-inch microchip!

You can see that innovations are often made before their use is needed, obvious, or practical. There is also the possibility that necessities can be created, particularly in relation to consumer goods, through advertising and the manipulation of consumer demand. And there are many cases of innovations that never become hooked to any human necessity and are never adopted on a wide scale. The archives of the U.S. Patent Office are literally full of such innovations, which are never needed and find no market. Thus it may be true that necessity is often the mother of invention, but an equally plausible case can be made that invention is sometimes the mother of necessity! What you can conclude from all this is that for an invention to become a social innovation it is somehow related to a need (necessity). Whether necessity always exists prior to innovation and motivates it is questionable.

FACTORS AFFECTING THE RATE AND PROBABILITY OF INNOVATION

The basic question to which I now turn is that of the (1) individual, (2) structural, and (3) cultural circumstances that make innovation more or less likely to occur.

Individual Factors

During the 1950s and 1960s there were many studies by behavioral scientists that attempted to discover the psychological basis of creativity. Dennis (1955) found that innovativeness in any given field is relatively rare. Studying creativity in seven different fields (including music, geology, chemistry, and gerontology among others) he asked a panel of judges in each field to rate the accomplishments of their peers. He found that about 10 percent of the contributors to each field contributed over 50 percent of the "creative contributions." Stein (1957) and Stein and Heinze (1960) had a panel of industrial chemists sort their peers into creative and noncreative professional chemists and then studied the characteristics of the two groups. They found, through a variety of psychological assessments, that creative chemists (in comparison to their noncreative peers) were (1) not more intelligent but were (2) less anxious, (3) more autonomous, (4) more likely to see their own attitudes as being divergent from those of their peers, (5) less authoritarian, (6) more relativistic—seeing rules as matters of convenience, (7) more likely to emphasize matters of practicality and utility, (8) placed less importance on the church as an institution, (9) more oriented toward accepting their inner impulses and less prone to avoid situations where they might be blamed, and (10) less prone to take risks in "unwarranted situations."

Looking at this profile of characteristics, one is struck by the similarity between these characteristics of creative persons and Maslow's (1971) description of "self-actualizing" persons. An interesting finding is that under some circumstances ("unwarranted situations") the innovative chemists were less prone to take chances than the noncreative chemists. This is contrary to the popular notion of creative people as reckless risk-takers. Another interesting finding confirms some of what was said above about the process of innovation. Stein and Heinze found differences in problem-solving styles between creative and noncreative chemists. The noncreative ones worked quickly gathering data and spent more time in synthesizing the data. The creative chemists worked slowly gathering data and information about a problem. After such an extended period (incubation?) they were able to more rapidly work toward a solution or synthesis.

In another study Getzels and Jackson (1962) studied innovativeness among elementary school students. They controlled for levels of intelligence among the children, in order to separate the effects of intelligence from those of creativity. Students were presented with an "ambiguous stimulus" (a picture) and asked to make up a story about it. Judges then sorted the responses into creative and noncreative categories. What the judges rated as creative was characterized by playfulness, stimulus-free themes, unexpected endings, humor, the heightening of incongruities, and high levels of violence. Getzels and Jackson explored the family environments of the creative and noncreative students. Families of the noncreative students were likely to be more restrictive, and to place more emphasis on "rule-abiding" behavior. Families of the creative students placed less emphasis on conventional behavior and were more likely to emphasize openness to experience for the child. Thus, in Getzels' and Jackson's view, creativity is a socialized capacity, rather than a genetic predisposition.

Wallace and Kogan (1965) studied the relationship between intelligence and innovativeness. In general their finding is that indicators of creativity are highly intercorrelated, but they are only weakly correlated with I.Q.

Age has been found to be related to creativity. Lehman (1953), in a massive study of creative products in scientific fields, medicine, art, music, literature, and architecture, finds that while creativity may be found at any age, it was most common between the ages of 30 and 40. Putting this in Usher's framework about the stage of the innovative process, it may be that one's early life and training represent setting the stage, followed by a creative act during the 30s or 40s, and that the rest of one's work represents a series of "critical revisions." There is another possible interpretation of this, however. Lehman's study dealt with creativity in conventional careers, and it has often been observed that such careers involve a process of moving through hierarchical stages of career advancement. It may be that one's ability to be innovative is limited by the stage of one's career. That is, early in one's career, when one is relatively low in status and autonomy, one may be compelled to follow the rules and produce fairly conventional products, while later one may possess career autonomy and freedom from supervision, so that one is free to be more innovative. Thus the relation between age and innovativeness may be partly caused by structural forces rather individual characteristics.

In sum, the research about individual qualities and innovation suggests the following: (1) that innovation is rare in any given field, (2) that there are some distinct psychological characteristics associated with innovation (although it is doubtful that there is an innovative personality type), (3) that innovativeness is distinct from intelligence, although creativity in certain fields may require high intelligence, (4) that the development of innovativeness may be related to one's family environment, and (5) that career innovativeness seems somewhat related to age, although the reasons for this are not clear.

Structural Factors

Several characteristics of social systems affect the probability of innovation. First, the rate of innovation is likely to be higher *when there are perceived internal inconsistencies that are stress producing.* Such internal inconsistencies (or "contradictions," as Marxians would call them) are inversely related to the degree of system integration, which is a variable property of social systems. That is, any social system is integrated to a degree, meaning that behaviors and cultural meanings fit together harmoniously, but no social system is perfectly integrated. In general the more heterogeneous the society or community in terms of different subpopulations, groups, or subcultures, the greater the probability that such inconsistencies will be perceived. Note that this generalization emphasizes that inconsistencies must be *perceived* inconsistencies. Any social condition can objectively exist for a long time without being perceived as a stress-producing condition. For example, such conditions as poverty and domestic violence are certainly not new to America. But it was not until such conditions were widely perceived by Americans as conditions inconsistent with American cultural values that innovative attempts were made to deal with such problems. In addition to the perception of widespread behavior inconsistent with cultural values, such inconsistencies can include situations in which conflicting demands exist within social roles, or in which legitimate effort fails to produce commensurate rewards, or in which established reciprocities are imbalanced in their rewards to each party. All such conditions establish stresses which are likely to produce innovations aimed at reducing such stresses and producing more integrative conditions within the social system.

A second condition which is likely to increase the rate of innovation exists *when a society is having difficulties regarding its adaptation to the physical environment.* The maintenance of a society is ultimately dependent upon successful adaptations to the physical environment, and when that adaptation becomes threatened and problematic, innovation is likely. For example, the widespread dustbowl conditions of the 1930s produced innovations related to existing patterns of agricultural land use. And many observers suggest that modern high-technology agriculture may be producing similar effects, by emphasizing productivity in a way that diminishes the fertility of the soil or subsurface water supplies. If they are correct, then one could predict that these practices, which destabilize the productivity of the environment, will require innovations in agricultural practices at some time in the future.

In this regard, energy crises are a chronic source of social innovation. They are not new. The cutting of trees in Western Europe (especially in England) forced innovators to search for new sources of energy (coal). There is an intriguing hypothesis here, though I know of no research that has studied it systematically: Every significant change in the modes of economic production was preceded by an innovation in the generation of energy, which was in turn stimulated by near exhaustion of the conventional energy sources. Early in the history of America there was an energy crisis of sorts when whales were hunted to near extinction (whale oil was at that time the major source of oil for lamps). This led to the development and production of kerosene as fuel for lamps. Today the dramatic rise of the price of petrochemicals has produced a plethora of innovations, including the development of more efficient extractive techniques for processing crude oil and natural gas, the development of more efficient appliances and automobiles, research and experimentation with exotic renewable energy sources, and the promotion of home insulation and energy conservation through a variety of tax credits. While today these innovative attempts are fragmentary and have not, as yet, been widely adopted, they surely will if the energy crisis intensifies. In any case, changes in the environmental circumstances of the social order are likely to be a fertile source of innovation.

A third condition that affects the rate of innovation has to do with social norms. *The rate of innovation will be higher in a system that has broad as opposed to narrowly defined social norms.* The question here is not the degree of integration of social norms, as implied above, but rather the precision with which behavior is specified. According to Ryan (1969:57), the "evidence suggests that ambiguity and latitude in structure offers innovative opportunity through both tolerance for normative deviance and misunderstandings of both norms and role expectations....loosely structured societies are more amenable to innovation through their tolerance of a variety of alternative behavior patterns within any given situation."

A fourth condition that affects the rate of innovation has to do with the rate of replacement and succession of personnel in a social system. *Higher rates of replacement and succession are related to higher rates of innovation.* New people who replace older ones are likely to be different for at least two reasons: they have different historical experiences, and, even when this may not be the case, there are enough uncertainties in the socialization process to ensure that they will have significantly different outlooks than the older generation. Thus newcomers are likely to attempt to reorganize social life so that it is consistent with their own outlooks. The relationship between rates of succession and social change has long been noted and it has long been argued that "generations cohorts" are the concrete carriers of change (Mannheim, 1950; Ryder, 1965). For groups and organizations, rates of succession are extremely variable; in some systems the turnover rate between old members leaving and new members arriving is very rapid, and in others it is very slow. Many investigators have found a positive relationship between the frequency of innovation and the rates of succession and replacement (Leighton, 1945; Gouldner, 1954; Firth, 1959; and Mc-Cleery, 1961; and Caplow, 1964).

A fifth condition that affects the rate of innovation is *growth in population size and in population density.* Growth has long been seen as producing "strains" that lead to innovation (Durkheim, 1893, 1947 edition). Growth produces strains on the system's mechanisms of social coordination and resource allocation. Thus, the mechanisms of social coordination and control which work in a small town meeting are not likely to be adequate for such coordination in a large urban political system. Mott (1965) has identified several sources of these problems related to growth. He argues that as a system grows (1) the level of integration that the system achieves from sharing common norms declines, and that (2) there will be an increase in problems of interacting vertically within the same hierarchy as well as between different hierarchies. Thus the potential for friction and conflict among the various parts of the system increases. As size increases the number of coordinative problems increases, and the need for more effective coordination increases. What is likely to occur is the elaboration of substructures with more specific roles and functions, and with more formalized (or bureaucratic) connections between them. Growth typically produces innovations that increase the degree of structural and functional differentiation within the social system.

Structural differentiation is not, however, the only response to growth. Another is *segmentation,* meaning that the system literally splits into autonomous parts. This is the strategy of the Hutterites of the Dakotas and Canada, among whom there are extraordinarily high birth rates. When a Hutterite community reaches a certain size, young people are encouraged to leave, purchase farmland elsewhere, and start new communities. The parent community typically provides some resources for the start-up costs of the new community.

A sixth condition related to rates of innovation is *the occurrence of catastrophes and disasters.* These—such as wars, depressions, floods, and plagues—are overwhelming events which cannot be dealt with by conventional means. Normally these overwhelming events produce innovations directed at restoring a condition of normalcy. Such innovations may be relatively short lived or permanent. Furthermore, innovations stimulated by a disaster may do much more than restore a previous state of the system. The New Deal programs of the 1930s, understood as innovative responses to the great depression, permanently altered the nature of the relationship between government and the economy (regardless of how successful such programs were). To take another example, the devastation of frequent tornados in the American Midwest has produced an effective early warning system, so that the loss of life from tornados today is typically much less than it was in the past. In general, overwhelming events produce innovations aimed at (1) dealing with the immediate effects of the disaster and (2) preventing or preparing for future occurrences.

Organizations and Innovation   Studies of innovation in bureaucracies, or complex organizations, have produced interesting insights about conditions conducive to innovation. Hage and Aiken (1970) summarize some of this literature by focusing on program change in complex organizations. *Program change* means the addition of new services or products, and the research summarized by Hage and Aiken included studies of the development of a new color TV by R.C.A., a molecular biology curriculum at Columbia University, and a new mental retardation program for Goodwill Industries. Such studies support the following generalizations.

The degree of centralization in organizations is *inversely* related to the rate of program change. Hage and Aiken suggest that when organizational power is concentrated in a few hands, people are less likely to experiment for fear of losing power. By contrast, less centralized organizations were likely to have wider participation in policy formation and a greater potential for bringing diverse and new ideas to attention. Rates of program change were found by most studies reviewed to be directly related to the degree of organizational complexity. Hage and Aiken suggest two factors at work here. First, organizations having a large number of specialists within the organization are likely to have more professionals, who are more likely than nonprofessionals to have ties outside of the organization and keep current with new ideas of organizational practice. Secondly, merely by virtue of being more complex, such organizations include people with varied perspectives and sources of information.

The degree of formalization was found inversely related to rates of program change. *Formalization* here means the degree of codification of jobs and procedures. Apparently highly formalized rules and roles offer less latitude to experiment with new ideas, and a high emphasis on rules may provide negative sanctions or penalties for innovative behavior. Studies reviewed by Hage and Aiken also report that the degree of stratification within organizations is inversely related to the rate of innovation. It may be that innovation has the potential for diminishing differentials between strata, and the well off may resist organizational innovation. A high degree of organizational stratification diminishes upward communication critical of organizational procedures. For fear of negative evaluation, subordinates may be less likely to communicate performance gaps and organizational problems to their superiors.

From Hage and Aiken the picture of a dynamic, innovative organization is one that is high in complexity, low in centralization, low in the degree of formalization of procedures, and low in the degree of internal stratification. Burns and Stalker (1961) suggest differences between dynamic and static organizations along similar lines. The assumption running through Hage and Aiken's model is that innovation originates from the lower participants and is likely to be opposed by organizational elites. This is a common perspective in the social science literature about innovation, but a questionable one. Perhaps the most important limitation of the perspective developed by Hage and Aiken is their failure to consider different stages in the innovative process within organizations. Zaltman, Duncan, and Holbek (1973), who review a wider range of literature, suggest that there are important differences between the "initiation" and the "implementation" stages of the innovative process, and that Hage and Aiken's model is more applicable to the initiation stage. They suggest that successful *implementation* of innovation is related to lower organizational complexity, higher formalization, and higher centralization of power within the organization. Apparently in this state organizations are capable of greater effectiveness and predictability in interpersonal relations and greater capability in conflict resolution and consensus building. In practical terms, then, the organization which is the most successfully innovative may be structured differently at different levels within the organization, or may develop different structures for the different phases of the innovative process.

Cultural Factors

Observers from both anthropology and sociology (Ogburn, 1938; White, 1949) have suggested that the rate of innovation is related to the *size of the cultural base*. According to Barnett:

> The size and complexity of the cultural inventory that is available to an innovator establishes limits within which he must function. The state of knowledge and the degree of its elaboration during his day, the range and kind of artifacts, techniques, and instruments that he can use, make some new developments possible and others impossible. The mere accumulation of things and ideas provides more material with which to work. A sizable inventory allows for more new combinations and permits more different avenues of approach in problem solution than does a small one. (Quotation from Homer G. Barnett, 1953, *Innovation: The Basis of Cultural Change,* p. 40. Copyright © McGraw-Hill, Co. Reprinted with permission of the publisher.)

This is an interesting but somewhat difficult notion to grasp. It is readily apparent when focusing on material items of culture: The greater the range of tools and materials available to craftsworkers and inventors, the greater the range of innovations possible. But it is also argued that this notion—the size of the cultural base—applies to the realm of ideas, values, and so forth. That is, the larger and more complex the culture's stock of ideas and, knowledge is, the more likely is innovation in the realm of nonmaterial culture.

A notion related to this is that *an innovation will not come into being until the cultural base is sufficiently developed to permit its occurrence.* At one level this is a self-evident and not very interesting proposition. Thus medieval farmers could not have invented a modern tractor, even though they could have used one. The cultural base was not ready: Such an invention would have required knowledge of the laws of gas expansion, the availability of refined petroleum distillates, and the mechanics of the internal combustion engine—all unavailable in European culture of the 1300s. A related proposition is much more interesting and contentious: When the culture is ready for an invention, it will come into being, whether people want it or not (White, cited in Cuzzort and King, 1980). If this is true, then culture is truly a self-generating force. This focus on cultural readiness is a perspective on innovation that contrasts sharply with the "great man" theory of innovation. As evidence for this view, large lists of simultaneous inventions have been developed. Ogburn (1922) has listed 150 such innovations. Here are just a few (Cuzzort and King, 1980):

> Theory of planetary perturbations, by Lagrange (1808) and Laplace(1808)
> Decimal fractions, by Rudolff (1530), Stevinus (1586), and Burgi (1592)
> Law of gases, by Boyle (1662) and Mariotte (1697)
> Process for reduction of aluminum, by Cowles (1885), Hall (1886), and Heroult (1887)
> Telescope, by Della Porta (1558), Digges (1571), Johannides, Metius (1608), Lippershey (1608), Drebble, Fontana, Janssen (1608), Galileo (1609)
> The phonograph, Edison (1877), Scott and Cros (1877)
> That the skull is made of modified vertebrae, by Oaken (1776) and Goethe (1790)
> Theory of infection by microorganisms, by Fracastoro (1546) and Kircher (1546)
> Solution of the problem of respiration, by Priestley (1777), Scheele (1777), Lavoisier (1777), Spallanzani (1777), and Davy (1777)
> Theory of natural selection and variation, Darwin (1858), and Wallace (1858)
> Theory of mutations, by Korschinsky (1899) and De Vries (1900)
> Centrifugal pumps, by Appold (1850), Gwynne (1850), and Bessemer (1850)
> Use of gasoline engines in automobiles, Otto (1876), Selden (1879), and Daimler (1885)

White (1949) finds in such lists evidence that culture is a self-generating force. When the cultural configuration of elements is ready for an innovation, it seems to appear simultaneously from several independent sources. This is an intriguing perspective: Any culture is "pregnant" at a given stage of development, that is, awaiting the development of innovations for which it is ready. An interesting project from this perspective would be to try to forecast exactly what innovations are just over the horizon at this stage of the development of contemporary culture (artificial organs? synthesizing new materials from subatomic particles? automated language translators? large-scale desalinization that is economically feasible? an integrated world economic and political order?). Another interesting project would be to search for singular innovations, which, to my knowledge, no social scientist has done. In sum cultural factors related to the likelihood of innovation are (1) the size of the cultural base and (2) the stage of development of the culture. These are limiting contexts shaping the rate of innovation, and I think others may be more important.

The rate of innovation will be higher in cultures where more cultural rules and norms are viewed as pragmatic and instrumental rather than as intrinsically legitimate, moral, or sacred rules. Every society has both types of rules: those that have intrinsic legitimation and those that have practical legitimation. In America, for instance, our rules governing economic production and distribution tend to be pragmatic and utilitarian, and we are very willing to innovate in these realms. On the other hand American cultural rules governing sexuality and family relationships tend to be intrinsically legitimated, and Americans are much more reluctant to accept innovation in these realms. But in some societies intrinsically legitimated rules are very extensive, and even the most minute and mundane rules governing social interaction are imbued with sacred meaning. Such situations are not conducive to cultural innovation.

Perhaps even more important is *the extent to which the culture normalizes and expects change.* The more the worldview of a culture sees the cosmos as being in a state of change, flux, and/or development, the more innovation will be encouraged. On the other hand where the cosmos is viewed as a static closed system, innovation will be inhibited and change viewed as an aberration. We tend to think of traditional and preliterate cultures as having a static picture of the universe and modern cultures as having an open-ended, evolutionary view. But the truth is a good deal more complicated than this. Some preliterate societies do have worldviews that inhibit innovation. Of the Zuni Indians of New Mexico, for instance, Barnett says:

> They are restrictive in their anticipations [for change]....They neither hope for nor anticipate changes in any part of their culture, and they are resolute against any suggestion of the idea. They are extremely ethnocentric and are uninterested in the world around them; they, in fact, regard their village as the center of the world. (1953:56)

Other groups of preliterates are different.

> The Navajo, who live close to the Zuni, take another view. They expect new developments in their culture; and their history, in so far as it is known, reveals that they have been receivers and adapters of alien customs throughout the period of their occupation of their present habitat....They welcome change, accepting it as a realistic adjustment to the world around them....The Samoans are also anticipators of change, but in a way different from that of the Navajo. They expect each individual among them to be unique in everything that he does. Imitation is deplored. Every woman has her own design for tapa cloth....Every person is expected to improvise songs and dance steps for himself. Likewise for house builders, tattooers, and other specialists. The expectation of deviation even extends to religion and political organization, both for individuals and villages. Innovation is the rule, and in conse-

quence the innovator receives only passing recognition. He is merely doing what is expected of him. (Barnett, 1953:56-57)

While there seems to be a great amount of variation among the preliterate cultures of the world, it is still probably true that modernization has everywhere promoted an open-ended worldview conducive to high rates of innovation. The Western Judeo-Christian notion of human beings having control over the environment, the idea of universal progress, deriving from Enlightenment thinking in the 1700s, and secularization, which gradually removed some cultural values and norms from sacred sanction, have all combined to produce a worldview that treats change as normal and legitimizes innovation in many spheres of social life.

Having explored the social science literature on the process of innovation and the circumstances most conducive to innovation, I now turn to issues about the spread, or diffusion of innovations.

HOW INNOVATIONS SPREAD

The spread of innovations has been a focus of much scholarly research during the last three decades. The research comes from diverse academic areas, such as anthropology, rural sociology, medical sociology, educational research, and mass media research. The results of these efforts have produced some of the best empirical literature on social change processes. There were over 1,500 diffusion oriented studies during the 1950s and 1960s, and the results of these studies have been summarized and codified by Rogers (1962), Rogers and Shoemaker (1971), Zaltman (1973), Rothman (1974), and Zaltman and Duncan (1977). While this body of research focuses on what are considered to be basic change processes, it has a strong applied flavor, often focusing on deliberate attempts to promote change. Researchers have studied, for instance, attempts to introduce new seed hybrids, drugs, health projects in developing nations, innovations in media, and educational reform. Research findings about innovation in these diverse areas have been remarkably consistent and cumulative. In this chapter I will attempt to summarize this research tradition as well as raise some questions about it.

Concretely, this chapter focuses around three issues: (1) How the characteristics of innovations affect their diffusion, (2) how the nature of communication and advocacy networks through which innovations flow affects their diffusion, and (3) how the characteristics of populations and social structures affect the likelihood that innovations will be adopted.

Diffusion Research in Anthropology

The oldest disciplinary interest in the study of the diffusion process was among anthropologists (see Linton, 1936; Redfield, 1936; Kroeber, 1937; and Herskovitz, 1947). Anthropologists in the early twentieth century focused on the diffusion of innovation as an alternative to the evolutionary theories of the nineteenth century, which had come under considerable criticism. Their general approach focused on the diffusion that resulted from the contact between cultures. I concentrated in the first part of this chapter on conditions conducive to innovation within a society or culture, but anthropologists generally argue that culture contact is the source of most innovation and social change, rather than indigenous innovation. Whether or not this is true is debatable, but it is certainly true that culture contact is a major source of innovation.

Anthropologists have studied the diffusion of discrete cultural items, but also *acculturation*, a more global term than diffusion that means "the influence exercised by one culture on another, or the mutual influence of two cultures, that results in cultural change" (Lauer, 1977:294). Contemporary research in anthropology has produced a number of useful generalizations about conditions of successful diffusion. Thus there is evidence that diffusion is more likely (1) when the new item is perceived as being consistent with the structure and values of the host culture, (2) when the culture item is material (versus nonmaterial), (3) when there are a greater number of people in cross-cultural contact, (4) when the quality of such contact is friendly rather than hostile, and (5) when the contact between two societies connects elites and central elements rather than peripheral or marginal elements of the two societies (Spindler, 1977).

Diffusion Research in Sociology

An interest in the diffusion of innovation began in sociology during the 1920s and 1930s, primarily among Chapin (1928) and William Ogburn (1922) and his colleagues. The major early contribution of sociologists was to demonstrate that the rate of adoption for many innovations generally followed an S-shaped curve, starting out slowly, accelerating rapidly, and reaching a plateau at which the rate of adoption slows. While this generalization remained unquestioned for some time, later research by Katz (1960) found that the S-shaped diffusion curve, as it was called, depends on the degree of social integration within a population, and that in weakly integrated systems the rate of adoption was more likely to be linear and not likely to vary much at various phases of the adoption process. The real growth of interest among sociologists in the study of diffusion took place in the 1940s and 1950s. Hundreds of studies were undertaken, particularly by those interested in technical innovations in agriculture, the spread of medical innovations, and the effects of the mass media.

CHARACTERISTICS OF INNOVATIONS THAT AFFECT DIFFUSION

In a study of medical innovations Menzel (1960) concluded that the extent to which innovations will be successfully adopted is related to three factors. First, it is related to the *communicability* of the innovation. That is, the easier the innovation is to communicate, the greater the likelihood that it will be adopted. Second, the likelihood of adoption is a function of its *perceived risk* by the adopting person or social unit. And third, it will is a function of the innovation's *pervasiveness*, by which Menzel means its scope of appeal. Rogers (1962) describes the characteristics of an innovation that affect its adoption in a different way. First, he argues that the likelihood of adoption will be affected by its perceived *relative advantage* over the existing scheme of things. Second, the likelihood of adoption will be a function of the innovation's *compatibility with the existing values and experience* of potential adopters. An example of this generalization can be found in the spread of Christianity to Samoa. In the 1880s Congregationalist missionaries had greater success than other Christian missionaries because the Congregationalist polity, emphasizing separate, autonomous congregations with no higher authority of Bishops or Synods, was compatible with the autonomous village structure of Samoan society. Third, according to Rogers the adoption process will be affected by the *simplicity* of the innovation. Other things being equal, simpler innovations will be more likely to be adopted than complex ones. Fourth, Rogers argues that if an innovation is *divisible*, that is, if it can be tried out on a piecemeal basis, it will have a greater likelihood of adoption. The remarkable spread of new seed hybrids among American farmers can be partly explained on this basis. A new seed hybrid could be tried out on an experimental plot, without a major investment or decision. On the other hand, a new plan for a city government, or a new school curriculum, is not so divisible, and one has to "take it or leave it." Divisibility facilitates the adoption of innovation because it reduces the risks involved. And fifth Rogers, like Menzel, argues that innovations that are easier to communicate will be more likely to be adopted.

Ryan (1969) thinks that what Menzel and Rogers describe as "communicability" is really the innovations's *observability*, that is, whether or not the innovation has clear, tangible effects. Thus innovations with *instrumental* (versus expressive or aesthetic) value are more likely to be adopted. This, according to Ryan, accounts for the common observation that material items are more readily adopted than nonmaterial culture items. It is easier, for instance, to demonstrate the instrumental value of steel axes or new seed hybrids than the relative advantage of a new religious or ethical system. As another example of the advantage of instrumental innovations, consider the importation of yoga and meditation into the United States. It emphasized the personal effects of these practices for self-improvement, a venerable American value. The Eastern worldviews and metaphysical systems in which these practices were embedded were deemphasized and have not been adopted to the same extent as have the disembodied techniques.

While the characteristics of the innovation itself are important determinants of the likelihood of its adoption, they should not be considered in isolation. Thio (1971) stresses the critical importance of *adopter-innovation compatibility*. This relationship explains some puzzling research findings. Fliegel and Kivlin (1966) hypothesized that high initial cost and slow cost recovery would "brake" the diffusion of agricultural innovations. While their hypothesis was confirmed by several studies of third world farmers, and American farmers "of modest means," it was not true of "successful commercial farmers" in the United States. The explanation is that the "successful" farmers were used to high capitalization expenses and long-term investments. Hence high initial costs and slow cost recovery were compatible with the way that the "successful" farmers operated, but incompatible with the way that the less successful and third world farmers were used to operating. There is another puzzle that focusing on adopter-innovation compatibility can help explain. Some researchers, such as Barnett (1953), have found early adopters to be marginal or socially deviant. Barnett notes for example that early converts to Christianity in India were to be found largely among marginal groups, who had "nothing to lose" because of their low status in Indian communities. Others (Coleman et al., 1957) have found that high status and social integration are conducive to early adoption of innovations. Coleman and his colleagues studied medical innovations, which had the probability of increasing the professional status of the adopter. Hence, such innovations were readily adopted by high status physicians. Innovations with the probability of reinforcing or enhancing power or status will readily be adopted by elites, but innovations that appear to threaten the existing scheme of things will be resisted by them and will be viewed most favorably by low status groups and persons with little at stake in the existing system. Again, the critical determinant is adopter-innovator compatibility, rather than the isolated characteristics of the innovation per se. Moreover, Thio argues that compatibility is a complex matter: It can be cultural, social, or social-psychological.

CHANNELS OF COMMUNICATION

Historically the diffusion of innovations required some kind of physical contact between people. Hence migrations and wars were always important sources of the diffusion of innovation, because immigrants and returning soldiers brought with them things that were regarded as innovations by the host society. The need for contact also meant that special categories of people (i.e., merchants, traders, explorers) have played a particular role in the historic diffusion of innovations.

The invention of the printing press in the fifteenth century provided a new possibility: the diffusion of innovation without physical contact between peoples. Literacy was historically in the hands of social elites or special categories of persons with supportive relations with them (e.g., scribes, monks). Thus the real impact of print media was dependent upon the development of mass literacy, which was a twentieth-century phenomenon in the Western world and has yet to occur in much of the world. With the development of electronic media a new threshold was reached. Radio and television have a great potential for the mass diffusion of innovation because they do not require literacy.

Diffusion and the Mass Media

There is a lot of research on the role of the mass media in introducing change, and surprisingly it shows that the mass media have limited *direct* effects. This is primarily because *mass communication* is one-way communication that has a limited capacity for feedback. That is, people who are the recipients of mass communication cannot really ask questions, get clarification, or talk back in any meaningful fashion. Effective persuasion to adopt change usually requires *interactive communication* between the change agent and the potential adopters. Thus a major limitation on direct effects of mass media communication is that it is typically modified by interpersonal communication among persons who are tuned to the same media message. People are likely to discuss the significance of media messages with friends, family members, and co-workers. And in this process the significance of the media message is critically reshaped and assessed in terms of the existing perspectives of the informal group.

Other factors are the selective *exposure*, selective *perception*, and selective *retention* of mass communications, all of which limit the effectiveness of such communication to persuade people to adopt change. For example, people who are initially the most favorably disposed toward an innovation are the ones most likely to be receptive to mass communication about it, and most likely to interpret it in a favorable light. Thus, using television to persuade people to vote for a constitutional amendment is likely to have the greatest effect on people who were inclined to vote for it anyway, and people who are favorably inclined to adopt a new contraceptive are most likely to pay attention to, favorably receive, and remember information about contraceptive techniques from the mass media.

The mass media have greater *direct effects* to persuade people under two conditions. One is when people are isolated (Larsen, 1964). A second is when social norms are not effective, or in other words, when a condition of "anomie" (or normlessness) prevails. Some interpreters (e.g., Wirth, 1957) have suggested that the direction of social change in modern societies will increase the direct effects of the mass media in introducing innovation. In this view, commonly called the "mass society thesis," modern societies are producing a greater proportion of individuals with ineffective and unstable interpersonal ties. Hence, more individuals are more susceptible to direct persuasive effects of the mass media. This view, however, is a controversial one and I am suspicious of it (see Chapter 2).

Klapper's (1960) summary of several decades of research emphasizes the complex effects of mass media communication: It can intensify existing attitudes and opinions; it can reduce the intensity of attitudes and opinions; and it can create new attitudes and opinions, and it can convert people to new attitudes and opinions that are contrary to prior ones. Of these diverse effects, most research suggests that the last one is the least likely, for the reasons cited above. In sum, the mass media appear to be more effective in disseminating new information than in changing behavior or attitudes. They appear to have little persuasive effect without reinforcement by interpersonal communication in an informal group context.

Mass Communication, Interpersonal Communication, and Diffusion   There have been interesting studies on the relationship between mass communication and interpersonal communication as they relate to the diffusion of change.[2] The studies suggest that there is a "two-step flow of communication." This means that communication originating within the mass media goes first to people termed opinion leaders before being transmitted to the rank-and-file population. I've always felt that this should be termed a "two-step flow of influence," since what these studies investigate is the flow of influence, rather than merely the dissemination of information. There are apparently two different types of opinion leaders. First there are cosmopolitan opinion leaders, who are more oriented toward the mass media and are likely to be more aware of the advantageous effects of specific innovations. Apparently such opinion leadership is issue specific, that is, it is exercised in discrete fields (art, music, politics, styles, health, etc.). Cosmopolitan opinion leaders are more likely than others to belong to secondary groups and organizations (for instance, professional organizations) than others. As the primary interpreters of mass communication, they are the disseminators, who channel information and influence to local groups. In contrast to the cosmopolitan opinion leaders are the local opinion leaders. They are more oriented to local groups and hold central and strategic power positions in them. At the same time, they are more likely than other local group members to have a relationship with cosmopolitan leaders external to the group. They are the gatekeepers who can effectively advocate innovations within the group or who can block the adoption of innovations by group members.

While most research has found at least these two types of opinion leaders, Menzel and Katz (1955) have suggested that there may be more than two links or stages in the influence process, that is, there may be a "multistep flow." For instance, research about innovations in agriculture has suggested that the flow of influence typically begins with an agricultural researcher (working in a college of agriculture or an agribusiness firm). When the results of this individual's research is published in an agricultural journal or research bulletin, it is likely to be picked up first by the county agricultural extension agent (the cosmopolitan leader), who in turn persuades locally prominent farmers (local opinion leaders) to try out the innovation. If they find the innovation a success, other farmers will adopt the new practice.

ADOPTER CHARACTERISTICS AND DIFFUSION

The adopting units of an innovation can be either individuals or social systems. Most of the research so far has focused on individuals: Rogers and Shoemaker (1971) cite 132 studies that focus on some characteristics of individuals as adopting units. Most such studies contrast the characteristics of early versus late adopters. In general, early adopters have been found to be higher in socioeconomic status, higher in education, and more likely to be active participators in voluntary associations than later adopters. Early adopters tend to be highly integrated in community and extracommunity social networks. Social participation has been measured in a variety of ways, for instance, as travel outside the community, reading library books, membership in organizations, and exposure to the mass media. However, regardless of how it is conceptualized and measured, it is found to be related to receptivity of innovation. By contrast later adopters tend to be semi-isolates with low rates of social participation (see Table 6-1). Inter-

TABLE 6-1   A Composite Picture of Adopter Categories

Adopter Category	Salient Values	Personal Characteristics	Communication Behavior	Social Relationships
Innovators 2.5%	"Venturesome"; willing to accept risks	Youngest age: highest social status; largest and most specialized operations; wealthy	Closest contact with scientific information sources; interaction with other innovators; relatively greatest use of impersonal sources	Some opinion leadership; very cosmopolite
Early adopters 13.5%	"Respect"; regarded by many others in the social system as a role-model	High social status: large and specialized operations	Greatest contact with local change agents	Greatest opinion leadership of any category in most social systems; very localite
Early majority 34%	"Deliberate"; willing to consider innovations only after peers have adopted	Above average social status; average-sized operation	Considerable contact with change agents and early adopters	Some opinion leadership
Late majority 34%	"Skeptical"; overwhelming pressure from peers needed before adoption occurs	Below average social status; small operation; little specialization; small income	Secure ideas from peers who are mainly late majority or early majority; less use of mass media	Little opinion leadership
Laggards 16%	"Tradition"; oriented to the past	Little specialization; lowest social status; smallest operation; lowest income; oldest	Neighbors, friends, and relatives with similar values are main information source	Very little opinion leadership; semi-isolates

Source: Adapted with permission of The Free Press, a Division of Macmillan, Inc. from *Diffusion of Innovations* by Everett M. Rogers. Copyright © 1962 by The Free Press.

estingly, the difference between early and late adopters is not in knowledge of the innovation. Studies suggest that later adopters knew of the innovation at a much earlier time, but for them, in contrast to the early adopters, there was a considerable time lag between the time that they heard about an innovation and the time that they adopted it. Rather, early adopters have (1) greater resources for risk ventures, (2) broad social contacts that enable them to conceptualize the unfamiliar, and (3) greater formal education, which is related to better understanding complex innovations.

Status, Marginality, and Adoption   The preponderance of the research finds that early adopters tend to be high in socioeconomic status and centrally located within social networks, In spite of this, the notion persists among some scholars that innovation is associated with marginality and deviance, and some studies find that those who are on the periphery are likely to adopt certain innovations earlier than others (Barnett, 1953; Becker, 1968; Robinson, 1976; and Rogers and Kinkaid 1981). These researchers suggest that *marginals*[3] are likely to adopt particularly risky innovations because they (1) have less to lose, (2) are less constrained by social control within the group, and (3) tend to rely on self-judgments rather than advice from others. Weinmann (1982) suggests that there are some structural advantages to marginality regarding the diffusion of innovation. He argues that marginality is associated with having extragroup ties, and cites Granovetter's view that marginality "serves as a crucial pathway for the flow of information between densely knit cliques or groups that would not be connected to each other at all were it not for the existence of weak ties (i.e., marginality)" (1973:1363). Weinmann's view is that it is the marginals with their weak internal ties but many extragroup ties who "serve to agglomerate microlevel behavior, attitudes, and opinions to large-scale patterns of macro-level processes" (1982:766). This seems to contradict the conventional model of the "two-step flow" process discussed earlier, in which high-status cosmopolitans who operate in a broad social field link together and channel information to local (micro) structures. But I'm not convinced that it is really contradictory. Cosmopolitans may have higher status within broader realms, but that doesn't always mean high status within local groups. Nor are cosmopolitans likely to be central within social networks at the local level.

Weinmann's research focused on types of communication within an Israeli kibbutz (gossip, general news, consumer information), and he used sociometric techniques to separate the centrals from the marginals in terms of their location within the intragroup social networks. He found that the centrals tended to dominate the flow of communication within groups, while the marginals dominated the flow of communication between groups. It is important to underscore that Weinmann's findings apply to the flow of information, not influence. Influence tended to be dominated by the sociometric centrals, both within and between groups. This research suggests the need to qualify the "two-step flow" model to distinguish between (1) the flow of information and the flow of influence, and (2) intra- and extragroup communication. While centrals apparently control the flow of influence, both within and between groups, marginals bridge groups and control the flow of information between groups. Weinmann suggests that the marginals can be viewed as external "scouts" who import information.

Structures as Adopting Units

Important as the characteristics of individuals may be, it is also critical not to ignore the impact of structures on the adoption process. Social structures have effects that facilitate or impede the adoption of innovation and that are independent of the characteristics of individuals. Van den Ban (1960) studied the adoption of agricultural innovations among various Wisconsin townships and found that township norms were a stronger influence on farmers' decisions to adopt new practices than individual characteristics (e.g., education, wealth). For example, a farmer with high education and wealth residing in a township with traditional norms was less likely to adopt innovations than a farmer with low education and wealth residing in a township with norms more conducive to innovation and change. Qadir (1966), in a study of twenty-six Philippine villages, found that in modern villages even individuals lacking in education, media exposure, or modern attitudes toward change were more likely to accept innovation than individuals with high education and wealth living in traditional villages. Similar findings have been reported by studies in India (Saxena, 1968) and Nigeria (Davis, 1968).

The Adoption Process in Structures   In many cases the adopting unit is not an individual, or the decision to adopt is only partly an individual decision. In some cases the decision to adopt is *authoritative*: a collective decision to adopt is made by some decision unit within a social system. In this case the individual has little direct control over adoption or option about the acceptance of the innovation. Examples would include the adoption of a new city charter, an altered system of welfare services, fluoridation, or a new school curriculum. In other situations there is *optional collective* adoption, in which there is a collective decision about adoption, but the innovation requires individual acquiescence. In other words, there is authoritative or collective support (or resistance) for an innovation, but individual options regarding adoption. Examples of this would be a public health campaign, the spread of new educational techniques, or the adoption of cable TV.

The process of adoption by individuals can be understood as having separate stages: (1) knowledge, (2) persuasion, (3) decision, (4) action. The adoption process has been seen differently when the adopting unit is a social system (Rogers and Shoemaker, 1971; Beal et al., 1964). First is the *stimulation* of group interest in the innovation. The stimulators are likely to be similar to cosmopolitan opinion leaders. Second is the *initiation* of the new idea, in which the initiators are likely to be similar to local opinion leaders. In terms of the research of Weinmann discussed above, stimulators are more likely to be the marginals, and initiators are likely to be the centrals. Third, and perhaps distinct for the collective adoption process, is *legitimation* of the innovation by power holders within the group or organization. In other words, an innovation must be sanctioned by those who control values within the groups. Such legitimation can be an open or a covert process, and it can be a formal or an informal procedure. Fourth, there is a *decision* to act, which is made by some kind of decision unit within the system.

Adoption and Structural Characteristics   In general, the more cohesive (or highly integrated) a social system is, the more successful it will be in collectively responding to an innovation. A collective response in this sense does not always mean adoption; it can also mean resistance to adoption. *Cohesion* here means the degree to which members perceive themselves to be strongly tied to the social system, but it is also a system state condition as well as an individual variable. Group pressure to change will be more strongly felt by those who are more strongly attached to the system. As an example of this generalization, Eibler (1965) studied innovative and noninnovative school districts and concluded that one characteristic of innovative districts was high staff cohesion. However, the converse is often true: High cohesion can be a source of resistance, if the innovation is perceived as contrary to dominant values and the interests of power holders in the system (see Kelly and Volkhart, 1952).

The likelihood of adoption of a collective innovation has been found to be positively related to the *degree of concentration of power* within a social system. Hawley (1962), for instance, found that among a sample of ninety-five cities the tendency to adopt urban renewal programs was positively related to the concentration of political power. Similar findings were reported by Gamson (1968) and Rosenthal and Crain (1968) regarding the adoption of fluoridated water. Apparently the higher the concentration of power the less the ability of the nonpowerful to resist innovation. Conversely, the greater the degree of power pluralism among legitimizers, the more likely the resistance to the adoption of innovations. These findings are consistent with those of Zaltman, Duncan, and Holbeck, 1973, cited earlier in this chapter, who studied the innovation process in complex organizations. Apparently, the process of creating innovation is related to complexity and pluralism, but the probability of successful adoption is related to homogeneity and concentrated power.

In spite of this evidence I think that the situation is more complex. Like cohesion, I think that the concentration of power should either facilitate or inhibit collective adoption. The concentration of power gives power holders the ability to act more decisively. If they favor the innovation in question then concentrated power would work to facilitate collective adoption. But if they don't favor an innovation then concentrated power should inhibit the likelihood of collective adoption. However, I know of no research that has addressed the question in this way.

Finally, there is extensive evidence that *member satisfaction and widespread participation in the decision to adopt* are positively related to adoption by groups and organizations. Participation can be of many sorts; it can mean surveys, referendums, petitions, and public hearings. Participation in collective decision making has been found especially important for adoptions of the optional-collective type (see above). This generalization has extensive empirical support (Couch and French, 1948; Giffin and Erlich, 1963; Davis, 1965; Queenley and Street, 1965).

But if widespread participation in adoption decisions and concentration of power are both related to adoption by groups, there is a dilemma for organizational policy. Collective decisions to adopt innovations may be easier when the concentration of power is very great, or in other words, when participation in such decisions is narrow. But a price for such ease in decision making may be paid: Members may be less satisfied with the decision and—where they have the option—may resist and sabotage the innovation. In situations where the system is less than completely authoritative, elites may choose to widen the scope of participation in decision making, even though it may make initial adoption more problematic.

BASES OF RESISTANCE

No discussion of the diffusion of innovation would be complete without at least mention of the various bases of resistance to adoption. Many of these have been treated, by implication, in the foregoing discussion of circumstances conducive to adoption, so I will treat them here only in summary fashion.

First, innovation is often resisted because of fear of the new and untried. This is in a sense the inverse of what was discussed earlier as the perceived relative advantage of an innovation. Second, innovation is often resisted because it is perceived to be incongruent with prevailing values and social mores. For instance, many in contemporary America have suggested advantages of decriminalizing the so-called victimless crimes (e.g., prostitution, gambling, some forms of narcotic use). Notwithstanding the advantages of decriminalization, such proposals usually do not get very far because they violate widely shared social mores. Americans by and large simply feel that such activities are wrong and should not be sanctioned by the state.

Third, innovations are often resisted because they violate existing aesthetic tastes. Several decades ago it was suggested that nutrition in many third world countries could be substantially enhanced by supplementing or mixing locally produced flour or cornmeal with algae flour processed from algae and seaweed. Such algae flour is a rich source of protein, and is dark green with a taste reminiscent of grass or processed alfalfa. While tests suggested that this was economically feasible, people were reluctant to adopt the practice because food cooked with this concoction didn't taste right and was the wrong color. People resisted eating green bread, however superior in nutrition it was to the standard item. Similarly, there have been many suggestions by visionary architects and planners that building high-rise cooperative housing units for middle class Americans would have considerable advantages. Such advantages include the avoidance of urban sprawl and inefficient land use as well as considerable savings for space heating, energy, and transportation costs. Such ideas have never sold among middle class Americans, who seem firmly wedded to a preference for separate single family dwelling units, even in highly inflationary times.

Finally, an important basis for resisting innovation is the threat it often presents to vested interests, that is, their fear of losing money, status, or prestige. In the United States, the implementation of public accommodation laws (guaranteeing equal access to public facilities) and school desegregation was widely opposed on such bases. As another example, the energy companies doing business in natural gas and petrochemicals have been major opponents of in funding research and development for exotic energy sources (solar, biomass, wind), which may threaten the existing system of energy production, which is highly centralized and under firm corporate control. Status threats like those suggested above are more likely to be operative as a basis of resistance among elites or higher status individuals, since lower status and marginal groups have less vested interest in the preservation of privilege.

IN RETROSPECT: THE DIFFUSION OF INNOVATIONS RESEARCH TRADITION

I find much to recommend in this research tradition about social change. There is much cumulative knowledge and many congruent findings from researchers with different disciplinary and substantive interests. As a body of literature, it has a strong empirical base. It is a compact literature, which has been usefully catalogued and codified. It has a strong applied orientation and has been widely used by those concerned with implementing change (more about that in Chapter 9).

There is in this body of literature no explicit acknowledgment of recognized theory, but there is a strong connection with functional theory and liberal political values about change. From this perspective, change is usually viewed as a top-down process, organized and promoted by specialists and elites. The target population, or the adopting unit, is likely to be viewed as passive.

Rogers is one of the few who has commented explicitly about this distinction between top-down and bottom-up change. He says that in top-down change elites act as gatekeepers to prevent "restructuring" innovations from entering the system, while favoring "functioning" innovations that do not immediately threaten to change the system (1973:81). I think that much of the attention to "restructuring" innovations has focused on the "latent" or unintended consequences of such innovations. The anthropological literature is especially rich in this regard (e.g., Sharp, 1952).

Top-down change, according to Rogers, is more likely to succeed than bottom-up change, which involves a greater degree of social conflict and is most likely to succeed in times of perceived crisis. Certainly many of the innovations studied in this literature are technical innovations which may increase the efficiency of the system but also enhance the power and/or resources of elites. And the suggestion is strongly supported in this literature that the probable success of an innovation is inversely related to the degree to which it conflicts with the existing scheme of things. Ironically then, the less change, the more of it there is, or, as Fairweather has phrased it, "an invention is acceptable to a society in direct proportion to the degree that the innovation does not require a change in the roles or social organization of that society" (1972:7).

But is this really true? Is Fairweather's generalization an attribute of social reality or an artifact of the focus of sociological inquiry? This is a thorny epistemological question that I cannot answer, but we need to recognize that social science is itself a part of the social life it studies. Has there merely been more attention to, and funding for, studies of elite-supported change? Anyone interested in understanding bottom-up change would be better advised to look at the literature on *social movements*—which is the focus of the next chapters.

There is one striking observation about the diffusion of innovations research: While it was a vastly popular focus in social science during the 1950s and 1960s, it has diminished greatly in popularity since the 1970s. In surveying several major journals of sociology, I could find only six or eight research papers utilizing this focus during the 1970s. This contrasts sharply with its earlier popularity. Why is this? I can only speculate. In the 1950s and 1960s there was a great deal of optimism that the mysteries of how change takes place were being unlocked and that this would result in a greatly increased ability of change agents to induce change in desired directions. Diffusion research was widely subsidized by both public and private agencies interested in promoting change. While this effort to produce practical knowledge about promoting change did not totally fail, it did not live up to the optimistic expectations of the fifties and sixties. Improving the lot of mankind by deliberately inducing innovations proved more complex and difficult than it was thought to be. And even when isolated innovations were successfully introduced, they often had unintentional consequences that were counterproductive. This frustrated expectation may have led to a decline in funding sources and the breakup of research centers and training networks among scholars.

In addition to the possible change in funding sources, the shift away from the diffusion of innovations perspective reflects shifts in the theoretical interests of scholars. As I mentioned above, this perspective was intimately connected with functional theory and liberal political attitudes toward change. These are both now widely thought to have resulted in an inadequate understanding of social change, for both industrial societies and the developing nations of the third world. The functional perspective is still viable, but it is no longer *the* way of understanding society and change. Many social scientists have moved in the direction of undertanding social change from the conflict, neo-Marxian, or critical perspectives (more about these in Chapter 11).

In spite of its decline in popularity as a research framework, the diffusion perspective is still being used today, although it has not been greatly expanded. The major compendiums of generalizations and research materials are still in print, and many have been recently reprinted and updated. Their use, I suspect, is mainly among those with applied interests in social change (more about this in Chapter 9). And I think that it is still a very useful and insightful orientation, if you understand its limitations.

NOTES

1. One could focus on other change processes, for instance on demographic and ecological change processes, or on urbanization as a change process. Urbanization was mentioned briefly in Part I, and I have chosen to discuss demographic and ecological processes in the context of global change in later Chapters, particularly chapters 12 and 13.

2. See Katz and Lazarsfeld, 1955; Gross and Ryan, 1943; Beal and Rogers, 1959; Wilkening, 1960.

3. Being *marginal* means being less centrally located in a group in terms of influence and the communication network. Marginal individuals often have lower status *within* a particular group, but they are also likely to have connections with groups and people outside of the group in question.

CHAPTER SEVEN
SOCIAL MOVEMENTS

Modern societies abound with groups of people who organize attempts to promote (or prevent) change from taking place. Sociologists call such attempts *social movements,* and if you've ever worked for, signed a petition for, or donated money to a cause, you've been a part a part of a social movement, even if only in a small way. In America it seems like there has been a movement for almost everyone in recent times. There have been movements with an amazing variety of contradictory goals: to protect the environment, to save the whales from extinction, to promote more spending by the government, to promote less spending by the government, to reform the tax system (in a *variety* of ways!), to promote solar energy, to restrict the possession of handguns, to remove restrictions on handguns, to promote a "freeze" on the production of nuclear weapons, to restrict abortion, to preserve freedom of choice about abortion, to restrict the areas where people can smoke, to change the traditional gender and family relationships, to preserve the traditional gender and family relationships, to restore prayer in the public schools, to prevent the restoration of prayer in the public schools, to find missing children, to promote the rights of minorities, to end job discrimination for homosexuals, to ban homosexuals from teaching and public employment, to address such social problems as hunger, poverty, domestic violence and drugs, to remove public funding from programs that address such problems, to overthrow foreign governments (e.g., South Africa), to prevent the U.S. government from overthrowing foreign governments (e.g., Nicaragua). As if this is not enough, there have been (as always in America) a bewildering variety of cults, sects, and messianic movements that propose to save the world! This list could go on and on. But you get the point.

Social movements are one of the basic processes by which social change emerges and is processed in societies like the United States. They are often the carriers of innovation, particularly in nontechnical realms. They shape attitudes, define public issues, and effect social policy in a variety of ways. They may seek to effect only the lives of individuals, but most become political at some point in their career.

This chapter addresses two issues: (1) What are social movements? and (2) how and why do they develop? In the first part of the chapter I will try to define social movements more precisely and describe various types of movements, and in the second part of the chapter I will discuss various perspectives about the origins and causes of social movements. Most sociological studies of movements have focused on this latter issue.

WHAT ARE SOCIAL MOVEMENTS?

Social movements can be distinguished from other social forms because they (1) exist outside the institutional framework of everyday life and (2) are in some way oriented toward a degree of social change (Hannigan, 1985:437). Social movements have been more formally defined as unconventional collectivities with varying degrees of organization which attempt to promote or prevent change (adapted from Wood and Jackson, 1982). The word *collectivity* is used instead of *group* in this definition to emphasize that they are only partly organized phenomena. There are organizations associated with social movements, but they also include a broader population of sympathizers, adherents, and publics.

Social movements usually involve issues surrounded by intense emotion and therefore may produce intense conflict with other movements and causes. As mentioned, they may not be overtly political (e.g., religious movements or enthusiasms such as jogging and love of nature), *but* any movement can become politicized if public conflict about its causes is intense enough. The Sierra Club, for instance, has evolved from a society of nature lovers into a highly politicized movement concerned with environmental issues. And motorcyclists have organized a public crusade in some states to prevent the passage of mandatory helmet laws.

Descriptively, social movements have several characteristics that differentiate them from more integrated structures and organizations (Gerlach and Hine, 1970). First, they have "segmental organizations" that compete for loyalties of the adherents in what can be described as a "multiorganizational field." Second, they are characterized by face-to-face recruitment in small groups. Large rallies and demonstrations publicize the issues of movements, but they are not the settings in which converts are made. Third, participation is typically motivated by high levels of personal commitment rather than by external rewards such as money. Fourth, movements develop ideologies which articulate their rationales, goals, and causes. Fifth, they seem to need opposition—real or perceived—which provides external pressure and helps to create solidarity within the movement. Both political and religious movements seem to need an image of evil and villains.

Social movements are usually understood as representing change from the bottom up, that is, originating among the masses and stimulating responses from social and political elites. However social movements may also be stimulated and manipulated by elites to create solidarity and commitment. Nazism, for example, grew from the widespread social and economic frustrations of the German people prior to World War II, but the movement was also extensively manipulated by Hitler and the Nazi elite to gain political power. Political elites often try to generate or control popular mass movements in support of their goals, not only in totalitarian societies. Indeed, one recent theory (the "resource mobilization" perspective) suggests that mass unrest may be less critical in the formation of social movements than is ordinarily assumed, particularly under conditions like those that exist in contemporary America. We will return to this issue.

TYPES OF SOCIAL MOVEMENTS

There are many ways of describing differences between different kinds of social movements. There are (at least) four important overlapping dimensions to describe differences among kinds of movements. First, there are differences between *general* and *specific* movements (Blumer, 1962). *General movements* spring from widespread but poorly articulated sentiments and have vaguely defined, inclusive goals. Examples would include the counterculture movement of the 1960s, or the new religious consciousness of the 1970s that gave rise to religious cults and meditation oriented movements. *Specific movements* have more narrowly focused goals, ideologies, and organizations. They *may* arise from more general movements. For instance, the general ecology movement gave rise to more specific movements with narrower focal issues, such as the movements to oppose nuclear energy, save the whales, and control pollution. Specific movements create specific social movement organizations (hereafter, SMOs), such as the Clamshell Alliance (a New England-based antinuclear group that opposed a specific power installation), the Union of Concerned Scientists (a national lobby against nuclear weapons), and Greenpeace (an organization devoted to saving whales and aquatic mammals). Such specific SMOs are part of a multiorganizational field (as suggested above) of related SMOs having somewhat different goals, ideologies, strategies for change, and constituencies. Specific movement may, however, *not* be part of a more general movement, such as the movements against child abuse and domestic violence, or ABATE, an SMO formed by some motorcycle enthusiasts to prevent mandatory helmet laws.

A second important distinction is between *radical* and *reform* movements. *Radical movements* seek fundamental changes of the system, rather than within the system. Most familiar are political revolutionary movements that seek change in the total system, but focus particularly on the political system as the key to larger system change. Radical movements may, however, focus on a particular subsystem of society (e.g., radical movements against racism, sexism, or capitalism). Even among religious movements, millenarian movements seeking the second coming of the kingdom of God can be viewed as more radical than other religious movements. The fact that radical or revolutionary movements seldom succeed at total system change is beside the point: Their intention to do so shapes their strategies and development. *Reform movements*, by contrast, seek more modest changes within the existing system. They are likely to aim at specific issues rather than total transformation. Such movements that seek to reform politics, medicine, education, and so forth are far more common, at least in democratic polities, and seem more likely to succeed. Radical movements can be transformed into reform movements, and vice versa. We will take up this issue later on in the chapter.

A third distinction is between *instrumental* and *expressive* movements. *Instrumental movements* seek to change the structure of society. Examples of instrumental movements would be the civil rights movement and contemporary feminism. *Expressive movements*, on the other hand, seek to change the character of individuals and behavior. Examples would be the temperance movement of the early twentieth century, religious revivals, and the human potential movements of the recent past. The same general movement may contain both tendencies. Contemporary feminism, for instance, contains SMOs such as the National Organization of Women, which seeks instrumental and political change, as well as many expressive SMOs devoted to consciousness-raising.

At this point we can consider how some of these distinctions overlap. There are, for example, radical movements that are instrumental, and radical movements that are expressive. Similarly, there are reform movements that are instrumental and ones that are expressive. Using the combinations of these two dimensions (radical-reform and instrumental-expressive), Wilson (1973) has described four types of combinations: (1) reformative, (2) alternative, (3) transformative, and (4) redemptive. See Figure 7-1 for a schematic representation of these types with examples.

FIGURE 7-1 TYPES OF SOCIAL MOVEMENTS

	Instrumental	Expressive
Reform: Permutations of existing social arrangements and culture	1. **REFORMATIVE** labor movt, NAACP, ERA, tax reform, anti-abortion	3. **ALTERNATIVE** Christian evangelicalism, Human potential movt, various "enthusiasms" (Star "trekkies, "joggers)
Radical: significant departure from existing social arrangements, may have esoteric knowledge	2. **TRANSFORMATIVE** Bolsheviks, Islamic fundamentalism (classic revolutions)	4. **REDEMPTIVE** millenarian movts, cults People's Temple, Synanon, (isolated environments)

There is one further distinction among types of movements that is useful: the distinction between *left wing* and *right wing* movements. *Left wing movements* have been described as progressive or utopian. They typically seek to bring about historically unprecedented conditions and often seek to improve the conditions of submerged groups. In this sense, the Russian Revolution, the American ecology reform movement, and the gay liberation movement can be described as left wing movements. *Right wing movements* are conservative by contrast. They seek to prevent further change or perhaps to resurrect the past. Examples of such movements are the Gaullist movement in France in the 1950s, and the neoconservative political movement in the 1980s that brought the Reagan administration to power. If left wing movements are utopian, right wing movements are usually oriented around the vision of some real (or mythical) golden age of the past. They often represent the interests of the dominant groups in society. While I am not happy with these old political labels because they are often used in a pejorative sense, it does seem important to recognize that a key dimension of social movements is whether they are oriented toward a vision of the golden past or a brighter tomorrow.

EXPLAINING THE ORIGINS OF SOCIAL MOVEMENTS

We now turn away from these descriptive issues to address issues that have been major concerns of analysts of social movements: How and why do they develop? What are the conditions that stimulate the development of social movements? Jenkins (1983:530) has identified these questions as the "sine qua non of the study of social movements," and most sociological studies have focused around these issues. In this section I will review various perspectives about the origins of social movements, including psychological, social psychological, and structural explanations.

Psychological Explanations

I will discuss psychological theories of social movements only briefly here, since they seem to me limited as *sociological* explanations of the emergence of social movements. It is important to mention them, however, since they are historically important in the study of social movements, and other kinds of explanations do make psychological assumptions about the emergence of social movements.

Psychological theories focus on the aggregate characteristics of individuals. The oldest of these has been termed "crowd psychology" (LeBon, 1896, 1960 edition; Hoffer, 1951; McCormack, 1951), and emphasizes the "irrational" nature of social movement participation. In this view mob action which results in social movement convulsions is the result of the breakdown of restraining structure which results in unregulated crowd behavior in which people are anonymous and suggestible, and behavior is contagious. The contrast is drawn between individual behavior (viewed as rational and restrained) and crowd behavior, viewed as irrational and impulsive. In this perspective the participants

in social movements are compensating for frustrating lives. In a study of movement activists and "extremists," Hoffer (1951) described the "true believer
syndrome" in what has come to be called the "riff-raff" theory of movement participation. Hoffer argues that movement activists are misfits and losers whose
participation is fueled by the futility of wasted lives (this is not exactly neutral
"scientific" language!). The ideal converts are those who feel inadequate and
who attach themselves to movements to enhance their self-esteem and hope: The
types of movements or goals they pursue are interchangeable, according to Hoffer; paramount is their need to belong. While there may be some grains of truth
in these assertions, they are not now held to be adequate either as description or
explanation, and this sort of explanation has rather obvious conservative political biases.

In contrast to these older views, more recent psychological approaches
(Berk, 1974; Oberschall, 1973) suggest rational calculative involvement of actors in social movements, and they see social movements as attempts at collective problem solving. The danger here is the mirror opposite of the irrationality
assumption of former psychological perspectives: the assumption that humans
are rational, calculating beings. This approach minimizes the influence of ideology and social influence in stimulating movements.

Psychological theories attempt to explain the development of social movements by telling us something about the underlying motivations, or psychic
states, of individual participants. They have some utility in describing the attraction and recruitment of individuals to movements. Particularly, it seems to me,
they have some utility in explaining the attraction of *expressive* movements, such
as cults and enthusiasms (e.g., meditation or muscle-building), whose adherents
have been described as "seekers engaged in a search for identity" (Klapp, 1969).
Beyond this, psychological explanations are limited. The older ones suggesting
irrational behavior overemphasize the role of crowds and riots, but many movements develop without them. In any case, such underlying psychic
states/problems are assumed to be constants, and tell us very nothing about the
varying *social conditions* that trigger movements for change.

Social Psychological Explanations

Social psychological explanations for the origins of social movements
focus on the relationship between social conditions, psychological dispositions,
and the emergence of movements. Although various social psychological explanations exist, I will focus on the two that have been most well developed as
explanations of social movements, (1) relative deprivation theory and (2) status
strains theory.

Relative Deprivation   Some scholars have argued that *absolute deprivation* is a motivating force in the generation of social movements (Toch, 1965;
Fanon, 1968). Absolute deprivation includes such material deprivations such as
hunger, illness, and lack of safety which bring people close to the minimal conditions of survival. These analysts argue that changes in objective social condi-

tions, such as extreme poverty and rises in the price of food, are the causes of collective behavior and social movements. Yet it is obvious that until recently, such absolute deprivation was the lot of perhaps most of humanity and usually did not produce social movements. Also, it has been observed that much social movement activity is not directed at alleviating absolute deprivation.

These and other considerations have led some scholars of movements to reject objective conditions/deprivations as causative factors and to argue that *relative deprivation* (or subjective deprivation) is the psychological condition underlying the emergence of social movements (Davies, 1969; Gurr, 1970). Relative deprivation (hereafter RD) exists when there is a significant gap between value expectations and value outcomes, or in simpler language, between what people expect and what they get. It has to little to do with absolute deprivations but rather with subjective feelings of being deprived relative to expectations. RD theory also implies the importance of *reference groups*, which are the source of such expectations. People thus feel satisfied or deprived by comparing their condition to relevant categories of others. RD explains why (1) protest movements are often common during periods of sustained improvement in objective conditions (expectations rise faster) and (2) people involved in movements are often not the most objectively deprived people.

RD has been used to explain the development of urban protests among American blacks during the 1960s. In spite of objective improvements in social conditions for blacks, there was still a gap between blacks and whites, and the perception of that gap was most intense among "middle class" blacks. According to Pettigrew (1964), during the 1950s blacks began to contrast their situation with that of similarly educated whites, rather than with their own history of slavery and extreme deprivation. Thus "this approach focuses on the comparative deprivation between groups....groups can be reasonably well off in terms of wealth, power, and prestige, yet still feel deprived relative to other groups. When this occurs, the underprivileged groups are likely to protest" (Wood and Jackson, 1982:37).

The RD approach to social movements was vastly popular during the 1960s, but its popularity among analysts has declined somewhat since then. Why? There are some limitations to the RD approach. It obviously has more relevance for political protest movements than for what has here been termed expressive movements, which also produce change. And while some saw RD as a sufficient (fully predictive) explanation of the emergence of movements, this conclusion is not warranted by existing evidence. Summarizing studies from the 1960s, McPhail concludes that "there is considerable reason for rejecting the notion that RD and ensuing frustration...is the root cause of rebellion" (1971:106). More recent assessments of research evidence also find only mixed support for RD theory (Gurney and Tierney, 1982). But although not as popular as it once was, RD theory continues to appeal to analysts of movements for a number of reasons: (1) The RD perspective is conceptually clearer than older arguments about "mass discontent"; (2) it does not involve a derogatory view of participants as riffraff enraptured by the irrationalities of crowd behavior; (3) it is viewed as having some utility when combined with other approaches, but is not seen as a necessary or complete explanation of the origins of social movements (Gurney and Tierney, 1982; Wood and Jackson, 1982).

Status Strains   Many have argued that the motivation to participate in social movements results from threats to one's status in society. Such threats, or *status strains*, are likely to arise when one's status is threatened by social change (e.g., demographic change, immigration, occupational or political change), or when there is an increasing influence of formerly subjugated groups, or by erosion of a cultural perspective which served to legitimate social status. Since the status strains theory (hereafter, SS) deals with threats to privilege, it has mainly been used to explain the attraction of people to right wing movements, which seek to preserve or restore the traditional status order.

Lipset and Raab (1970) have exhaustively documented the relationship between SS and the emergence of a variety of rights wing movements in American history. I will mention three of their examples only briefly. The nativist movement (and its major organization, the American Protective Association) emerged in the late-nineteenth century; it attempted to protect the political and cultural dominance of the "old Americans" (WASPS) from growing Catholic and immigrant influence in the urban Northeast. Similarly, the Ku Klux Klan developed after the Civil War to protect the political privilege of southern whites in the wake of the postwar Reconstruction period. The movement was revived during the 1920s to protect the interests of rural white Protestants who were losing influence to urban immigrants. It thus became an anti-Catholic and anti-Jewish as well as a white racist movement. It was revived again in the 1960s to protect against gains made by blacks during the civil rights movement. Analysis of the adherents of these movements suggested that they were disproportionately composed of those whose social status and prestige was most threatened by the incorporation of new or previously subjugated groups into the American system. Another such movement was McCarthyism, an anticommunist movement led by U.S. Senator Joseph McCarthy in the 1950s. The adherents of this movement were attracted by his claim that the troubles of the nation were caused by the infiltration of communists into American political and cultural life. While McCarthy had support among powerful elites, several studies of his followers found that they were disproportionately composed of small-businessowners, the self-employed, and manual workers, all categories whose economic status was being progressively affected by social change. They all represented in various ways, the old middle classes whose status was being eclipsed by the rise of large corporations, skilled labor, and powerful unions.

It is possible to interpret the resurgence of right wing movements in the 1980s as being caused by SSs. In the late 1970s there was the growth of a highly politicized New Religious Right among Christian evangelicals (most familiarly represented by Jerry Falwell's Moral Majority organization), that developed in response to social changes of the 1960s and 1970s which threatened traditional lifestyles. According to some analysts (Gannon, 1981; Simpson, 1983; Yinger and Cutler, 1982), these changes (changing gender roles, affirmative action programs, and "welfare state" programs) along with the economic stagnation of the 1970s produced SSs particularly for the Protestant evangelicals, whose social status was most precarious. Hence, the emergence of a vigorous right wing religiopolitical movement. Also, I think the emergence of right wing anti-Semitic groups in the rural Midwest in the 1980s (the Posse Comitatus, the Aryan Nation, and other "survivalist" groups) is related to SSs associated with the economic farm crisis in rural America, and to threats to the status of small Midwestern farmers.[1]

In spite of the intuitive appeal of the SS perspective, there have been few systematic attempts to assess the adequacy of the theory. There are, furthermore, many problems with it as a general theory of movements. First, it is primarily an intriguing theory of *right wing* movements, and it is not clear how it could be applied to other types of movements. Second, the theory is reductionistic: The overt claims of protest groups are not taken as real, but as a kind of sublimation for status difficulties. Third, systematic studies of supporters of the New Religious Right, mentioned above, have in general concluded that adherence to that movement is at best only weakly related to SSs (Page and Clelland, 1978; Harper and Leicht, 1984; Simpson, 1985), if SSs are interpreted as threats to hierarchical statuses. These studies suggest that the support for the New Religious Right is at best related to defense of a cultural lifestyle, rather than threatened economic or political statuses. This suggests a fourth weakness of SS theory: It is conceptually muddied. That is, it conflates threats to cultural tradition, prestige, political power, and economic position. And sociologists ever since Max Weber have cautioned, that these different dimensions of stratification do not have an automatic equivalence in complex societies. In sum, SS is a useful but limited theoretical perspective; it requires much theoretical specification.

To summarize, social psychological theories focus on the interaction between individuals and social structure mainly as it relates to understanding the sources of the mass discontent.[2] That is certainly useful, but far from a comprehensive explanation of the emergence of social movements. In addition to explaining the motivational sources of movements, we need to know more (1) about the broader structural circumstances within which the development of mass discontent is likely, (2) about the differential availability of resources—both material and ideological—for the development of movements, and (3) about the ongoing interaction of social movements with other movements and the surrounding social order. These questions are not likely to be answered adequately by social psychological theories, and they require full-blown structural theories.

Structural Explanations of Social Movements

Structural explanations are *macro* theories of the origins of social movements. That is, while they may incorporate some of the perspectives of psychological and social psychological theories, the emphasis is on understanding the development of social movements in larger structures within which they develop.

The dominant macro view of social movements that developed in American sociology during the 1950s understood them in relation to a broader kind of phenomenon called "collective behavior." First, I will discuss some assumptions about social movements and collective behavior and a specific theory that developed within this framework (Smelser's "value added theory"). Second, I will discuss a newer perspective on social movements that developed during the late 1960s, called resource mobilization theory, which differs dramatically from the collective behaviorist tradition in American sociology. Third, I will discuss briefly some recent macro theories of social movements in the Marxian tradition, the so-called "French school," which presents an alternative view to both of the above.

Social Movements and Collective Behavior   Most human social behavior is routine in that it takes place within established social relationships. In other words, much of human social behavior is broadly guided by cultural norms and social control processes along preestablished patterns. People often enact established social roles within (imperfectly) integrated groups, organizations, and structures. In some situations, however, there are no clearly defined guidelines, and behavior is novel, spontaneous, creative, and rather unpredictable. *Collective behavior* is the technical term sociologists use for situations in which a significant number of people are acting in the relative absence of integrated social control. There are many *elementary forms* of collective behavior, such as the transmission of rumor, crowd behaviors, mobs, panics, and protests. Sociologists have assumed that such elementary forms of collective behavior develop in the context of the breakdown of traditional order (often associated with rapid social change) and always assume some underlying shared source of excitement, stress, anxiety, tension, or frustration.[3]

Blumer (1969:8) writes that in its beginning a social movement is typically "amorphous, poorly organized and without form" and is characterized by collective behavior "on the primitive level" as well as by mechanisms of interaction which are "elementary" and "spontaneous" (cited in Hannigan, 1985:438). Blumer (1962) argues that in spite of the negative images of protests, mobs, and panics, they may contribute to the creation of new social forms. In short, elementary forms that persist may lead to the formation of social movements, and these, in turn, may evolve into integrated structures and new established forms of behavior (see Table 7-1 for the schematic illustration of these relationships).

The development of the American labor movement illustrates this process. In the 1890s the labor movement was often characterized by volatile mob action (on the part of *both* strikers and the authorities!). As the union movement developed it evolved into an established set of structures and interests which are now a routine part of the American economic system. This illustration should not be taken to mean that social movements always succeed in evolving new structural forms. Just as the elementary forms of collective behavior are often short-lived, the emergent forms (social movements, with their organizations and

TABLE 7-1   Collective Behavior and Group Structure

Elementary Forms of Collective Behavior	More Developed Forms of Collective Behavior	Integrated Structure
Characteristics: lacks structure; fluid, spontaneous interaction, volatile	evolving structure; change oriented, non-institutionalized	stable structured interaction; institutionalized
Examples: crowds, mobs, protests, panics, rumor networks	social movements, movement organizations, publics, audiences	organizations, bureaucracies, families, stable peer groups

publics) often fail to result in any stable forms or produce any meaningful change. Social movements may transform society, but history is also full of the wreckage of lost causes!

In sum, the collective behaviorist perspective emphasizes that the breakdown of traditional patterns of order and social control produce elementary forms of collective behavior and that these may crystallize into ongoing social movements that attempt to promote or prevent further social change. This is, as mentioned above, broadly consistent with the functionalist image of order and change, in which change is a reaction to disequilibrium and stress. Social movements can be viewed as adaptive responses to such states of social disorganization.

Smelser's "Value-Added" Theory of Social Movements   Value-added theory (Smelser, 1962) attempts to explain not only the structural origins of movements but also the stresses that motivate actors and well as the development of the movement in terms of its ongoing interaction with the larger social environment. As such, it is the most ambitious and elaborate explanation of social movements from the functionalist and collective behaviorist tradition in American sociology. Smelser argues that there are six conditions that are necessary for the emergence and development of social movements. Each of these six conditions is necessary for the development of movements, but none is alone sufficient. They operate in an additive fashion (hence the name "value-added") but not necessarily in chronological sequence. The theory is not—strictly speaking—a stage model of the development of movements.

Smelser outlines the six conditions as follows:

1. *Structural conduciveness*: Preexisting structures in society are more likely to generate certain kinds of movements than others. For example, a society with racial cleavages is likely to develop racial movements, and free market societies are likely to develop panics and movements aimed at stabilizing the cycles of the economy. The structures of particular societies encourage or rule out certain kinds of issues around which collective behavior and movements develop.

2. *Structural strains:* Strains (perceived ambiguities, deprivation, inconsistencies, tensions) emerge in relation to the way that conducive structures are perceived. For ex-

ample, the vast inequality in a caste system is a *conducive* factor which may or may not produce strains. In this case strains only develop if such inequality is perceived as an oppressive fact. Thus strains are based upon *perceptions* of the structural order and are inversely related to the perception of its legitimacy. Such strains become relevant to collective behavior when they become collectively shared.

3. *Growth of a generalized belief system:* A preexisting or emergent set of ideas is required to galvanize widespread strains into an on-going movement. Such idea systems, or *ideologies*, define the sources of strains and point toward solutions that would alleviate them. In America, for example, ideologies that analyzed the sources of restricted opportunities for minorities and women as deriving from a fundamental aspect of American culture—as racism or sexism—have facilitated the development of the civil rights and feminist movements.

4. *Precipitating events:* Dramatic events sharpen and concretize issues. They can focus attention, galvanize public support and awareness, and draw the attention of media and the authorities. Examples of precipitating events include the Watts riot in relation to the black power phase of the civil rights movement; the collapse of the French credit system and the Petrograd food riots in relation, respectively, to the French and Russian revolutions; and the Santa Barbara oil spill and the Three Mile Island nuclear disaster in relation to the ecology and anti-nuclear power movements.

5. *Mobilization of participants:* This includes the emergence of leadership and spokespersons for the movement, and the development of organizations, as well as general processes of agitation, recruitment, and claims-making about grievances regarding the issues that animate the movements.

6. *Operation of social control:* The activation of forces in the larger society to respond to the movement. Such responses may be by governmental authorities or by countermovements that develop in relationship to a movement (examples of the latter would be the mobilization of anti-ERA forces, and the anti-cult movement that developed to combat the influence of religious cults during the late seventies). (Adapted with permission of The Free Press, a Division of Macmillan, Inc., from *Theory of Collective Behavior* by Neil J. Smelser. Copyright © 1963 by Neil J. Smelser.)

Smelser identifies three types of responses by the authorities to social movements. First, they can open channels of communication and influence, bringing the movement, its issues and leaders partly within the framework of the institutional system. This has been called cooptation. Second, the authorities can, while not coopting the movement, nonetheless seek to alter the underlying structural conditions that gave rise to the movement. In the German Empire of the late-nineteenth century, for example, Bismark did not open the regime to the influence of the socialist movement, but rather created "welfare state" reforms to deal with the issues that animated it. Third, the authorities can attempt to suppress a movement with all the resources of the state.

It is important that Smelser's theory addresses the ongoing interaction between the movement and forces in the society. This interaction can be a powerful force that shapes the development and direction of the movement. Thus a radical movement that is successfully coopted can become more moderate, while a reform movement that is brutally repressed may become more radicalized (more about this in the next chapter).

Smelser's intent was to create a theoretical scheme that is like a funnel, in which the initial variables are abstract ones relating to the macroscopic features of the social order and subsequent variables become more concretely related to specific episodes of collective behavior and movement development. Its comprehensiveness is appealing but it is also difficult to empirically refute. There are several critical questions about its adequacy as a theory. For example, the causal linkages between the six factors in the model are not clear, and they would not seem to operate in the same way. Structural conduciveness, for instance, is a "permissive" variable and may or may not lead to the emergence of strains. Strains, on the other hand, are treated as causally linked to the emergence of generalized beliefs and the mobilization of participants.

Smelser's depictions of structural conduciveness and structural strains are so abstract that they are of questionable usefulness in developing an explanatory theory. It is useful, and undoubtedly true, that certain kinds of structures are likely to generate certain types of movements, but is this more than an airy tautology? What kinds of structures generate which kinds of movements? Smelser's theory is of little help. There are similar difficulties with the notion of structural strains. There are no clear "criteria for identifying a 'structural strain' in a real society....Virtually any type of social problem or inconsistency seems to qualify as a strain" (Useem, 1975:9). Furthermore, Smelser is not clear as to whether structural strain reflects an objective condition in the society (e.g., disequilibrium or malintegration) or the perceptions of those conditions by its citizens (Berk, 1974:41). It seems to me that the latter (perceptions) is a more defensible interpretation. Furthermore, Smelser argues that "any kind of strain may be a determinant of any kind of collective behavior" (1962:49).

Precipitating events are different from the other factors, in that they can be seen as unpredictable collective "accidents" which come to have a significance for the development of social movements in the context of existing strains and generalized beliefs. Furthermore, there is evidence that some movements (particularly nonpolitical ones) develop in relation to the accumulation of individual biographical "events" rather than the occurrence of such dramatic collective events (see Harper, 1974:322).

In sum, I find Smelser's explanation more descriptive than explanatory, but the generality of the theory which makes it so universally applicable also makes it hard to refute. It is very useful as an orienting framework, however, since Smelser defines levels of things and issues that would have to be taken into account in explaining the emergence of any particular social movement.

The Resource Mobilization Perspective Recent explanations of social movements by American sociologists differ from the conventional functionalist and collective behaviorist (CB) approaches. Rather than emphasizing the grievances arising from structural strains, the newer resource mobilization (RM) perspective argues that social movements arise at a particular point in time because of the "changing availability of resources, organization, and opportunities for collective action" (Jenkins, 1983:530). So rather than viewing social movements as emerging from the spontaneous and amorphous mass discontent of collective behavior, this newer theory sees social movements as extensions of interest-group organizations which attempt to produce social reforms and to gain entry into the established structures of society. The RM perspective focuses more on the "role of power and power struggles in mobilizing people for collective action" (Burton, 1984:48).

The originators of this newer explanation began with some intriguing observations about American social movements during the 1960s. There was a dramatic increase in social-movement activity during this period. Why? During the 1960s there was a sustained growth in both affluence and apparent social conflict. There was no evidence of increase in the rates of participation in voluntary associations, and no dramatic increase in individual discretionary time and money that might explain the growth in social-movements activity. And there was no evidence that suggested increases in relative deprivation in comparison to previous decades (McCarthy and Zald, 1973; Gamson, 1974).

The RM theorists argued that the increase in social movement activity was related to a number of important trends in American society during the 1960s. First, there was the growth of private foundation and church support (financial and otherwise) for reform causes of all sorts. Second, the mass media gave greater attention to the dramatization of social issues. Third, there was extensive government sponsorship of social movements through agencies such as the Office of Economic Opportunity and the Civil Rights Commission. Fourth, there were improvements in the technology of fund-raising for social causes, in particular the development of cross-listed computerized mailing lists. Fifth, there was the emergence of "career social-movement organizers" who rejected traditional institutional roles, careers, and reward structures. These were, for instance, ministers, community organizers, and public relations specialists as well as doctors, scientists, and lawyers who opted to work in nontraditional settings for the advocacy of change. Sixth, during the 1960s there emerged a special body of literature for social-movement organizers.[4] Seventh, and most important, there was the development of "professional social-movement organizations" (SMOs). McCarthy and Zald (1973) have described the professional SMOs that developed during the 1960s as follows: They have full-time "professional" leadership, and in comparison to older SMOs they are driven by bureaucratic organizers rather than charismatic leaders or compelling ideology. A large part of their resources originate outside the aggrieved groups that the SMO claims to represent, and the actual membership base may be small or actually nonexistent. Or it may be a paper membership base of people who receive newsletters and make occasional financial contributions. Such SMOs attempt to impart the idea that they speak for an aggrieved constituency and to influence public policy.

I think these are important observations about movements in contemporary America. On my desk are letters soliciting support (and, more importantly, money!) from the Save Our Children Federation, the Solar Lobby, Nebraskans for Peace, and TransAfrica—which seeks to rescue South African blacks from the system of apartheid. And while I have some ideological sympathy with these causes, they are not SMOs that I helped to create from deeply personal grievances. Those on other mailing lists get appeals to restore prayer to the public schools or to prevent the regulation of handguns, and the multitude of other causes that are being mobilized at any given time. Advocates of the RM perspective thus argue that U.S. society now possesses the generalized resources that can used to mobilize a variety of (contradictory) change efforts that all have the appearance of mass-based movements. In this view there has been a decline in the importance of a mass membership base in the generation of social movements, and "the definition of grievances will expand to meet the funds and support personnel available" (McCarthy and Zald, 1973:23). The development of movements can then, to a certain extent, be planned or even manufactured.

The RM perspective deemphasizes the role of mass discontent—by treating it as a constant—and emphasizes the ongoing transformation of movements through the interaction of competing SMOs in the broader political environment (more about this later). It also assumes a liberal pluralistic political structure. That is, it assumes a political system in which elites are not firmly in control and there is continual political realignment that makes the success of activist SMOs possible. Hence it may not be applicable to authoritarian societies in which there is less freedom to mobilize. Yet critical questions about American society have been raised by the RM perspective. For instance, "Does the piper call the tune?" That is, if social movements in contemporary America reflect the influence of professional organizers and SMOs, to what extent do they reflect *their* needs and interests rather than the mass clienteles they purport to serve? And can such movements be channeled in less politically threatening directions?

There have been a variety of criticisms of RM theory. It seems too tied to recent trends in the United States (which may be reversible) to be a generalized explanation of social movements. Some research has been critical of the assumption that the relative deprivation and strains related to mass discontent have been relatively unchanging (Useem, 1980; Walsh, 1981; Law and Walsh, 1983). An important limitation of the RM explanation is that it is a better explanation of the social movements of the affluent than those emerging from lower status groups. Law and Walsh comment that

> collectivities at the lower end of the socioeconomic hierarchy are more likely to experience widespread, serious, and chronic discontent while having relatively...little organizational leverage. Higher status collectivities...have relatively few common grievances and abundant personal as well as organizational resources at their disposal. (1983:135)

In other words, as a general explanation RM theory has a social class bias. Most of the critics of RM theory argue that it has made an important contribution by emphasizing the role of SMOs, but that it minimizes the continuing role of mass grievances and strains in the emergence of protest movements. Hence it is not so much wrong as limited and needs to be reintegrated with the traditional macro explanations that emphasize the structural basis of mass discontent.

Neo-Marxian Explanations of Social Movements   No discussion of the emergence of social movements is complete without mention of explanations in the Marxist tradition. This approach shares with CB theory a focus on the *structural* sources of social movements, but their emergence is explained not in terms of structural conduciveness, disorganization, or shared states of psychic stress, but rather in terms of cleavages in the institutional structure of society—particularly in societal power relationships. Recall (from Chapter 3) Dahrendorf's assertion that society is composed of dichotomous structures of domination and authority between those in power—with an intrinsic interest in preserving their status—and those without power—with an intrinsic interest in increasing their share of power. In the neo-Marxian view these cleavages are the structural basis from which social movements emerge as major vehicles in the ongoing struggle for autonomy and constraint between various groups in the social order. Having dealt with Marx's and Dahrendorf's views at length in Chapter 3, I will not reiterate that discussion here, but rather will focus on newer a neo-Marxian perspective of European origins, the so-called French School as represented by the views of Alain Touraine and Manuel Castells.[5]

Touraine and Castells argue that the old Marxist conception of an economic base determining the political and ideological superstructure is no longer adequate to explain social change in advanced industrial societies. Instead, they view society as an interacting complex of three levels—economic, political, and ideological—in which contradictions develop both within and between each level. Since movements emerge from these contradictions, the neo-Marxists are closer to CB explanations (i.e., that movements emerge from the basic structures of society) than to the RM approach. In fact, Castells has criticized the RM approach for denying that movements "have a life of their own," and for assuming that movements in modern societies are bound by the "institutional rules of the game" of interest-group politics (Hannigan, 1985:438). But unlike the traditional American approach, the French School does not argue that movements emerge from amorphous "strains" which can develop in any direction, but rather from "spontaneous" moral protests as forms of opposition to established structures. They are thus movements of "social liberation" that can take a variety of forms: expressive as well as political, reformist as well as radical. Underneath the neo-Marxian language of the French School there are strong currents of echoes of the traditional mass society perspective. Thus Touraine speaks of

> the crisis of industrial culture in which the old anchoring institutions, the family and the Church, have burst apart, and where the channels of society no longer correspond to the cultural content they are meant to bear. (1981:15, cited in Hannigan, 1985:440)

Because of this, industrial societies have not only movements of political opposition but also a plethora of community utopias, cults, and messianic movements which are viewed as paving the way for more enduring social and political change.

While the thinkers of the French School recognize that to succeed or survive emergent movements must become organized, they (in contrast to the RM perspective) focus on movements as wholes rather than SMOs. They argue that movements are greater than the sum of the SMOs that comprise them, and that SMOs are important insofar as they "link contradictions" of various kinds. In fact the French School thinkers are quite suspicious of SMOs, and argue that they *can* weaken a cause by substituting organizations which coopt issues and interests for those of the mass base (more about this later). They argue that movements can make a lasting impact when the participants in movements are able to (1) identify the "stakes" over which the conflict is being fought—not just rolling back a new technology such as nuclear power but reshaping the wider structure of power, (2) identify the "opponent" as a class or institution, not just the state, and (3) transform this analysis into a program for action (Hannigan, 1985). In other words an effective movement must be able to transcend both localism and a narrow issue focus and transform its concerns into a systematic critique of the existing social arrangements.

The French School and CB theories are also similar in that they emphasize the *noninstitutional* origins of social movements. Touraine and Castells argue that there are two major dimensions that shape the ongoing character of social movements: (1) the degree of awareness of the need for institutional change and (2) the degree to which there is an emergent group identity shared among movement participants. Hannigan (1985) has suggested that there is a typology of social movements implicit in this thinking based on the permutations of these two dimensions (see Figure 7-2). This typology produces types of movements similar to those suggested by Wilson earlier in this chapter, though the dimensions are very different.

A *cultural movement* is similar to what I previously described as an expressive movement. It has a highly developed sense of group identity among participants, but lacks connections between its goals and a critique of the wider

FIGURE 7-2 NEOMARXIST "FRENCH SCHOOL": TYPES OF SOCIAL MOVEMENTS

		Emergent Group Identity	
		High	Low
Emergent Anti-institutional Awareness	High	social liberation movement	revolutionary movement
	Low	cultural movement	professional reform movement

Source: Figure adapted from John A. Hannigan, 1985, "Alain Touraine, Manuel Castells, and Social Movement Theory: A Critical Appraisal, "*The Sociological Quarterly*, 26, 4:435-54. Copyright © *The Sociological Quarterly*. Reprinted with permission of *The Sociological Quarterly*.

system. Examples include most religious movements, cults, and recreational movements such as those to which joggers and gun enthusiasts belong. When and if these movements become political, they tend to be perceived as "just another interest group engaged in coalition politics" (Castells, 1983:323). A *social liberation movement*, by contrast, has both a highly developed sense of group identity *and* a systematic critique of the social order within which its problems and goals are understood. Having such, it aims at broad-scale transformations of the political system, social institutions, and established culture. An example studied by the French School is the Warsaw branch of the Polish Solidarity movement, which aimed not only at political change but also a variety of cultural changes (e.g., increasing intellectual freedom and revitalizing work in industrial settings). Social liberation movements differ from *revolutionary movements* in that revolutionaries have as their first priority the overthrow of the existing political regime. They have a strongly developed group identity, and even though they are anti-institutional in the sense that they are the political outs, they still view the most significant change as taking place within the established political institution. They may or may not have goals for broader cultural change. I discussed *professional reform movements* earlier within the context of RM theory. Since these movements are led by professional organizers the mass participants have a low degree of group identity. And since they are likely to focus on single issues and seek entry into the established political system, they are not likely to develop a far-reaching critique of the established system. For instance Greenpeace, a significant ecology SMO in the mid-1980s, sought a wide number of reforms, from saving the whales to stopping the dumping of toxic wastes in the ocean, but purposely avoided direct political challenge based on the interconnectedness of these issues (Hannigan, 1985:450).

I think this is indeed a creative and interesting way of understanding different types of social movements, but it leaves many questions unanswered about the *emergence* of the different types (as does Wilson's older typology). We need to know much more about specific factors that lead to the emergence of the different types, and the transformation of one type to another. In particular I would like to know more about social liberation movements, which are the most distinctive contribution of the French School. What social conditions produces the "dual consciousness" (strong group identity and the awareness of the need for institutional change) that gives rise to them? While there have been calls to integrate the RM and the older F/CB perspectives, the French School has produced the first major attempt to create a comprehensive theory of social movements since Smelser's value added theory.

Some Similarities Between Neo-Marxist and Traditional Theory   It is conventional in sociology to contrast functionalist and Marxian or conflict theory, as I have done in Chapter Three. Yet there are some underlying similarities, and I have mentioned a few of these in relation to explaining the origins of social movements. There are some other similarities between neo-Marxist and CB approaches to social movements that are important. First, both approaches see structural conditions as necessary but not sufficient causes of the emergence of social movements. This is contrary to simplistic interpretations of Marx, which view protest as inevitably flowing from structural contradictions. Second, both theories emphasize the importance of ideas in the emergence of social movements ("generalized beliefs" in Smelser's approach and "ideologies" in the neo-Marxist framework). While traditional Marxism tended to emphasize structural factors and view ideas as derivative of them (that is, "epiphenomenal"), neo-Marxians are much less likely to do so. As we have seen from the theories of Castells and Touraine above, ideology and consciousness play a significant role in shaping the emergence of different types of movements from structural conditions fraught with various contradictions. Third, both CB and Marxist approaches emphasize the importance of particular precipitating events. While these are systematically incorporated into Smelser's explanation, Marx recognized the importance of "sparks" (e.g., military defeats, panics) as catalysts that ignite collective protests. Fourth, both approaches to the origins of movements emphasize the importance of leadership and organization if movements develop beyond short-lived and limited concerns. The French School has been particularly concerned about the possibility of the betrayal of a movement by its leaders and organizations.

To summarize, we have now explored a variety of explanations about how and why social movements develop. I have described psychological explanations (irrational versus rational emphasis), social psychological explanations (relative deprivation and status strains), and structural explanations (collective behavior, resouce mobilization, and neo-Marxist). Having described types of movements and examined different theories about their origins, in the next chapter we move on to more direct questions about movements and change.

NOTES

1. To say that the SSs of small farmers was a basis of these movement organizations is *not* to infer that all small farmers found these groups attractive.

2. This discussion is only an illustration of social psychological approaches to social movements, rather than a comprehensive review of them. I have not discussed Turner's "emergent norm" theory, which is a well-established perspective. Nor have I mentioned Brown and Goldin's (1973) suggestion that the stresses which underly social movements are caused by the existence of two (or more) competing and mutually contradictory "reality constructs" or definitions of the situation. I find this latter suggestion intriguing because it relates to the general symbolic interactionist perspective on change (outlined in Chapter 3), but unfortunately it has not been well developed as a theory. See Wood and Jackson (1982) for a more comprehensive discussion of social psychological theories

3. While collective behaviorists argue that the breakdown of order means that actors are "under the dominance of restlessness and collective excitement" (Blumer, 1969:11), I think it is important to emphasize that such collective states of tension are not necessarily irrational states of individuals. Such states may be rational ways of responding to frightening and frustrating aspects of the way that the social world is organized—or disorganized.

4. Here are a few of the titles to give you the flavor of this literature, which reflects the issues and the mood of the 1960s: *Political Action: A Practical Guide to Movement Politics, How People Get Power, Rules for Radicals, Manual for Direct Action, and The Organizer's Manual* (McCarthy and Zald, 1973:24).

5. For a fuller account of the "French School" of neo-Marxism in specific relation to social movements, see Hannigan, 1985, on which this account relies heavily.

CHAPTER EIGHT
MOVEMENTS
AND CHANGE

Movements sometimes transform society in dramatic ways, but often their impacts are minor and transitory. Furthermore movements grow and develop in various ways as they interact with the society in which they develop. That is to say, movements themselves have histories, and many scholars have argued that there are predictable stages in the development of movements themselves. In this chapter I will explore two issues: (1) how movements are transformed as they interact with society and (2) the kinds of impacts that movements are likely to have on society. At the end of the chapter I will illustrate the relationship between social movements and change by an extended analysis of feminism as a social movement in America.

THE TRANSFORMATION OF MOVEMENTS

While the major sociological focus on movements has been on their emergence, some of the classic sociological thinkers were concerned with how movements develop and change. I will briefly examine some classic views and then describe some newer perspectives about the transformation of movements.

Classic Perspectives

There are two important strands of sociological thinking about the transformation of movements that derive from classical sociological theory. First is the assumption that social movements begin in collective behavior and evolve to higher degrees of organization and, if they are "successful," to institutionalization. Connected with this assumption in older sociological literature is the second assumption that as this process of structural development and institutionalization takes place, movements come more and more to accommodate their goals and to comnpromise with the demands of the established system. Radical movements become tamed. Even "successful" revolutions wind up with a series of compromises that betray revolutionary ideals and often result in new regimes that are profoundly conservative. For example, many supporters of the Russian Revolution, such as Leon Trotsky and John Reed, ultimately felt that the revolution had "been betrayed" and that a repressive Bolshevik regime had been substituted for a repressive Tsarist one, with only minimal implementation of the utopian Marxian ideals.

Oligarchy and the Routinization of Charisma   Many scholars have analyzed this tendency for movements to compromise and become more conservative. Max Weber, for instance, focused on change in leadership. He observed that radical movements are often lead by *charismatic* leaders who exercise personal control over followers. A crisis of succession is inevitable, in which the successors to the charismatic leader must, if the movement is to survive, convert his personal charisma into an abstract theory of authority, based on traditional or bureaucratic rather personal criteria. As this "routinization of charisma" (as Weber called it) develops, stable structures of organized authority emerge. This change is signaled by changes in leadership. The successive generations of political movement leaders are more administrators than revolutionaries, and in religious movements there is a transition from prophets to Popes, who administer religious bureaucracies rather than dynamic movements. Weber's student, Ernst Troeltsch found what he claimed to be a predictable pattern whereby dissident Christian sectarian movements evolved into stable and somewhat conservative religious organizations. The transformation in America of the Methodists and Baptists from frontier sects rebelling against the religious establishment of the times to large established religious denominations are cases in point. Robert Michels (1903, 1949 edition), another of Weber's associates, documented the transformations of socialist labor unions and parties in Germany at the turn of the century from "radical" anti-establishment movements to reform-oriented "party" structures engaging in routine parliamentary politics and compromises with the more conservative establishment. Michels argument is that in the process of organizing, radical movements develop cadres of professional leaders who negotiate in practical rather than ideological terms with their opponents, and whose interest in their own careers and organizations may displace concern with the grievances that gave rise to the movement. As they become organized, Michels argues, mass movements become more hierarchical and come to reflect the structural characteristics of the surrounding social order. Michels argued that this was an invariant "law" of social movement development. In the words of Michels' famous "iron law of oligarchy," "whoever says organization says oligarchy" (1949:401). The important corollary is whenever movements become "organized" they inevitably come to accommodate the established order and therefore to become more conservative.

The Life Cycle of Movements   A second sociological strand of thinking about the transformation of social movements is the notion that they have a "life cycle" or a "natural history" akin to stages of development in the lives of individuals. That is, there are a predictable set of stages of development through which movements pass (Edwards, 1927; Brinton, 1938, 1965 edition; Blumer, 1969). Rex Hopper (1950), for instance, has argued that social movements pass through four stages of development. First is the *preliminary stage* characterized by high levels of shared unrest, excitement, and stress. People are unhappy about some condition, but they are not organized to promote change. Second is the *popular stage* in which disconnected individuals find that many people share their discontent. In this stage there is interaction between affected groups, often dramatic forms of elementary collective behavior (e.g., crowds, riots, demonstrations, etc.), the emergence of charismatic leaders, and widespread agitation for change. Third is the *formal stage* in which there emerge more organized SMOs, an articulate ideology, and attempts to negotiate with centers of power. Charismatic reformers may be partly replaced by pragmatic organizational leaders, who know how to get things done. Fourth is the *institutional stage* in which—for successful movements—there is the legalization and societal incorporation of the movement. When this happens the movement becomes a stable bureaucratized form, and leaders may become administrators charged with maintaining an organization and its interests. As such, they may become skeptical of further proposals for change. Thus the life cycle approach argues that successful movements undergo an evolution from unorganized collective behavior to become part of the established institutional framework of the society.

Hopper's life cycle stages assume that social movements become institutionalized as permanent structural forms. While this is often the case it is also often true that the reforms advocated by successful movements are institutionalized, while the movement and its SMOs decline after their programs become widely accepted. Mauss (1975) has constructed a set of developmental stages that reflect this fact (i.e., that even successful movement are likely to decline). According to Mauss, there are five stages in the life cycle of movements: (1) *incipiency*, in which there is widespread concern over issues, (2) *coalescence*, during which there is the emergence of organization and leadership, (3) *institutionalization*, during which the movement achieves its largest following and may achieve legitimization of its goals, (4) *fragmentation*, which follows either success or failure and may involve cooptation, repression, or intramovement factionalization, and finally, (5) *demise*, during which the movement disintegrates as a viable social force. According to Mauss, this rise and fall life cycle occurs for both successful and unsuccessful movements. Looked at in this way,

American society is full of reforms which are the programmatic remnants of long-dead movements. The social security system, the regulation of narcotic drugs, educational reforms, and prison reforms, for instance, are the institutionalized residues of what were once contentious public issues around which powerful movements and countermovements took shape. While the reforms remain, the actual movements and SMOs have passed into the dustbin of history. On the other hand, the American labor movement not only promulgated lasting reforms, but has survived as an entity. But it has survived to become incorporated into American society as a set of stable interest-group organizations; its dynamic phase as a *social movement* is long past.

Critique of the Classical Approaches   While these two themes (the compromise of radicalism and the life cycle notion) will continue to inform sociological thinking about the development and transformation of social movements, they are both, I think, critically flawed as adequate explanations about how social movements develop. While it *often* happens that radical movements become more conservative and accommodate themselves to society, it does not *always* happen. There are many movements that start as reform movements and become progressively radicalized (the New Left of the 1960s and the Gay Liberation movement would be examples). And there are religious sectarian movements, such as Jehovah's Witnesses, that never mature into established denominations. There is not any inherent tendency for movements to accommodate and compromise. The life cycle approaches suggest that there is an invariant "career" of movements, and give too little recognition of different developmental paths. They do not explain why some movements fail, or fail to undergo significant transformations during their life span. The growing conservatism and institutionalization of a movement depends not only upon the internal character of the movement, but importantly upon how it interacts with authority structures in the larger society. It is not that the classic Weber-Michels theory and the life cycle perspectives are wrong, but rather that as general explanations they do not do justice to the complexities of the way that social movements can develop.

Recent Approaches

Newer approaches seek to address these issues and complexities in a fragmentary way, although there is as yet no comprehensive theory of the complex variety of possible developmental paths of social movements. I will briefly discuss two such approaches.

Contingencies of Radicalization   Beach (1977) studied a Catholic SMO in Northern Ireland known as the People's Democracy, which during the 1970s evolved from a moderate liberal civil rights organization to a militant leftist movement formally committed to the revolutionary goal of creating a workers republic. Based on this study, he suggests that there are a number of circumstances that can lead to the progressive radicalization of a moderate reform movement. Radicalization can be produced by attempts of the police and the authorities to physically repress a movement. The effect of this repressive treatment is to erode the legitimacy of the authorities and the system they represent in the eyes of the movement adherents. Beach found that in Northern Ireland the authorities attempted to suppress all protest movements, not differentiating between modest and fundamental challenges to political authority. It is worth noting in this context, that the Russian Revolution was preceded by several decades of political reform movements which were brutally suppressed. When reform fails movement organizers may turn to more radical programs.

Radicalization can also be related to a change in the popular constituency of an SMO. Clientele of the People's Democracy gradually shifted from a popular base of college educated people and college students to a base of younger urban workers, who had different outlooks and needs. In America, the progressive radicalization of the Student National Coordinating Committee, a liberal civil rights organization of the 1960s, is also partly explained by a shift in constituency from relatively well-educated middle class blacks to less-well-educated, urban, working class black youths. In general, movements with middle class clienteles will experience more pressures to accommodate their objectives than movements with less affluent clienteles, who have less stake in the legitimacy of the existing order.

Movements are more likely to undergo radicalization in certain types of societies, particularly, in dual societies that are polarized with no middle ground between the cleavages that divide political interest groups. With its strong polarization between Protestants and Catholics, Northern Ireland is such a society, as is South Africa, in terms of the polarization between whites and blacks. In such societies there is very little support for moderate reform movements, and the ruling group is often unable to differentiate between requests for modest reforms and challenges to legitimacy. Hence elites in dual societies are more likely to respond with undifferentiated repression of protest groups (mentioned above), and are less likely to seek to coopt them. In Northern Ireland Beach found that Catholic reform groups were inevitably viewed by the government as subversive and were treated as such. "In time, they generally either *became* subversive, or gave up" (Beach, 1977:313).

Other sources of radicalization are internal. One is the degree to which SMOs can control and discipline members to act responsibly. In SMOs with less control, members are more likely to engage in undisciplined and perhaps violent acts that produce a climate of polarized confrontation with the authorities and promote radicalization. Beach argued that the ideology of participatory democracy within the People's Democracy in Northern Ireland weakened internal control within the movement and indirectly stimulated radicalization. This was also arguably a factor in the progressive radicalization of the Students for a Democratic Society, a New Left SMO from the 1960s in America.

Finally, the relations of an SMO with its competitors in an interorganizational field can promote radicalization, but the manner in which this may happen is complex. An SMO may become more radical in order to compete with others. Thus in the 1970s the NAACP became somewhat more radical in order to compete for clientele with other civil rights organizations. In the case of the People's Democracy however, it became more radical in order to differentiate itself from more moderate groups such as the Northern Ireland Civil Rights Association (Beach, 1977:315).

Factors Related to the Transformation of SMOs   In an influential theoretical work Zald and Asch (1966) discuss the pressures related to a variety of possible transformations of SMOs. They treat such transformations as *variable*, that is, some SMOs change more than others, and in different ways. One common type of transformation is a shift away from original goals to a concern for organizational maintenance (as manifested in a heavy emphasis on recruitment drives and fund-raising). They argue that this goal displacement underlies much of the "accommodationist" tendencies of movements observed by Weber, Michels, and many others. But there are other possible changes in SMOs. They can form splinter movements. They can die out both after failure and after success. Or they can survive success by adopting new goals and programs.

Zald and Asch recognize that *external factors* affect change in SMOs. They suggest that the ability of an SMO to survive and/or grow is related to (1) the size of the potential support base, (2) the amount of societal interest in the social movement and its SMOs, and (3) the direction of that interest (favorable, neutral, or hostile). These propositions are undoubtedly true, but almost too obvious. Zald and Asch also argue, like Beach, that the transformation of an SMO and its goals is related to interorganizational competition for support among similar SMOs. Their most unique and interesting hypotheses are about how internal factors effect the transformation of SMOs.

Zald and Asch make a number of distinctions about the internal character of SMOs that relate to their transformation. First, they distinguish between groups that have *inclusive* versus those that have *exclusive* membership requirements. Inclusive SMOs require only minimal commitments from their members—a pledge of support with few specific duties. They attempt to create as broad a support base as possible. Exclusive SMOs on the other hand seek a narrower base of support from those with intense commitment to the cause among whom they can require heavy investments of time and energy in movement affairs. They are likely to "hold the new recruit in a long 'novitiate' period, to require the recruit to subject himself to organizational discipline and orders, and to draw from those having the heaviest initial commitments" (Zald and Asch, cited in McLaughlin, 1969:467). Second, Zald and Asch analyze SMOs in terms of their goals—as I did in the last chapter—distinguishing between those that have goals to change individuals and those that have goals to change society. The former are generally perceived as less threatening to dominant values and other institutions. Third, they distinguish between SMOS that are created by larger parent organizations and those that are autonomous. Autonomous SMOs have their own membership and fund-raising support base, while the former are likely to be dependent upon support from the parent organization. Fourth, Zald and Asch distinguish between types of incentives for participation. There are *material incentives* (money and goods), *solidarity incentives* (prestige, respect, friendship), and *purposive incentives* (ideological and value fulfillment). Although SMOs may offer all three types of incentives to elicit support, they vary considerably in their emphasis.

Zald and Asch suggest a number of propositions that relate these distinctions to a variety of possible SMO transformations.[1] Several relate to the pressures for the displacement of goals and a shift to organization maintenance (the "accommodationist" tendencies of Weber and Michels):

1. The more insulated an organization is by exclusive membership requirements and goals aimed at changing individuals, the *less* susceptible it is to pressures for goal displacement and a shift that emphasizes organizational maintenance.
2. A "becalmed movement," which has managed to survive without achieving major successes, is most likely to follow the Weber-Michels model of conservatism and goal displacement because it comes to rely more on material incentives. The lack of major successes produces membership apathy and allows leaders to gain control of such material incentives, thus facilitating oligarchization and growing conservatism.
3. Goal displacement and a shift to maintenance activities is likely to conservatize the dominant core of the SMO while simultaneously producing increasingly radical splinter groups.

A number of the Zald-Asch propositions deal with the ability of SMOs to survive both failure and success ("surviving success" means that when the major objectives of an SMO are achieved, it is able to add new goals or broaden old ones):

4. SMOs created by other organizations are more likely to go out of existence following success than SMOs with their own linkages to individual supporters.
5. SMOs with relatively specific goals are more likely to vanish following success than organizations with broad general goals.
6. SMOs that aim to change individuals and employ solidarity incentives are less likely to vanish than are ones with goals aimed at changing society and employing purposive incentives.
7. Inclusive SMOs are likely to fade away faster than exclusive organizations; the latter are likely to take on new goals.

Some of the Zald-Asch propositions relate to changing interaction among SMOs:

8. Inclusive SMOs are more likely than exclusive SMOs to participate in coalitions and mergers with other SMOs.
9. Coalitions are most likely when they increase the resource base, and when success is close, or when one indivisible goal is at stake.
10. Exclusive SMOs are more likely than inclusive ones to be beset by schisms.
11. The more the ideology of the SMO leads to a questioning of the basis of authority, the greater the likelihood of factions and splitting. (From Mayer M. Zald and Roberta Asch, "Social Movement Organizations: Growth, Decay, and Change," *Social Forces*, 44:327-41. Copyright © *Social Forces*. Used with permission of *Social Forces*.)

I believe this is an interesting set of propositions which goes considerably beyond arguing that there is some "iron law" of development or an invariant life cycle toward specifying variables related to the different types of changes that SMOs can go through as they develop. There are two empirical field studies that lend general support to the Zald-Asch propositions: a comparative study of two antipornography SMOs (Zurcher and Curtis, 1973) and a study of the development of a religious communal organization (Richardson, Stewart, and Simmonds, 1979).

Here then are two somewhat fragmentary attempts to account for the differential outcomes of the developmental careers of social movements and SMOs. I would like to summarize by describing more coherently the possible types of outcomes of movement development that seem possible.

The Transformation of Movements: A Summary

First, there is the outcome of accommodation and cooptation embodied in Weber-Michels' classic theory. In this development, the movement changes its structure and ideology to become more congruent with those values and social forms found in the social environment. The movement's agendas and programs for change may be adopted by the established authorities and become a part of the larger societal goals for change. To *some* extent this is the fate of many contemporary American reform movements, such as the civil rights, feminist, and environmental movements. Second, a movement may disappear for a variety of reasons. It may disappear after success if the authorities respond by initiating reforms that undercut its reasons for being. It may disappear after initial failures, because it does not have the ability to mobilize support and resources to continue the struggle. It may disappear because it is effectively repressed and harassed by the authorities. It is important to note that because movements are composed of different wings and factions, parts of them may succeed and thrive while other parts fail and disappear. Thus the radical wings of the civil rights movement (e.g., the Black Panthers) and of the antiwar movement (e.g., the Weathermen) failed because of both lack of public support and effective government harassment, while the more moderate reform wings of the movements were more successful. Furthermore, a movement can—such as the feminist movement did—disappear at a given time, only to be revived at another time (more about feminism at the end of this chapter).

A third possible outcome is that a movement can continue to exist without being either very successful or a total failure. In doing so it often becomes an isolated sectarian organization, or what Zald and Asch (1966) call a movement "becalmed." Such movements create a stable but marginal ecological "niche" in the society. They undergo goal displacement, that is, deemphasizing their goals for social change to emphasize activities that help to *maintain* the movement and its SMOs (what Zald and Asch have termed a shift from "purposive incentives" to "solidarity incentives"). This is the fate of many American radical fringe movements that have managed to survive. Thus American socialism became a socialism of study groups and pot-luck dinners while the reality of "transforming the system" became increasingly remote. Likewise Jehovah's Witnesses spend their time and energies supporting their organizations and distributing millenarian literature, while the events they predicted—the battle of Armageddon and the triumphant arrival of the "Kingdom" of those saved by God—become distant visions remote from the daily activities of the movement.

A fourth possible outcome, and perhaps the rarest one, is that a social movement can succeed on such massive terms that it *becomes* the framework of a new society. This is the aim of revolutionary movements. Successful revolutions are rare historical and political events. Here I use the term revolution in its strict sense, as a sudden overthrow of a political regime followed by a rapid transformation of other institutional realms rather than in the looser usage of the "sexual revolution," or the "computer revolution." These latter usages are how we talk about what I have previously called trends, when we want to be dramatic about them. I think that political revolutions—in the strict usage—are more likely to be successful in societies undergoing a rapid transformation from agrarian to industrial. They are more likely when there are rapidly changing economic, technical, and demographic contexts and rather static political contexts. Certainly, the political revolutions in France, Russia, Egypt, Cuba, and Nicaragua were such.[2] Such revolutions, rare and dramatic events as they are in transforming society, never manage to completely transcend the structures and values of the old order.

We have examined how movements are variously transformed as they interact with society. Now I will turn the question around: How do movement change society?

WHAT KINDS OF CHANGE DO SOCIAL MOVEMENTS ACCOMPLISH?

I began this chapter by asserting that movements are one of the basic processes by which social change is processed in society. While this is true, their degree of success in creating change, as well as their significance and the kinds of social change they create is often debatable.

Movements and Social Inertia

As just mentioned, even successful revolutions do not completely transform society. Change outcomes are even more complex and ambiguous for successful reform movements, which are likely to wind up in a series of practical compromises with other interest groups and the authorities. Thus one of the reasons that social movements find it difficult to be completely successful is that they have very complex developmental careers as they interact with society. This is what the Weber-Michels thesis was all about, although as we have seen, the possible outcomes are more complex than Weber and his students envisioned. A second reason that most movements are incompletely successful is that popular movements do indeed represent change from the bottom up, that is, they face an

uphill battle in seeking to alter the social system. There are usually more resources and loyalties available to social elites seeking to perpetuate existing social
arrangements than there are available to those seeking change. Thus popular
movements for change seek to modify (1) established patterns of material interests, power, and status, and (2) established cultural values and norms.

Additionally—to restate what I hope by now is obvious—movements do
not operate in a vacuum but in the context of other types of trends that are simultaneously taking place. That is, movements as deliberate attempts to produce
change often develop from and respond to long range (undeliberate) trends and
the stresses that they create. Sometimes they accelerate existing trends, as in the
case of the feminist movement's demands for expanded female job opportunities
in relation to a highly inflationary economy and increased pressures for more
family income. They may also seek to slow or reverse long-standing tends. Examples of this would include the environmental movement's goal to reduce industrial pollution produced by prior trends of industrial growth and
environmental despoliation, or the aim of the New Religious Right to reverse
long-term trends toward a more secularized society and nontraditional family
roles. In sum, movements are important sources of social change, but (1) it is
difficult for them to completely realize their goals and (2) there are social trends
that underlie the failures and successes of movements.

Movements and Dimensions of Change

What kinds of changes are movements likely to create in societies like
America? I think it's important to look at three kinds of consequences of movements for change: (1) dramatizing social issues, (2) creating normative change,
and (3) creating structural change. I will use examples from some of the more
successful American reform movements of the decades after World War II, such
as the civil rights, antipoverty, women's liberation, and the ecology movements.

Whether successful in achieving their goals or not, social movements do
dramatize issues that require public attention (such as racial and sexual inequality, pollution, abortion, mental health, chemical abuse, domestic violence,
or the threat of nuclear war and the safety of nuclear power). In that sense, they
are instrumental in the creation of social problems that have concerned publics
with agendas for public action. And in that sense movements provoke controversy and change, even if—ironically—the political resolution of controversies
produces change in the opposite direction from the intentions of particular movements.

One of the most obvious changes that such movements create are *changes
in social norms and values*. This is illustrated by recent changes in American
popular culture. Movements have introduced new styles, songs, and jokes; they
have transformed the tone of American language and culture. Thus Negroes became blacks, and Americans struggled to find appropriate nonsexist words for
such titles as *chairman*. Thus there has been significant pressure to eliminate
sexist and racist language from public discourse, and also to eliminate
stereotypic portrayals in the mass media. Changes in forms of address and

popular culture reflect deeper normative change promoted by movements: toward increasing equality in interpersonal relationships. Social movements can broaden the scope of application of existing cultural values (e.g., democracy, equality, respect for nature). They can extend the application of these existing values to new issues and aggrieved groups and can stimulate the formulation of new norms and policies related to them (such as environmental impact requirements and affirmative action policies). In doing so, movements can often affect the course of public policies about social issues. For example, though the Nuclear Freeze movement that developed in the early 1980s was not successful in its goal of creating a bilateral freeze on the production of nuclear weapons, it can be partly credited with altering the behavior of the Reagan Administration—which had previously been talking about the ability of the United States to "win" a nuclear war. After the rapid emergence of the freeze movement and peace activists pressure groups, administrative pronouncements on the subject of nuclear war became much more moderate in tone.

It is in the area of *structural change* involving access to resources that the accomplishments of American reform movements is most ambiguous. Certainly, movements can cause or accelerate the speed of some changes, for example, the growth of a sizable black middle class; growth in opportunities for women; growth of access to education, employment, and medical care by a broader spectrum of the population. These are real changes, which are improvements from the perspective of the movement activists converned with them. Yet leaders of movements often claim that such successes are incomplete, ambigous, and sometimes trivial in terms of their expectations for societal transformation.

The Political Context of Social Movements   I mentioned the changing sympathies of national political admininstrations above, and more needs to be said of them in assessing the changes stimulated by American reform movements. The political climate created for movements by presidential administrations is an important factor in the "structural conduciveness" (in Smelser's sense) to the development and success of movements. The achievements of the civil rights, feminist, and environmental movements were facilitated by the sympathies of the Kennedy and Johnson administrations. These administrations created investigative commissions on the status of women and on civil rights to help deal with the problems and sponsored legislation on housing, public accommodations, civil rights, environmental safety, and other issues raised by reform movements. They created permanent agencies to oversee enforcement of these laws, such as the U.S. Civil Rights Commission and the Environmental Protection Agency. While it may well be that these Democratic administrations supported issues in order to gain more voter support for the Democratic Party, they nonetheless supported the grievances raised by minorities, feminists, and environmentalists. With the election of the more conservative Republican Reagan administration in 1980, the political support for such reform movements has eroded. The Reagan administration has weakened enforcement of the residue of legislation and programs from earlier decades and has given visible support to more conservative movements, such as the New Religious Right and antifeminist groups, which would like to undo the reforms of the sixties and seventies. While it is obvious-ly possible for administrations to shape the course of social change by control of legislation and budgets, my own view is that it is not possible to entirely roll back the changes of the last three decades, since some of these changes are sup-ported not only by movements but also by economic, demographic, education-al, and family trends. For example, in spite of attempts by the government and conservative movements to revive the "traditional family," such a revival seems possible only to a limited degree, since changes that have occurred in the fami-ly and in gender roles are rooted not only in the activity of social movements but in changing economic conditions. Even so, the sympathies of the government are powerful contextual forces that determine the extent to which movements succeed in creating change.

The Impacts of Movements: A Summary

Let me summarize the argument I have been making. The impact of social movements for creating social change in societies like the United States is not trivial. Few succeed completely in their goals. Many have partial successes. They can leave permanent social, cultural, and social policy residues long after their demise as living social forces. Their most likely success is to reshape the cultural and normative order by changing the language we use and how we in-teract with each other. They can create structural change—in the distribution of wealth, power, privilege, and opportunities—but such change is more difficult because movements inevitably find themselves in conflict with other interests and groups for such resources. As controversial as it often is, changing symbols can be a "variable sum game," with no real losers. Changing the distribution of resources—the availability of jobs or housing, for instance—is almost always a "zero sum game," with real winners and losers. Yet even symbolic change is rarely trivial. If movements don't *directly* create structural change, they can *de-legitimate* structural arrangements by changing the normative system and thus make structural change more likely in the long run.

EXTENDED APPLICATION: THE FEMINIST MOVEMENT IN THE UNITED STATES

The feminist movement is one of the most visible social movements in America and its issues and spokespersons have been prominently featured in the mass media since the late 1960s. In one way, the feminist movement is different from most social movements that address the concerns of specific interest groups. Since it deals with matters of sexual and gender equality, the issues raised by the movement potentially touch the lives of *all* persons, and we are all likely to have opinions about them.[3]

There have in fact been two visible phases of the feminist movement in the history of America: one that existed from the 1840s to the 1920s (sometimes called the suffrage movement) and the contemporary one that has existed from the 1960s to the present. The earlier phase came to be organized primarily around the issue of political equality and the right of women to vote. The contemporary movement is organized around a broader set of issues—not only political equality but also equality of opportunity in jobs, pay, education, and a whole range of issues that deal with the family and sex roles in American culture. But despite the differences between the two phases, there is continuity between them. The contemporary movement has taken up the unfinished agenda of the earlier one.

In what follows I will use Smelser's value added perspective to analyze the movement because it identifies important features of the emergence and dynamics of movements.

Structural Conduciveness

What are the underlying structural sources of the feminist movement in the United States? As in most societies, sex is understood as one of the basic and important differences between human beings, and this assumption led to the perpetuation of different stereotyped gender roles for males and females in American society. Consistent with our European history, men had the right to control things, and women played dependent and supportive roles, and were "cared for" by men. As the nineteenth century began, there was marked inequality between men and women in the United States.

> Married women could not sign contracts, have title to their own earnings, vote, hold office, inherit property independently, or have custody of their own children. Divorce was all but impossible for them to obtain without their husband's consent. In fact, the legal status of women as wives was not much different from that of indentured servants. (DeFleur et al., 1984:358)

While women did contribute to the economic support of families by domestic labor and work on farms, most women who were employed outside of the home worked for low wages in industrial sweatshops. Women's work was much like child labor in the early 1800s. Women needed to be married to avoid being a "burden" on relatives, and families worried a great deal about "marrying off" their daughters. While the status of women has improved since the early nineteenth century, the basic structure of male-female inequality persists, and this is the basic structural fact that has given rise to feminist movements in America.

Structural Strains

Given the underlying continuity of the basic structural fact of male-female inequality, why did the feminist movement become active at particular times? Both phases of American feminism developed during decades during which there was a relative increase in (1) the number of women in higher education and (2) the number of women in the labor force at higher levels. In the 1830s a number of women's colleges, seminaries, and teacher training institutes were founded, and some (such as Oberlin) began to admit women as well as men. The growing number of educated women in the nineteenth century made a disproportionate contribution to the founding of the feminist movement. One study of ten prominent nineteenth-century feminist leaders found that seven of the ten were college graduates (O'Neill, 1969). Also, as the American industrial and commercial system developed, a bourgeois class—of businessmen, politicians, and ministers—was coming into existence. If they did not marry, women of this class were not expected to go into factories, but it was socially acceptable for them to teach the children of those who did. Thus teaching, social work, and other types of socially benevolent work emerged as female occupations.

The contemporary feminist movement emerged during the 1960s, after an unprecedented increase in the enrollment of women in higher education. Between 1950 and 1960 women in higher education increased by 230 percent, while male enrollment increased by 130 percent (Howard, 1974:143). Likewise the slow but steady entry of larger numbers of both single and married women into the labor force began. There was an increase of women in technical and professional jobs, but most of the increase in female employment was in lower paying jobs. While there were more educated women coming into the job market, even they were being channeled into low-paying, less responsible jobs.

Why were education and work outside of the family important to the emergence of the American feminism? Women in families are wives, daughters, mothers, and lovers, and these intimate ties mute and personalize the subordinate position of women. "No other subordinate group has such an intimate relationship with the dominant group" (Gurin, 1982:5). It was only outside the family that the disadvantage and exploitation of women came to be experienced as an objective social fact. Women who worked found that they were given less responsible positions than men and, even when doing the *same* work as men, they were paid less.

The effect of education was twofold. It gave larger numbers of women opportunities to compete in the same occupational areas with men. But more importantly it gave women the conceptual sophistication to understand the nature of the problem.

Besides increased labor force participation by women and more opportunities for women to receive a higher education, there was another feature that both decades during which feminist movements emerged in America had in common. Both were times when women had had experience working in another movement for social justice. Many of the early activists of the suffrage movement had experience working in the antislavery movement of the nineteenth century, and many activists of contemporary feminism had worked in the civil rights and antiwar movements of the sixties. But even in these movements for social justice and reform, women played only a subordinate role to men. In the civil rights and antiwar movements women made coffee and ran the duplicating machines while men made the decisions. Out of the alienating experience in these movements women came to see the necessity of organizing movements to address the status of women in America.

In sum, increasing labor force participation outside the family, increasing education, and experience in prior social movements operated jointly to produce the consciousness among some women to see their problems not as personal problems but as status limitations imposed by a male-dominated society. As the position of women relative to that of men improved somewhat, the awareness of the disadvantages of women intensified. In terms of the concepts introduced earlier in this chapter this can be viewed as *relative deprivation*. A Marxian might see it as the stripping away of false consciousness. However it is labeled, the reaction to this situation was moral outrage—strains, in Smelser's terms. How were these strains interpreted by the thinkers and writers of the movement?

Emergence of Shared Beliefs

Feminist writers and thinkers created many interpretations of the situation that became the ideology[4] and beliefs that sustain the movement and its goals. While they vary in emphasis, there are common elements: (1) that many of the problems of women transcend individual problems and stem from the fact that women—as a category—are subordinate to men, (2) that this subordination is socially rather than biologically imposed, and (3) that it is unjust. The Women's Rights Convention at Seneca Falls, New York, in 1848 produced a "Declaration of Sentiments" which was perhaps the earliest statement of feminist grievances. Here are a few excerpts that will give you the flavor of this statement:

> The history of mankind is a history of repeated injuries and usurpations on the part of man toward woman, having in direct object the establishment of an absolute tyranny over her....He has compelled her to submit to laws, in the formation of which she had no voice....He has made her, if married, in the eye of the law, civilly dead....He has monopolized nearly all the profitable employments, and from those she is permitted to follow, she receives but a scanty remuneration. He closes against her all the avenues to wealth and distinction which he considers most honorable to himself. As a teacher of theology, medicine, or law, she is not known....He has endeavored, in every way that he could, to destroy her confidence in her own powers, to lessen her self-respect, and to make her willing to lead a dependent and abject life. (Grimke, 1848, 1970 edition)

A number of resolutions were passed at the meeting, calling for economic and educational reforms, as well as the right of women to vote. Oddly, given the strong language of the statement, the resolution calling for the right to vote for women was hotly debated as being perhaps too "radical" and "impractical." It nonetheless became the central goal of nineteenth-century feminism.

Among the literary works which stimulated contemporary feminist consciousness and ideology was *The Feminine Mystique*, written by Betty Friedan in 1963. She wrote about the plight of the middle class housewife, cut off from doing anything society considered important and pressured into conforming to the stereotype of the "feminine" homemaker. The book became a best seller, and "once more large numbers of women began to question their dependence on men and their subjugation to a male-dominated world" (DeFleur et al., 1984:359). Since then there has been a vast and varied outpouring of feminist literature which is in varying degrees polemical, political, and scholarly.

Feminist Ideologies   Polk (1974) has described four overlapping types of explanations of women's problems that exist in the feminist literature of the 1970s. First, there are writings that see women's problems as related to *sex-role socialization*. In this view the socialization process arbitrarily parcels out a wide variety of human characteristics into "masculine" and "feminine" categories, and thus deprives all (not only women) of full humanness. Second, there is the *conflicting cultures perspective* which emphasizes that men and women tend to have different cultural values. "Masculine" values include things like competitiveness, aggressiveness, and independence, while "feminine" values include cooperation, emotionality, and dependence. This perspective emphasizes that the values held by women have many positive aspects, and that there are problems (excessive competitiveness and aggressiveness) because the "male" culture so dominates society. Third is a *power perspective* which does not deny the importance of sex roles and cultural differences but sees them as symptoms of the underlying problem, which is the domination of women by men. Men have privilege by virtue of their sex, and they do not want to lose those benefits. Men can control women through brute force, but much of the control is through roles and culture, which are shaped by that domination. A fourth approach relates feminism to the *socialist perspective*, arguing that "the oppression of women originated in the concept of private property...[and that] sexism is functional to capitalism because...women provide cheap labor...holding down labor and increasing profits" (Polk, 1974, cited in Freeman, 1979:595). Some who hold this position argue that the struggle of women should not be separated from that of others who try to change the capitalist system. These are four different interpretations of the problems of women that appeal to different subgroups within the contemporary feminist movement.

The Mobilization of Participants

I have already mentioned the women's conference at Seneca Falls, New York, in 1848, which was one of a number of meetings that helped mobilize the nineteenth-century feminist movement. Then, as now, there developed networks of feminist newsletters and publications that helped galvanize concern about women's rights issues. And then, as now, there were a variety of subgroups within the feminist movement with a variety of opinions about how to improve the condition of women. There were those who worked to improve conditions for working class women, those who advocated avoidance of relations with men, as well as some who advocated "free love" and the removal of sexual taboos. Some developed ties with the temperance movement. Some worked to develop educational institutions for women. Some, as in the contemporary movement, saw the suffragist movement as too narrowly focused and worked within the socialist movement of the late-nineteenth century. "Among the few issues on which women and women's groups across this broad spectrum could agree was the importance of obtaining the vote" (Howard, 1974:139). The result of this effort was the passage of the Nineteenth Amendment in 1920. It took seventy-two years!

Feminist Factions, Networks, and SMOs   The mobilization of the contemporary movement was facilitated by the liberal political climate of the Kennedy and Johnson administrations. A National Commission on the Status of Women was established in 1963, followed by the establishment of fifty state commissions which documented the existence of sexual inequality. They produced recommendations for change (many of which were ignored). A network of leaders emerged (including Betty Friedan, Kate Millet, Germaine Greer, and Gloria Steinem), who were the movement's intellectual spokespersons and "traveling evangelists," active on lecture circuits and TV talk shows. Independent women's organizations developed such as the National Organization for Women (NOW), founded by Betty Friedan, the National Women's Political Caucus, which encouraged women to enter politics, and the Women's Equity Action League. They were largely interested in improving the occupational and political opportunities of women. They engaged in interest group politics on behalf of women and were conventionally organized with boards of directors, executives, and occasional internal power struggles (Freeman, 1979).

By the late 1960s a younger generation of feminist activists with experience in the civil rights and the antiwar movements began to create different kinds of movement organizations. These were a multitude of local groups that (unlike the older ones) deliberately tried to create organizations without hierarchies and traditional structures of authority. Also reflecting the influence of the sixties, these groups were less interested in conventional political action than in consciousness-raising about a variety of gender-related issues that transcended formal sexual equality. Contemporary feminism illustrates my earlier description of social movements as a network of diverse and sometimes competing SMOs. It is conventional but overly simplistic to divide contemporary feminism into reformist and radical wings or branches. The *reformers* are typically older political activists who advocate an *equalitarian ethic* which focuses on sexually based discrimination in jobs, educational opportunities, and so forth. They work toward overcoming the barriers to such discrimination. The more *radical* feminists are typically younger and tend to be committed to an ethic of *liberation*. They focus more on educational efforts to transcend gender-based distinctions in various forms and manifestations, not just on changing the legal barriers and institutional barriers to sexual equality. The reformers tend to have a well-organized elite network of organizations with an ambiguous popular base, while the radicals have a large popular base of support without a national network to articulate such efforts. You can see that as parts of the broader movement they are interdependent and need each other. Furthermore, it is important not to overemphasize the differences between the two wings of the movement. "It is structure and style of action rather than ideology that more accurately differentiates the various groups, and even here there has been much borrowing on both sides" (Freeman, 1979:560).

Nonetheless, these relative distinctions reflect the issues in contemporary feminism. The most integrative issues that attract the widest support are those having to do with jobs, educational discrimination, and unequal rewards for males and females. Not only are these issues relatively clear-cut, but they potentially touch the lives of all women, and most men at least recognize discrimination against women in these arenas. The more divisive issues relate to sexually based gender roles and cultural values which affect male-female relationships, the socialization of children, portrayals of males and females in the mass media, and the possibility or desirability of a "gender-blind" society. There is much less consensus among women generally and within the movement on these issues.

Societal Reaction

All movements that are pervasive enough produce some kind of reaction from society. This is particularly true of the feminist movement since it raised such basic issues about the roles and privileges of men and women in society. It is possible to distinguish between the reactions of individuals and the reaction of groups and organizations. Individual reactions to contemporary feminism vary widely. Most women are attracted to the goals of equal opportunities for women in jobs, education, and so forth, but for a variety of reasons many remain committed to the traditional female role and are less sympathetic to changing basic gender roles. And though men have more to "lose" from feminism, many men are at least sympathetic to the movement. Nonetheless, the movement has encountered much opposition, ranging from overt hostility to ridicule.

During the time that the broader political climate was more liberal and sympathetic to the grievances of such movements there was much support by corporations, governments, and education for the goals of the movement. Most responded by at least seeming to implement antidiscrimination policies. But women, like blacks, discovered that institutions and organizations are hard to change. There was much organizational inertia even when they were sympathetic, and some cynical tokenism that dressed up the images of organizations but produced little substantive change.

As the American political climate changed from liberal to more conservative in the late 1970s official support for the feminist movement began to erode. Countermovements developed seeking to reinforce and support the traditional family and gender roles, and these movements overtly opposed the goals of feminism, as they saw them. Countermovements included the emergent politicized Christian evangelical movement and organizations such as the Eagle Forum, led by Phyllis Schlafly, which actively lobbied against the programs of feminist political leaders. Antifeminist organizations opposed the liberal abortion policy and the passage of the Equal Rights Amendment to the Constitution (which failed after a decade of agonizing efforts).

Even with these developments, the major thrust of opposition to feminism has been limited to opposing some, but not all, goals of the feminist movement.

Antifeminists, both males and females, accept the consensual goals of feminism. According to Himmelstein

> anti ERA women approve of proposals aimed at providing women a greater role in the public sphere (equal pay...encouraging more women in professions...) but oppose those proposals that attack the traditional sexual division of labor or the coherence and autonomy of the family (day care, abortion...), and they reject those proposals that symbolically undermine the traditional image of women (using "Ms," keeping one's maiden name...). (1986:10)

THE IMPACTS OF CONTEMPORARY FEMINISM

How successful has the contemporary feminist movement been? This is a highly debatable and emotion-ridden judgment. Tavris and Wade (1984:32) evaluate some of the successes and failures of the movement (from *The Longest War*, Second edition, by Carol Tavris and Carol Wade. Copyright © 1984 by Harcourt Brace Jovanovich, Inc. Reprinted with permission of the publisher.)

GAINS	LOSSES
1. More women "firsts" and in traditionally male jobs...	but the great majority still clustered in "woman's work."
2. Women entering law, medicine, and business in greater numbers...	but still earning less than men in the same fields.
3. More than half of the labor force is now female, with up to 80 percent of all women working at some point in their lives...	but women earn, on average, only 59 percent of what men earn.
4. The Equal Credit Opportunity Act ended legal economic discrimination against women (for example, denying credit to married women, cutting off employed women's credit when they divorced, disregarding women's income in deciding eligibility for a bank loan)...	but today's credit laws offer little protection for women who worked before the legislation was passed (1975-1977), and who will lose their entire credit history if they get divorced.
5. Divorce is easier, on a no-fault basis; more cases of joint custody are awarded by courts; women are paying alimony in rare cases...	and divorce is creating an underclass of poor women and children; these women are not getting alimony and child support.
6. Many more women are now running for public office....	but there are only two women in the Senate and twenty-one in the House (Ninety-eighth Congress).
7.The majority of the nation is in favor of the Equal Rights Amendment....	but the amendment was defeated.

8. Men no longer regard wives' working as a threat to their masculinity....

unless their wives earn more than than they do.

9. Rape laws were reformed so that the victim is not on trial; rape crisis centers were set up to help victims....

and the incidence of rape is increasing (extramarital rape and marital rape); rape myths are still prevalent.

10. The vast majority of young high-school and college women assume they will work for a large percentage of their lives, and that they will combine work with family....

but neither business institutions nor young men plan to make professional accommodations or compromises for child care.

Is the glass half full or half empty?

The Future of the Feminist Movement

The American feminist movement in the nineteenth century came to be organized around a concrete but narrow goal—getting the right for women to vote. While having such a goal is a short-run advantage in organizing a movement and producing a consensus, it is a long-run disadvantage. Once it was achieved, there was a sense that the "victory had been won," and feminism disintegrated as a viable movement.[5] By comparison the contemporary feminist movement has a broad range of goals, some having to do with consciousness and cultural change that are not would not be easily satisfied by legislative action of any kind. There have been some successes, but as you can see from the above there is much unfinished business on the feminist agenda for change.[6] The fact that this agenda has some concrete and consensual goals and some that are controversial, abstract, and far-reaching means that the movement has more factions and is perhaps less cohesive than the suffrage movement, but also that the movement is less likely to disappear after success in one particular dimension of its goals.

While the effectiveness of the movement may be shaped by (1) changes in the larger political climate that may (or may not) facilitate the movement and (2) the shifting focus of national controversies that compete with feminism for public attention, the movement is not likely to die out in the future. The most important reason is demographic. There are three significant long term changes in the characteristics of American women as a population that will produce a continuing base of support for feminist issues. First, the gap between men and women in higher education continues to diminish so that substantial proportions of American women will have college degrees. Second, the majority of American women have significant experience in the labor force, and younger women are more likely than older ones to want to combine families with careers. Third, there is an increase in the proportion of women who marry late and have small families or no children. Historically American feminist movements were supported most strongly by women who had higher education, worked to support themselves and their families, and did not have large numbers of children.

This is likely to be true in the future. And the proportion of American women with these characteristics is increasing.

NOTES

1. I have not listed here all of their seventeen propositions. Also I have reordered them somewhat into different categories than those they use, and I have modified the language somewhat to be consistent with the terms I am using here.

2. There is a vast scholarly literature on revolutions. Although I have mentioned revolutionary movements in several places, a detailed discussion of the phenomenon of revolution is far beyond the scope of this discussion of social movements. See Brinton (1965) for a classical historical perspective, and Goldstone (1986) for a more wide ranging contemporary account of the nature of revolutions.

3. The terms "sex" and "gender" have different meanings, although I will use them interchangeably here. *Sex* relates to differences between males and females that are rooted in biology. *Gender* relates to the roles that come to be associated with sex differences in any given society. While male and female are universal biological categories, gender is considerably more variable, historically as well as cross-culturally. It relates to our learned notions about masculinity and femininity, as well as behavior and rights thought appropriate for males and females in a given culture.

4. I am not using the term ideology in the negative sense in which Americans usually think of it. Ideology, as I use the term here, is merely a system of ideas and beliefs that interprets a situation and justifies action—and in the case of social movements, goals for change. Ideologies are not necessarily false, but they do selectively organize facts in relation to particular interests.

5. There was, of course, more to it than this. After the passage of the Nineteenth Amendment the attention of Americans was absorbed not by issues of the rights of women but by the great depression and World War II.

6. As I write this there is on my desk a letter from the National Organization of Women soliciting my support—and money—in a renewed attempt to pass the Equal Rights Amendment.

CHAPTER NINE
CREATING CHANGE

All of us have at times been so frustrated by our lives at work, as students, in families, or as citizens in the political community that we have wanted to change things. And we often have ideas, both large and small, about how things could be better or more effective than they are. Indeed, the issue—how one goes about trying to change things—is such an important "nuts and bolts" issue that it rarely needs any elaborate justification as an important topic to consider. The problem, of course, is that understanding how and why change takes place is complicated enough, but trying to tell someone how to go about creating change is doubly difficult. While there was some optimism during the fifties and sixties that social scientists were beginning to learn a great deal about the planning of change, that confidence turned out to be partly an illusion. Instigating social change, particularly on a large scale, was much more complex than anyone realized. Partly this is because the social world is an interconnected system of things, and it is rarely possible to change just one thing without ultimately implicating other things, people, and interests. In fact, some of my more cautious professional colleagues would argue that to try to extract any practical wisdom from the social-science literature on change is something that only a fool would attempt. Nonetheless, I believe that students and laypeople are justified in asking—at some point—just what social scientists have learned about social change that is of any practical relevance. It is also my considered judgment that there *are* some useful implications in the social science literature on social change that do have relevance for creating change, although they must not be oversold. The most useful insights about creating change come from the literature on the diffusion and adoption of innovation, and (secondarily) from the social movements literature, and I hope you will see the connections between this chapter and those earlier ones. This chapter is an attempt to spell out some of those implications.

The extent to which change is deliberately induced by human actors is itself a factor in the historical development of societies. Karl Mannheim (1940) has suggested that early in human history most social change was the result of chance discovery through trial and error. Later, as the development of science produced systematic inquiry, came deliberate innovation in the form of what we would today term research and development. Thus systematic, deliberate innovation is now widely practiced, most obviously in technological matters, but also with regard to organizational and social policy. Mannheim predicts that as systematic innovation becomes more pervasive, it will eventually result in more systematic social planning at the societal or total system level. The last part of Mannheim's career was spent grappling with how such pervasive social planning—which he saw as an inevitable evolutionary development in industrial societies—could be made consistent with the political norms of democracy. Mannheim is not, of course, the only scholar who grappled with the dilemmas of democratic planning. Etzioni's innovative work *The Active Society* (1968) is a more extensive argument that modern societies are becoming deliberately "active" and reflexive entities in terms of their ability to shape their own destinies.

Whether or not one accepts the desirability of such system-wide planning for change, or the validity of these evolutionary arguments, it is without question that the interest in the planning of change is more pervasive in the contemporary world than in the past. Moore has observed, "The proportion of contemporary change that is either planned or issues from the secondary consequences of deliberate innovations is much higher than in former times" (1974:2). Thus today corporations have a great interest in planning the expansion of their markets and promoting their products, such as cable TV or personal computers, and public agencies spend a great deal of time and energy in planning for full employment, economic growth, public health, and the like. Similarly, the plethora of social movements in contemporary America have an interest in deliberately promoting—if planning is too strong a term—their own vision of the "good society." One effect of the high level of interest in the deliberate creation of change is the burgeoning quasi-scientific applied literature about the planning of change related to business (Zaltman, LeMasters, and Heffring, 1982; Bennis, Benne, and Chin, 1985), social services (Rothman, 1974), and community development (Warren, 1976). There is also much literature for social movement organizers based on social-science insights as well as the accumulated wisdom of practice (Alinsky, 1972).

I will begin this chapter on creating change with (1) a discussion of two actual cases of attempts to introduce fairly complex and unpopular community change in Omaha, Nebraska, that took place during the mid-1970s, followed by discussions of (2) basic change strategies appropriate for different situations, (3) the role of violence as a strategy for the creation of change, (4) mixed change strategies which are more complex and involve the combination of several basic strategies, and (5) the role of the change agent, including some nuts and bolts strategies for reducing the resistance to change and a "cookbook" of issues that change agents need to consider. Finally, (6) I will address what I see as some important ethical and practical issues that surround the deliberate instigation of social change.

SUCCESS AND FAILURE IN OMAHA:
AN ANALYSIS OF TWO CASES
OF PLANNED CHANGE

Scattered-Site Housing for the Poor

The Omaha city government applied for a five million dollar community development grant from the federal Department of Housing and Urban Development (HUD). The grant money was to be used for a variety of community development projects, but probably the most important, from the city's standpoint, was the refurbishing and redevelopment of the downtown central business district. Over the past two decades Omaha (metropolitan area population about 580,000) had, like most urban areas, witnessed the outmigration of people, business, and money from the older urban core to the outlying suburbs. And like most urban areas in the United States, the downtown business district was in danger of becoming a squalid zone of deserted office buildings and retail stores. The grant application was part of a larger ongoing effort to revitalize the downtown area as an attractive recreational area and to encourage businesses to stay or relocate in the downtown area. These efforts were enthusiastically endorsed by the Chamber of Commerce and the Omaha business community in general. Other provisions in the grant provided for refurbishing inner city residential neighborhoods judged to be in danger of "becoming blighted." Every metropolitan area in the country has had to cope with similar trends and problems in recent years.

A provision in community development grants (required by HUD) was that the applicant community must provide funds for the development (construction or subsidization) of housing for low-income families. Such housing programs were to be located on scattered-sites throughout the community, to prevent the further ghettoization of the poor in isolated and dilapidated areas of the city. The city had to develop, in other words, a reasonable plan to locate publicly supported housing in otherwise rather affluent neighborhoods, to facilitate (in HUD's terms) the social integration of the poor and to prevent federal monies from being used to further intensify housing patterns that reinforced economic class segregation. Furthermore, HUD specified that the city had to hold public hearings to ascertain the level of community support for such plans (not only the "scattered-site" provisions, as they came to be called). The city did faithfully develop such scattered-site provisions (they planned to build multiple family dwellings for low income families on vacant property in the middle of an affluent area in an outer northwestern suburb, as well as in several other locations to be later announced). It did indeed hold public hearings. The city's community development plans were extensively reported in the local media prior to the scheduled hearings, but aside from the business community, whose support was deemed crucial, the city made only few and fragmentary efforts to sell the plan to the public at large prior to the actual publication of the plan in the local media.

At the first public hearing, the room was packed with residents of the northwestern suburb in question, who had begun to mobilize to oppose the plan to build low-income housing in their neighborhood. Fears and rumors had developed among the largely white upper-middle-class residents that the city was planning to build cheap "tenements" (soon to become dilapidated) which would be populated by unemployed black welfare mothers with large families. The residents alleged that the "quality" of the neighborhood and property values would be ruined by the program. Furthermore, they lobbied individual elected city council members with thinly veiled threats to lead campaigns to dump them at the next election and hired a lawyer to seek a court injunction preventing the city from implementing such a plan—should the grant materialize. The press, of course, widely reported the high drama of the confrontation between the city and the neighborhood. In spite of the valiant attempts of the city's community development director to defend the plan and provide evidence that the objective consequences would not be as the residents feared, the city council directed the department to return to the drawing boards and develop a new scattered-site provision.

It did. Which is to say, that another neighborhood was targeted as the recipient of the city's multiple housing complex for the poor with precisely the same result: an angry and rancorous hearing, lurid press accounts, and the council's refusal to approve the plan. This was repeated several times with different neighborhoods targeted. The issue became a hot item of community discussion and dialogue. There were those who opposed the scattered-site provision on principle, as well as the larger effort of the community development program, and saw them as city and federal "meddling" in private local affairs. Most, however, supported the city's larger effort and viewed the scattered-site provision as legitimate at least in the abstract. But no one wanted a low-income housing complex in his or her particular backyard. In the final version of the grant proposal, the city had chosen to locate such a complex on cheap and poorly drained land in an area of the city which was rapidly becoming a lower-income area anyway. HUD rejected that grant proposal.

As a footnote, and in fairness to the Omaha city government's efforts, it should be mentioned that the city has been notably successful in the last decade in the larger goal of promoting downtown revitalization as well as providing resources for neighborhood development across the city. HUD continues to promote the development of small-unit, scattered-site housing for the poor, and by 1987 several dozen scattered-site housing units had been acquired by the Omaha Housing Authority. In March of that year the Board of Commissioners authorized the purchase of twenty-five additional units, in spite of the fact that the public hearing related to the purchase was attended by over a hundred vocal opponents of the purchase program. Thus the goal of scattered site housing for the poor remains a contentious community issue.

School Desegregation

In the mid-seventies school desegregation came to Omaha, as it did to many other American communities.[1] Such a program was mandated by the Federal District Court in St. Louis which, after hearing the plaintiff's arguments against the Omaha Public School District, agreed that the district had been negligent in promoting a racially integrated educational system. There was, of course, widespread opposition to court-mandated desegregation ("forced busing") in Omaha as well as across the country, and there were widespread fears that such a program would become as disastrous and disruptive in Omaha as had prior desegregation attempts in other cities (e.g., Boston and Pontiac, Michigan).

The school district—begrudgingly—began to develop a plan for the implementation of desegregation along guidelines specified by the court. The plan the district developed was complex but ingenious. First, there was an appeal to consensual values. The district did not publicly promote the virtues of integrated education (widely debated at the time), although it did not publicly deny them. The district urged citizens to "abide by the law"—a higher-order value about which there was little dissent. Second, the district formed—at the specification of the court—an independent voluntary association (Concerned Citizens for Omaha) which included a panoply of community notables from the educational, business, and religious communities as well as ordinary citizens to promote "peaceful implementation of desegregation." Although the association cooperated with the district, it was legally independent of it. Third, the architects of the district's plan decided to "pair" white and nonwhite elementary schools and to bus students between the paired schools so that each school had a racial mix that approximated the court's ultimate target goal of a 40 to 60 percent racial balance. No school was exempted except those few which naturally met the court's racial balance guidelines. At the junior high and high school levels, many of the schools naturally fell within the racial balance guidelines. The district promoted here a policy of voluntary "selective migration," that is, black students were encouraged to transfer to predominately white schools, and curriculums were upgraded in several predominantly nonwhite schools to attract white students. A black high school which had had declining enrollments for some time was developed as a "magnet school" specializing in vocational and technical education (while such curricula were pruned back at other schools) and a predominantly black middle school was developed as a magnet center for science and math—and given some of the best teachers in the district, along with superior laboratory and computer facilities. The actual plan was not leaked to the press in bits and pieces, but published all at once, which took up about three pages in the local newspaper.

During the summer before the plan was to be implemented, the Concerned Citizens operated bus tours for parents to visit the elementary schools their children would attend (complete with tea and cookies served by the principals and staffs of the schools). They operated a telephone hot line to provide information about the desegregation plan and to defuse rumors. They sponsored a speaker's bureau of community leaders and academicians to promote peaceful desegregation. They sponsored media adds promoting peaceful compliance with the plan, emphasizing again the virtues of compliance with the law and community harmony. Also during that summer there emerged a counter association, the Citizens for Educational Freedom, which sought to oppose desegregation and urged parents and students to boycott the schools if the plan was implemented in September. There were a few public demonstrations and vague threats of community disruption, but none that could be clearly linked to the counter association. The Archbishop of Omaha announced that the Catholic schools of Omaha would *not* accept new students from the public school system whose main motivation appeared to be to escape the desegregation plan.

That September the schools opened and the plan was implemented without a significant event of any kind, contrary to many predictions. By the end of the first year when it became apparent that the schools were conducting business as usual, the only vocal complaints about desegregation were about the costs of gasoline for the school buses. Within three years all of the secondary schools except one had voluntarily altered the racial enrollment patterns to fall within the court's guidelines. There was a brief but minor acceleration of the normal rate of outmigration of whites to suburban districts, which diminished in about two years to its customary predesegregation rate, again, contrary to the expectations of many. Almost ten years later the plan is still in effect, and the buses are still running, long after the legal mandate by the federal court has been terminated. According to a knowledgeable high school principal (in 1985) there have not been many complaints about the desegregation program in recent years, nor a significant community initiative to roll back the program, even though federal interest in promoting desegregation has lessened considerably in recent years.

Analysis

Why did one plan fail and the other succeed? What factors account for the difference? The two changes had at least some similarities. They were both vastly unpopular with the majority of the population affected. They both threatened cherished values of the influential white middle classes—property values, educational quality, and welfare of their children—and they both triggered latent racial prejudice that existed, although this was never openly admitted. They were both perceived as unwarranted meddling by Washington "bureaucrats" in local options and affairs. Beyond those similarities, there were some obvious differences between the two initiatives. Scattered-site housing was a required feature embedded in a larger grant proposal which was itself voluntary and optional. HUD provided no guidelines as to how communities would satisfy the scattered-site requirement, nor how the city should go about promoting its acceptance among the public. Desegregation was mandated by the court, and was coming to Omaha, ready or not, under *some* conditions. The court, having the experience of desegregation programs in other cities, specified some things about the method of implementation, and the plan to be developed by the school district.

Beyond these differences, though, there were some dramatic differences between the plan of implementation developed by the city government and that of the school district, and my argument is that the differences between these plans dramatically shaped the differing outcomes. First, the school district, and to some extent the voluntary association that it created, appealed to higher-order consensual values ("peacefully abide by the law and preserve community harmony"), rather than the merits of integrated education. The local media overwhelmingly endorsed these values. The city, on the other hand, became drawn into a public controversy over the specific (and in the eyes of many, questionable) merits of scattered-site housing. The larger benefits of the community development grant became a vague background to the high drama of the near-weekly televised shoot-outs between the city planners and the targeted neighborhoods. And the terms of the debate were shaped by the opponents of the plan rather than by the city, which continually *responded* to the arguments of critics but which they were never able to effectively refute. Second, the city's plan appeared to arbitrarily and unfairly place the costs of scattered-site housing on a few neighborhoods, while leaving most untouched. The school district's plan, on the other hand, equitably distributed the "costs" of desegregation. At the elementary level, none were exempted. No group of parents or neighborhoods could feel singled out to bear the "burdens" of desegregation. Third, the school district was able to close ranks and cohesively promote the plan, while there existed a visible rift between the planning department and the elected city council, who came, as often as not, to be sympathetic to the neighborhood groups opposed to scattered-site housing. Indeed, the scattered-site proposals came to be identified more with the "bureaucratic planners" in the city planning department than with the city government as an undifferentiated entity, and many city officials sought to distance themselves-and their careers—from such plans. Fourth, and perhaps most important in my view, was the relatively effective mobilization of community support for the peaceful implementation of the desegregation plan using widely respected community opinion leaders and preexisting community organizational networks—contrasted with the relative absence of such efforts by the city planners. In retrospect, the school district and its civic allies developed a complex and ingenious campaign lasting for several years designed to mobilize public sentiments around the goals of peaceful implementation of court mandated desegregation, whereas in the city's efforts to implement scattered-site housing, such a premeditated campaign was conspicuous by its absence.

I am uncertain about the extent to which the architects of the school district plan consciously drew on the practical implications of the social-science literature about implementing change. Nonetheless, it seems that the school district's plan did indeed conform to many of these implications while the city's plan did not. It is to these implications that I now turn.

BASIC CHANGE STRATEGIES

Any effort to instigate change can be conceptualized as having three elements: (1) the change agent who seeks to promote change, (2) the change itself, which for practical purposes can be viewed as either changes in *behavior* (or relationships) or changes in *attitudes* (or norms and values), and (3) the target population or system which the change agent wants to convince to adopt the change. A target population or system can be individuals, groups and organizations, communities, or whole societies. Preliminary to any attempt to instigate change, the change agent should delineate (1) exactly *what* she or he wants to change and (2) the precise boundaries and characteristics of the target population or system. Change agents can then select from among several broad strategies to promote change, depending on the nature of the target population and the change itself.[2]

Facilitative strategies should be used when (1) the target group or system recognizes a problem and the need for change, (2) is open to external assistance, and (3) is willing to engage in self-help. Within this strategy the change agent acts as a facilitator who provides resources, information, advice, and expertise. His or her task is often to make the target group (who are really clients in this case) aware of options and the existence of resources and to clarify issues. It is a *cooperative* strategy—the change agents and their clients collaborate in seeking solutions to problems already felt by the client. But though they perceive the need for *something*, clients may be only dimly aware of what kinds of changes are required, and the strategy may require a self-study or a needs-assessment study. When this is the case the change agent's agenda must remain open-ended.

In other cases the needs of clients may be fairly well defined, and the problem is to convince clients that certain changes will work. For instance, efforts to introduce modern medicine in third world nations addressed fairly well-understood needs (sickness and health problems), but convincing third world people that Western medicine was in any way superior to traditional folk medical practice often was a considerable task. This is a particularly acute problem when the discrepancy between the technical knowledge and the worldview of the change agent and the client population is very great.

Facilitative strategies work best when (1) there are a multiplicity of broad goals (e.g., community improvement) and (2) the change requires the active participation of a diversity of people. They are most inappropriate where (1) there is significant resistance to change among the client population, (2) the change is contrary to the values and interest of powerful segments of the client population, and, usually, (3) where the change must occur quickly.

Two additional things must be said. First, the change agent must often be prepared to provide long-term support for *sustaining* the change after its initial adoption. To use again examples of induced change in the third world, one can find many examples of schools, water systems, and so forth which were enthusiastically built at the instigation of outside change agents who quickly departed after their construction and provided little long-term support or incentives for their long-term utilization. Second, the facilitative strategy is often more effective if it provides benefits *beyond* the formal goals of the change itself (e.g., interactional needs, status enhancement). Several years ago I participated in a program evaluation study of a project sponsored by the United States Department of Agriculture called "Project Green Thumb" which was to employ retired farmers to refurbish small-town facilities (parks, fairgrounds) in southeast Nebraska. The program was designed not only as an economic benefit to the retired farmers—many of whom had no adequate pensions—but also to provide them with health, legal, and educational assistance. The program was largely successful in its formal goals, but that was not the major reason the retirees participated. They enjoyed the physical activity itself but most of all, they enjoyed socializing with each other. They had fun. It is important for the change agent to try to construct the change process so that participating in the change process will be enjoyable and engaging for the client population.

Reeducative strategies are "relatively unbiased presentation(s) of facts...intended to provide a rational justification for action....[they] assume that human beings are rational beings capable of discovering facts and adjusting their behavior accordingly when facts are presented" (Zaltman and Duncan, 1977:111). The strategy has been termed *re*education because it usually involves *un*learning or overcoming prior learning. Reeducation takes time—to build new knowledge or skills—and hence is most important when time is not critical. Reeducation is effective, and in fact necessary, when the target population or group does not possess the knowledge or skills to utilize an innovation or when there are fears, anxieties, and moral barriers to adoption. Reeducation can involve broad-based media campaigns that attempt to address moral issues and reduce fears about the consequences of adoption, or, when more specialized skills and competencies are involved, reeducation often means the creation of structured programs and workshops for specific groups of potential adopters. Thus both public and private agencies often create free (or nominally expensive) classes and workshops to develop skills related to the programs and products they seek to disseminate (e.g., contraceptives, personal computers).

Reeducation can be used both (1) to provide a *rationale* for adopting a change and (2) to provide the target system with new knowledge and skills necessary to adopt a change. The former is usually easier than the latter, but the latter may often be necessary. When it is necessary to provide a rationale for change, reeducation becomes a campaign to promote change, rather than a facilitative or cooperative strategy practiced among those already committed to some kind of change. *Segmentation* of the total target population may also be necessary to make the message about the change understandable and appealing to different groups. Demographic characteristics (age groups, sex, education, socioeconomic class) are the most obvious categories for segmentation, but the change agent may also segment in terms of developing a different approach for opinion leaders versus rank-and-file members of the target population. Finally, it is important to say that reeducation is most effective when the advantages of and facts about the innovation are clear and unambiguous.

What are the limitations of reeducation as a change strategy? One limitation should be obvious to you from the last sentence of the previous paragraph. Facts surrounding the advantages and hazards of adoption are often ambiguous and unclear. Ironically, the major limitation of reeducation strategy is a function of its major characteristic: It appeals to the rationality of the actors in the target population. It is often an *overly* rationalistic approach to change. Reeducation is usually not effective—no matter how sensible the change is in the eyes of the change agent—when there are strong and conflicting emotions surrounding the change. Similarly, reeducation is not likely to be effective *by itself* in promoting innovations that require dramatic alterations of behavior or groups structure, because these are embedded in larger structures, values, and interests which may reinforce stability. Hence rational suggestions for social reform (e.g., to decriminalize marijuana, legalize prostitution, prevent poverty by redistribution) often fail because they are contrary to established values and moral sentiments, as well as material vested interests. In this context, it is important to note that scientific studies and blue ribbon panels appointed to study social problems (e.g., pornography, crime, poverty) and make policy recommendations are often ignored in the absence of a larger political climate conducive to change. There is a final difficulty with reeducation as a strategy of change: It is difficult for change agents to practice it in a pure form. Is information really objective, neutral, and uncontestable? Rarely. And given an overwhelming interest in instigating change, does the change agent tend to stack the deck or strategically withhold certain information from the target population? Probably. In other words, the line between reeducation and persuasion is often fuzzy.

Persuasive strategies are "attempts to bring about change partly through bias in the manner in which a message is structured and presented" (Zaltman and Duncan, 1977:134). Persuasive strategies can be based on facts and rational appeals, or they can be totally false. Thus persuasion differs from reeducation by degree, in terms of the extent to which the change agent (1) arranges or selectively ignores facts and (2) utilizes emotional and nonrational inducements (e.g., "hidden persuaders"). Persuasion is most appropriate when the target population is unaware of the need for change or has a low commitment to change.

Unlike reeducation, persuasion is relatively effective when the facts are ambiguous and the costs and benefits of adoption are difficult to discern, which explains its widespread usage in advertising and political campaigns. When the relative advantage of adoption is in doubt, the change agent can easily combine persuasive efforts to change people's minds with material incentives. This means that persuasive strategies can sometimes short-circuit the need for long and extensive reeducation by media campaigns. Persuasion does have another advantage in overcoming resistance to adoption, since the change agent is not required to present unbiased facts or the whole story—in contrast to reeducation. There are limits to the extent to which this is possible, however. Gross factual distortions may backfire and jeopardize the credibility of the change agent, particularly when the target population is sophisticated. As a rule of thumb, the more sophisticated and critical the target population, the more the change agent should rely on reeducation rather than persuasive strategies. There are other limits to the effectiveness of persuasion that are obvious: It is not effective when the target population has neither the skills or the material resources to adopt. There are also obvious ethical problems with persuasion strategies, but (as mentioned) I will deal with these separately below.

Power strategies use coercion or threats to obtain the compliance of the target population with some sort of change. The effective practice of power strategies requires that the change agent (1) possess resources to reward or punish the target system and (2) be able to monopolize access to such rewards and resources by the target system. Power strategies are effective when the commitment to change is low, but they may be the *only* available strategy when change is perceived highly risky, irreversible, or undesirable. Furthermore, power strategies are most effective when (1) time is very short and (2) the changes sought are *behavioral* rather than *attitudinal*. In other words, where the change sought requires mainly outward compliance rather than inward commitment.[3]

To speak of the use of power to induce change evokes very negative and unsavory images. Nonetheless, power strategies are quite commonly used and involve widely varying degrees of deprivation on the part of the target system. Moreover, I argue that they *can* be used within the framework of a democratic political process. The case of successful court-mandated desegregation analyzed earlier would be an example of such democratic coercion, as would attempts to regulate environmental pollution, promote auto safety, and civil rights. In each of those cases, the change to be promoted was instigated by the established democratic political process (either legislative or judicial) but the change promulgated with legal penalties and sanction and was not voluntarily accepted by portions of the target system. There is probably a generalization in this: namely, that power strategies are most effective when supported by broadly accepted social values and the larger political community—that is, when used to coerce segments of a population to abide by widely accepted rules.

What are the costs and limitations of power strategies of inducing change? Unlike the previous strategies, power is almost always *alienative* in that it creates strains and estrangement in the relationship between the change agent and the target system, and it does not produce a stable commitment to the change itself. Power strategies may require ongoing surveillance by the change agent to insure continuing compliance. The costs of such surveillance may be quite high, both in terms of its intrinsic costs to administer, and in terms of its damage to the quality of relationships within the social system. Additionally, power is less effective for promoting changes that are highly complex so that they may *require* voluntary participation, or at least cooperation, on the part of the target population. Where this is the case, reeducation or persuasion is more appropriate.

I have now outlined what are usually considered to be the basic types of strategies available to change agents. It remains to discuss how they can be combined into mixed forms. That discussion appears below, but first a brief detour about about the uses of violence in the creation of change.

THE ROLE OF VIOLENCE IN CREATING CHANGE

Power is often identified with violence. And while it is not always the case—violence is really a subform of power —it is a common observation that violence often accompanies significant social change, in the forms of riots, guerrilla war, oppressive measures by the state, terrorism, and—the ultimate form—revolution (Vago, 1980:301). Violence is often advocated as a coercive power strategy to promote social change, and in fact is so commonly associated with change that some analysts (Huntington, 1972:282) argue that in no society does significant social, economic, or political change take place without violence or the imminent likelihood of violence. I am not certain that I agree with this, but it is certainly true that violence *is* commonly associated with significant change. Violence is often advocated as a strategy by which disadvantaged groups call attention to their plight, and may be perceived by lower status groups as the only feasible strategy. Indeed, Emerson (1962) and others have argued that the only ultimate resources that "lower participants" hold is the power to disrupt the system, often violently. Wilson (1973) has written in a similar vein of the "politics of disorder" as a strategy to promote change.

As a deliberate strategy, the use of violence often involves two stages: (1) the disruption of the social system in a significant way to get attention and dramatize the seriousness of an issue and (2) overtures to elites to come to the bargaining table to negotiate concessions. Such strategies have been commonly used by revolutionaries and terrorists (e.g., the student radicals and "Weathermen" of the late 1960s) as well as reform movements. Indeed, the history of American reform movements cannot be understood without recognizing the frequent adoption of violent strategies to promote change by otherwise respectable citizens, ranging from the Whiskey Rebellion of the 1790s by the corn farmers of Pennsylvania (a tax revolt) to the bombing of abortion clinics by prolife activists in the mid-1980s.

Do such strategies work to produce change? The evidence is that they often do. Looking again at major American reform movements—the abolitionists, the populists, the labor movement, the civil rights movement, the antiwar movement, and the ecology movement—were all characterized by significant deliberate episodes of violence and other forms of the politics of disorder which helped to trigger major changes in social policy and the direction of change. The civil rights movement, for example, did result in significant reforms (jobs, increased welfare benefits) which followed the outbursts of urban violence in the hot summers of the 1960s. Following the Birmingham riot in 1963, President Kennedy pressed Congress for the passage of his Civil Rights Bill to "get the struggle off the streets and into the courts." Failure to pass the bill, Kennedy warned, would lead to "continued if not increased racial strife—causing leadership on both sides to pass from the hands of reasonable and responsible men to the purveyors of hate and violence" (cited in Huntington, 1972). Hence the threat of continued civil disruptions by the lower participants galvanized the political elite to promulgate reforms.

Gamson (1975) conducted one of the rare systematic studies of violence in relation to change by examining the characteristics and circumstances of fifty-three "violence prone" protest groups in American history in relation to the success and failure of their formal goals for change. Violence, Gamson found, was more likely to succeed when the goal sought by the group was narrow and concretely defined rather than a broad and comprehensive one, and particularly when the goals were defined in terms of gaining concessions and advantages rather than winning social acceptability. Related to this, Gamson found that violence-prone groups were more likely to be successful when the group was more interested in removing others from power or displacing the privileged position of other groups rather than achieving power and privilege for themselves. Successful groups also were larger, more able to effectively and rapidly mobilize resources, and had a more centralized power structure—with power vested in an individual or an executive committee. Less successful violence-prone groups were found to be more decentralized, in that they allowed considerable leeway to local chapters to act on their own without approval from the top, and the protest organization exercised less discipline throughout its entire system of members and subgroups. Successful violence-prone groups were more successful when they chose unpopular targets (groups, leaders, or policies). Only one successful violence-prone group in Gamson's sample relied *exclusively* on violence (the Kentucky Night Riders, who coerced recalcitrant tobacco farmers into joining a trade association by whipping them and burning their barns and crops). Most used it as a supplement to other strategies, such as strikes, bargaining, and propaganda. Finally, Gamson found that successful use of violence was related to the larger societal context. Some groups which had been having little success for a long time were able to succeed during an intensified crisis. For example, the Steel Workers Organizing Committee was able to win concessions that steel companies had been effectively blocking for years from the National War Labor Board during World War II.

Having said all this, I must add that violence is a volatile strategy that doesn't always work and is particularly ambiguous as a strategy of change. Successful use of violent strategies requires a large base of public sympathy, if not outright support, for the broader goals of change. Even then others may support the larger cause while distancing themselves from violent strategies to promote that cause. Furthermore, violent strategies may have a boomerang effect. They may erode public support for goals that would otherwise find significant public support. Thus at the 1968 Democratic convention, violence by the police *against* demonstrators ultimately eroded the credibility of the police and drew onlookers into the action on the side of the demonstrators. A more recent example is the effect of the bombing of abortion clinics which eroded the legitimacy of the prolife movement among potential sympathizers. And though the leaders of the prolife movement distanced themselves from those strategies, they did not seem to be able to prevent them.

Another problem with the use of violence is the kind of society that develops when violence is commonly used to promote change. Oppenheimer (1969) argues that the use of violence prevents the emergence of a democratic and humane social order. People who are successful in the use of violence become habituated to its use in problem solving. Where this is the case, Oppenheimer argues, what is likely to develop is the antithesis of the Western vision of rule by law. Clearly, the deliberate encouragement of violence as a strategy for change is a grave choice, which may be justified only in extreme circumstances. Those circumstances do, however, exist.

Finally, it is important to note another thing about violence in the context of the social order. Most of the foregoing discussion is about violence "from below" by dissident groups and social movements (as indeed are most sociological writings about violence-as-a-change strategy). But violence "from above" is a fact of life for many people in the world. It is impossible, for instance, to understand the violence-as-tactics of insurgent groups in the Philippines, South Korea, Central America, or South Africa without considering them in the context of state-sponsored terrorism that limits nonviolent responses and provokes violent ones. Such was also the case in the outbreaks of labor violence in the United States at the turn of the century.

MIXED AND COMPLEX STRATEGIES

While one strategy may predominate in any particular change effort, most efforts require a combination of strategies. Complex and mixed strategies are particularly required when the changes sought are themselves broad, complex changes operating at different structural levels, and the target population is heterogeneous and diverse. There are a variety of ways of using complex strategies.

First, one might *segment* the target population into various subgroups, according to the appropriateness of different strategies. Thus for some subgroups reeducation may work, for others persuasion may work, while others may require the use of various power strategies. This depends upon the characteristics of the target population in relation to the change. Reeducation may be most appropriate, for instance, for very intellectually sophisticated sectors of the target population, who would be critical of the stacked deck implied in persuasive appeals. Facilitative strategies may work for those initially predisposed to adopt the change, while persuasion and/or power may be required to overcome the resistance of those not so predisposed. And different strategies and appeals may be required for cosmopolitan opinion leaders, local opinion leaders, and rank-and-file-members of the target population (see Chapter 6 for an elaboration of this distinction). A second way of combining strategies is to use different strategies in different stages of the adoption process: reeducation at the *awareness* stage, during which the target population is becoming aware of the possibilities of change; persuasion at the *evaluation* stage, in which the target population is evaluating the relative advantages of the change; and facilitative strategies at the *adoption* stage, which make it easy for the target population to actually adopt the change. For example, attempts to introduce school desegregation (both in the Omaha instance cited earlier as well as in other communities) used reeducation, persuasion, and power strategies, both with regard to different subgroups in the target community as well as at different stages in the implementation process. A third way of combining different strategies is in a "freeze" and "thaw" combination, that is, alternating the use of power and persuasion. This is frequently done in labor management negotiations, when attempts to persuade the adversary of the justness of the cause are followed by attempts to impose sanctions. This strategy is also frequently employed in international diplomatic relations. Thus "in East-West relationships, both sides have tended to employ power to gain concessions and to follow that with overtures of peace and friendship" (Lauer, 1977:365).

It is very delicate and difficult to successfully practice this combined freeze-thaw strategy, however, and it may place contradictory demands on the role of the change agent. As I indicated above, power is typically *alienative*, since it implies at least the threat of coercion, while persuasion stresses trust between the change agent and the target system. And while power strategies encourage change agents to monopolize resources and information to deprive the target population of them, other strategies (facilitative, reeducative, and persuasive) press the change agent to at least *appear* to put resources in the hands of the target system and be open and honest regarding resources relevant to the change. Such contradictions implicit in the freeze-thaw strategy may hinder its effectiveness so much as to outweigh whatever advantages it has to offer. At the very least, the change agent who practices such a strategy will have to give considerable thought and effort to address such dilemmas and choose actions that minimize them.

Nonviolent Direct Action

No discussion of multiple strategies is complete without mention of the combination of strategies for change that grew out of the movement for national independence in India. These have since been widely developed, codified and practiced in other movements that represent the interests of the lower participants in society. Mahatma Gandhi, the creator of this strategy, called it "satyagraha," which literally means "the force which is born of truth and love." Satyagraha includes both persuasion and power, but emphasizes nonviolent uses of power. It depends critically on the ability of change agents to mobilize a cadre of supporters capable of self-discipline, adherence to ethical principle, and— most of all—a willingness to endure deprivations. Bondurant (1972) has outlined nine steps in a satyagraha campaign:

1. Try to resolve the conflict or grievance by negotiation and arbitration, (without compromising fundamentals).
2. Prepare the group for direct action (including preparations to suffer the consequences of the action).
3. Engage in propaganda and demonstrations.
4. Try once again to persuade the opponent to concede demands, explaining the further action to be taken if this is refused.
5. Begin various economic boycotts and various kinds of strikes.
6. Initiate a program of noncooperation with established authorities and institutions.
7. Engage in civil disobedience to selected laws.
8. Take over some of the functions of government.
9. Establish a parallel government to handle those functions.

As you can see, this is a progressive strategy which begins quite modestly but could continue to a radical social transformation (a political revolution or the departure of a colonial power), but it is important to emphasize, as do its practitioners, that the strategy could stop at any point that concessions are made. Alternately, it could be abandoned at any point, if the costs of the later stages are judged too high in relation to the benefits associated with the change.

Such nonviolent direction action has been widely influential among leaders of movements of the powerless directed toward gaining concessions from the powerful. Gandhi and the Congress party movement were able to finally force the powerful British colonial government to "quit India." It was adapted by Martin Luther King and used in the in the early days of the Civil Rights movement, as well as by Jesse Jackson (Operation Breadbasket) more recently. It has been used by community organizers such as Saul Alinsky on behalf of the poor and by Caezar Chavez who spearheaded the drive among California farm workers for better working conditions. Nonviolent direct action does not always succeed, but it has often been a powerful tool when used by lower participants who ordinarily have little influence on the course of social change. How so?

There are, I think, three keys to the success of nonviolent direct action. First, since it is a strategy often used by relatively powerless groups, its practitioners must think creatively and imaginatively about what tactics and resources they will use. According to Alinsky, a master tactician of community organization in the United States:

> I have emphasized ...that tactics means you do what you can with what you've got, and that power has always gravitated towards those who have money and those whom people follow. The resources of the Have-Nots are (1) no money and (2) lots of people....How can people use them?...Use the power of the law by making the establishment obey its rules. Go outside the experience of the enemy, stay inside the experience of your people. Emphasize tactics that your people will enjoy. (1972:138-39)

The practitioners of nonviolent direct action not only organized voters and created consumer boycotts, but also created a variety of imaginative tactics (such as sit-ins, swim-ins, and pray-ins) directed at the targets of change. Alinsky himself graphically and humorously illustrated the need for creativity by citing a suggestion he made during a campaign by blacks in Rochester, New York, to gain concessions (jobs) from Eastman Kodak, a major employer in Rochester. He suggested a demonstration at the local concert hall, which had been donated to the city by the company.

> I suggested that we might buy one hundred seats for one of Rochester's symphony concerts. We would select a concert in which the music was relatively quiet. The hundred blacks who would be given the tickets would first be treated to a three-hour preconcert dinner in the community, in which they would be fed nothing but baked beans, and lots of them; then the people would go to the symphony hall—with ob-

vious consequences. Imagine the scene as the action began! The concert would be over before the first movement! (If this is a Freudian slip—so be it). (1972:139)

Second, and perhaps most obviously, the successful practice of nonviolent direct action requires the creation of a core of activists who are willing to suffer some deprivations in order to draw attention to an issue or embarrass the authorities. Third, such strategies succeed because they are likely to provoke the authorities into unprincipled violent reactions. This is the real core of successful nonviolent direct action strategies that progress beyond the initial polite negotiation stages. Thus the British bludgeoned demonstrators during the Indian independence movement, while Gandhi threatened to embarrass the British further by starving to death in their jails. During the 1950s white sheriffs unleashed their dogs on civil rights marchers in Alabama, and in the 1960s police and national guardsmen clubbed, teargassed, and shot student antiwar demonstrators. In the 1980s, South African police beat and jailed demonstrators of the black nationalist movement. These kinds of brutal responses are likely to be widely reported in the mass media. They draw distant onlookers and third parties into the controversy. While third party sympathies may be polarized, nonviolent direct action strategies succeed to the extent that they are able to mobilize sympathetic public opinion and embarrass the authorities. The British ultimately quit India at the point where they could no longer suppress the independence movement without further erosion of the legitimacy of the British government policy in the eyes of world opinion, and of many Englishmen themselves.

What are some of the limitations of nonviolent direct action as a complex strategy? Some are obvious from the foregoing discussion. First, the issue must be one of enormous importance to the people seeking the change if they are to be willing to suffer the deprivations associated with such actions. Second, change agents must invest heavily in the creative use of resources and tactics and the maintenance of disciplined loyalty. These requirements may be unmanageable. Third, the strategy is likely to be ineffective when the grievances involve only conflicts of material interests with no *moral* or *ethical* basis. Not only must the grievance have a moral basis, but the insurgent group must be able to co-opt the moral high ground. Fourth, the strategy is not effective where there are no third party onlookers or where the overwhelming sympathies of such third parties come to side with the authorities. This is always a possibility, particularly in complex social systems where onlookers are likely to be polarized. Fifth, nonviolent direct action is probably not effective in authoritarian systems that are so secure that favorable public opinion (either internal or external) is entirely irrelevant to the maintenance of control. Such systems may exist. The Russian dissident movement, for example, probably had a limited ability to affect major policy change in the Soviet Union. Even in such circumstances adverse international publicity has some limited effect.

Soviet emigres have suggested that to the extent that the Russian dissident movement or the condition of Soviet Jews have become objects of international attention and embarrassment to the regime, its behavior was often moderated. Similarly, Amnesty International has found that by publicizing the plight of political prisoners they have often—but not always—been able to secure their release from jails by authoritarian regimes of both the left and the right. One might argue, however, that even with such a limited impact, the dissident movement *did* embarrass the Soviets internationally.

Let me pause now to review this discussion about creating change. I began by underlining the distinction between trends and deliberate attempts to instigate change, and then analyzed two cases of attempts to create change. Next, basic change strategies were discussed (facilitative, reeducative, persuasive, and power strategies). Following that was an extended aside about the role of violence in creating change, and finally, I have discussed the necessity for complex and mixed strategies, with a special emphasis on nonviolent direction action strategies. Now I will redirect the discussion toward more nuts and bolts issues and discuss some issues that I think are of practical value to would-be change agents (a category that I think includes all of us at some time or another).

THE TASKS OF THE CHANGE AGENT

I believe that the job of being a change agent should start with two kinds of questions. First is a *structural* question, that of identifying persons and subgroups who are the "strategic levers" of change in any particular target population. This means identifying the opinion leaders and community influentials (see Chapter 5) who can influence others in the system to adopt change. Second, is a *social psychological* or an *interactional* question: How do you change the behaviors or the minds of the persons in question? The different strategies discussed above represent alternative ways of going about changing the minds and/or behavior of persons. But within any of these strategies, there may be some things that change agents can do to reduce resistance to change. What are some of these things?

Drawing again on the materials of Chapter 6, one can reduce resistance to the adoption of a change by attempting to make the particular innovation (1) simple and easy to communicate, (2) divisible, and (3) maximally compatible with the status quo (values, needs). This is no easy task, particularly when dealing with broad-scale change, but change agents should attempt to think in these terms. The change agent may also be able to reduce resistance to change by shaping the climate in which such efforts take place in a number of ways. In general, resistance to change is less when

1. The clients feel that the change project is "their own."
2. The change project is supported by top officials (unless the relations between the target population and top officials is itself a hostile and/or mistrustful one).
3. The clients see change as reducing their burdens.
4. The change involves new experiences which interest the clients.
5. There are no threats to the security or autonomy of the clients.
6. The clients join in diagnosing the problem.
7. The change project is supported by group consensus.

8. There are many similarities between the change agent and the clients in terms of background, outlook, and so forth.
9. There is a great deal of empathy between the change agents and the clients.
10. There is a high degree of trust between the clients themselves.
11. The change program has built-in provisions for feedback from the clients.
12. The change program is open to ongoing revision.

Certainly, if all of these conditions were in place, chances of adoption would be maximized. But, alas, in an imperfect world, that may not be possible. I should emphasize, however, that change agents may be able to *produce* some of these conditions by their own efforts (e.g., facilitating a group consensus, securing the support of the top officials.) where they do not naturally exist. Obviously, also, a great deal of ingenuity and inventiveness is required by change agents.

Creating Change: An Elementary Cookbook

It is possible to create a sort of checklist of issues that change agents need to address in roughly sequential fashion. What follows is such an attempt (see Figure 9-1). I chose the term "an elementary cookbook" for this deliberately. As anyone who has attempted to cook a complex meal using a recipe from an elementary cookbook knows, the exact parameters are always missing and the recipe contains many vague instructions. "Add salt to taste." How much is that? "Cook until vegetables are crisp, but do not overcook." What does this mean? (As you might guess, I've had some exasperating experiences as an amateur cook!) The point I'm trying to make is that a "recipe" for creating change can only provide rather vague guidelines and is not a substitute for experience, for making do with imperfect ingredients, or for occasionally muddling through (more about muddling through later).

The first task of a change agent to define what kind of goals the change is to effect. Such goals are of two sorts. There are *conceptual* goals which ask exactly *what* it is to be changed (What's the problem? What do I want to change? How could the situation be improved?). Second, there are *operational* goals that need consideration. These are more concrete than conceptual goals, and ask for specification of exactly the behaviors, attitudes, structures, or groups processes that are to be changed. These I have termed operational, because they also provide clues to how one might measure the extent to which the change has actually occurred.

After clarifying the goals of change, the change agent needs to specify as precisely as possible the target or client population. Who—precisely—is to change? This includes delineating the relevant individuals, population categories, groups, and structures to be affected by the change. Besides merely identifying the target group, it is important for the change agent to attempt to identify channels of communication and particularly channels of influence within the target system. This means, as earlier suggested, the identification of opinion leaders within the system.

FIGURE 9-1 CREATING CHANGE: AN ELEMENTARY COOKBOOK

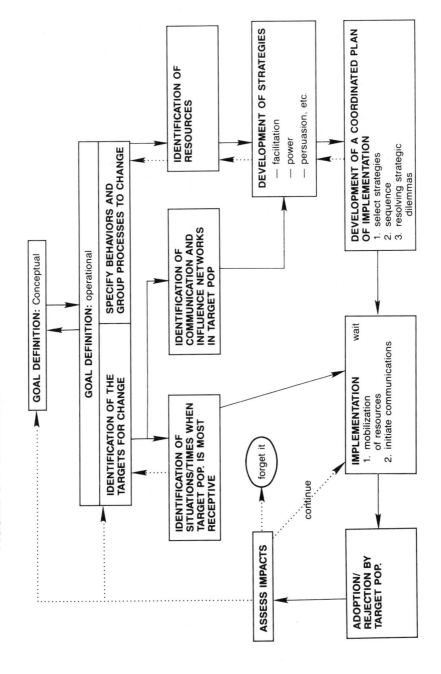

After the relevant change target system has been defined, the change agent needs to try to identify situations or times when the target population is *most* receptive to change. In general, these "change conducive" situations include (1) times when the target group is experiencing stress about the present situation, (2) when there are cross-pressures from conflicting group affiliations that tug the individual in different directions[4] and (3) when the target group has the time to consider adopting the change. For example, if one is interested in promoting economic reforms, it may be advisable to wait until the bottom of a business cycle when the level of stress about economic issues is relatively greater. Often change agents are convinced that there is a crisis situation requiring change, but the target population does not. In this case the change agent may seek to persuade the target population that there *is* a crisis, or even try to *induce* stress in a variety of ways. As to the importance of time, consider the experience of the organizers of the American Agriculture Movement in the late 1970s. The movement was directed at reforming government agricultural policies. Its organizers found that they could successfully mobilize farmer for demonstrations during February, when the farmers had the time to do so, but not in May when they were busy with crops. They were able to mobilize farmers to drive their tractors in a convoy to Washington and around the White House to publicize their cause. And then, they were successful mainly at mobilizing wheat farmers—whose work is more seasonal—than diversified and livestock farmers—whose farms are more likely to require year-round attention.

After defining the goals of change and specifying features of the target system, it is important for the change agent to develop an inventory of resources available. Resources can mean persons (and the prestige of particular persons), money and material resources, as well as loyalties and commitments that can be used as change relevant resources. As I previously suggested, the change agent should approach the problem of developing resources with imagination, looking for unobvious resources or creative ways of using the obvious ones.

Taking cues from the above, the change agent is then in a position to consider which basic change strategy is appropriate (e.g., facilitative, reeducation, persuasion, or power). These should be developed into a coordinated plan of implementation, which includes not only (1) the selection of basic strategies and more concrete tactics, but also (2) the sequencing of strategies, if multiple and mixed strategies are appropriate, and (3) attempts to resolve strategic dilemmas (by the freeze and thaw process mentioned earlier or segmentation of the target population). At this point some consideration should also be given to the kinds of resources or support required to *maintain* the change when—and if—it is adopted by the target system.

The actual *implementation* of change efforts means the mobilization of resources and initiating communication with elements of the target system. It is followed by the beginnings of the process of adoption or rejection by the target system, processes that may begin only slowly and continue for a lengthy time period. While this is going on, the change agent needs to continually monitor this process, so that ongoing efforts to promote change can be modified and/or fine-tuned. At some point, an overall assessment of the success or failure of the change effort is required, and the change agents must decide whether to continue such efforts, to provide ongoing support services for adopters, or to abandon such efforts entirely. This latter judgment should not be made prematurely, but at some point it is inevitable.

The "elementary cookbook" is certainly an idealized image of the process of instigating change. If taken too strictly it would imply omniscience on the part of the change agent, that is, that one must have complete knowledge of the target population and perfect control of resources. But this misconstrues the present intent. I am merely arguing that before attempting to instigate change, one should strive for clarity about the goals of change, the nature of the target population, the resources available, appropriate strategies, and strategic dilemmas that are likely to present themselves. There are those who would argue, on the contrary, for the virtues of muddling through without the development of an elaborate design for inducing change. Such arguments usually emphasize that the development of such a plan is not a practical possibility for complex change and that the plan itself may force the change agents into narrow and rigid forms of thought and strategies, which may prevent adaptive modification of the change effort and serendipitous learning on the part of the agents. *Serendipitous learning* means that we usually learn things accidentally "in process" that we could not foresee and that we can profit from those experiences. Change agents will undoubtedly learn unanticipated things during the change process itself, but (alas!) they may not always be able to profit from them. A muddling-through strategy may lead one to commit such irreversible strategic blunders that no amount of serendipitous learning will allow one to repair the damage done. To the extent that muddling through implies remaining open and flexible to ongoing revision, I am for it; but as a basic approach I favor as much planning and foresight as is possible and practical.

THE ETHICS OF INDUCING CHANGE

I promised to return to the subject of ethical issues involved in creating change. If you have been bothered by the manipulative and deceptive overtones of strategies described in the previous discussion, I will admit that I am too. To speak of *clients* of change as involved in a collaborative enterprise is not a problem for me, but to speak of a *target population* is. Targets are, after all, things we shoot at.

I will arrange the various change strategies along a continuum in terms of the extent to which I believe that they involve ethical problems, as follows:

Facilitation	Reeducation	Persuasion	Power/Coercive

◀───▶

Few ethical problems   Many ethical problems

Let me elaborate. Ethical problems in inducing change exist to the extent that change efforts do not respect the autonomy, rationality, and dignity of persons to choose whether or not they wish to change, or to be fully informed about the consequences of such choices. When there is lack of candor or full disclosure about such choices, there are ethical problems. In terms of these criteria, *facilitation* and *reeducation* (to the extent that the latter can be honestly practiced) *do* respect the autonomy, rationality, and dignity of persons who are the targets of change. *Persuasion*, in comparison, respects the voluntary choice to adopt change but may overwhelm the person with distorted (or false) information, withheld information, and nonrational appeals to emotion. The target population is not aware of how information is arranged and loaded to persuade. It is, moreover, contrary to the accepted values of truth and full disclosure. By these standards, much contemporary advertising and political persuasion is unethical. *Power and coercive strategies* carry the greatest number of ethical problems because they deny voluntary adoption and rejection and maximally violate the autonomy and dignity of persons.

Regarding ethical problems, social psychologist Phillip Zimbardo and his colleagues (1977:189 cf) have suggested several criteria under which "intervention" is justified.

1. If there is informed consent
2. If there is accessibility to one's usual sources of information and social support
3. If there is the absence of threats of dire consequences of the failure to change
4. If there are no "non-ordinary techniques" used that overwhelm reason (e.g., isolation, deprivation)
5. If there are no uses of special vulnerabilities, such as those associated with age, sex, education, or financial status

These are very strict standards that, if taken literally, would mean that facilitation and reeducation are the only permissible strategies for the ethical change agent. But I believe that this is an overly restrictive view. Obviously, the ethical concerns surrounding manipulation and coercion are matters of degree. In everyday life when the degree of coercion is modest we are ordinarily willing to use it for socially sanctioned purposes (for example, to manipulate children to behave, get drivers to obey traffic laws, or prevent environmental pollution). Our willingness to use coercion depends not only upon the degree to which we perceive its side effects on the subjects to be moderate, but also upon how important we perceive the ultimate goal to be. Thus we may be willing to consider the use of capital punishment (the ultimate form of coercion) if we believe that it will achieve the important goal of lowering the rate of homicide.[5] My argument is not that ethical issues are secondary or unimportant issues in the planning of change, but rather that they should be considered in the context of the importance and potential benefits of the change itself, either to the change agents or the target population (though these are *very* different criteria of judgment!).

This discussion of ethical problems is gradually devolving, as perhaps all do, into the age-old ethical conundrum: Do the ends justify the means? It is obvious that no single answer can be given. That is, *some* ends justify *some* means. But other than looking to the existing social values and norms for guidance, this is clearly a matter of judgment in each situation for which the agents promoting change must bear responsibility. Rather than attempting to discuss my reading of current social norms regarding what is permissible, or developing guidelines which reflect my own individual outlook, let me pose a series of questions so that you can explore your own values.

Would *you* use extreme forms of manipulative persuasion or coercion to:

1. Guarantee equal access to public facilities?
2. Gain the adoption of demonstrably superior techniques of food production in a third world country?
3. Prevent people from having abortions?
4. Redistribute land in third world countries?
5. Redistribute vastly unequal wealth in industrial countries?
6. Gain the adoption of a form of government you believe to be significantly better than the existing one?
7. Get an individual to take a lifesaving drug?
8. Get people to quit smoking cigarettes?
9. Promote family planning in third world countries?
10. Promote the sale of a product that will make you rich?
11. Convert someone to a new system of religious beliefs (yours)?
12. Isolate a community to prevent the spread of a deadly plague?
13. Promote energy conservation in the United States?

My answers to the above are yes on some and no on other issues. Clearly, the burden of ethical justification remains squarely on the shoulders of those seeking to induce change. Nor does it help to argue that you can use questionable strategies merely because others are doing so (you know...everybody's doing it...). Thus using the scientific literature about change does not remove one from the burdens of ethical choice. They are an inescapable part of social life.

SOME FINAL THOUGHTS ABOUT THE FEASIBILITY OF CREATING CHANGE

With all of the difficulties I have raised about creating change, a would-be change instigator might say, at this point, "Why bother?" Considering the complexities and difficulties of any particular case, this may indeed be a rational response. To recapitulate, the difficulties are of two sorts: practical and ethical. Having discussed the ethical difficulties, let me return briefly to the practical ones. They boil down to four types: (1) lack of clarity about the goals of change (What would be better than the present?), (2) lack of control over the resources necessary to bring about change, (3) unpredictability about the outcomes of one's efforts, and (4) unpredictability about the longer-range ramifications of change even when the short-run goals are successfully achieved. Although I alluded briefly to the fourth type of difficulty at the beginning of this chapter, I would like to expand on it by illustration.

The long-range ramifications of change are often unpredictable because it is impossible to change "just one thing" without ultimately implicating other things. This is because the social world is a *system* of elements (subgroups, levels, institutions) that are interconnected in subtle and complex ways. Consider the case of the Green Revolution, a good example of unintended, long-range, and sometimes bizarre ramifications of change. The problem was precisely that the change agents' concern with the immediate success of changing "just one thing" led them to be inattentive to the broader system context within which that "one thing" was embedded. The Green Revolution was a world-wide effort to address the problem of world hunger by increasing agricultural productivity in the third world countries. Miracle seed varieties having extraordinarily high per-acre yields (primarily wheat and rice) were developed by Norman Borlag and others at Iowa State University, and their global distribution was sponsored by the Rockefeller and Ford Foundations in the 1950s and 1960s. By the 1970s these efforts were pronounced to have been counterproductive in many nations (Lauer, 1977:213-14; Freeman, 1974:89-90). Why?

To begin with, the new seeds, while being marvelously more productive, required much heavier inputs of water, fertilizers, and pesticides. Thus, in spite of the sponsorship of governments and foundations, the new seeds were primarily beneficial to the more prosperous farmers and larger landowners, who could afford to invest in the support systems for the new seeds, or who were deemed good credit risks by local banks. As these large producers raised larger crops and began to upgrade the technological level of production, they came to have an even greater market advantage over the small farmers. The large landowners began to buy up even more land from the smaller ones. The upshot of these trends was to increase unemployment among the small farmers, who sold out, and tenants, who were kicked out, as the large-scale producers consolidated their holdings and shifted to a higher level of commercialized production. The Green Revolution projects therefore benefited the small number of large landowners, while marginalizing the (vast) majority of agriculturalists.[6]

The social, economic, and political implications of these changes were profound. Urban economies became even more overburdened with displaced rural people. The efforts of governments to subsidize credit and price supports for the new seeds drained existing (inadequate) budgets for health, education, and social services. As the economic dominance of the large landowners increased, so did political unrest in the rural areas. National economies were increasingly penetrated by multinational corporations from the industrialized world, who sold the fertilizers and pesticides. Governments subsidized the prices of the new crops, and producers shifted more to production for more lucrative external markets than for domestic consumption. This was the most bitter irony of all: In many areas the price of food actually increased so that many of the poor had worse diets than before. The Green Revolution was supported by most of the world's policymakers. In retrospect, it is not clear to me whether the promoters of the Green Revolution *could* have foreseen the tangled web of system interconnections that would result from the seemingly benign introduction of high yield seeds.

What are the implications of the practical difficulties mentioned and of the woeful tale of the Green Revolution? One possible implication is the conclusion that since the difficulties of bringing about desirable change are so profound, one who attempts to do so is merely being foolish. This is the perennial wisdom of conservatives, who argue that one is best advised to "let nature take its course" and not exacerbate problems by well-intended but naive efforts to change things. Benign neglect, so the argument goes, is often the only prudent course. This is indeed often compelling advice. But it is not the only implication one could draw from considering the difficulties of deliberate change efforts. There are at least two others. First, it is not planning for change itself but the *absence* of an adequate plan that often causes change efforts to miscarry. Efforts to induce change are frequently driven by our passions in the absence of a well-thought-out plan. And when we *do* plan, we often focus on the practical difficulties related to initial adoption rather than the longer-term systemic consequences. Elementary sociological wisdom suggests that the unintentional ramifications of intentional change are very important, and the planners of change should attempt to comprehend them. It is also true that this is often very difficult or, in some situations, impossible.

Setting aside for the moment the problems of the long-term systemic ramifications of change, the second implication I will draw here is that there is a virtue in thinking small about the goals of change. It is often intellectually more satisfying to think of making sweeping changes in the whole scheme of things, but it may be more feasible to strive to change smaller and more limited parts of the total scheme of things. I recognize that this is not popular counsel to those desiring to change the whole system, but if one wants at least some successes, it may be the only practical possibility. The wisdom of thinking small about change is supported by Gamson's research, mentioned earlier. He found that successful groups had more limited goals, pursued a single issue rather than multiple ones, and did not aim at displacement of their opponents (1975:38-54). Etzioni (1968a) puts this idea of thinking small in a somewhat different way. He argues that we tend to think of society in terms of a "medical model." That is, we view problems as symptoms of deeper causes, and we are always trying to get at the "root causes" and not merely the symptoms. But changing the root causes of problems is very difficult. Etzioni argues that it is often possible to find short-cuts that address problems by controlling the "symptoms" rather than changing the more intractable "underlying causes." Thus it is easier to provide more adequate street lighting and escort services than it is to address the underlying causes of street crime. And though effective affirmative action programs are difficult, they are not as difficult as trying to eradicate racism from American culture and society. Though the symptoms of underlying conditions may keep reoccurring, it may be more feasible and less costly to the society to address them than the deep causes. "True believers may insist on waiting for the needed revolution, but the victims will welcome the treatment of the symptoms" in the meantime (Lauer, 1977:357).

None of this should be taken to mean that I would urge those interested in change not to search for basic causes, or even to undertake to change them, if that is required and feasible. What I am urging is that if this becomes impossible or too scary, given the imponderables involved, one need not give up entirely. In such cases significant improvements can often be made by creatively aiming low.

There is a bottom line here. Granted that creating social change is often costly and demanding. Granted that success, even partial success, is always uncertain. Granted that the long-term systemic consequences may be counterproductive to one's original intent. But even so, should one refuse to make efforts to change things if the issues are really important? The civil rights movement of the fifties and sixties was a long, costly, and difficult effort that only partly succeeded. Being aware of its high costs and limited successes, should its organizers have given up? I don't think so. The lives of millions of minority Americans are better today for those efforts, even though the goal of complete racial justice remains elusive. Or should Gandhi have given up the Quixotic goal of organizing the world's poorest peasants to throw out one of the world's strongest colonial powers? Should one do nothing because the hope for improvement is small? To do so is to live fatalistically and without hope, unless one expects circumstances to improve naturally without human effort. Confronted by the realists of his day about the slim chances of success for the Indian independence movement, Gandhi responded, "To believe what has not occurred in history will not occur at all, is to argue disbelief in the dignity of man."

NOTES

1. At that time Omaha's population was about 12 percent black, and there was also a smaller but substantial Hispanic community.

2. The following conceptualization relies heavily on Zaltman and Duncan (1977).

3. There *is* of course a relationship between attitudes and behavior. Attitudinal change sometimes follows behavioral change. The converse is also often true. Decades of research by social psychologists has been unable to unsnarl the tangled web of causality between attitudes and behavior, and so the issue will not detain me here. My argument is that in the long run attitudes and behaviors are often reinforcing, so they are roughly compatible. But in the short run, it may be possible to change behavior without affecting attitudes very much—or vice versa. It *is* important for the change agent to have sorted out which is the most important to change, because they imply different change strategies.

4. The concept of cross-pressures comes from political scientists, who developed the term to describe the behavior of a voter who is cross-pressured by membership in reference groups that pull the individual's vote in different directions. The assumption, supported by much evidence, is that when the group affiliations of the individual all consistently pull the individual to vote for particular parties or candidates, voter behavior is relatively unproblematic and can be understood as a direct function of those group affiliations. For instance, if one is white, wealthy, college educated, and a Presbyterian, one's vote for Republican candidates becomes rather predictable. This person is minimally open to political persuasion by Democratic candidates. When, on the other hand, such group affiliations pull politically in different directions—so to speak—the resultant voting behavior is more problematic. Consider the case of the black physician, whose professional

affiliations and ethnic affiliations pull in politically different directions. The outcome not only becomes more unpredictable, but the individual in these circumstances is more amenable to political persuasion of various sorts. In the broader context of advocating change, the individual who is rooted in multiple and somewhat conflicting reference groups is more likely to be open to persuasion and adoption than one who is not so cross-pressured.

5. Personally, I find the evidence in support of that belief not convincing. But many do find it convincing.

6. Some nations avoided these effects by subsidizing credit for small producers. But many did not.

CHAPTER TEN
GLOBAL DEVELOPMENT AS MODERNIZATION

Our focus shifts again. In Parts II and III we explored theories of change and change processes from two different bodies of sociological literature and ended with an examination of the implications of these for creating change. Now we shift back to the more concrete and descriptive aspects of change, as in Part I. The chapters in Part I focused on social change in the United States, and I hope from reading them you recognize that social change in America (or in any society, for that matter) is embedded in the broader contexts of change that is taking place on a worldwide basis. I argued in Chapter 1 that you cannot go very far in understanding the changing lives of persons without considering how these are embedded in broader currents of societal change. In an analogous way, the same is true of nations, that is, understanding changes that occur in nations requires understanding how they are embedded in international contexts. This global "embeddedness" of nations and their growing global interdependencies is what the rest of this book is about.

Most of us are aware at least abstractly that the world is becoming a global "system" of some sort, in which everything ultimately affects everything else. This may be a vague common perception, but I want to explore in more depth the extensiveness and implications of this global system, because we still often think and act in ways that do not recognize the growing importance of our connections with people and nations in remote parts of the world. These connections are certainly not historically new: Societies in diverse parts of the world have interacted economically and politically since times of ancient civilizations. But such global interaction is deeper and more extensive in the modern world, as a much larger human population becomes increasingly intertwined in economic, political, and ecological terms. Hence it is more important than ever that we understand the nature of such global interconnectedness.

This chapter and Chapter 11 focus on processes of modernization and development in the less developed nations, and the nature of their ties to the industrial nations of the world. Chapter 12 develops a systems perspective on understanding global change and focuses mainly on the interpenetrating relationships between population growth, resource use, and ecological consequences. The last chapter explores the implications of these subjects for some different visions of the human future.

DEVELOPMENT AS MODERNIZATION

Consider the life circumstances of two different peanut farmers: one in the American state of Georgia and the other in the West African nation of Senegal, both internationally important regions for the commercial production of peanuts.[1]

The Georgia grower cultivates about 540 acres of peanuts and another 650 acres of corn. His fields are prepared by a large tractor, and he uses improved varieties of seed and fertilizers that have been developed by government-sponsored research. Pesticides are sprayed on his crops from an airplane, and they are harvested by a mechanical combine, which separates the peanuts for drying. They are stored in a modern warehouse. He sells his crop to a regional broker, who resells it to larger brokers in Atlanta, New York, or Chicago. The prices he gets are maintained well above the world market price by government price-support programs. The government also restricts imports and limits domestic acreage—all of which protect him from rapid price fluctuation. Research, mechanization, government support, and hard work enable him to net (after costs) as much as $100,000 in good years, and his family lives in comfort enjoying the wide variety of basic and luxury goods and services available to affluent Americans.

The Senegalese grower cultivates a small farm near the village where he and his family live. Like the American farmer he inherited his farm, which is the sole source of support for his family of five and three other relatives. Until recently his crop was hand-planted and picked, but he has recently begun to mechanize. Fertilizers and pesticides are either too expensive or unavailable. His per-acre yield is about one-fifth of that of the American grower. Storage facilities are rudimentary and there are losses because of insects and blight. The Senegalese grower sells his crop to a government corporation at well below the world market price; the corporation resells it on the world market at a higher price. The difference between what the farmer is paid and the government export price is a major source of government revenues.

Small farm size, poor yields, storage losses, and low prices keep the typical Senegalese farmer very poor. His net income is about 400 dollars per year (by contrast, the field workers on a Georgia farm, who are poor by American standards, earn 100 dollars per week when they work). In addition to the peanut crop, which he sells, the African farmer also grows food for his family, mainly millet which is made into gruel. His village has no electricity, and is likely to have no school or health clinic. His wife draws water from a well near the village. One-fifth of the children born in the village do not survive to adulthood. While most of the Senegalese are poor small farmers, the minority who live in the capital city (Dakar) live much better. Government officials are likely to have nice homes, drive cars, and work in air-conditioned offices.

In both America and Senegal the political process affects and distorts the economic process. The Georgia farmer is represented in Washington by a member of Congress who is responsive to his need to maintain price supports. The poor Senegalese farmer has little or no political influence. The government is controlled by the minority of urban dwellers and is responsive primarily to their interests and needs.

Two Worlds of Development

The lives of the American and Senegalese farmers sharply define two worlds—one "developed" the other "less developed"—that are vastly different in geography, standards of living, and economic, social, and political structure. Of the two worlds it is easier to define the developed world—which includes the modern industrialized nations of Europe and North America (as well as Japan, Australia, and New Zealand). The less developed world includes most of the nations of South Asia, Latin and Central America, Africa, and the Middle East. Putting it another way, the developed world is the nations of the northern hemisphere, while the less developed nations are concentrated in the southern hemisphere. The developing nations are also called third world countries, which describes a historical sequence of development and modernization that began in Northern Europe and America (the first world), continued in Southern and Eastern Europe (the second world) and continues today in the rest of the world (the third world).

Lumping all these countries into a single category called the third world or less developed countries (LDCs) obscures their diversity. They are similar only in that (1) compared to the developed nations their economies are less productive, (2) they are more likely to be dependent upon a single or a few commodity exports, and (3) they have relatively larger subsistence economy sectors. Beyond that they differ from one another. Some have vast natural resources (Brazil, Zaire); others are virtually barren of usable natural resources (Chad, Central African Republic). They have diverse cultures and histories: Some have been politically independent for centuries (Ethiopia, Brazil, China), while others are former colonies of the Western nations (India, Nigeria). Some have a highly literate if not a highly skilled work force (Sri Lanka, 85%; Cuba, 96%), while in others literacy is rare (Mali, 9%; Senegal 10%) (World Bank, 1982).

Notwithstanding the differences within the third world, it is important for you to recognize that on a global basis many more people live like the Senegalese farmer than the American one. And the human meaning of underdevelopment is that the "great mass of the people in the developing countries continue to live in dire poverty. They have barely enough to eat and rarely have enough potable water. Health services are thinly spread. When work is available, pay is low and conditions are close to intolerable. Insecurity is permanent; there are no public systems of social security to condition the unemployment, sickness, or death of the family wage earner. Malnutrition, illiteracy, disease, high birth rate, underemployment and low income close off in turn each avenue to escape" (Dadzie, 1980:4). The American writer Thoreau wrote long ago that "The masses of men live in quiet desperation." But the peoples of the world are no longer content—if they ever were—to live in quiet desperation; "a passion for bread and freedom has swept over the world" (Lauer, 1973:299). Even in the developing nations people are aware that abject misery is no longer the lot of all people. People in the developing nations do not want to surrender all of their cultural uniqueness to the forces of change, but they universally want development in terms of better material security, literacy, health, and life expectancy. They want freedom, self-determination and a better life. And they have come to believe that it is possible. The process of trying to achieve that and the difficulties involved are what this and the next chapters are about.

WHAT IS DEVELOPMENT?

It is hard to precisely define the concept of development. It reminds me of the old joke about the man who couldn't define what a giraffe was, but was sure that he knew one when he saw it. Furthermore, most definitions of development are ethnocentric—in terms of the ideas and values of Western societies. To complicate matters further, we use some other terms as rough synonyms for development. Two of these are *modernization* and *industrialization. Modernization* is a broad concept that at its root means Westernization (the diffusion of Western or European social, economic, and cultural forms to the non-Western world). *Industrialization* involves economic development and is a narrower term than modernization. It has four primary dimensions: (1) aggregate economic growth through transformations in the sources of energy used (from animate to inanimate), (2) a shift from primary production (agriculture and mining) to secondary production (manufacturing), (3) growth in per capita incomes, and (4) diversification of occupations. Though modernization and industrialization are often linked, you can have modernization—particularly of cultural and political forms— without much industrialization (more about this later).

Development, as I use the term here, is a more general and in some ways a less ethnocentric term. Like industrialization, it means growth in the material base of the society (production, consumption, and per capita income), but not necessarily a shift to manufacturing as the dominant core of the economy. Mining, fishing, and agriculture can be highly developed. Development implies not only material growth, but also qualitative improvement in the lives of people. In the words of Dadzie, an Indian economist, development is "the continuous liberation of peoples and societies" (1980:6). Like modernization, development means a growth in social complexity and the scale of social life, but does not necessarily imply the emulation of Western cultural and political institutions. Saudi Arabia is a society that is rapidly being developed without becoming significantly Westernized. Still, the notion of development is not entirely free of Western values. Its use often focuses on material improvements, sometimes to the neglect of nonmaterial dimensions of human life. Among scholars there are two broad types of explanations of development and obstacles to development. Oldest is the *modernization perspective* and more recently elaborated is its alternative, the *world systems perspective.*

In this chapter I will first explore the reality of global development, both in contemporary and historical terms. The rest of the chapter explores how development is explained from the modernization perspective. The next chapter examines development from the world systems perspective, and concludes with an assessment of development and development policy.

THE REALITY OF DEVELOPMENT

Since the idea of development is a complex one, it is not surprising that the facts and perceptions about the degree and success of development among the nations of the third world is in dispute.

Among the more positive and optimistic views are those of the economist Reynolds (1983), who uses a fairly narrow economic yardstick. He defines economic development as simply a stage of "intensive growth," in which the capacity to produce rises faster than increase in population. The opposite is "extensive growth," in which economic growth is absorbed by population growth and no per capita increase in incomes is possible. In his study of forty-one LDCs Reynolds found that all except seven had reached the turning point to intensive growth by 1965 (the laggards were Afghanistan, Bangladesh, Ethiopia, Mozambique, Nepal, Sudan, and Zaire). Surprisingly, the majority had done so prior to 1910. I think Reynolds' analysis is very narrowly cast, however, since such measures of aggregate economic growth do not mean that economic improvements are by any means evenly distributed throughout the population. Typically, in fact, they are not, and the economic and social differences between national elites and the urban and rural masses is vast.

There are those, on the other hand, who, viewing the miserable condition of the world's masses of people, pronounce development to have been an unmitigated global failure. The consensual view among most students of development is more differentiated: Some nations are doing fairly well; some marginally well, but are fragile; and others are developmental disasters.

Degrees of Development within the Third World

It is useful to think of the LDCs in terms of their developmental "success" in three tiers. The *upper tier* is the newly industrializing countries including Argentina, Brazil, Mexico, Korea, and Taiwan, which have had an average economic growth rate of 5 to 9 percent in the 1970s. Many, but not all, of the petroleum-exporting and OPEC nations are also included in this category (Saudi Arabia, Kuwait). These countries have about a fifth of the population of the LDCs and account for about 40 percent of the economic output of the third world. The *middle tier* of some forty-five middle income countries, with intermediate rates of growth during the 1970s (5-6%) have about one-fourth of the LDC population and produce another 40 percent of the total economic output of the third world. This middle tier includes Kenya, Indonesia, Bolivia, Egypt, and Guatemala. The *lower tier* of the third world grew at just under 4 percent in the 1960s and at less than 2.5 percent in the first half of the 1970s. The average per capita income in this tier is less than 250 dollars. Their people subsist on a fifth of the total income in the third world. Indonesia and the three nations of the Indian subcontinent—Bangladesh, India, and Pakistan—have two-thirds of the population. Most of the remaining third live in the contiguous poverty belt countries of Africa and Asia. In Gambia, for example, over half of all rural children die by age five; and in Nigeria, one of the better nations of sub-Saharan Africa, one-third of the urban and one-half of the rural families are unable to obtain a calorie-adequate diet (Clausen, 1985). These are designated by the United Nations the "least developed" countries in the world; their 1.2 billion people live at bare subsistence levels, hedged from disaster only by slim margins. In the early 1980s disaster became manifest in the form of famine in sub-Saharan Africa (Dadzie, 1980:24). Table 10-1 depicts some social and economic characteristics of countries within the three third world developmental tiers in comparison to some first world nations.

Development and Historical Periods

In addition to these national and regional differences there are time periods in which the third world nations have collectively fared better and worse in their efforts at development (Reynolds, 1983). Between 1850 and 1914 there was a world economic boom that stimulated the economic growth in the developing world as well as the industrial world. The rapid rise in world trade during this period produced growth in the developing countries primarily as exporters of cash crops and commodities. In the period between 1914 and 1945 there were two world wars and a world depression which inhibited growth and development in *all* nations. This was followed by the greatest boom, from 1945 to 1970, in which there was an unprecedented growth of world trade with national growth rates well above those of the earlier periods. The most recent period, beginning about 1970, has been disappointing from the standpoint of the third world. Growth in the upper tier of newly industrialized and oil-exporting countries has

TABLE 10-1   Characteristics of First and Third World Countries, 1984

Countries	GNP Per-Cap.,US $	Energy Consumpt. Per-Capita[a]	% Jobs in Agriculture[b]	Life Expectancy[c]	%Adults Literate[d]
Industrial nations[e]	11,430	4,877	7	73	99
Soviet Union	4,550[f]	4,627	20	65	100
Upper tier					
Saudi Arabia	10,530	3,602	49	60	16
Mexico	2,040	1,308	37	64	81
Brazil	1,720	753	31	62	76
S. Korea	2,110	1,121	36	64	93
Middle tier					
Philippines	660	271	52	61	75
Bolivia	540	267	46	51	63
Senegal	380	118	55	45	10
Indonesia	540	205	57	53	62
Lower tier					
China	310	485	69	68	66
India	260	187	70	56	36
Mali	140	26	86	44	9
Ethiopia	111	17	80	43	15

[a] Kilogram of oil equivalent.
[b] 1980
[c] Males
[d] 1979-80
[e] Weighted average for 19 industrial market economies with per-capita incomes of over $4,880. Includes all of Western Europe except Greece, plus Canada, the United States, Japan, Australia, and New Zealand.
[f] 1980

Sources: World Bank, World Development Report 1986 (NY: Oxford University Press), Annex Tables 1,8,27,30; and World Development Report 1982, Annex Tables 1 and 21. Adapted from The World Development Report, published by the Oxford University Press. Used with permission of the International Bank for Reconstruction and Development.

slowed, while in the lower tier countries the per capita GNP declined by .4 percent between 1970 and 1974 (Pirages, 1978:227). It is important for you to note that *these historically varying rates of development generally follow the economic conditions of the world market.* In the late seventies and early eighties the entire world market system, including the developed industrial nations, was in a state of slow growth and recession. The relative stagnation of the American economy during the 1970s (see Chapter 3) was connected through global financial and trade relationships to a slowing of the pace of development among the LDCs.

In sum, most observers of development in the third world are rather pessimistic. Even in the most successful LDCs (the newly industrialized and OPEC nations) there is cause for concern. While the GNPs of many grew dramatically in the 1960s and 1970s, this economic improvement did not "trickle down" to the masses. Thus, while the Brazilian economy grew remarkably during this period, at an average rate of 7 percent a year, "The underprivileged half of the population has never been so underprivileged. The majority of those with relatively stable jobs earn less today than they did twenty years ago" (Andrade, 1982:165). Concern is particularly widespread about the most recent period. Contrary to expectations there has been (1) a widening gap between the developed nations and the LDCs and (2) a widening gap between the most and least successful LDCs.

DIMENSIONS OF MODERNIZATION

In the decades after World War II the idea of modernization dominated thinking about economic and social change in the third world, and it held out the expectation that the economic prosperity and democratic political institutions found in the developed industrial nations would spread throughout the world (Johnson, 1986:679). At its core the modernization perspective argues that the introduction of complex Western technology produces not only economic development but a variety of other structural and cultural changes. People become more oriented to the future and open to change, and the rights of individuals become more important. Social relationships shift from traditional to bureaucratic, and populations become more urban. Social inequality increases in the early stages of modernization (as elites profit from the toil of unskilled laborers), but as industrialization proceeds and requires a more literate and skilled work force, the middle segments of society grow—which decreases social inequality. Status relationships based on the rigid criteria of race, age, and gender tend to be replaced by ones based on skills and competence, and social mobility increases. Traditional sources of authority— such as respect for the elderly—tend to weaken as bureaucratic institutions such as schools and the state gain increasing responsibility and power (Johnson, 1986:679). That is how the modernization of Western Europe and North America since the 1700s is perceived to have taken place. The modernization perspective argues that the Western model of modernization has components and sequences that are of global relevance and can be replicated in other nations regardless of their history, culture, and geography (Lerner: 1958:46).

The study of modernization emerged in the 1950s as a loosely connected intellectual movement among prestigious social scientists from several disciplines. But the intellectual perspective also had political and official support because

> the United States suddenly found itself the leader of the Western world and the only defender of its economic and ideological interests against the Soviet Union and what then seemed to be a growing united world Communist revolutionary movement. The basic notion was that because it was the richest and the strongest of all nations, the

U.S. must also be the most morally advanced of societies. It therefore became the model of how to be properly modern. The U.S. was bound by interest and duty to show the rest of the world how to follow in its path. (Chirot, 1981:259)

The perspective embodies not only a set of scholarly interests but also idealism and humanitarian impulses—a desire to improve the human condition— and U.S. strategic and geopolitical interests as they were understood in the postwar decades. It functioned as an anticommunist ideology and developmental strategy. The modernization perspective is a description, an explanation, and a set of prescriptions for change in the third world. It is very much related to the diffusion of innovations literature that we explored earlier.

Economic Modernization

While not all modernization is economic, economic change is at the heart of the modernization processs. In the most abstract terms economic modernization means the shift from a stable subsistence economy to one of self- sustaining economic growth (Lerner, 1968). In more concrete terms this involves (1) the technological upgrading of economic production, (2) the development of an extensive money economy (as opposed to an exchange economy), and (3) the development of large-scale markets (Levy, 1966).

One influential model of economic modernization is Rostow's "takeoff" stage model, in which he compares successful economic growth to an airplane moving down a runway—it gradually builds up enough momentum to take off into self sustaining flight (or in the case of an economy, to self sustaining growth). Here is how Rostow (1962) describes the stages of economic development:

1. *Traditional setting.* Using traditional technology the economy has a limited potential for production; there are large subsistence sectors and few or weakly developed markets.
2. *Preconditions for growth.* There is a widespread psychological desire for growth, a degree of mass literacy, and a central government. Importantly, there is the development of an infrastructure (communications, transportation, banking, investment, and credit systems).
3. *The "takeoff."* There is a rapid growth of industrial technology in a few economic sectors (typically in agriculture or mining), and between 5 and 10 percent of the GNP is reinvested economic growth.
4. *The drive to maturity.* There is the application of high technology across many sectors of the economy.
5. *The mature industrial economy.* A diverse, mass consumption economy develops.

I think Rostow's model is a useful one, but it has many difficulties. It is more descriptive than explanatory (this is a general weakness of modernization theory). Some stages seem arbitrarily separated, especially the "preconditions" and the "takeoff." Does one really *precede* the other? Another difficulty is that most LDCs have long ago evolved beyond a traditional subsistence economy, but have somehow not managed to "takeoff" or achieve a "mature" industrial mass-consumption economy. Why? These questions are largely unanswered by Rostow's economic perspectives on modernization.

Social Modernization

Far reaching social change accompanies economic change. As it is depicted, the typical bases of relationships between people begin to change in a developing society. First, the dominant pattern shifts from relationships based on binding traditions to ones based on rational interests and exchanges. Second, relationships based on loyalty to particular persons, such as kin and tribe, begin to be replaced by relationships based on more universally applied standards and principles, such as competency and citizenship. This is what Parsons has called a shift from "particularism" to "universalism." Third, whereas relationships in traditional systems tend to be functionally diffuse involving broad commitments between persons, modernization signals an increase in more segmented relationships where people have limited rights and obligations, such as relationships between employers and employees or practitioners and clients. Fourth, modernization produces an increase in the avoidance of intimacy and growth of large-scale, secondary relationships (Levy, 1966).

At the level of *structures* (rather than relationships) social modernization has been abstractly described as an increase in specialization, centralization, and a decrease in the self-sufficiency of "local units" such as families and villages (Levy, 1966). Stated in these abstract terms you will notice a strong similarity between how change is described by the modernization perspective and functional theory perspectives on change described earlier. Both emphasize structural growth and differentiation. This is not accidental. Modernization theory was created at the same time that structural functionalism was the dominant mode of explanation in American social science.

Political Modernization

Politically, modernization involves nation building, that is, the knitting together of diverse ethnic, linguistic, and tribal regions into an integrated national and administrative system. In many former colonial LDCs such as Nigeria and Malaysia, the *only* political common denominator among different peoples and regions was the colonial heritage. Nation building had to start from scratch. And in those LDCs that were long independent, such as Ethiopia and Thailand, nation building means transforming a traditional regime into a modern bureaucratic administrative structure. Nation building is a process in which "tribal or village authority systems give way to a system of universal suffrage, political parties, and a civil service bureaucracy" (Smelser, 1966). Such structural changes in the polity usually involve the creation of new integrative ideologies and principles (e.g., African socialism and *ujamaa* in Tanzania). Political modernization involves an increase in popular participation in government, although exactly how this takes place is a very controversial issue. Levy (1968) argues that it means a shift toward Western-style parliamentary democracy, yet it is common knowledge that many LDCs are ruled by authoritarian regimes, even when they have the superficial trappings of a parliamentary system. Yet all LDCs develop mass-based political parties (as opposed to tribal or ethnic parties) that are vehicles for national mobilization and generating commitment to the state. In this sense popular participation may increase, but this is not democracy—Western-style. Many LDCs are single party states, but there is also the possibility that democracy is in fact played out and preserved among factions *within* the dominant party (as seems to be the case with the Institutional Revolutionary Party in Mexico). For political modernization to occur I think it not so important that LDCs replicate Western-style democracy, but that (1) comprehensive political structures emerge that can integrate and command the loyalties of diverse regions and factions and that (2) a climate of long-term political stability be created. There is a consensus among development economists that the creation of such domestic order and stability is critical for economic modernization to take place. Reynolds (1983) argues in fact that "the single most important explanatory variable...[regarding economic development]...is the political and administrative competence of government."

Modernization, Authority, and Inequality   Modernization transforms the basic status and authority differences in important ways. In brief, this can be described as a shift in emphasis from *ascribed statuses*, based on such given characteristics as age, sex, and family lineage, toward an emphasis on *achieved statuses*, based on such characteristics as education, competency, and so forth. The implications of this change are profound because the latter are (in theory) open to change within the life span of an individual, while the former are not. Thus the transition from a castelike system of stratification to a classlike one provides at least the basis for an *increase in social mobility*.

This transition from a traditional to a modern status and authority system should not be taken too simplistically, however, as the wholesale replacement of one system of status and authority with another. One study of the efforts of the national government of Ghana to introduce modern public health and sanitation programs in two Ghanian towns illustrates this point. In one town the changes were not widely accepted partly because the persons responsible for promoting them were national civil servants who were perceived as a threat by the existing tribal chiefs and authorities. In another town the changes were implemented more successfully because the traditional authorities had an extensive role in promoting the new programs, one that reinforced rather than eroded the traditional basis of authority (Wunsch, 1977). A more familiar example is the role of Mahatma Gandhi in the creation of modern India. He was the leader of a modern national independence movement and a mass-based national political party, but at the same time he was the epitome of the traditional Hindu ethical leader. The point is that while modernization involves the development of more modern bases of authority and status, it often works by a creative fusion of the traditional with the modern.

In spite of this qualification, most scholars argue that in the long run modernization means not only an increase in social mobility, but also the growth of a sizable middle class, and a broader distribution of wealth and power with some decline in inequality (Moore, 1974). This is a controversial point, as the quotes above about the Mexican and Brazilian experience indicate. Some argue that the *initial impact* of modernization is to increase inequality but that its *long-range impact* is to decrease it. This is at least the experience of modernization of the Western nations.

Modernization and the Family

Modernization is accompanied by a shift from *extended, consanguine* family systems toward *nuclear, conjugal* ones. There is a general weakening of the binding power of kinship ties and a decline of family characteristics as the basis of status and authority. More concretely, Goode (1982:183-87) has itemized eight family changes that have been occurring on a global basis which are associated with modernization: (1) marital selection is taken from the hands of elders; (2) ethnic endogamy declines, but class endogamy does not; (3) an increase in the proportion of the population that is unmarried; (4) age-discrepant marriages increase; (5) the dowry or bride price begins to disappear; (6) concubinage and polygamy decline; (7) infanticide decreases; and (8) family size *ultimately* decreases.

There is a danger of seeing change in the family and kinship as only *a response* to changes in other realms (e.g., the impact of industrialization on the family). The structure of the family itself can be a significant independent factor in the modernization process. For example, the family systems in China and Japan, while similar in some ways, have had a very different impact on the development process. In China rules of inheritance specified that land be equally divided among the sons, which led to the fragmentation of land-holding and wealth. And the ultimate loyalty was to the family elders, who often resisted modernization. In Japan, by contrast, inheritance rules specified that family wealth and land be passed on to the oldest son. This had the effect of preserving large pools of land and capital that were instrumental in the modernization process of Japan. Another significant difference was that in Japan the ultimate family loyalty was not to one's elders, but to the emperor. Thus when state-sponsored modernization began in Japan in the 1800s, the loyalties to the emperor and the existence of large pools of wealth greatly facilitated the process (Goode, 1982:191-92). The point is that changes in family and kinship systems are not always effects of the modernization process. They can shape it as well.

Modernization and the Individual

The process of modernization changes individuals as well as social structures such as the economy, politics, the family, and the stratification system. Lerner (1968) thinks that modernization involves a dramatic transformation of the "modal personality" of people, in terms of their cognitive functioning and value orientations. As you might expect, there is not agreement about just *how* the process of development changes individuals. Some, such as Peter Berger and his colleagues, see modernization as having a negative effect on the psychological makeup of persons, both in the LDCs and in the developed industrial nations. They argue that the premodern conception of reality in traditional societies is "a living and interconnected fabric," and that modernization destroys the organic unity of this "lifeworld." Specifically, they argue that modernization entails a "pluralization of lifeworlds" that has led not to freedom and maximization of individual potentialities, but instead to a condition of "homelessness" and to feelings of helplessness, frustration, and alienation (1973:148).

Most analysts do not view individual modernity in such a negative way. Kahl has defined individual modernity in this way:

> A "modern man" is an activist; he attempts to shape his world instead of passively and fatalistically responding to it. He is an individualist, who does not merge his work career with that of his relatives or friends. He believes that an independent career is not only desirable, but possible, for he perceives both life chances and the local community to be low in ascribed status. He prefers urban life to rural life, and he follows the mass media. (1968:37)

Kahl's cross-national research used survey items corresponding to this definition and studied populations in Brazil, Mexico, and the United States. He found in all countries that the above modern traits were strongly related to socioeconomic status and weakly related to urban living. A similar study by Inkles and Smith (1974) included samples from Argentina, Chile, Bangladesh, India, Israel, and Nigeria. They found that modern traits (similar to Kahl's) were strongly related to levels of education and media exposure within each country. In both of these studies

> a set of modern characteristics of the individual are said to arise from and to facilitate the development of a modern society. In neither case is unidirectional causality suggested; no claim is made that the modern individual causes the development of a modern society or vice versa. Rather, there is interaction, with individual modernity facilitating societal modernity and, in turn, societal modernization generating greater numbers of modern individuals. (Lauer, 1977:107)

One criticism of this conception of individual modernity is that it takes characteristics of the American middle class as a model (Safilios-Rothschild, 1970). Nonetheless, the researchers argue that their depiction of individual modernity is a collection of traits most conducive to functioning in modern societies.

ALTERNATIVE PATHWAYS TO MODERNIZATION

While industrialization is usually seen as central to the modernization process, Chodak (1973) has questioned this view and has proposed an interesting model about the different "pathways" to modernization. He thinks that the various pathways to modernization are determined by two primary dimensions: (1) whether it is the result of industrialization or broader "culture contact" and (2) whether it is "spontaneous" or organized by the government.

Industrial modernization is how the process took place in the first world of Europe and North America, starting the 1600s. Modernization was driven by industrialization, which produced new material conditions, technologies, and needs. This in turn stimulated new (modern) attitudes, values, expectations, and a transformed division of labor. New interdependencies and new social and political forms grew that were consistent with the economic structure and demands of industrialism. In Western Europe and North America industrial modernization took place spontaneously as the capitalist free market system took shape, while in Eastern Europe and the Soviet Union industrialization was organized and promoted by the government in the absence of such free market institutions.

Acculturative modernization, according to Chodak, is the typical path for modernization in African colonial systems as they became independent. Modernization in these societies emerged not from economic development but from the direct confrontation and superimposition of European colonial cultures on traditional African ones. This had the effect of creating among the more modernized colonials a new "semidevelopmental buffer culture that was marginal to both and that promoted a duality in norms, patterns of behavior, attitudes, and structural affiliations" (Chodak, 1973:263). This is illustrated by Turnbull's description of an individual who led a dual life in these two cultural worlds:

> In Accra I stayed in the town household of a Kwahu family... In his country home the family head was a chief—"kwame," or "he who was born on Saturday." In his Accra house..[in the city]...the chief became Harold, a prosperous merchant and politician. His town house was large and rambling, on two floors. He occupied the upper floor with his wife by Christian marriage and their small children. It was a magnificent apartment, with every possible luxury—including a well stocked cocktail cabinet, for the one tradition that dies the hardest is the tradition of hospitality. In this apartment lived a happy, settled, thoroughly westernized family. But downstairs lived his other family, the family of Kwame as opposed to that of Harold—all his nephews and other appendages of his extended family which, as Kwame, he felt obliged to support, even in Accra.

> It was like going from one world to another... Upstairs we drank whisky, danced the cha-cha and the mambo, ate bacon and eggs for breakfast and drank tea at tea time. From upstairs, we sallied forth for evenings at the various smart night clubs (evening dress compulsory), or to elegant private dinner parties. But downstairs I ate *fufu* (a kind of unsweetened dough made from manioc flour, from which one tears pieces to dip in a sauce) with my fingers, drank palm wine, danced Abalabi, and learned what real family life is like. (1962:32)

The upshot of acculturative modernization was to produce individuals who are partly alienated from both cultural worlds, or as Franz Fanon (1968) described them, who have a "black skin and a white mask." They are the "superior inferiors," that is, they are treated as being superior to unacculturated individuals, but still inferior to Europeans. This supports Berger's depiction of modernization as involving a "fragmentation of lifeworlds." In the long run Chodak thinks that the process of acculturative modernization will result in a process of *detribalization*, in which there is a gradual substitution of traditional roles for more modern ones based on individual achievements with a new social and political organization of the society.

Acculturative modernization is a process of cross-cultural diffusion that can exist alone where there are no significant attempts of governments to promote modernization. In fact, governments may try to promote or restore tradition and to roll back acculturative modernization (e.g., Iran after the fundamentalist revolution). But in most of the third world today the cultural diffusion of modernism is accompanied by *induced modernization* whereby the government sponsors the introduction of Western administrative, educational, and economic systems and values in a developing nation. The goal is *nation building*, meaning the transformation of the population into a new national entity, while at the same time retaining selected aspects of the traditional culture and trying to integrate these traditional elements into the new social order. Induced modernization can be attempted in terms of a Western "free-market" strategy (as in Kenya or Malaysia) or in terms of a socialist model (as in North Korea or Tanzania).

Induced modernization in Tanzania illustrates the attempt to combine Western and traditional social forms. The traditional system of agrarian villages was supported by the government, and in some instances new villages were created by the forced resettlement of scattered subsistence farmers (Rigney, 1986). But villages were incorporated into the new national system and economy. The model for doing so was socialistic, in terms of government control of markets, but the ideological symbols for the new synthesis were only vaguely Marxian and defined more in terms of *ujaama*, the traditional African concept of *familyhood*. Thus traditional structures and symbols were incorporated in the process of nation building in Tanzania.

Typically, induced modernization occurs in a one-party system whereby the government and the ruling party are its chief organizers. It results not in detribalization, as does acculturative modernization, but in a "stratified supratribal society" that is superimposed on a traditional or tribal structure. It seeks to incorporate not only the most Westernized (or detribalized) groups living in the capital city and wholly identified with the aims of development, but also the melange of other less Westernized ethnic, linguistic, and tribal groups in various parts of the country. Different groups and regions can be identified in terms of their degrees of belonging to the national system (Hutter, 1981:64).

In sum, Chodak's approach to alternative pathways of modernization suggests that while economic development was central to the historic modernization of Europe and North America, it can and does take place differently in the LDCs. His theory is a broad, comparative one, and represents a significant improvement over much earlier theorizing about modernization, which tended to assume an invariant causal sequence producing a uniform type of modern society. It explicitly recognizes that the historic experience of Europe and North America may *not* be replicated in the third world.

EXPLAINING MODERNIZATION FAILURES

The recognition that modernization may be fundamentally different in the third world than was the modernization of the West is often coupled today with pessimism about global progress. Particularly in its economic dimensions, development is perceived to have widely failed in recent decades, as I mentioned above. The current pessimism is particularly notable when compared with the buoyant optimism of modernization theorists in the 1950s. At that time, stimulating modernization seemed deceptively simple. All that was requried was (1) enough capital investment from the developed world, (2) the transfer of western technology, (3) an international climate of free trade and low tarrif barriers for the sale of the products of the LDCs, and (4) the widespread diffusion of western ideas and the "revolution of rising expectations."

What happened? How have modernization failures been explained from the modernization perspective? Variously. First, and most simply, it was argued by some that the capital investment and technology transfer from the industrial nations was simply not sufficient to stimulate development in the third world. Second, some argued that even if the capital and technological inputs were sufficient, that the LDCs lacked the human capital—in terms of skilled labor and administrative resources—to utilize them. Third, others argued that the persistence of traditional culture in the LDCs—and in particular the lack of a cultural ethic valuing hard work and economic growth—have sabotaged economic modernization. Fourth, some have argued that modernization is deflected by the existence of antiquated political and land-holding structures, and by the political dominance of those groups who profit not from improving the lot of the poor masses, but from exploiting them. Others, fifth, put the matter more simply. Modernization is deflected by rampant official corruption at all levels. Sixth, there are those who argue that modernization has failed because governments of the LDCs have been too much attracted to socialist versus capitalist models of development. From this perspective, modernization failure results from too much government interference in free markets and too much economic planning. The seventh and perhaps the most persuasive argument is that modernization has widely failed because in most of the third world *population growth* has outstripped *economic growth* and continues to to so. This last argument is a particularly complex issue, and I will return to it again in Chapter 12.[2]

These are ways that modernization failures have been explained from within the modernization perspective. But in the 1960s there emerged a different type of explanation about why modernization has not proceeded on a global basis as expected. It suggests that the development of LDCs is related to and limited by their position in an emerging global political and economic system. It argues that the fate of the third world is shaped decisively by conditions external to any given nation. It is not only a newer perspective on modernization and its failure, but a fundamental critique of the whole modernization perspective. It is called *world systems theory*, and it is to this alternative perspective that we turn in the next chapter.

NOTES

1. The following is freely adapted from a television film by Otto C. Honegger, "The Nguba Connection," jointly produced by WGBH, Boston, and Swill TV, Zurich.
2. See the anthology edited by Thompson (1978) (*The Third World: Premises of U.S. Policy.* San Francisco, CA: Institute for Contemporary Studies) for an elaboration of these arguments. See in particular the essay by economists Bauer and Yamey.

CHAPTER ELEVEN
THE WORLD SYSTEM AND DEVELOPMENT POLICY

The last chapter examined development in the third world from the modernization perspective. In this chapter I examine development from the major theoretical alternative to modernization theory, which has come to be called *world systems theory*. The chapter concludes by discussing (1) changes in recent decades in development policy recommendations by experts and (2) factors that I think are related to the success and failure of development. You should be forewarned that this summary is my own and that there are others who would summarize things quite differently.

WORLD SYSTEMS THEORY

World systems theory (WST) is an alternative perspective about development and particularly about why development has so often not happened the way modernization theorists argued that it would. As such, it is more than another perspective on development, it is a radical and fundamental critique of the modernization perspective. WST has its historical roots in Marxist-Leninist theory of colonialism and colonial expansion, although it is a significant modification of this.

WST thinkers reject the most basic tenet of modernization theory—that contact with Western societies would stimulate development and modernization in LDCs. In contrast WST thinkers believe that *underdevelopment* in the LDCs arose at the same time and by the same processes as did *development* in the richer industrial nations. "There was, in other words, a simultaneous and intertwined development of some countries and underdevelopment of others" (Stokes, 1984:492). Rather than promoting modernization, WST thinkers argue that the intrusion of Western capitalism destroys the self-sufficiency of third world economies, loots them of resources, and blocks the ripening of diversified capitalist development. For example, Paul Baran has argued about India:[1]

> At the beginning of the eighteenth century, before Britain assumed control, India was a relatively prosperous country with a growing industrial system based largely on textiles. The countryside was organized into village communities that farmed communally and provided for themselves. Britain took conscious steps to destroy Indian industry so that the British could sell their own industrial products in India without competition. Furthermore Britain introduced cash-crop farming on a massive scale to secure raw materials and encouraged the development of large landholdings to facilitate this process. As a result, the village economy was destroyed, leaving millions of landless and destitute peasants at the mercy of landlords for their survival. (Baran, 1957, cited in Stokes, 1984:492)

Baran and contemporary WST theorists argue that the current poverty and underdevelopment in India—and in the third world generally—is the result of economic exploitation by the industrial nations of the West. They think that to argue that the underdevelopment of LDCs results from the inadequate introduction of Western values and technology or the persistence of tradition (as do modernization theorists) misses the critical point of their domination by Western nations.

There was a forerunner of contemporary WST called *dependency theory* that was stimulated by Argentinean economist Raul Prebisch as early as 1949. He thought that development in Latin American countries was stunted because their economies were too dependent upon primary commodity exports and manufactured imports from Europe and America. By the 1960s the views of Latin American *dependencistas* were widely known among American economists and social scientists. University of Chicago economist Andre Gunder Frank (1969) developed the argument this way:

1. The "underdeveloped" countries are in fact highly developed adjuncts to the capitalist countries of Europe and North America.
2. The rich countries could not have become that way without exploiting the poor ones, so that underdevelopment is simply the reverse side of development.
3. Modernization theory focuses on factors internal to the poor nations and ignores their embeddedness in a world economy dominated by the rich ones.

Furthermore, Frank and others in this perspective argue that the modernization perspective can simply be dismissed as the ideological justification for continued capitalist domination of the third world.

The Growth of WST   In the last chapter I mentioned that the modernization perspective was a scholarly theory that had political and ideological support for its development in the post-World War II decades. Similarly there are social circumstances that surrounded the meteoric rise in popularity of WST as an alternative perspective. Its popularity grew among younger social scientists during the 1960s when the moral and political optimism of the 1950s began to erode and America entered a period of pessimism and uncertainty. Chirot describes these circumstances in which supported the growing popularity of WST.

> The almost simultaneous start of the American debacle in Vietnam and the eruption of major racial troubles in the mid-1960s, followed by chronic inflation, the devaluation of the American dollar, and the general loss of America's self-confidence in the early 1970s, ended the moral conviction on which modernization theory had come to base itself. A new type of theory became popular among younger sociologists, one that reversed all of the old axioms. America became the very model of evil, and capitalism, which had been seen as the cause of social progress, became a sinister exploiter and the main agent of poverty in most of the world. Imperialism, not backwardness and lack of modernity, was the new enemy. (1981:259-60)

These shifts in the circumstances and mood of America provided fertile ground for the growth of conflict theory as a general sociological perspective and for WST as a means of understanding the relationship between the industrial world and the LDCs. There is now a generation of scholars trained in the perspective who have elaborated and criticized it (more about that later).

The Assumptions of Contemporary WST

The most comprehensive and systematic formulation of this alternative theory of development was by Immanuel Wallerstein (1974) and his students, who coined the term WST. Since the 1970s their orientation has dominated thinking about development and the global economic system. Wallerstein begins with three assumptions about the evolution of the modern world. First, since about the year 1500 most of the world has been in contact with the modernizing nations of Europe, and by 1800 the scope of that contact had increased so that through the development of colonial empires the Europeans controlled most world trade. Second, since 1900 the colonial empires have broken up to be replaced with economic control through the world system of trade. Third, in the contemporary world there has evolved a *world economic system* of trade and investment which is a global economic exchange network divided among competing national political entities (or at least those in the noncommunist world). Wallerstein views this contemporary *world system* as in fact an international system of economic and political stratification in which nations compete for control. Thus he takes the old Marxian notion of class conflict within society and broadens its meaning to understand international economic and political conflict.

The Structure of the World System   There are three tiers of nations within the world system. First, there are *core societies*. These are the Western industrial and capitalist nations, which have developed highly diversified economies. They import raw materials, export manufactured goods, and through the control of prices and investments they control the terms of trade in the world system. At the other end of the system are *peripheral societies*. According to WST these are not merely underdeveloped societies, but societies that have historically been *differently* developed: They have a narrow economic base with little diversification. They are the commodity producers that are likely to depend upon the export of a single crop or mineral resource. They are dependent on the core societies and powerless to control the terms of trade in the world market system.

> Peripheral countries find it virtually impossible to transform their status in the world system....They are highly dependent on the core for capital, technology, and for markets for their products....[WST theorists view relations between the core and periphery as]...highly asymmetrical because the core countries have far greater discretion over the terms of their participation in the global economic system. The peripheral countries, precisely because they are so poor, are politically as well as economically weak, and must generally accept the term of trade they are confronted with as a set of "givens" over which they have little or no control. (Lofchie and Commins, 1984:4)

In between the core and peripheral extremes of the world system are *semiperipheral* societies. These are intermediate societies in terms of their wealth, political autonomy, and degree of economic diversification. These are countries like Taiwan, Korea, Brazil, and Mexico, where development has been relatively successful compared to the poorest third world nations; yet they are still dependent upon investment and trade from the core nations. They provide good places for investment when well-organized labor forces in the core nations bid up domestic labor costs.

The Roots of Underdevelopment

Modernization theory views underdevelopment as an original premodern state involving traditional social organization and culture. The prescription for development was more complete contact with modern societies. In contrast, WST views underdevelopment as resulting from the long interconnection between core and peripheral societies in an international division of labor. In other words, development and underdevelopment arose simultaneously and are causally related. In the colonial past colonial administrators directly manipulated the periphery. Even in third world countries that have been *politically* independent for some time there is a legacy of the colonial past. Thus in many parts of Asia and Latin America the semifeudal agricultural system (which WST analysts regard as a major barrier to growth) was consciously created during the colonial era to more efficiently exploit natural resources. The system of large agricultural estates is not the remnant of some traditional period but a relatively modern off-spring of the world system that was created to produce cash crops for a capitalist world economy (Griffin, 1969).

In the contemporary world the dependent status of the LDCs is indirect and economic rather than direct and political. There are at least four sources of dependency: (1) the nature of world markets for the commodity products of the LDCs, (2) the debt trap, (3) the role of multinational corporations in the world economy, and (4) the inherent weakness of "extraverted" economies. Let me explain.

The World Market for Commodity Products Most of the LDCs earn money by exporting primary commodity products such as coffee, fruits, tobacco, peanuts, tin, or copper. Many are largely dependent upon a single or a few commodity exports (e.g., peanuts in Gambia, coffee and tobacco in Kenya). In the world market for these products there are *many* producers. For example, Kenya, Tanzania, Ethiopia, Uganda, Brazil, Colombia, and *all* of the Central American nations export coffee. On the other side of the market, there are only a few significant buyers, which are the multinational trading corporations (such as General Foods, Nestles, and Lipton). As a result coffee tends to be a buyer's market: The few buyers can shop around, and the many producers tend to bid down prices. In addition these markets tend to have what economists call an *elastic demand*, which means that the demand for such goods fluctuates so that a decrease in supply simply lowers demand. In comparison with the products of tropical countries, the commodity products of temperate-zone countries (e.g., corn, wheat, beef) tend to be traded in robust inelastic demand markets, where demand remains relatively stable regardless of supply or price. They tend to be sellers' markets. In addition, many of products of tropical countries are not necessities (such as bananas), and when the price is high there are many substitutes for overseas buyers. Finally, there is a danger that some of the commodity products of LDCs will be replaced with synthetic products (as happened to rubber and hemp).

All of these market characteristics means that *producers* have little price leverage in international markets. The long-term trend has been for falling commodity prices. Since the mid-1970s there has been a dramatic collapse in the world prices for Chile's copper, Ghana's cocoa, and Morocco's phosphates.[2] As the prices for their commodity products fall, so do national and per capita incomes. In Latin America, for instance, economic distress has been general since 1980.

Per capita income has dropped 9 percent.
Unemployment is higher than ever (50 percent in some areas).
Inflation is rampant (150 percent for the region as a whole).

Commodity prices are lower in real terms than at any time since the 1930s.
Nearly 40 percent of all export earnings go to service debts from the industrial nations (Lowenthal, 1986).

The social consequences of such economic vulnerability are equally disastrous. It translates into more hunger, more crime, and less money in national budgets for development projects related to improving health, education, and human services. The point is that such dependence and vulnerability is *structural*: It is built into the role of the LDCs in the world economy. As long as the LDCs remain narrowly developed as the exporters of tropical agricultural and mineral products there is a high risk of economic catastrophe as a result of fluctuations in world market prices.

The Debt Trap   LDCs have sought (and have been encouraged to seek) foreign loans and investments to provide capital for modernization and development programs. In recent decades foreign money has been sought to supplement export earnings and to cushion the effects of fluctuating commodity prices. Major lenders in the core used to be governments, but since the 1970s private banks and international agencies have become the largest lending agencies. Today the major source of loans to LDCs are the International Monetary Fund (IMF) and the World Bank.

Given the trends of recent decades, LDCs have become increasingly dependent upon such international loans and, as mentioned above, larger proportions of their national earnings go to service such debts. Most LDCs are now heavily in debt. Between 1970 and 1978 the average increase in external debt among the ninety poorest countries in the world was 400 percent. And even in the most successful tier of developing nations, debt has skyrocketed. Brazil, for example, had an external debt of 3.5 billion dollars in 1970. By 1983 Brazil's foreign debt exceeded 82 billion dollars. Collectively, the third world owes at least 500 billion dollars to the core nations (World Bank, 1982). The level of indebtedness is so large that many nations are chronically on the verge of default, unable to pay even the interest to service the loans, much less payments on the loan principal.

By the mid 1980s this debt crisis in the third world was so general that the lending agencies were petitioned by LDCs to renegotiate the conditions of loans by (1) developing plans to declare temporary moratoriums on payments, (2) reducing interest rates, (3) stretching out payments, and (4) in some cases, forgiving entirely portions of loans. But there were *strings attached* to such adjustments. In general, loan adjustments are made if the petitioning country agrees to a program of economic austerity, weakens restrictions on imports from the core, controls wages, cuts social development programs, removes price controls, and tightens internal credit systems. "The overall effect is that the standard of living of average persons inside the country is lowered and the foreign takeover of local businesses as they become unable to borrow capital is hastened" (Stokes, 1984:496).

It has been noted by WST analysts that the express purpose of such agencies as the IMF and the World Bank is to stabilize the conditions of world trade and promote the unimpeded flow of capital and goods throughout the world (Payer, 1975). As such their primary purpose is *not* to promote diversified economic development in the periphery, but to ensure that the LDCs could keep exporting cheap raw materials and importing manufactured goods from the core when their export revenues were exhausted. In addition a number of observers suggest that the policies of the IMF and the World Bank promote the spread and power of multinational corporations.

Multinational Corporations and the World System   Multinational Corporations (MNCs) are business organizations that operate on a global scale. They are typically headquartered in the core nations, but have manufacturing plants, sales divisions, and raw material production facilities in the LDCs. Their names are household words: Du Pont, Ford, Exxon, ITT, Procter and Gamble, Unilever, Volkswagen, Shell, and so forth (Stokes, 1984:496). Since MNCs invest capital in the third world, they have often been envisioned as the "engines of development" by their defenders. But in fact they often *drain* scarce capital from the LDCs and wrench control of the economy from indigenous owners. In Latin America, for instance,

> for every dollar of net profit earned by a global corporation fifty-two cents left the country, even though 78 percent of the investment funds used to generate that dollar of profit came from local sources. [In mining, petroleum, and smelting]...the capital outflow resulting from the operations of global corporations is even worse. Each dollar of profit is based on an investment that was 83 percent financed from local savings; yet only 21 percent of the profit remains in the local economy. (Barnet and Muller, 1974:153-54)

When MNCs control the economies of the LDCs in such a manner, the LDCs lose the capacity to implement their own economic policies. "MNCs, by their very nature, place their own profit and growth ahead of the needs of their host countries" (Stokes, 1984:497). Since this is the case, economic resources are generally allocated in ways profitable to the MNC and only secondarily in terms of the development needs of the host country. If they are compatible, that is fine, but often they are not.

Among the most striking misallocation of resources is the intrusion of agribusiness firms that encourage production for export rather than production for domestic consumption. While many LDCs have chronic food shortages, farmland is being converted to production of products other than food for more lucrative export markets. In Colombia for instance a hectare of land growing carnations sells for about a million pesos per year, while a hectare of land planted in wheat or corn brings only 12,500 pesos. MNCs naturally favor the growing of carnations rather than wheat or corn. And most of the profits will be sent to the United States or Western Europe. That which remains in Colombia will be used to buy more land to grow more carnations. Such is the result of using MNC profit, rather than domestic needs (calories and protein), to determine what will be grown (Barnet and Muller, 1974, cited in Stokes, 1984:498).

Extraverted Economies   In the most general terms, the weakness of the peripheral nations is that they have *extraverted economies*, that is, (1) they function as appendages of the world economy and (2) lack internal integration (Amin, 1976). They function as appendages of the world economy because increasingly basic economic and social decisions are not made by nationals of the LDC but by the corporate board of MNCs in Europe or North America, or by executives of the IMF or the World Bank. And the economies lack integration because the enterprises in LDCs often have closer ties with economic firms and banks in the core nations than they have with economic entities in the LDC. A vivid example of the lack of integration can be found in the transportation systems in many LDCs. Railways and roads are likely to run

> from the interior to the nearest seaport, rather than knitting the country together as is the case in developed countries. It is thus often easier to ship goods from the interior of many African countries, for example, to Europe than to elsewhere in the same country. (Stokes, 1984:494)

This is a physical reflection of what Amin means by extraversion. The central weakness that produces dependency of extraverted economies is that they lack the capacity to generate autonomous economic growth. Thus they do not develop the economic dynamic for self-sustaining economic development, which modernization theorists describe as the "takeoff" (see Chapter 10).

These then (the nature of tropical commodity markets, the debt trap, the intrusions of MNCs, and extraverted economies) are the roots of contemporary economic dependence among the peripheral nations of the world system. World systems theorists argue that even in those LDCs that seem to successfully modernize, development is often dependent and deformed. Consider the case of Brazil.

In 1964 civilian president João Goulart was overthrown by a military coup, and a ruling coalition of businessmen and generals embarked on a bold program of economic development. The doors were thrown open for foreign investment and multinationals were welcomed to Brazil, by enabling them to invest virtually without any restrictions or taxes. In a narrow sense, it worked. Brazil was hailed as the "miracle economy" of the late sixties and early seventies. The GNP tripled in a decade, and the Brazilian economy diversified to the extent that Brazil became a regional exporter of manufactured goods, not just an exporter of coffee (the historic mainstay of the Brazilian economy). But it was a strange development process, and the economic miracle exacted a high price in terms of social conditions in Brazil. The Brazilian economy became increasingly owned by foreigners. Civil liberties were curtailed, labor unions were suppressed, and wages declined. Industry was allowed to operate in the virtual absence of environmental or safety regulations, and today Brazil has one of the worst industrial safety records in the world. As agribusiness corporations entered in Brazil to produce for export, the production of black beans—the staple carbohydrate of the Brazilian diet—declined. The result is that malnutrition is more widespread in Brazil than before the economic miracle. Perhaps the most telling aspect of the deformed development in Brazil is what has happened to the distribution of income in the last decade. It has become dramatically more unequal. In 1960 the lowest half of Brazilian wage earners controlled 17.7 percent of the total national income: By 1976 they controlled only 11.8 percent. In the same time period the proportion of total national income controlled by the top 5 percent of wage earners grew from 27.7 percent to 39 percent (Reichstul and Goldstein, 1980 cited in Andrade, 1982:172).

As a former president of Brazil, Emilio Medici, put it, "Brazil is doing well, but its people are not" (cited in Barnet and Muller, 1974).

Economic Development from the WST Perspective

At this point you might be thinking that WST is only an explanation of developmental failures, but in fact there *is* a theory of development implied in WST. In general the basic notion is that the peripheral nations should strive for autonomy and self-reliance within the world market system. Raul Prebisch, for instance, has urged a policy of "import substitution," in which the LDCs substitute local manufactured goods for imports as a means of freeing them from dependent status as mere suppliers of raw materials. I think that Dudley Seers (1963) has made the most articulate statement of a development model from the WST perspective, although he wrote several years before the term WST was in vogue. His model, which follows, is based on the Latin American experience.

First in Seers' model is the *open economy*. This is the extraverted economy described above by Amin, in which the society is an exporter of primary commodities. Exports depend on demand and the rate of growth of the customer countries. Economic growth depends upon external influences and circumstances: There is an inflow of capital, few tariffs or import restrictions. In this stage there is a *dual economy*, with a highly developed export sector and an underdeveloped domestic economy. The distribution of income is highly unequal. The economy is highly susceptible to stress because of (1) the tendency for decline in external demand and/or commodity prices and (2) political pressures for development.

These stresses produce a transition to the second stage, the *closed economy*, in which the government attempts to control the inflow of capital and develop a more diversified domestic economic sector. There are two subphases of this stage. First there is the *easy import substitution phase*, which is characterized by (1) a national plan with targets for growth, (2) restrictions on certain imports, (3) the growth of internal markets and market integration, and (4) the growth of light industry, such as the manufacture of cigarettes, beverages, clothing, cement, and household goods. As this succeeds, the society moves into the *difficult import substitution phase*. There is a push to new areas of industrial diversification and self-sufficiency, but these new projects require heavy capitalization and much more effective planning. At this stage there is likely to be (1) a foreign exchange shortage, (2) high inflation and currency devaluations, (3) lowering of bank reserves, and (4) resort to external borrowing and deficit financing. In addition at this phase the economy is likely to face physical constraints—in terms of shortages of electricity, power, and technological constraints. At this stage there is likely to be an increase in political conflict and tensions. There are political pressures for higher incomes (which bleeds capital from development projects). And there are tensions between landowners and workers, between new industries as they complete for scarce capital resources, and between those with links to external markets and those linked to the domestic economy.

If the LDC successfully negotiates this difficult phase, it moves into the third stage of *export diversification*. At this stage the economy has achieved a high degree of internal integration and control, and the society becomes an exporter of manufactured goods. It again begins to link up with the world market system and hence becomes more dependent on external demand, but with a much more diverse set of products. The LDC seeks markets either in the core nations or elsewhere in the periphery and seeks membership in a trading community in which it is an important part, not an extraverted appendage.

Seers' model of economic development is both descriptive and prescriptive. It envisions the possibility of successful development, but Seers is aware of the possibilities of "breakdowns" and barriers in the developmental process, which can become "stalled" at any stage

> by the political strength of one or more developed countries, or by internal pressures, from raising barriers against imports and progressing beyond the open economy. If the internal market is very small, and nothing is done to widen it by commercial policy, progress in import substitution will be limited. The push through into the final stage, when the country exports manufactures, requires an aggressive search for big new markets overseas, which means overcoming not merely the technical difficulties of satisfying foreign buyers, but also the obstacles raised by manufacturing interests in the developed countries, interests which are, of course, politically very powerful. Such failures to move on are quite common. (Cited in Rhodes, 1970:176)

Seers argues that his model fits the Latin American experience. In 1929 all countries were open, extraverted, exporters of primary commodities. By the 1930s nine countries were closed in varying degrees. Bolivia and Paraguay lacked internal markets for much import substitution. Cuba became stuck at the hard phase of import substitution. Argentina, Brazil, Chile, and Mexico were more successful in that they became developed, large, diverse, internal economies. Brazil and Argentina particularly have become successful exporters of manufactures, while Mexican development has depended heavily on the exploitation of oil resources. But in the current world economy even these more successful cases are, as mentioned above, plagued by inflation and debt. And even among them there is no guarantee that economic development is accompanied by political democracy and an equalitarian distribution of the fruits of development.

In sum, WST theorists have argued that for development to occur, the LDCs must engage in a process of "delinking," that is, withdrawing as much as is possible from the world market economy, which perpetuates dependence. This involves striving for diversified internal development, relying mainly on internal resources, and producing primarily for domestic consumption. The strategy implies working toward an introverted economy with its implied protectionism and trade barriers, and this contrasts dramatically with the policy implications of the modernization perspective, emphasizing, as it does, specialized commodity exports and free trade. I should emphasize that the closed economy is not viewed by most as a final stage, but as an intermediate one, preliminary to reopening trade within the world market system in a better bargaining position.

Though seeking autonomy and self-reliance represented a viable option for many earlier WST scholars, most now see these strategies such as those proposed by Seers as unrealistic. Most now argue that (1) many LDCs are so lacking in resources that such autonomous development is not likely with a world capitalist economy and (2) that even when capitalist development takes place it is a savage and deformed process that produces only wealth for the elite but poverty, hunger, and squalor for the masses and frustrates the popular desire for human liberation. Some WST scholars argue that taking steps to a more just world economy (e.g., redistribution between the first and third worlds) is the key. But exactly how this might happen is not clear. Others, perhaps most, argue that nothing short of the creation of a world socialist economy will provide the appropriate conditions for the autonomous and humane development of the nations of the third world. Again, the mechanisms by which this might happen under present circumstances are not clear.

WST and Modernization Theory

The two perspectives on development I have presented are dramatically different. *Modernization theory* is older, more detailed, and more descriptive. It is really a loosely connected set of ideas and definitions (of modernity) rather than a coherent explanatory theory. It assumes that development in the third world will takes place roughly as it did in the original modernization of the industrial nations (although I think modernization theorists had a somewhat idealistic view of how smoothly this all went). The central assumption vis-à-vis the third world today is that close contact with the Western nations will produce self-sustaining economic growth, a reduction in material inequality, and an increase in social and individual welfare in the LDCs. *WST* is a more coherent explanatory theory which is better at explaining why development does not take place than why it does. Its central tenet (dogma?) is the converse of modernization theory: that close contact with the West has produced underdevelopment and dependency, growing inequality, and a decrease in social welfare. While the modernization perspective has an elaborate—if incoherent—theory about the *internal* social, political, and cultural changes that accompany development, these are notably lacking in WST. Thus if modernization theory gives inadequate attention to the external context of national development, WST pays little attention to internal factors. The conflict between the two perspectives is not only about the consequences of contact between the core and the periphery but, more abstractly, about how much weight to give internal national factors (e.g., resources, population growth, political factors, literacy) and how much weight to give external ones (the nature and state of the world market system). And most importantly, it is not merely a debate about theories of development, but also a controversy about development strategies.

DEVELOPMENT POLICY: FADS AND FASHIONS

Since World War II there have been many changes in the advice given to LDCs not only by social scientists of different theoretical persuasions, but by government agencies, United Nations agencies, and agents of financial institutions such as the World Bank and the IMF. The problem is that little of the advice and technical assistance has really worked.

Western "Advice and Aid"

In general the advice of the U.S. government and financial agencies, operating within the assumptions of the modernization perspective, has advocated a free market strategy and has urged the LDCs to avoid export taxes and restrictions on foreign investments. The major stumbling block to development is seen as the shortage of capital and advanced technology. These needs have been addressed by programs offering investment, loans, and the transfer of technology. The advice to LDCs was to pursue a strategy of export-led growth. In economic terms this policy was based on the 200-year-old notions of David Ricardo, a contemporary of Adam Smith, about the "comparative advantage" of nations in the context of free trade. Ricardo's argument was that, given differences in resources, geography, and climate, particular nations had a "comparative advantage" over others for the production of certain products, and that their economic development should emphasize whatever they could produce best and most efficiently. Thus the LDCs were urged to develop their commodity exports and then to use their export earnings to invest in industrialization schemes, again in the context of free trade and low tariffs. This advice seemed plausible in the 1970s because of the dramatic growth of the few successful newly industrialized nations (South Korea, Taiwan, Brazil) that had opted for export-led, free market strategies. Other LDCs were urged to emulate their model. But their growth was supported by the booming international economy of the 1970s and has been sharply curtailed by the global recession of the early 1980s. In retrospect this sort of advice has been disastrous for most nations. According to economist Theodore Schultz of the University of Chicago,

> Most of the poor countries were being advised by the rich countries and also from within, that the best way to achieve economic growth was rapid industrialization if need be at the expense of agriculture. It turned out in country after country to be a disaster. (*NY Times*, July 28, 1985:8).

Third World Responses

As you might imagine, the nations of the third world have not been merely passive recipients of aid and advice, but have sought to articulate their collective interests through a variety of strategies and coalitions. There are three general types of coalitions (Wriggins, 1978:43-76). There are *commodity coalitions* based on the locations of strategic resources. They seek to withhold resources until prices go up and/or importing nations agree to their political demands (Bassis, Gelles, and Levine, 1982:137). Their power depends upon the global demand for their resources and on the member nations' ability to do without earnings until the loss is felt. OPEC is the most successful example of such a coalition. Less sucessful coalitions have been based on phosphates, copper, and tin. Second, there are *regional coalitions* based on common economic interests and cultural ties of neighboring countries, such as the Organization of African Unity (OAU) and the Andean Pact. These try to deal with local conflicts and formulate coherent international policies for the region. A third type of coalition is the *universal coalition* that acts as a generalized pressure group on behalf of certain third world nations (Wriggins, 1978:63-76). Examples of this type are the Nonaligned Nations coalition that grew at the height of the Cold War and Group-77 which grew from the United Nations Conference on Trade and Development (UNCTAD). UNCTAD called for reforming the world economic system with a New International Economic Order that would help the third world by stabilizing mineral and commodity prices, lowering tarrifs on their manufactured exports, and providing both renewed financial aid and debt relief.

Because large numbers of nations are represented by such universal coalitions they have great potential influence as voting blocs in the United Nations. So far they have dealt "largely in words, resolutions, and symbolic positions" (Wriggins, 1973:73). But even though "they have won few concrete concessions from the North, their symbolic victories should not be undervalued...they have succeeded in altering the agenda of international meetings, shifting the focus from East-West security problems to North-South economic problems (Bassis, Gelles, and Levine, 1982:137).

In the 1970s many LDCs embarked on individual programs of self-reliance, import substitution, and attempts to create diverse and integrated domestic markets. This shift was encouraged by the widespread diffusion of dependency theory and WST among third world economists and policymakers. The weaknesses of this approach are now apparent. According to one assessment:

> Those who seek to isolate themselves under the illusion that they have found an "autonomous path"...find it extremely difficult to attain the minimum levels of economic efficiency required for survival, and their economies are corroded by contraband and multiple forms of parallel markets. (Furtado, 1983:115)

First, notwithstanding the injunction to "rely on internal resources," many LDCs have few resources to rely upon, save primary commodities, which give them little leverage in international markets. Second, import substitution implies protectionism and high trade barriers which are policies that find disfavor with international aid and lending agencies that provide essential scarce capital for import substitution. In addition, such policies usually are disfavored by deeply entrenched vested interests, that is, economic elites in the LDCs who gain wealth and power by serving as agents of the world economy. This has been recognized by WST analysts such as Frank (1972) who in an article entitled "Who Is the Immediate Enemy?" argues that the most immediate stumbling block to development is not international dependency but the *internal* political class structure of the LDCs. He argues that as long as the policies of an LDC are dominated by persons whose own fortunes are derived from the world system, it is foolish to expect any major change and that the first priority for development is to wrest political control from traditional elites who have little economic interest in developmental change..

Development Policies in the 1980s

In the 1980s things came almost full circle. Economists, advisors, and policymakers, both in the first and third worlds, advocated once again that the LDCs pursue growth through the export of primary commodities (Kristof, 1985:3). The thing that is different this time, however, is that agriculture is emphasized as a permanent basis for economic growth, rather than for the rapid shift to industrialism. This trend was encouraged not only by the resurgence of neoconservative free market economic thinking, but also by the growing realization that the worldwide neglect of agriculture in favor of industrialization is one of the prime causes of the global problem of hunger. There are some obvious difficulties with this shift.

> Countries turned to industrialization to escape the slowness of development and the tyranny of commodity prices. Ironically, they are moving back into production of agricultural commodities at precisely the period when prices for many of these exports are at their lowest levels in years. Some nations are trying to diversify exports within agriculture...but in general such nations will not soon be able to escape dependence on a few product whose price may be dropping. (Kristof, 1985:8. Copyright © 1985 by The New York Times Company. Reprinted by permission.)

The shift back to agriculture is beneficial at a basic level, since it may increase the food supply in a hungry world. But as important as food is in the short run, development ultimately means more than just food. In the last chapter I mentioned that, in the aspirations of people and nations, development also means "human liberation" in the broadest terms of cultural and political improvements. These require more than food. They require economic resources that a food first strategy may not provide.

In spite of the contradictions in these policies of the 1980s there seems to be an emerging consensus about developmental policies in some areas. These would include the following:

1. To provide foreign aid more selectively to avoid the creation of dependencies
2. To target foreign aid at local projects, which bypasses the domination of urban elites, promotes rural development and empowers the peasants and small landowners
3. To provide direct aid only for dire emergencies
4. To provide the LDCs with freer access to commodity markets through bypassing the large multinational firms that presently dominate the international marketplace
5. To maintain and encourage consumer demand in the developed countries for the products of the LDCs
6. To stabilize international commodity prices
7. To limit the intrusions of MNCs by tariffs and taxation policies.

You don't have to be too perceptive to note that these concrete proposals are fraught with contradictions, and to implement them assumes that you could do so against the interests and will of major actors in the global political scene (e.g., urban elites of the third world, workers in the developed nations, MNCs). In spite of these dilemmas, there is in the 1980s a curious consensus emerging around the themes of self-help and the dangers of continued dependency. This may be viewed by conservative thinkers as "benign neglect" or by more leftist thinkers as "de-linking" from the world system. But there is much disagreement about the particulars of a self-help developmental strategy.

DEVELOPMENT RECONSIDERED: SOME CONCLUSIONS

With all of these difficulties in development and development policy, you may be getting the idea that (1) development has been an unmitigated failure throughout the third world and (2) that there are no generalizations that can be made about conditions for successful development. I don't think either conclusion is warranted. As I pointed out in the last chapter, some nations have done rather well. If you take the third world as a whole (an assumption that masks the developmental disasters in some societies) the economic growth rates of the LDCs since World War II compare very favorably with the rates of growth of the industrial world in the earlier phases of its development.

Average Third World economic growth, as measured by per capita GNP change between 1950 and 1980, has been about 2.2 percent per year. This is as high as average American per capita GNP growth from 1870 to 1913, and at that time America had the fastest-growing economy in the world. Average growth in Latin America from 1950 to 1980, and in many Asian countries—such as Turkey, Thailand, Indonesia, the Philippines, Malaysia, Taiwan, South Korea, and even in most North African countries, including Egypt—has been significantly above this rate. (Chirot, 1986:248)

Chirot argues that it is only because people in the LDCs expected that they might actually catch up to the industrial nations in a fairly short time that these results have been so disappointing, but that in historical terms average economic growth in the third world has been "nothing short of astounding" (1986:248). Even in the lower tier of development, progress has occurred. India's growth rate between 1950 and 1980, for example, was equal to that of France and England between 1870 and 1913. In 1986 Indian Prime Minister Rajiv Gandhi argued:

> One tends to forget that India today has a very substantial middle class which didn't exist 30 years ago...[which] numbers upward of 100 million people... more than the total population of most developed countries. Included among them are twice as many doctors as a decade ago, even though the population of the country has grown by only 25 percent....The single most important group to join the ranks of the middle class, however is the entrepreneur: the number of people running their own industrial establishments has more than trebled..in the last decade. (Cited in World Development Forum, 1986)

And, according to the periodical *India Today*

> Ten years ago the goals were more food, water, steel, aluminum, hospitals. Now it is all that plus telephones, TV sets, scooters, cars, [and] refrigerators. (Cited in World Development Forum, 1986a)

It is more difficult to find generalizations about conditions that contribute to successful development than to recognize that some progress has occurred. Nonetheless, let me end this chapter by spelling out what I think are some of the conditions promoting successful development.

Physical and Human Resources

Most obviously the presence of rich human and physical resources are relevant to developmental success. By *physical resources* I mean such things as fertile soil, climate, mineral deposits, and so forth, and by *human resources* such things as literacy, skills of the work force, administrative skills, and levels of commitment to the development process. Successful development requires both types of resources. But there are countries, such as Zaire, with vast physical resources without the human resources to exploit them. And there are countries, such as Ethiopia, that are virtually barren of any exploitable resources, where it would be difficult to imagine successful development taking place, even if there *were* a surplus of human resources. But there are many cases of successful development where human resources are highly developed even though physical resources are sparse (but not absent). In the modernization of the first world, Denmark and Japan would be examples of nations that successfully modernized by having superior literacy levels, work force skills, and political will in the relative absence of natural resources. South Korea and Taiwan would be contemporary examples. On balance, it seems to me that human resources are relatively more important than physical ones, but, as in the case of Ethiopia, there are limiting cases. The resource base—either physical or human—does not, however, guarantee successful development. Resources are limiting contexts that determine the potential for development. They determine the starting points of various nations.

The Political Context

Another important context of successful development is political. Such diverse observers as Reynolds and Bienefeld (from a free market and neo-Marxian perspective, respectively) argue that *political stability* is an absolute precondition for successful development. Given political stability, there are three other political characteristics that are directly relevant to successful development. First is a government that is strongly committed to development as a priority. Some are not. Some represent those classes whose overwhelming material interest is in perpetuating a state of dependence and underdevelopment. Second, beyond a commitment to development, a strong interventionist government is required. This means a government that can shelter the economy from the hazards of extraversion or the unrestricted predations of MNCs. Such a strong interventionist state can regulate investment flows, in terms of developmental priorities, and stimulate capital accumulation toward long-term strategic goals. It can diffuse the social and material benefits throughout the population, organize the acquisition of technological capabilities, and promote aggressive export policies to get foreign currency. This is not to say that a strong state *will* do these things, but they will not occur if the state is unable or unwilling to intervene in the economy in these matters.

A strong interventionist state was characteristic of the development of Japan at an earlier time, and it is characteristic of the more successful nations in recent decades, both in a capitalist context (South Korea, Taiwan) and a socialist context (North Korea and Yugoslavia).[3] Whether democracy is required is debatable. Most of the newly industrializing nations, including those just mentioned, have been governed by authoritarian regimes, of either the left- or the right-wing variety.[4]

Third—and this is very important—LDC governments must not only promote economic development, but must be committed to ensuring the diffusion of the benefits of such development to the bulk of the population. Economic growth does not guarantee improvements in the lives of the masses of people, as the Brazilian example mentioned earlier graphically illustrates. There is always the danger of deformed development in which economic growth does not benefit most of the population, and the modernization perspective largely overlooks this possibility. But there *are* many cases where deformed development has not occurred, and where in fact economic development has been connected to an upgrading of mass living standards (North and South Korea, China, Taiwan, Costa Rica, and Sri Lanka). In South Korea, for instance, the distribution of income resembles that of the United States, rather than that of Brazil and Mexico, where wealth is considerably more skewed in favor of the dominant groups (Chirot, 1986:255). There is some evidence that government interest in diffusing the benefits of development follows the structure of property holding—especially land. That is, in many of those nations where the benefits of development have become widely diffused, the ownership of land was widely decentralized *before* development. In general, the countries that have the *worst* record for the democratization of internal development are the oil exporting nations, followed by those that have large cash crop estates. The best record for having an egalitarian distribution of benefits is in those nations where the backbone of the economy is small landholders (e.g., Taiwan, both Koreas). Thus there may be a *structural* basis for equalitarian development.

The International Economic Context

As the foregoing suggests, *internal factors*, such as political stability and the structural basis of support for the regime, are very relevant to the conditions of successful development. The *external international context* is also very important. During the 1960s, when many LDCs made great progress, the international economic climate had the following characteristics: (1) There was much foreign aid available from the Western powers, international credit was easy to get, and interest rates were relatively low. (2) The industrial economies themselves were rapidly growing and there was a high demand for the primary commodity exports of the LDCs. (3) Liberal trade policies and low tariffs dominated the world market, (4) There was a deepening of economic interdependencies as a result of international capital and trade flows. And (5) energy supplies—primarily petroleum—were relatively cheap. The last point was particularly significant in that countries such as India and Pakistan were able to buy petroleum to manufacture fertilizers and thereby significantly increase agricultural production.

In the 1970s these conditions changed rapidly. There were shifts in the pattern of competitive dominance among the industrial nations; the United States and the United Kingdom declined relative to the growing economic power of Germany, France, and particularly Japan. But more important than the changing dominance patterns in the world market system was the fact that growth rates and profits began to decline generally throughout the world system. In comparison to the buoyant boom times of the 1960s, most developed nations embarked on economic strategies of higher tariffs and protectionism. Prices rose and consumer demand for LDC products began to weaken. There was a decrease in government aid and increases in loans from private banks and international monetary agencies. Between 1960 and 1980 government aid from Western nations dropped from an average of 1 percent of GNP to 0.35 percent of GNP. There were higher interest rates from private agencies and increased penetration by MNCs (Dadzie, 1980). Most importantly, the meteoric rise in the world price for oil devastated the development plans of many of the poorer LDCs. The oil-producing nations were the temporary beneficiaries of such a rise in the price of oil, but as the attempts of OPEC to cartelize the world market failed in the early 1980s, those nations dependent upon oil for export earnings were in turn devastated. Thus Mexico and Nigeria saw significant economic growth throughout the 1970s, but as the price of oil fell dramatically, those economies became increasingly vulnerable. Export earnings plummeted and the Mexicans increasingly tried to maintain economic growth through borrowing. In sum, the result of these changes in the international climate has meant slower growth in all LDCs, and a widening of the gap both between the first and third world, and between nations within the third world.

Summary

Let me try to summarize the argument that I have been making. Both the modernization theorists and the WST theorists have perceived a part of the riddle of global development, but both have significant blind spots. Modernization theory correctly argues that such internal factors as capital resources, political structures, culture, and technology are relevant to development. The naiveté of the modernization perspective of the fifties and sixties was to think that (1) development was primarily an internal event and (2) the modernization experience Western-style was readily translatable into the twentieth century and to the third world. WST theorists have, on the other hand, correctly argued that the development of any particular society is importantly shaped by its position in an interconnected global economic system. But it is *not* true that internal factors are irrelevant, as by now most WST analysts realize. Nor is it true that integration into the world system automatically produces underdevelopment or deformed development. The nations having the most developmental successes *do* have close, organic ties to the world system. But not all societies so connected have been successful. On the other hand it is difficult to think of a single case of successful development by a nation that is "unlinked" to the global economy. Even the Chinese, who have made the most coherent attempt at autonomous development have, in post-Maoist times, sought to establish ties to the world economy. It is not economic linkage per se that produces underdevelopment, but linkage under the conditions of extreme extraversion in which the domestic economy of a nation becomes controlled by international actors.

Finally, it is obvious by now that the fates of developed nations and the LDCs are inextricably linked. The LDCs do not benefit from economic stresses, such as depression or inflation in the industrial world. It has become increasingly clear that collectively the LDCs have great potential leverage to affect economic conditions of the developed nations. Even though it seemed to have failed in the 1980s, the OPEC oil boycott of the mid-1970s sent shock waves around the world. And it is not just oil: The global reserves of dozens of strategic materials, such as tin, copper, and other minerals, increasingly lie in the hands of the LDCs. A steady and uninterrupted cheap supply of these materials is the backbone of the industrial economies.

The mutuality between the core and the periphery is not only a matter of resources, it is also monetary. Low commodity prices mean that the LDCs must borrow heavily. Initially the power and leverage is in the hands of creditors. But beyond a certain point of indebtedness, some leverage begins to shift back to debtors. Thus in the mid-1980s Mexico, Peru, and Brazil have all threatened to default on loan payments if "adjustments" were not made. A default of the largest debtor LDCs, which owe billions to Western banks, would initiate a world fiscal crisis, and perhaps some of the largest Western banks would themselves go into default. The political ramifications of such an increasingly interdependent *but fragile* world economic system are grim. Historically, *war* is often associated with widespread economic collapse (more about this later).

The point I am trying to make is that because the contemporary world has such deep economic and geopolitical interdependencies a "zero sum game" (I win, you lose) is not going to work in the longer run. A way *must* be found to develop a "variable sum game" (everybody wins something). In the broadest terms this means renegotiating the terms of trade and benefits between the first and third world. Finding a way to do this will obviously not be easy. But there are two reasons why such an international strategy must be pursued. *Ethical reasons* ought to be compelling enough: A world in which most people live in unbelievable squalor, hunger, and poverty while a minority live in relative opulence with a material surfeit is simply unconscionable. But if ethical reasons are not compelling enough, there are *practical reasons*. To pursue a lifeboat strategy, where the developed nations prosper while the rest of the world sinks into misery, is simply not workable, as I have argued above. We inhabit an interconnected world where, as the English poet John Donne said centuries ago, "No man is an island..." Neither is any nation. The final two chapters explore issues of global interconnectedness.

NOTES

1. Paul Baran was an American Marxist economist and an early dissenter from the modernization perspective.
2. Copper, which used to sell for $1.34 per pound at its peak sold for $.66 per pound in 1985, and sugar (a stable export of the Caribbean as well as many other parts of the tropics) which sold for $.66 per pound in 1974 sold for about $.025 per pound in the mid 1980s.
3. Although it is not generally considered as such, North Korea is almost as much as great a developmental success as South Korea, in terms of successful "marketing" of its extensive mineral resources and rising standards of literacy, health, and material standards. According to White, "the country has achieved a high rate of socio-economic growth and development over the past three decades through a conscious strategy of politico-economic self-reliance, eschewing a high degree of economic integration with either capitalist or socialist international economies" (1982:323).
4. Among the newly industrializing nations, Mexico seems exceptional in terms of its degree of internal democracy. Although it is formally a one-party state there are large, well-established internal factions, and it is not appropriate to characterize the regime as authoritarian.

CHAPTER TWELVE
GLOBAL INTERDEPENDENCE, CHANGE, AND THE "WORLD PROBLEM"

The last two chapters focused on change in the emerging world system in terms of development in the third world and the interconnections between nations in the world economic system. This chapter explores the emerging world system in a different way. Here I am not using the term *world system* to refer specifically to the world systems perspective about development as in the last chapter, but in a more general descriptive way. It focuses on the connections between population growth, energy, and food resources and on some ecological consequences—in other words on the changing relationship between human social activity and the resource base of the planet. But before doing this I want to describe more concretely what is meant by "systems" and "ecological perspectives" as they relate to understanding global change. This chapter explores some important environmental and resource dimensions of global change as they relate to the changing quality of human life now and in the future. The next chapter examines various speculations about the future of the world.

PERSPECTIVES ON GLOBAL CHANGE

I think you need two important perspectives to understand contemporary global change processes and their implications: (1) a "systems" perspective about the world and its problems, and (2) an ecological perspective about the relationship between human social activity and the capacity of the planet to support life.

Perspective I: Growing System-ness

A *system* is a network of interconnected parts that affect each other so that changes in various parts affect all the others as well as (ultimately) the nature of the system as a whole. The opposite of a system is an aggregate of parts or pieces that may occupy adjacent space but are minimally interdependent. As I mentioned above, human societies have always had some systemlike connections between them, but societies increasingly have systematic linkages between them as we come closer in time to the modern world. This is the abstract meaning of global interdependence. What are some of the more obvious dimensions of this growing global system-ness and interdependence?

Economic Interdependence   International trade, in terms of the flow of raw materials, manufactured goods, and technology, is increasingly important to the domestic economies of all nations. Also, as discussed in the last chapter, there is an increasingly important global financial system of investments, loans, and currency regulations by banks, international agencies, and governments that knit together the economic fates of nations in various parts of the world. Such economic connections should be obvious to American consumers as they view the volume and variety of goods on the shelves in American stores that are manufactured by our trading partners in other industrial nations. Our economic ties to and dependence on the less developed nations is not as obvious but nonetheless extensive. Here are a few examples noted by Maxwell Hamilton, a former World Bank official:

> Farmers in Commerce, Texas, suffer from a drop in exports to third world markets.
> A manufacturer in Cleveland depends on raw material, such as cobalt from Zaire and other developing countries, to stay in business.
> Longshoremen in Duluth, Minnesota, earn half their annual income loading food sent by the U.S. government to poor nations in Africa and Asia (World Development Forum, 1986c).

Imagine if you will that the United States is suddenly prevented from importing foreign goods or selling our products to other nations. There would be immediate shortages of petroleum, iron ore, copper, chromium, and dozens of other strategic minerals that drive the industrial economy. In the short run some workers and industries would benefit from the absence of foreign competition, but others would be devastated in the absence of international customers. In the longer run there would be significant price increases and a general deterioration of the economy so that the wages and living standards of most Americans would decline.

Political Interdependence The political connections between nations are as important as the economic ones. National governments not only seek to regulate the problems created by trade and economic interaction, but seek to promote the sovereignty and the interests of nations as they interact. This is obvious, but less obvious has been the emergence and importance of international political entities. Most well known of these is the United Nations and its many agencies, but there are also many others, such as the World Court, the association of nations that negotiates trade and tariffs (G.A.T.T.), the European Parliament, and a host of other regional economic and political alliances such as the Organization of Petroleum Exporting Countries (OPEC). Today political events in remote parts of the world have increasingly global ramifications.

The systematic character of contemporary politics is visible not only in international cooperative arenas; political conflict is also coming to have a more systematic nature in the modern world. Revolutions and the fall of governments (for example, in Iran, the Philippines, or Nicaragua) are no longer only local events to be briefly noted in other parts of the world, but events of international importance that have the potential to reshape the international order of relations between nations and the world economic system. In the 1930s a war between Iran and Iraq would have been briefly noted in American newspapers as a curious war among foreign nations. In the 1980s it is an important international event because of its potential to disrupt the flow of oil from the Persian Gulf. Local wars anywhere have an increasing potential to pull regional and international actors into the conflict.

Cultural and Ideological Connections Along with the international flow of goods and technologies comes the flow of ideas and lifestyles. The global diffusion of Coca Cola and autos implies, for better or worse, the diffusion of different ideas about life and how it should to be lived. Many of the political events in the third world nations are a reaction not only to economic intrusions, but also to the intrusions, positive and negative, of Western ideas and values. Such diffusion of culture and technology has not produced wholesale adoption of Western cultural patterns, but it has produced at least a growing awareness of the ideas and values of people around the world. In a cultural perspective the global political events and disruptions are not only conflicts about resources and power, but in a larger sense often conflicts about the spread, meaning, and dominance of some of the big ideologies, such as freedom, democracy, capitalism, socialism, and—in the Middle East—Islamic fundamentalism.

The Complex and Volatile Global System It is important not only to recognize growing interdependence and system-ness, but that the emerging world system is *highly complex, disorderly, and unstable*. Nations and interest groups both within and between nations interact in highly volatile and seemingly unpredictable patterns. You have only to watch the international news on television to get a highly personal sense of this: Political alliances become fraught with internal conflict, terrorists hijack airliners to dramatize their grievances, there is worry of economic collapse of markets and currency values as nations argue about trade barriers and protectionism, politicians of the third world articulate grievances against the industrial nations, industrial accidents (both conventional and nuclear) have frightening transnational health and ecological ramifications, and the Americans and the Soviets threaten each other (and implicitly the rest of the world) with bellicose language in the context of the horrendous possibility of a nuclear holocaust. The list of things that one could worry about seems endless. I guess it always has been, but somehow today the stakes in these global issues seem more serious because of the growing system-ness of the world. The prospect of an orderly, stable, and equitable world system seems distant.

Normal Crises   The world today seems in a constant state of interacting crises. Perhaps that is an overstatement, but it is at least reasonable to perceive the contemporary world as having an increasingly unstable and potentially dangerous dynamic on a scale that is historically unprecedented. The problems and crises of today's world are different from many of those in the past because they seem constant rather than periodic and they interact on many different levels. In the past, widespread crises with international ramifications (floods, droughts, epidemics, famines, wars) seemed caused by accidents or acts of nature beyond human control. What is different about the crises of the contemporary world is that more of them are normal crises, that is, problems caused because of *the way the system itself is structured* (Perrow, 1979). The likelihood of such normal crises is most obvious in complex technological realms. For example, in the long run nuclear accidents are predictable and likely, given the complexities of managing nuclear facilities and the difficulties of nuclear waste disposal. Events like the near disaster at Three Mile Island and the actual disaster at the Chernobyl reactor in the Soviet Union are predictable possibilities given that method of generating electricity. Beyond purely technological realms, normal crises occur because of the increasingly complex social structure of the modern world. Examples are not hard to find. Famine is no longer caused only by periodic crop failure, but is a routine event in parts of the world, such as sub-Saharan Africa, where the pressure of a large a population makes too many demands on a fragile agricultural environment. In the political realm, the more parties become involved in global political negotiations and treaties, the more likely they are to break down. The more that economies rely on products and labor from diverse sources, they more things can go wrong. In general, the more complex the system gets, not only are more disruptions possible, but increasingly they are not accidents, but probabilities built into the nature of the system itself.

Perspective 2: An Ecological View

Underlying the growing interconnectedness of human life around the world is another obvious but often overlooked level of interdependency: that between humans and the natural environment. Humans share the life-support system of nature with other species. Even though they are often understood separately, all human economic, technical, political, and cultural activities are in fact ultimately rooted in and dependent upon resources of the biophysical environment of the planet. The relationships between living things and the planet form complex and delicately balanced webs of energy transformations and food chains that are called ecosystems by biologists. More formally, an *ecosystem* is an interdependent biotic community that depends in turn on the resources of the physical environment.

Put differently, the survival of all living things depends upon the carrying capacity of Earth to support life. The interaction between the resources on the earth's crust and living things is a vast recycling system, in which living things make withdrawals from the natural environment as they use air, water, soil, and minerals, and return wastes to that environment, most of which are reabsorbed and recycled. In addition, you must recognize that all living things have the capacity to alter the carrying capacity of the physical environment. When their natural predators are eradicated, for instance, herbivore populations (e.g., deer) may multiply to the extent that they strip the environment of vegetation. And human societies have been known to overuse the environment (e.g., soil fertility and water resources) in such a way that the basis for economic production is altered. When that happens, the short-run consequences are disastrous. Deer begin to starve, as may humans, although human populations generally have migrated out of an ecologically devastated region before starving. As the demands of living things diminish, because they starve or migrate, many aspects of the natural environment gradually rebuild (vegetation, soil fertility). But it is significant that many of the natural resources relevant to the maintenance of industrial societies are not recyclable in the same way that fresh water, vegetation, and soil minerals are. Using petroleum and natural gas for energy destroys them for good. Technological change can enable humans to find and use them more efficiently. But they are finite. When they are gone, they are gone for good.

You might be wondering at this point why I am reviewing these elementary concepts about ecology, because they are developed (in considerably more depth!) in high school biology texts. The reason is that we often behave as if they were not true. Or, perhaps more accurately, we only see half of the picture. We are aware of how we use and exploit the environment for our consumption, but seem unaware of the consequences of our capacity to modify that environment and our ultimate dependence upon it. This seems particularly true of Americans—with our recent frontier history and "vandal ideology" about the wide open spaces that could be tamed and conquered willy-nilly, with no regard for the ecological consequences of doing so. But this *environmental myopia* is also characteristic of most people around the world, both now and in the past. It has characterized the outlooks of most sociologists and other social scientists as well as ordinary people. Most social science literature gives minimal recognition to the ecological rootedness of human economic, cultural, and social systems and implicitly assumes that human technological inventiveness has enabled homo sapiens to somehow transcend the limitations of nature.[1]

The fact that ecological myopia is so widespread is understandable. Historically human populations were much less dense, human technological capacity to exploit the environment more rudimentary, and human consumption (withdrawals) rarely reached the threshold of permanent damage to the environmental balance. Throughout most of human history the ability of homo sapiens to greatly modify the biophysical environment was quite limited. The earth was an open system with seemingly limitless space and resources that could be freely used. Things are much different in the modern world. Human populations are much larger and more dense (in both the developed and LDCs), most of the world possesses high technology with a capacity to significantly alter the natural environment, and most people today desire a level of material consumption that is historically unprecedented. Under these circumstances an ecological perspective should become a much more important outlook for understanding human affairs, change, and problems.

From it a number of disturbing possibilities flow. Do industrial societies have the capacity to overwhelm the absorptive capacity of the earth to recycle pollutants and wastes? Does the extensive reshaping of the natural world in modern times disrupt the food chains and energy transformations between species in ways that are subtle but critical for maintaining the equilibrium of the ecosystem? Is the scale of human material consumption now such that renewable resources (such as fertile soil and fresh water) cannot be regenerated rapidly enough? Also frightening is the possibility, raised since the 1960s, that the human consumption of many nonrenewable resources may be approaching absolute finite limits in the future. Is the potential of human ingenuity and technical inventiveness sufficient to transcend these finite limits (If there are any)? Are such technological fixes extravagantly expensive when their real ecological costs are accounted for, and are they so inordinately complex that they have built in instabilities (normal crises)? And, perhaps most disturbing of all, to what extent does the combination of international political volatility in combination with nuclear technology increase the possibility of a thermonuclear holocaust that could once and for all destroy the ability of Earth to support human life on any meaningful terms?

These are indeed scary possibilities. But my intent is not to scare you, for there is not sufficient evidence to say that any of these things are certainly going to happen. But there is enough evidence that they are at least possibilities. I raise them here not as predictions, but rather as important reasons for understanding change and problems in a global perspective.

DIMENSIONS OF THE WORLD PROBLEM

Let me tie these two perspectives together. An understanding of global change and problems needs to consider (1) the growing social, economic, and political relationships and interdependencies between societies around the world, and (2) the relationship between the scale of human economic and social activity and the capacity of the planet to sustain life.

French scholars have used the term *world problematique* to describe the interacting problems of the world as a dynamic system in which (1) there is a growing functional interdependence of nations and regions, and (2) the causes of routine crises and problems have many intertwined dimensions (e.g., ecological, demographic, economic, political, technological) that cannot be understood separately. There are a number of implications of this view of the *world problem* (as I will call it). First, contemporary crises are not likely to be temporary but chronic. Second, moderating such interlocking crises will not occur through traditional methods, but will require rethinking human-environment relationships as well as the relations between nations.[2] Third, while there may be national strategies to deal with dimensions of the world problem, policies that significantly moderate their intensity will be found in international, rather than national contexts. Fourth, I think that *in part* the world problem is more likely to be successfully addressed through international cooperation than entirely through the dynamics of economic and political conflict. All of this raises questions about the limits of *nationalism* and the independent pursuit of national interests as forces for positive social change. The problem is that while our interests have become global, our loyalties and outlooks often remain national. Whether the world problem *will* indeed be addressed in terms of a cooperative global context is questionable.

Among the important dimensions of the world problem are those demographic and biophysical issues that relate directly to the maintenance of human life. The remainder of this chapter explores these issues. More concretely, these are questions about (1) the enormous world population growth in modern history, (2) food resources and the incidence of hunger, (3) energy resources that support all forms of human economic activity, and (4) the implications of human activity in all its forms for depleting and polluting the natural environment.

Dimension 1: Population Growth and the World Problem

We are used to thinking of growth in linear terms. But world population has grown *exponentially*. This means that human population grew very slowly for centuries, but is now growing very rapidly. As long ago as A.D. 1 there were only about 250 million people on the entire planet. By the 1600s that had doubled to about a half billion. The second doubling occurred about 1850, and then again by about 1930. By 1970 the world's population had reached about 4 billion (Pirages, 1984:59). In 1986 it was 6 billion, and by 2020 it is expected to reach 8 billion (see Figure 12-1). While these numbers are staggering, the consequences are even more so, for such growth increases the population pressure on food and economic resources of all sorts. A larger population eats more, consumes more, and pollutes more. According to one observer, the current world population "probably puts the world...at about its carrying capacity. It will be difficult to feed, clothe, shelter, and employ many more people at more than a subsistence level of life" (Cutler, 1986). Not all observers are as pessimistic, however, and many think that the world can indeed support a much larger population. How

FIGURE 12-1 WORLD POPULATION GROWTH

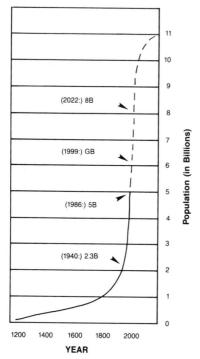

Sources: U.S. Bureau of the Census, *Statistical Abstract of the United States*, 1987:814, and Population Reference Bureau, 1985.

large, is a matter of conjecture. Furthermore, there is some evidence that the rate of world population growth is beginning to level off: The rate of world growth declined from roughly 1.9 percent per year in 1970 to 1.64 percent in 1975 (Douglas, 1976).

The Distribution of Population Growth   Brown (1976) has noted that the global reduction in the population growth rate has been accounted for by the declining birth rates in the industrial nations and parts of East Asia. This change in the developed nations can be understood in terms of what demographers have called the *demographic transition model*, which is a relatively simple conceptual model having three stages of population change.

"Primitive" social organization (Stage I) where mortality [is]...relatively high...and fertility is correspondingly high; "transitional" social organization (Stage II) where mortality is declining, fertility remains high, and the population exhibits high rates of natural increase; and a "modern" stage (Stage III)... where mortality has stabilized at a relatively low mean value, fertility is approaching the level of mortality, and a stationary population size is possible in the near future. (Humphrey and Buttel, 1982)

This model is represented schematically in Figure 12-2. What caused this demographic transition to occur in the industrial world? First, industrialization upgraded both manufacturing and agricultural productivity so that the economic base could support much larger populations. Second, medical advances in the control of epidemic disease and improvements in public services (urban sewage and water systems, garbage collection, etc.) contributed to improved health and reduced mortality rates. Third, as populations became increasingly urbanized family changes occurred. Children—their education and rearing—became more of an economic burden than an asset. Industrialization was coupled with opportunities for women to work outside the family and the establishment of national social security programs apart from kinship. Industrialization, therefore, had a variety of incentives for smaller families. In other words, as economic incentives changed, cultural norms promoting large families began to weaken. Finally, research shows that while industrialization is inversely related to fertility, another important consequence was the level of economic equality.

In the European nations the demographic and economic transitions led to a general improvement in living standards for all persons and a gradual reduction in income inequalities. (Birdsall, 1980)

However it came about, birth rates in all industrialized countries began to decline as economic development proceeded. I should emphasize that though the rate of population growth of the industrial nations is declining, their population base is very large in absolute numbers and even their lower rates of growth still add significantly to the absolute increases in world population.

FIGURE 12-2 DEMOGRAPHIC TRANSITION MODEL

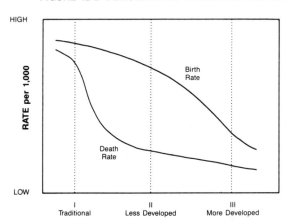

Stages of Socio-economic development

The third world is a very different story. Nine of ten babies born today live in the poorer regions of the globe. The reason that third world populations are growing very rapidly relative to the first world nations is that since World War II there has been a very rapid introduction of enough improvements in nutrition and public health care facilities to dramatically reduce the death rate. Babies born in the poor nations today have a historically unprecedented chance of surviving to adulthood. But economic development—with its widespread improvement in living standards, changed economic incentives, and establishment of social security systems not tied to kinship—has not kept pace with the rapid decline in mortality rates. As we saw in the last chapter, many of the LDCs are still mired in stalled, dependent, or deformed development, and the global recession of the 1970s and 1980s has exacerbated these trends. Traditional cultural norms favoring large families still exist in much of the third world. There may well be more Brazilians or Indians who are now vaguely middle class. But there are at the same time larger numbers of Brazilians and Indians than ever before in history who are landless peasants living in unprecedented squalor, chronic hunger, joblessness, and despair. In the terms of the demographic transition model, many third world nations seem stuck in Stage II, with rapid decreases in mortality but no reductions in fertility in sight.

In the third world there are large masses of displaced farmers pushed off the land by the consolidation of small subsistence farms into large cash-crop estates. But they are also demographic refugees, pushed off the land by the less visible but powerful population pressure of high birth rates in rural areas. Some have migrated to other countries where economic conditions are better: There is a small but growing stream of international migration from the LDCs to the industrial nations. But more significant is the pattern of internal migration from the countryside to the cities of the third world. Migration from the country to the city is an ancient pattern, but the *urbanization* of the first world nations was caused not only by the push of rural poverty but also by the pull of exploding economic opportunities in the industrializing cities. Urbanization in the third world is today largely a matter of the push of rural poverty without the concomitant pull of dynamic economic growth in the cities. Thus the cities of the third world, such as Calcutta, Cairo, Dakar, and Rio de Janeiro, are rapidly becoming awash with displaced peasants with grim prospects for fruitful urban employment. Perhaps the outstanding case is Mexico City, which by the year 2000 is expected to have a population of 31 million persons, eclipsing the size of New York and making it the largest urban area in the world (United Nations estimate, cited in Demerath, 1984:39). Urban populations in the third world, particularly in the largest cities, have increased much too rapidly for urban services to handle. Such populations have overwhelmed the ability of cities to provide jobs, water, sanitation, and food resources, and the resulting misery and degradation among recent urban immigrants is unprecedented.

Population Policy: Birth Control or Wealth Control?   There is disagreement about the significance of world population growth in the contemporary world problem (more about that later). But even among those who recognize population growth as a significant threat to global stability there is disagreement about how to address the problem. On one level this is an intellectual debate about cause and effect, but it is also a highly politicized debate, which became quickly apparent at the United Nations Conference on Population Policy held in Bucharest in 1974. Seven countries refused to send delegates to even discuss the problem, and the countries that did attend quickly separated into different factions (Pirages, 1978).

The major cleavage was between the representatives of the Western industrial nations and those of the LDCs and socialist bloc nations. In general, the representatives of the Western capitalist nations argued that the world is poor because it is becoming overpopulated. They argued that exponential population growth is a prime cause of global instability because it increases pressure on resources, creates scarcities, and undercuts economic development efforts in the third world. They were quick to point out that since the growth rates in the developed world were declining, the major responsibility for curbing world population growth lies with the LDCs themselves. Representatives of the LDCs argued to the contrary that the world is becoming overpopulated because it is so poor. They argued, consistent with the demographic transition model, that to expect exponential growth "to level off *before* economic development and redistribution of wealth takes place is to put the cart before the horse...that when people perceive no improvement in the living standards they will not change their behavior patterns on the promise of future benefits" (Pirages, 1978:60).[3] They argued that the prime cause of poverty in the developing nations was not population growth per se, but the economic constraints of dependent development vis-à-vis the developed nations. They also were quick to point out that if the concern is overconsumption of global resources, the real locus of the problem is with the developed nations, which consume 60 to 70 percent of the earth's annual production of natural resources, that are increasingly being used to meet nonessential wants of the Northern lifestyle, while obtaining raw material to satisfy basic human need in the poor countries is becoming much more difficult.

The rejoinder from the Western nations was that under present global circumstances it is simply not possible to support the world's population at a level consistent with Western living standards without devastating the resource base of the planet. There is some data to support this contention. Consider the consequences of miraculously and suddenly raising the Chinese alone with a population of over one billion to American consumption standards. The average American was supported by 11 tons of coal-equivalent energy in 1974, while the average Chinese consumed only two-thirds of a ton. Sustaining the Chinese at an American level would "require 9 million metric tons of coal equivalent in additional energy each year, which would increase present world energy consumption by more than 100 percent...and these figures do not even consider...[the high levels]...of other minerals that would be required to develop the industrial infrastructure needed to raise China to these high levels of development" (Pirages, 1978:62).

The Bucharest conference ended in a state of inconclusiveness. But the debate continues today about population policy. The third world nations in general still advocate policies that would require the redistribution of wealth from the North to the South and reorganize the world in more "equitable" terms. They have advocated the creation of a "New International Economic Order" (NIEO—as it has come to be called). Needless to say, this proposal is not popular with the dominant political and economic interest groups in the capitalist world. The Western nations largely continue to urge third world government to aggressively pursue programs of family planning and population control, even in the absence of significant economic development and in spite of the fact that such efforts have often failed abysmally in recent decades.

Population Growth and the World Problem   How significant a factor is population growth in terms of the current world problem? As you might guess, experts' answers to this question vary. There continue to be neo-Malthusians[4] who argue that population growth is creating a global disaster of the greatest magnitude, that it will lead only to widespread environmental despoliation, famine, disease, and war. But I think that the growing consensus among scholars is more moderate in tone. This consensus argues that world population growth is a significant component of the volatile world situation, but perhaps not the most important. A study by the National Academy of Sciences (NAS) in the mid-1980s took a middle-ground on the debate about the relationship of population growth to the well-being of people and economies. According to a member of the NAS working group on population and economic development "the rate of *populatiK*wth is an important variable, but there are many other variables that can have a greater effect on people's welfare," such as government pricing policies that discourage farmers from growing food (World Development Forum, 1986b). Similarly, Humphrey and Buttel suggest:

> One of the more important findings to come from a study of the relationship between population size and the environment is the misplaced importance given to world population size as a cause of natural resource scarcities and pollution....[we do not] imply that world population growth should be ...neglected as a cause of environmental problems, [but] a fixation on it as *the* major reason for pollution and energy crises would be sociologically misguided. (1982:60)

There are two bases of this more recent moderation about the significance of population growth *per se* as an inherently destabilizing force. First, as mentioned above, most analysts foresee that the world population growth rate is now beginning to level off and could stabilize in the future. Explanations for this vary: Some emphasize that population growth is leveling off in parts of the world because of widespread famine and material deprivation. But it is also true that the efforts of third world nations to brake population growth have had some significant successes, as well as many failures. Population limitation programs have been particularly successful in parts of East Asia, for instance in the Koreas (both), Taiwan, Malaysia. The rapid decline of fertility in China, with its over one billion people is very significant in terms of impact on world population growth. China is beginning to look more like a first world than a third world country in terms of its demographic growth rate. Evidence from the 1960s suggested that fertility control programs were mainly effective in countries with significant economic growth under conditions of relative social equality (Cuca, 1980). More recent and encouraging evidence suggests that such programs can be effective in nations that define development priorities primarily in terms of the alleviation of poverty rather than economic growth and high average income levels (Birdsall, 1980:10). A second, reason that world population growth is now judged by some to be a significant but not inevitably disastrous problem is that recent estimates suggest that *under certain conditions* the planet could comfortably carry a much larger population than exists at present. This judgment depends upon assessments of the resource base of Earth, technological potentials for its exploitation, and the political feasibility of developing efficient, equitable, and stable systems for the distribution of material resources on a global basis.

Dimension 2: Food, Hunger, and the World Problem

When we think about resource problems we often think about energy and mineral resources, but for many people on the globe the resource question is much more simple and concrete: What—if anything—is for dinner? The scope of the problem is vast: Hundreds of millions of people in the world suffer from chronic nutritional deficits. Hunger is certainly not a new problem; periodic famines are as old as humanity. Historically famines were caused by rather unpredictable events such as drought or wars that destroyed food supplies. But increasingly hunger is not caused by these whimsical events that create temporary food scarcity, but it is becoming a normal crisis that is likely to be an ongoing problem in certain parts of the world. Some 70 million people were starving in the mid-1970s, representing about 2 percent of the world's population at that time (Mastrand and Rush, 1978:82). In the 1980s there were regions of ongoing mass starvation, such as in Ethiopia and sub-Saharan Africa, that were displayed in vivid terms in the American media. But *the wider problem is chronic malnutrition.* Most people in the world are able to get enough food to survive, but over 700 million suffer dietary deficiencies (Mastrand and Rush, 1978:82). At least 25 percent of the third world population does not have a diet that meets minimum nutritional standards for amounts of protein or calories (Murdoch, 1980). Even in the developed United States there were at least 30 million people living in a state of poverty in 1980 who were likely to suffer malnutrition (Phillips, 1984:1). Such chronic malnutrition may not be as grotesquely visible as massive famine, but its consequences are nonetheless devastating: In children it delays physical maturity, impairs brain development, and reduces intelligence, even if replaced by an adequate diet later on. Malnourished adults are unable to work hard or long and have a lower resistance to disease. The danger of epidemics is always high in overpopulated and underfed areas (Coleman and Cressy, 1984:533).

Food and Population Growth   It is often argued, particularly by the neo-Malthusian thinkers mentioned above, that the growing problem of world hunger exists because population growth has relentlessly outstripped growth in the food-producing capacity of the world. *Surprisingly, that is not true.* Since the 1960s increases in food production have outstripped population growth on a global basis. By 1976 food production had grown 40 percent over the 1961-1965 levels, enough to effect a 10 percent per capita increase in global food supply (Food and Agriculture Organization, 1977). Increases in food production occurred during this period in all regions of the world, and production grew more rapidly in the third world than in the developed nations (Humphrey and Buttell, 1982:196).

But the whole story is not as optimistic as these global aggregate figures suggest. First, looking at world aggregate figures of the ratio between food and population we find that the margin of safety for food production has tightened considerably in recent years (see Table 12-1). Not accidentally, the slowdown in food production relative to population growth coincided with the first dramatic rise in the world price for oil, a significant component in agricultural production (e.g., for the manufacture of diesel fuel and fertilizers). Second, while per capita increases in food production for all regions was increasing until the mid-1970s, since then regions have begun to diverge, with some declining. The major food exporters can now be counted on the fingers of one hand (Argentina, Australia, Canada, France, and the United States) and food deficits have grown severe in Africa and the Middle East and parts of South Asia. Since 1978 food production has also fallen in Eastern Europe and the Soviet Union, not just in proportion to population size but also in absolute terms (a fact which is explainable more in terms of the political organization of Soviet-style agriculture rather than in technical and agronomic terms!). There are, however, some bright spots in the global picture. Western Europe, and—most significantly for the world population—India and China have recently become self-sufficiant in terms of food (Brown, 1986a:14).

Hunger and the World Problem   In a nutshell, then, the growing problems of starvation and world hunger are not due to the lack of resources or technical

TABLE 12-1 Annual Growth in World Grain Production, Total and Per Capita 1950-1973 and 1973-1985

Period	Grain Output(%)	Population(%)	Grain Output/Capita
1950-1973	3.1	1.9	1.2
1973-1985	2.2	1.8	0.4

Sources: Brown et al., 1986:14; U.S. Department of Agriculture, Economic Research Service, World Indices of Agricultural and Food Production, 1950-85, Washington, DC, 1985.

capacity to feed the world's population. They are rather a *maldistribution* problem: Many of the world's most efficient food-producing regions have small or low-density populations, and many of the densely populated and rapidly growing regions are increasingly less self-sufficient. This maldistribution is not only because the high output regions are superficially more efficient at producing food, though that is certainly true. Food productivity in most regions has increased (until recently), but a major problem is that the development policies of the poorer nations have not, until recently, emphasized food production for domestic consumption as a priority. To put it another way, the world hunger problem is not because population is outstripping the growth in food production, but rather because of *inequality* both within nations and between them. The poor simply are not able to consume their share of the world's food, and increases in food production itself will not address this problem without the global redistribution of wealth or the capacity to produce food—making most nations self-sufficient. The problem of world hunger is more political and economic than technical.

That is true of the present, but what of the future? There are indeed causes for the alarm that has been voiced for years. There is concern that the land in many parts of the world is being overfarmed, so that soil fertility is declining. This concern is not only for parts of the tropics with very fragile soil systems that are being rapidly depleted, but also with the prospects for continued productivity increases in temperate climates. The vaunted American agricultural productivity is, for instance, of doubtful stability in the longer run, because topsoil is being systematically eroded, and in many areas the water tables are being exhausted or seriously polluted by fertilizers and pesticides. Yet even with these fears, projections about the future of world food productivity are rather optimistic. They indicate that the world as a whole can theoretically produce enough food to feed projected populations for the foreseeable future. In 1984 the World Bank estimated the maximum global food output is 7.5 billion tons grain equivalent a year, enough to support some 11.5 billion people, which is the projected level of worldwide stationary population growth (World Bank, 1984:91). The situation of individual countries and of the poor within those countries is far less reassuring. Here is how another authoritative source described the situation:

> We...conclude that regulation of world food supply will be important at least for the next thirty years; that South East Asia and Latin America will continue to be the most vulnerable regions; but that even the worst assumptions about increased food production provide for a basic minimum diet for all between 2000 and 2030 and a 'Euro diet' by 2050. The most optimistic assumptions produce a world-wide 'Euro diet' between 2000 and 2030. (Mastrand and Rush, 1978:92.)

World hunger could become a less important problem if (1) population growth begins to level off sooner rather than later, (2) more land can be brought into production, (3) increases in productivity can be sustained and increased in the world's poorer regions, (4) more effective utilization of the seas as food resources is possible, (5) much of the land currently used for nonfood production (e.g., tobacco) can be shifted back to producing food for domestic markets, and (6) a global "deal" can be struck among nations to distribute global food resources on a more equitable basis. Those are *very big ifs*. Nevertheless, it is possible that everyone will have enough to eat in the next century. The central problems may not be supply but distribution. Distribution problems are not trivial or easy to solve. They involve very hard choices among limited options and inevitable conflicts among nations and interest groups within nations. And there is a hitch in the supply side of the issue that may prove to be intractable. All schemes to sustain increases in food productivity require higher inputs of *energy resources* to manufacture fertilizers and other essential material inputs.

Dimension 3: Energy and the World Problem

It is no longer news to talk about problems with the world's energy supplies, but there is little popular agreement about the seriousness of these problems. Certainly there was less popular concern about the "energy crisis" in the mid-1980s than there was in the 1970s because of the increasing supplies and decreasing prices of oil in the 1980s (whether these conditions will last into the 1990s and beyond is an important question). The opinion of energy experts is also varied, but I think that there is some consensus among contemporary analysts that sustaining the world's energy consumption will be technically and politically a *most* difficult aspect of the world problem. Furthermore, the way that we deal with energy problems will condition our ability to successfully cope with problems of population, food, and problems of economic development and equity.

One fact is indisputable: world energy consumption has dramatically increased in the last half century. It has increased not just in aggregate terms, but per capita consumption has increased in all parts of the world.

> Commercial energy consumption increased about tenfold between 1900 and 1974, the rate of increase being particularly rapid in the period since 1950. The relative importance of the Western market economies in total consumption declined to 60 percent (...of the world total...) in 1974, whilst that of Eastern Europe and the USSR increased to 23 percent and that of poor countries to 17 percent. (Chesshire and Pavitt, 1978:118)

Along with this phenomenal growth in energy consumption, the "mix" of resources used changed as well.

> The relative importance of coal declined steadily from over 90 percent in 1900 to 32 percent in 1974, whilst that of oil increased over the same period from 4 to 45 percent and natural gas from 1 to 21 percent. The substitution of oil and natural gas

for coal as been particularly rapid since 1950. In poor countries, the "non-commercial" fuels such as wood, dung, human and animal power have been steadily replaced by fossil fuels. (Chesshire and Pavitt, 1978:118)

You can get some subjective sense of this enormous level of energy consumption in the contemporary world by considering that in 1980 the world consumed almost 300,000 gallons of petroleum each *second* (Barnet, 1980:21).

Assuming present and probable technologies of production and other optimistic circumstances, it is also a fact that the historic increase in the growth of energy consumption cannot be sustained far beyond the next hundred years (or very far beyond about 2100). That is a fact, but not an indisputable one. It is at least the middle of the road opinion among energy analysts. While growth rates in energy consumption have changed somewhat in recent years (more about that below), the underlying and *important fact* is that the fossil fuels upon which the world relies are *finite*, and are someday going to be very scarce. At some point in time the world will literally run out of gas at a price that anyone will be able to afford. I will return to contemporary trends and energy problems, but first let's briefly survey the situation and prospects regarding various energy resources.

Energy Resources and Supplies   Most of the world's energy needs are supplied by *finite resources*, mainly fossil fuels such as petroleum, natural gas, and coal. Another finite resource, uranium, fuels nuclear reactors that supply a small portion of the world's energy (about 3 percent). *Renewable resources* that are not used up as finite resources are also supply a portion of the world's energy needs. Hydroelectric power is a major such resource, and in the third world a variety of organic materials (firewood, dung, crop wastes) are still major sources of energy and fuel. There are other potential renewable energy sources (solar, wind power, geothermal, tidal) but at present none supplies a significant portion of the world's energy budget.

Estimating supplies of world energy resources is very complicated, technical, and speculative, yet it is unlikely that there are *vast* supplies of conventional energy resources that are yet to be discovered. Table 12-2 is an authoritative estimate of U.S. and global energy reserves made a decade or so ago by M. King Hubbert, a widely respected geologist and for years chief geologist of the U.S. Geological Survey.

Hubbert's estimates were made on the basis of projecting the growth rates of energy consumption and estimates of known reserves that existed in the early 1970s. Even though these consumption rates have changed since then, more recent estimates of known energy reserves have modified Hubbert's estimates only marginally (see, for example, Chesshire and Pavitt, 1978:122; Holdren, 1975; Brown, 1986; Flavin, 1986; Yergin and Hillenbrand, 1982). Table 12-3 (p. 249) summarizes in a more descriptive way the situation for both finite and renewable energy resources.

TABLE 12-2 Hubbert's Analysis of Conventional Fossil Fuel Supplies

	Estimate of Ultimately Recoverable Resources (10^{18} kJ)*	Year of Peak Production (year)	Year When 90 Percent Is Gone
U..S. petroleum	1.4	1970	2000
U.S. natural gas	1.6	1980	2015
U.S. coal	42.8	2220	2450
World petroleum	12.4	2000	2030
World coal	218.0	2150	2400

*kJ = kilojoules, an energy measure; the amount of work required to move 1 newton of mass (N) over 1 meter multiplied by 1,000.

Source: Reprinted from John Holdren, 1975, "Energy Resources," in Murdock (ed.), *Environment: Resources, Pollution, and Society*. Copyright © 1975 by Sinauer Associates. Used with permission of the publisher.

The numbers that express the energy-producing potential (10^9 tons of coal equivalent) of various energy sources don't have much subjective meaning for us, but they are index numbers that give you a relative sense of the availability and potential of various resources.

From Tables 12-2 and 12-3 you can see that oil and natural gas are in very short supply, and most analysts don't think that future resource discoveries will be very large. There is a vast supply of coal, but coal is hazardous to mine and a dirty, toxic fuel to burn. The by-products of coal-burning plants (sulfur dioxide and nitrogen oxides) are not only toxic to humans, but destructive of the natural environment. The acid rain produced at least in part from coal-fired plants is damaging lakes, streams, and forests in many areas of the world (e.g., in eastern United States, Europe). Coal is everybody's least favorite fuel, but there is a lot of it. There was once great optimism about producing oil from shale rock formations and tar sands, but this has faded as it has become aparent that this process is so destructive of the environment and requires so much energy and water that it is almost inherently uneconomical.

While nuclear power supplies about 3 percent of the world's and 10 to 15 percent of the industrial world's power needs, enthusiam for its further development has faded. The hazards of nuclear energy are well known: (1) There is always risk of a nuclear catastrophe like the ones at Three Mile Island or Chernobyl; (2) no one knows how to safely dispose of radioactive nuclear wastes (of which the typical plant produces about 2,400 tons a year!); (3) a vast increase in nuclear energy would greatly increase the costs of uranium, of which world supplies are very uncertain; and most importantly, (4) nuclear plants are *very* expensive to build. The strongest barriers to the expansion of nuclear energy are not the safety hazards (though they are considerable) but economic ones. In 1984 a nuclear plant cost three times as much to build as a coal-fired plant with state-of-the-art pollution control equipment, and the costs differential has

TABLE 12-3   Energy Resources: Characteristics, Problems, and Uncertainties

Resource	Supply Estimate		Problems, Uncertainties
Finite resources	*Proven/possible reserves (109 tce*)*	*Theoretical recoverable*	
Coal	1,000	much more 5-7700	supply vast; problems with toxic pollutants, mining hazards; not as versatile as oil for many uses
Oil	300-375	very uncertain 150-2760	energy use competes with uses for fertilizer, plastics, etc.; rapidly dwindling supply; at 1985 rate of consumption ultimate depletion 50-100 years away
Natural Gas	200	uncertain 150-1500	high caloric value; burns clean; difficult to transport; bulky to store
Shale Oil	negligible	1400	very expensive to produce; may be inherently uneconomical; 1 barrel requires much water and moving 1.7 tons of earth; destructive of natural environment
Nuclear Fission (uranium)	80-100	uncertain	supplies uncertain; very costly to build plants; problems with nuclear disasters, sabotage, and radioactive waste disposal
Nuclear "Breeder" Reactors	none	vast; reaction makes own fuel	problems proving technical feasibility, containing reaction
Geothermal	12-60	large	problem proving technical feasibility; using low grade heat
Renewable resources	*Proven potential*	*Theoretical potential*	
Direct Solar	uncertain	80,000	limitless supply, vast potential; problems with storage and large-scale applications
Hydro-Electric	uncertain	uncertain	high capital costs; use of water competes with residential/ industrial/agricultural uses
Wind Power	uncertain	400	problems with storage
Firewood, Dung, Waste Crops (forests)	1-2	40	major resources in less developed countries; problems with environmental destruction and net energy gain—it may take more energy to collect and use than you get in return

* *Equivalence in tons of coal* calculated on a thermal basis for hydrocarbons and geothermal, solar, firewood, dung, and waste crops; on a primary fuel equivalence basis for nuclear energy, hydroelectric, and wind power.

Sources: Adapted from John Chesshire and Keith Pavitt, 1978, "Some Energy Futures," in Freemand and Jahoda (eds.), *World Futures 1978*, London: Martin Robinson. Copyright by the Science Policy Research Unit, University of Sussex. Used with permission of the Science Policy Research Unit; Flavin, 1986:89; and Bassis, Gelles, and Levine, 1982:95.

been steadily widening (Alexander, 1984:34). Hard, cold economics is preventing the expansion of nuclear energy in a way that thousands of hot-blooded antinuclear demonstrators could not (Flavin, 1984). Similarly enthusiasm has faded for the development of nuclear breeder reactors that produce their own fuel. Such nuclear fusion reactions are so intense that it is doubtful that they could be contained.

Most of the renewable energy sources have a limited potential for contributing to the world's energy budget. While organic materials (firewood, dung, plant fibers) provide fuel in many parts of the world their contribution on a global scale cannot be increased much. Since they take much energy to collect and use, there is not much "net energy gain" in using organic fuels. Wood, in fact, has been overexploited as a fuel source. Since World War II, fully *half* of the world's forests have been cut, some for commercial lumber, but most for firewood. This growing shortage is not only significant in its own right, but has devastating effects on the environment: When the tree cover is removed, soil erodes rapidly and water tables may fall. Wind and tidal power have a significant but limited potential. Solar energy has the greatest potential. An enormous amount of radiant energy falls on the earth's surface which—if trapped and converted into usable forms—could supply the needs of the globe. The technology does not now exist to convert solar energy directly into electricity on a large scale at an economical cost, and there are problems with storage and transmisson. Though the rudiments of such technology are known, it would take several decades of investment and technological effort to develop.

Solar energy is not now practical for the mass production of electricity, but it is now practical for *space heating*—to heat homes, offices, and buildings. The technology of using solar collectors for space and water heating is relatively simple and well known, and it is possible to retrofit an older home to significantly reduce the dependence on natural gas or coal-generated electricity for heating water or rooms. Though more feasible in some regions than in others, the potential for reducing America's aggregate energy bill in this manner is enormous, and it will become a more attractive option if the cost of natural gas rises significantly—as is expected—in the 1990s. It would require public investment and a lead time of several decades to convert existing housing stock to decentralized solar space heating in this fashion.

Technological "Fixes" and Speculative Ideas About Energy   There have always been suggestions about more far-fetched technological breakthroughs that could provide quick technological "fixes" to the world's energy problems. What are some of these speculations? One suggestion is to produce hydrogen gas from ordinary water[5] and use it as a fuel on a massive basis. Problems with this idea are that it now takes as much or more energy to produce the gas than you get in return, and there are many safety problems in handling hydrogen, a highly combustible gas. Another idea is to develop the high frontier in outer space, by moving a substantial human population into colonies in orbit as sites for industrial production, to construct satellites that beam solar energy to the earth, and to mine the moon and asteroid belts for minerals and energy materials

(O'Neill, 1977). Another possibility would be the development of the technology to drill "deep" wells (below four or five miles) to exploit very deep natural gas formations that are widely thought to exist in areas such as the Anadarko basin geological formation that underlies most of North America. Exactly how much gas could be added from these deep formations is unknown, but it could be substantial (Osborne, 1984). Finally, among the more speculative theories in vogue is the theory by a few maverick scientists that crude oil is in fact of abiogenic geological origin (rather than from fossil sediments) and in fact is not limited at all. We just have been looking in the wrong places (Osborne, 1986). These are all certainly possibilities, but they are low probability ones, according to more conservative assessments of likely technical developments. They don't deserve to be ignored, but they are "wild cards," so to speak. One can't depend on their being in the deck.

Having briefly surveyed the contemporary situation regarding energy resources, let me turn to some critical issues about the relationship between energy consumption and the quality of social life.

Energy and the Quality of Social Life   It is a well-established fact that among the nations of the world there is a strong positive correlation between per capita energy consumption and the gross national product (Darmstadter, 1971; Cook, 1971; Humphrey and Buttel, 1982:156). But equally important is the considerable variation among nations between levels of consumption and *per capita* incomes. The correlation between energy consumption and per capita incomes still exists, but it is quite small, particularly among the developed industrial nations. Among them, per capita incomes are similar (within 10% of each other) but there are major variations in their levels of consumption (Makhijani and Lichtenberg, 1972). The United States, for instance, consumes roughly twice as much inanimate energy on a per capita basis as does Sweden, but Sweden's per capita income level is very similar to that of the United States. The point is that some societies are much more energy-frugal than others, and it is possible to support a relatively high Euro-American standard of living at far less than current American levels of energy consumption. These are partly due to differences in climate, but also to differences in the importance of energy-intensive industries, lifestyles, and the general efficiency of energy conversion and use (Darmstadter, 1971).

In spite of these variations, the energy crunch of supply shortages and price increases expected by the late 1990s would have negative effects on all national economies. That is because an adequate energy supply is so basic to the maintenance of economic production, food supplies, employment, and ultimately all aspects of human social life. You only have to look at the 1970s to get some understanding of the social consequences of such an energy crunch. During this decade, when the price of a barrel of oil tripled, there was a world economic recession that affected all nations. In the industrial nations the costs of living rose, there were gasoline shortages, production cutbacks, increases in unemployment, and economic problems of all sorts. Many third world nations, being virtually shut out of the expensive world oil market, were unable to purchase fertilizers and other material inputs to sustain food production, let alone invest in economic development. Foreign debts increased to pay for more expensive energy supplies and most development schemes were derailed and postponed. The energy crunch of the 1970s was indirectly responsible for much of the growing malnutrition, misery, and frustrated expectations within the third world. These economic dislocations had political consequences. During the 1970s there was an increase in political tensions within nations, between the first and third world, and among the industrial nations. Certainly not all of the economic and political volatility of the 1970s was caused by the "tight" global energy picture, but it was an underlying context that amplified the other causes of these problems. And if the improved energy picture of the 1980s has somewhat alleviated such global stresses it is certain that the return of a tight energy situation in the 1990s will bring back such problems with a vengeance.

Let me summarize the argument that I have been making: Although there is considerable variation between nations, there is indisputable evidence that the level of energy consumption is broadly and positively related to economic, political, and social well-being. As a corollary, there is historical evidence that resource shortages and high energy prices lower the levels of human well being and increase economic and political tensions, both within and between nations. Changes in the availability of energy are certainly not the sole or the most direct cause of variations in human well-being, but other factors that more directly affect social well being are broadly conditioned by the energy context. And in the absence of a miraculous technological breakthrough, most energy analysts think that supplies will become very tight in the near term future.

Contemporary Trends in Energy Consumption   First, *the good news*. In the industrial world which consumes two-thirds of the world's energy, oil consumption has declined significantly since the 1970s. Between 1979 and 1984 consumption declined 18 percent in Western Europe and 16 percent in both North America and Japan (Flavin, 1986:79). Some but not all of this decline was due to the economic sluggishness of the 1970s. But oil consumption *per unit of gross national product* also fell 36 percent between 1973 and 1984 (International Energy Agency, 1985). These improvements have outstripped even the more optimistic forecasts and continue to exceed official forecasts. Greater energy efficiency accounts for over half of this decline in the energy/GNP ratio. They stem in part from simple housekeeping measures (turning down thermostats, driving less often, and driving more slowly) and in part from the development of more energy-efficient technologies (in the design of homes, autos, appliances, etc.). Such energy-efficient machines take years to develop but can be expected to gradually replace older less energy-efficient stocks (Flavin, 1986:84-85). The changing mix of energy fuels accounts for another large part of the decline in oil use. Since 1973 oil's share of world energy use has fallen from 41 to 35 percent and continues to decline. Coal use has increased (from 25 to 28%) and the use of natural gas and renewables has increased modestly. These trends represent good news, for the most part, since oil is the most severely limited resource, though— as I mentioned above—a cloud of difficulties still hangs over the increasing utilization of coal.

What is *the bad news*? Ironically, some of the short-run good news may prove to be bad news in the longer run. The momentum to develop more energy efficiency and to conserve was undoubtedly stimulated by the rise in oil prices during the 1970s. New oil fields were exploited (in Mexico and the North Sea). The addition of these supplies combined with the internal conflict for control within OPEC had the consequence of increasing market competitiveness and lowering the price of oil, from $35 per barrel in 1981 to $27 in 1985. That is certainly good short-term news to the consumers of the world. But the new oil fields are not vast and will not last long—the deepest reserves are still in the Middle East. In the meantime there is danger that the complacent mood of the 1980s will begin to undermine efforts at conservation and investment in energy alternatives. "Declining prices have already led many countries to cut successful energy programs that would have provided substitutes for oil in the nineties" (Flavin, 1986:79). In the United States, for instance, tax credits for home insulation and research funds for developing solar energy have all but vanished. The hard part is continuing the political and technical momentum to develop innovative energy strategies at a time when it is easy to be complacent. It is to these strategies that I now turn. If there is an energy crisis *today*, it is the absence of energy policies that look to the future—even the near-term future.

Energy Strategies to the Year 2000   Energy strategies and policies of the nations of the world—to the extent that they even exist—have for the most part emphasized the *expansion of supply* as a means of coping with energy problems (Humphrey and Buttel, 1982:183). In the United States, deregulating energy prices and giving tax incentives for exploration and development have had the effect of modestly increasing domestic energy supplies. Such a policy is popular partly because it makes minimal demands for altering lifestyles, living standards, and modes of production. It is also politically easy because it benefits the vested economic interests that currently control the energy industry. As an exclusive policy, however, it is self-defeating in the longer run; it encourages us to use up finite fuel supplies at a more rapid rate. It only hastens the day of reckoning.

A second strategy emphasizes *conservation*, and, as I argued above, much can be gained from conservation measures alone. At least the day of reckoning (if there is to be one) is postponed. Conservation has at least three forms. One is *technological* and emphasizes developing more efficient machines and patterns of production. Second is an *economic* form of conservation, which raises prices to discourage consumption and conserve scarce resources. The third form of conservation is *social-psychological*, caused by changing the values and habits of people so that they use less energy and adopt frugal lifestyles. Of these three modes of conservation I think that the economic one is the most straightforward, and it undoubtedly works. In a private market context, when supplies become scarce, prices will rise and aggregate consumption will decline. But the economic market strategy is a way of adjusting to existing scarcity, not a way of altering energy consumption behavior before shortages develop. In addition, the economic solution to conservation is socially regressive; it makes far greater demands on the poor, and on poor nations in comparison to the wealthier ones. Social justice requires, in my view, that we not pursue an economic conservation strategy unalloyed with political policies that attempt to equitably distribute the costs of such a policy. However, I think that the other two strategies of conservation and cannot entirely work in the absence of some form of economic incentives. That is, it is difficult to see how consumer lifestyles (e.g., riding bicycles or using mass transit rather than personal autos) could be significantly altered without at least some economic incentives. The same is true of the technological strategy. Both of these must be long term efforts. Technological strategies for conservation require long years of investment and mobilization of research capabilities to bring to fruition. Social psychological strategies may entail vast public campaigns to produce social change by altering behavior and attitudes (see Chapter 10 about campaign strategies).

A further limitation of the conservation strategy is that most attention has been paid to the individual-residential sector of energy consumption, which accounts for only about 34 percent of national energy consumption in the United States (Leik and Kolmann, 1977). Hence if significant individual conservation were to occur, it would have an important but limited impact on national energy consumption. Most of the energy is consumed in production activities in agriculture, industry, and transportation. The development of a high tech capitalist economy with a large oligopolistic sector has its own "treadmill of production," as Schnaiberg (1980) has called it. In other words, the effort to maintain profitability and corporate growth has required ever increasing uses of energy in production. The same situation exists in American agriculture which, for its highly advertised efficiency has become increasingly energy intensive. It is difficult to see how significant conservation could be practiced in production without a substantial overhaul of economic production institutions both in capitalist and socialist nations, which—ideology notwithstanding—seem to possess similar growth dynamics. In spite of these complexities and difficulties with conservation strategies, they have demonstrably worked in recent years, and they are strategies that can work now while we develop longer-range alternative technologies and sources for the world's energy needs.

A third energy strategy involves *developing innovative energy conversion technologies from unconventional sources.* This means the expanding use of alternative resources, particularly the renewable ones discussed above. A considerable potential exists to develop such energy technologies. On one level the problems are technical, but to resolve them requires significant investment in research and the sustained mobilization of talent and political will. The solar option in particular has a considerable potential for development. Other renewable resource technologies could make significant but small contributions to the mix of energy sources. The most viable energy research policy would pursue a number of different options to maximize the chances that some combination of them would pay off.

In sum, I think that the most viable and responsible energy strategy in the near-term future would emphasize *conservation* and deemphasize the *expansion of supply* as a means of adjusting frugally to the world's limited energy supplies. Coal could gradually replace the consumption of oil and gas but only within the boundaries of responsible health and ecological constraints. The *longer-term strategy* for the year 2000 and beyond must depend on the development of alternative technologies using renewable resources, particularly solar energy. But the frugal use of conventional sources must make do until then, barring unexpected technological breakthroughs.

Dimension 4: Environment and the World Problem

The foregoing shows a qualified optimism about the potential to resolve global problems of population growth, food, and even energy. But before leaving these concerns let us return briefly to concerns about the environmental impact of human activity. At the risk of being redundant, let me reiterate a theme introduced at the beginning of the chapter: the growth, feeding, and material supply of human populations makes demands upon the environment. What is the state of the environment?

Damage to the Carrying Capacity of the Environment   Historically human populations and consumption levels were well below any threshold of permanent damage to the ecosystem. Even during the period of rapid global economic expansion since World War II, it has been possible to ignore ecological concepts such as carrying capacity, "largely because the human demands on biological systems were well below their sustainable yields. With the quadrupling of world economic activity since mid-century, however, human demands are beginning to exceed sustainable yield thresholds in country after country" (Brown, 1986a:38). In Table 12-4 there is a bill of particulars of contemporary environmental concerns.

As you can see, there are indeed visible signs today that the environment and atmosphere are being degraded in many ways. The effects of environmental and resource degradation are most evident in parts of the third world, particularly in Africa. In the industrial nations the short-run effects of such ecological processes can often be masked by increasing capital and technological inputs to sustain production. But in the longer run the industrial nations are not immune from the impacts of ecological change. The connection between ecological degradation, economic production, and the quality of social life is subtle, long range, but profound.

Longer-range Environmental Threats   There are longer-range threats to the global environment. Among the more important of these are the strong indications that human economic activity is gradually altering the climate and atmospheric conditions of the planet. Industrial production is adding significant amounts of carbon dioxide and other industrial wastes to the atmosphere. At the same time the earth's forests, the primary reconverters of carbon dioxide back

TABLE 12-4   Environmental Depletion That Has Adverse Economic Effects

Resource	Extent of Depletion
Forests	World's tropical forests are disappearing at 2 percent per year, far faster in Africa and Southeast Asia, where moist tropical forest will have virtually disappeared by end of century. Previously stable forests in temperate zone now suffer from air pollution and acid rain—dead and dying forests are plainly visible in West Germany, Czechoslovakia, and Poland.
Grasslands	Excessive pressure on grasslands, closely paralleling growing pressure on forests and soils, has led to deterioration, which is most advanced in Africa and the Middle East. Herd liquidation in pastoral economies of Africa is now commonplace.
Fisheries	Rapid growth in world fish catch during 50s and 60s is now history; overfishing is often the rule, not the exception. Fish catch per person, including from fish farming, is down 15 percent since 1970, with biggest consumption cuts in third world countries such as the Philippines.
Soil	Soil erosion exceeds new soil formation on 35 percent of world's cropland. The world is losing an estimated 7 percent on topsoil per decade. Effects are most evident in Africa, where 40 percent of people live in countries where land productivity is lower than it was a generation ago.
Water	Growing water demand exceeds sustainable supplies in many locations, leading to scarcity. Falling water tables are now found on every continent and in key food-producing regions. In some areas, including portions of the United States, water is being shifted out of irrigated agriculture to satisfy growing residential demands.

Source: Adapted from Lester R. Brown, "A generation of deficits," in Brown et al., eds., *The State of the World: A Worldwatch Institute Report*, New York: W.W. North, 1986, page 110. Used with permission of the Worldwatch Institute.

into oxygen through plant respiration, are being decimated both by being used as fuel and by industrial pollutants themselves (in the form of acid rain). The net effect of these two changes is to subtly alter the oxygen-carbon dioxide balance of the atmosphere. The increased levels of carbon dioxide and other pollutants may not be immediately toxic, but it is widely thought that their accumulation in the atmosphere will produce a *greenhouse effect* that will trap more of the sun's radiant heat energy and cause a gradual warming of the earth's atmosphere. This is not just idle speculation: The amount of carbon dioxide (due to the burning of coal, wood, oil, and gas) has increased about 25 percent in the last 100 years and is expected to double by around 2050. And studies show that the annual global temperature has gone up about 1 degree in the last century, and can be expected to rise by 4 to 8 degrees by 2050 (Newhouse News Service, 1986). The causal connection between increasing carbon dioxide concentrations and rising global temperatures is circumstantial. To some extent the earth's temperature may be gradually rising due to natural long-range fluctuations. But most climatologists are convinced that the greenhouse effect greatly amplifies such long-range fluctuations.

The effects of even these seemingly modest rises in global temperatures over an extended time period would cause significant alterations in the earth's climate and weather patterns. Some of the polar ice caps would melt, flooding many of the world's densely inhabited coastal areas. Some areas would become wetter, and in others, large areas of desert would gradually appear in what are now moist, fertile areas. The tropics would be stricken with unprecedented heat waves, and the prime agricultural areas in the temperate zones would shift northward (and southward), where in many instances the topsoil is thinner than it is in the present grainbelt regions of the world. American agriculture

> could be severely disrupted. Warmer weather will mean longer growing seasons, but more heat and less rainfall will also cause major shifts in both dry-land and ir-rigated farming. Overall, the nation's bountiful harvests are likely to drop sig-nificantly....Corn production is projected to drop 20 percent, soybeans 10 to 15 percent with a 3.5 degree Fahrenheit temperature increase and a 10 percent decrease in precipitation. (Newhouse News Service, 1986b)

Besides the rise in atmospheric temperatures there is another industrial pol-lutant threat to the atmospheric environment. As of 1986 some 770,000 tons of chlorofluorocarbon gases are released into the atmosphere each year (*Boston Globe*, 1986). Scientists have suspected for some time that these gases (includ-ing Freon used in air conditioners, refrigerators, aerosol sprays and plastic foam) are gradually accumulating in the atmosphere and that they chemically react to destroy the ozone gas layer in the upper atmosphere. It is this ozone layer that filters out much of the harmful ultraviolet radiation from the sun, and the weakening of this layer has the potential to increase radiation levels and sig-nificantly increase the long-term incidence of skin cancer among humans. Al-though the evidence of effect is speculative, it was discovered in 1986 that the ozone layer above the Antarctic has decreased more than 40 percent since 1975, and many scientists think this decline is due to the buildup of these man-made ozone-eating gases.

Ecological threats are often less obvious and harder to perceive than are the threats of immediate hunger or near-term threats of economic disruption. Ecological disruptions, except for dramatic events such as oil spills, accumulate slowly, and the thresholds of toxicity and points of no return in terms of the rebalancing capacity of the environment are very real threats to human welfare. In fact, exactly what these thresholds are is largely guesswork, even among ex-perts. But I think that is important for you to recognize that the concerns sug-gested by the ecological perspective are very real threats to the quality of human life on the planet.

SUMMARY: THE GLOBAL SYSTEM AND THE WORLD PROBLEM

This whole chapter has been an argument that there is an emerging world sys-tem and, consequently, a world problem with interpenetrating dimensions (population growth, hunger, energy resources, environmental problems). I hope by now you can see that these factors affect the future quality of life (if not the survival) of individuals and nations. The world problem today is not caused by any one dimension: It is rather sustained by the ongoing interaction between them. And coping with the world problem requires that we somehow attend to all of these dimensions and the ways that they interact.

Feeding the growing world population requires an increase in and a more equitable distribution of the world's food supply. Similarly, not only social justice, but the solution to the population problem itself seems to require increasing economic output in a manner that raises the living standards of much of the world's population. The ability of the world to do this depends, in turn, on how well we navigate the difficult choices about sustaining the world's energy supply. Since these three dimensions all require concern with with resources, consumption levels, and wastes, they ultimately fold into the ecological question. This is, I think, the supremely important long-range dimension, since it is about the maintenance of the geophysical carrying capacity of the earth to support human social life. The environmental dimension of the world problem is different from the others because it raises most profoundly the issue of possible geophysical limits to growth—a value and strategy that we often use in attacking the other dimensions of the world problem. Recognizing that as individuals we live in the short run, it is also important to realize that long-run human survival in any reasonably positive terms requires that we do not opt for short-run solutions that destroy the carrying capacity of the earth to support human life. Arriving at a reasonable balance between short-run needs versus long-term interests and between national versus global interests confronts humans with a complex and difficult range of choices.

All that is certainly enough to worry about. The problems of collectively producing a viable human future are enormous. But equally impressive—to me at least—are the possibilities of human inventiveness, and the abilities of humans to both adapt to necessities and shape the directions of change.

In this chapter I have focused mainly on demographic, resource, and biophysical dimensions of the world problem. In the next chapter I turn to the equally important political and social dimensions and to some contemporary thinking about the future of the world.

NOTES

1. Environmental sociology (a subdiscipline that grew in the late 1960s) has described conventional social science as being implicitly done in a "human exemptionalism paradigm," whereby humans alone among other species are treated as being more or less exempt from the limitations of the natural system. It has called for recasting social science theory in terms of a "new ecological paradigm," which views human social life as ultimately rooted in nature (see, for instance, Catton and Dunlap, 1980:22-26).

2. I have not talked about solving the crises of the world problem. You can solve once and for all contrived puzzles, but not problems deeply embedded in the structure of social life. While they cannot be solved, such problems can be ameliorated or moderated by policies so that their effects are less severe on the lives of humans. Thus I have *moderated the effects* of problems rather than *solving* them.

3. In a study of the failure of India's family-planning programs, Mamdani (1972) argues that the poor in developing nations have compelling reasons to have large families: (1) children provide a form of old-age support; (2) children provide economic support through their labor on the farm or the sale of their labor to others; and (3) children add little to household expenditures in a condition of deep poverty. In these conditions, he argued, chronic poverty does not provide the incentives for reduced fertility.

4. So termed because they repeat, in a modified way, the arguments of the eighteenth century thinker Thomas Malthus, who argued that there was an inherent tendency for population to grow faster than food supplies.

5. Every high school chemistry student has probably done this as a laboratory exercise.

CHAPTER THIRTEEN
WORLD FUTURES

The desire to look into the future is very ancient, and every society probably has had its seers, visionaries, and prophets who had a special role in envisioning the future. But in times when human populations were smaller and more isolated, and the resources of the earth seemed limitless, it was probably less important to be concerned with the future except in times of widespread crisis. Today *not* thinking about the future seems irresponsible, because both as individuals and nations we are being increasingly pulled into the future by the thickening web of global connections. More than ever today we need to be concerned with how the global events shape the nature of the world that our children and grandchildren will inherit. This is difficult, because as individuals and nations we naturally tend to be more concerned with "making do" in the present and let the future take care of itself. It is nonetheless true however, that how we behave now, in connection with other global actors, shapes the possibilities of what is to come.

While the visionary, prophet, or seer is a social role as ancient as mankind, since the 1960s a significant network of scholars has emerged that has made serious intellectual attempts to envision the future. These "futurists" come from different areas of expertise, such as philosophy and literature as well as the social and physical sciences, and have used methods as diverse as literary scenarios, panels of experts, and computer simulations. The futurist enterprise has been sponsored by business and government agencies around the globe, and their writings have been immensely popular.[1] Such speculations always fascinate us. To be quite honest their record for accurate and detailed prediction of the future has not been much better than that of traditional prophets and seers (given the pessimism of much of the thinking about the future, that is cause for hope!). In point of fact it is impossible to predict the future in any accurate detail. There are simply too many variables that interact in unpredictable ways.

Yet to dismiss futurism because concrete predictions often go awry misses an important point. I agree with Edward Cornish, an influential futurist who argued that the primary goal of futurism is not to predict the future accurately but rather to help people make better decisions so that a better future can be created. Similarly, physicist Dennis Gabor argues that "We cannot predict the future; we can only invent it" (cited in Pohl, 1981:7). In other words, the future is not some inexorable unfolding of trends that will inevitably come, regardless of what people think or do about them. People are not passive observers of trends. Once they become aware of trends that are underway they often behave—both individually and collectively—in ways that modify the likelihood that the trends will continue without modification. And it is also true that our *visions* of the future are—in themselves—important factors that shape which futures do in fact come into being. In short I think that it is important to understand major trends not because they proceed in an unaltered way, but because they contain *implications for possible alternative futures*. One can't "know" the future with any great certainty, but one *can* consider visions of alternative futures. That is what this chapter is about.

The last chapters focused on modernization, development, and the emerging world system and its problems. Together they form a background that is relevant to understanding possible world futures. First, this chapter begins with some speculations about the fairly short-term global political and economic futures (that have relevance to about the year 2000). They pick up the focus of Chapter 11 about the ongoing interaction between the developed and less developed nations, as well as a cyclical theory of social change outlined in Chapter 4. Since these are fairly pessimistic views, I termed them *nightmares*. I wanted to put most of the really catastrophic stuff in one section, so I have followed these nightmares with a brief discussion of the ultimately disruptive wild card in the human future: the prospect of war. Second, I turn to two longer-term views of the human future (that reach considerably beyond the year 2000) that contain two very different visions and options for the development of human societies. Third, I will conclude by considering more analytically some of the choices, options, and values that will shape emerging possibilities.

SOME SHORT-TERM NIGHTMARES AND THE SPECTER OF WAR

The Dialectics of Crisis

Johan Galtung (1981) argues that a fundamental process of global change continues to be the diffusion of western economic technology. This was also a major assumption of the modernization perspectives discussed in Chapter 10 but unlike those, he explores the stresses and contradictions that accompany the spread of economic technologies (you might review Chapter 4 about dialectical models of change). What are the future social implications of the global transfer of technology?

In the *cultural* realm the transfer of economic technology also transfers a hidden social code that stands behind the technologies. The introduction of electronics and fertilizers, for examples, carry with them not only changes in the organization of work, but also altered relations between communities, status relationships, altered family roles, and relationships between people generally. Technologies bring with them new sets of values and expectations. Ultimately, Galtung argues, the diffusion of economic technology has the potential to bring more thorough cultural Westernization than older political or economic colonialism. In the *social* realm the diffusion of economic technology is likely to produce the gradual emergence of a new "social formation" at the elite levels in all societies: capitalists, researchers, and bureaucrats who enable the new technology to be implemented. In the *political* realm ideological and national differences will not disappear, but in practical terms there will emerge a growing homogeneity of outlook between political elites who negotiate with each other in the global system. In the *economic* realm itself there will be a global decline in hand labor as a mode of production, and routine industrial production will be gradually transferred to parts of the third world and the newly industrialized nations where labor is cheap. Thus the less developed nations will become more economically developed in some sectors (though they will continue to be dual societies with large traditional subsistence populations). The Western industrial economies will continue to be deindustrialized in terms of routine production and assembly. As a proportion of global industrial output, the output of the third world nations will grow in relation to that of the developed industrial economies. This trend has been going on in fact for some time, as illustrated by the data and estimates by an agency of the United Nations in Table 13-1.

In short, what Galtung envisions is a new pattern of relationships between nations. There will still be control from the classical center (North America, Western Europe, Japan) but that control will be built around innovation and the research component of production. Parts of the third world, where cheap labor exists and deferred gratification can be politically enforced, will increasingly become the production centers of the global economy.

What are some of the consequences of this pattern for the developed industrial economies? According to Galtung they will survive increasingly by generating and exporting innovations and new technologies. Fewer people will

TABLE 13-1 Share of World Industrial Output (Percentages)

	1900	1950	1975	2000
Western countries	99	73	52	one-third(?)
Eastern Europe	0	20	30	one-third(?)
Third world	0	7	18	one-third(?)

Source: UNCTAD division for transfer of technology, WHO conference, 1979, cited in Galtung, 1981:115.

be employed in the *production* of material goods. But there will not be enough good jobs in finance, research, and trade for most of the population, whose employment is likely to become increasingly marginal (remember the process of *restratification* in America that I mentioned in Chapter 3?). But all people consume, and in the older industrial nations people have high expectations and living standards. In short, "the scenario would be that this social construction very soon will show serious cracks. It will simply no longer be possible to have so few people engaged in such high productivity ... for so many" (Galtung, 1981:125). Solutions may be sought in the corporatist social welfare state policies like those of West European societies, but those become very expensive solutions in economic terms. And when many must be supported from the earnings of a relatively small number of people and key industries, the potential for political stress and class conflict intensifies.

For the third world the future consequences of this new pattern are equally grim. As is now true, some third world countries will be more successful as industrial production/assembly centers. The third world will increasingly become internally differentiated, with some countries becoming dependent upon others, and some nations left out of the process entirely. Even where the diffusion of economic technology produces modest successes, Galtung envisions a growing duality whereby third world societies become increasingly dominated by urban sectors and Westernized elites. They will increasingly exploit the non-Western part by "depriving it systematically of production factors, buying its land or evicting the tenants, exhausting its raw materials, siphoning capital accumulated through banking systems...and so on" (Galtung, 1981:128). But the less modernized segments of third world populations are still relatively large and either left in neglect or as displaced migrants to the third world cities (see Chapter 12), can significantly disrupt the political stability of less developed nations. To this unstable urban-rural political stress add the fact of the continuing domination of Western over traditional cultural forms, not so much because of overt cultural imperialism, but because the diffusion of economic technology is a "Trojan Horse" that brings the covert penetration of Western ideas and culture. Thus there will continue to be a mood of "culturcide" among thinkers and intellectuals of the third world who resent the loss of national identity and tradition.

In sum, Galtung's vision of the near future is not a happy prospect for either the developed or the less developed nations as they interact in the emerging scheme of things. He envisions increasing stress within the industrial nations, increasing stress within the less developed nations, and inevitably, a stressful relationship between them in terms of trade and political interaction. In this dialectical perspective the future of the global system will become increasing stressful, volatile, and politically unstable because, according to Galtung,

> Once dominant social processes are geared to build a social construction so that not only a small minority but a vast majority is no longer materially productive, then a high number of conditions have to be satisfied and that can only be done at the expense of somebody and something. Sooner or later the precarious balance will topple, and the result will be a general crisis in that formation. It is the export of that

crisis which is currently a predominant global process.(Adapted from Johan Galtung, 1981, "Global Processes and the World in the 1980's," in Hollis and Rosenau (eds.), *World System Structure: Continuity and Change.* Beverly Hills, CA: Sage Publications. Used with permission of the editors.)

Cycles Again?

To this dialectical nightmare let me briefly add some of the near future implications of a cyclical theory of change that I discussed as an example in Chapter 4. Recall that Chirot (1986) argued that there were global "long cycles" in economic and political change, and that periods of economic innovation were followed by expansion, saturation, and ultimate decline of industries and markets based on particular technologies. The last phase of the cycle is accompanied by increasing competition in crowded markets, high rates of business failures, high rates of individual unemployment, family disruption, frustrated expectations as well as an increase in political stresses. The end of the last cycle resulted, in Chirot's view, in World War I, the global depression of the 1930s, and World War II. He does not argue that such catastrophic ends of an economic cycle are inevitable—they can be managed with more or less disruption—but that the potential for catastrophe is much greater at the end of a cycle. The important implication for the future here is that according to many observers the world economy has been in a long-term state of contraction and slower growth after its prolonged post-World War II boom (see Chapters 10 and 11). Thus if Chirot and other observers of such "long cycles" are correct, the world system is heading into a time of great potential for economic, social, and political catastrophe.

Chirot argues that the older ideological "solutions" to these problems (free market capitalism and socialism) are both "spent forces" incapable of dealing with the problems of global economic stagnation and social stress at the end of an economic long cycle. Pressures for governmental action to deal with these problems will make various forms of "corporatism" seem like attractive alternatives. By "corporatism" Chirot means a political economy in which the economy is still privately owned, but a strong government emerges to manage and manipulate the system to make each nation highly productive and competitive in the international marketplace. In any case corporatism, whether West German or Japanese style, implies the existence of a strong bureaucratic state. But in Chirot's view economic innovation has always been the product of a free competitive environment, and he questions whether it will take place in the context of strong state guidance. Thus the paradox: In the context of growing international stagnation there is a need for economic innovation to produce new growth industries. The key question is whether such progress, originally fostered by free-thinking rational intellectuals and businessmen, can occur if it is increasingly subject to state-sponsored intervention and manipulation. In Chirot's view, "competition between states, economic and political rivalry, and international tension are the best guarantees of continuing progress" (1981:296). Such international tensions and rivalry may be the best ways of guaranteeing continued

economic innovation, but in the context of the interlocking dimensions of the world problem and advanced military technology they are also very dangerous. The possibility of an unprecedented global disaster, either military or ecological, becomes more possible and ominous.

Both of these visions, one dialectical and the other cyclical, suggest an increasingly unstable world in the immediate future. The *worst case* political scenario of this growing instability of the global system is increased probability of wars, large and small.

The Prospect of War

Wars are among the most frightening and destructive events in the human experience. They are pervasive, discontinuous events that disrupt the lives of individuals and families as well as stable expectations about the way societies function, develop, and change. In the contexts of the emergence of a world system with its multidimensional, seemingly intractable problems and the existence of thermonuclear weapons with immense destructive capacity, the specter of war, particularly a big war, is *the* ultimately frightening human nightmare. The possibility of another world war would mean an end to the human future on any reasonably decent and civilized terms.

It is common to associate the outbreak of war with fanatical and unstable individuals (the mad man theory of war), but wars are fought not only because unreasonable men can come to power: There are deeper social and cultural circumstances. First, wars are fought for control of limited resources. In a world of growing population and resource constraints (for food, energy, and minerals) such competition will become more intense and will increase the threat of war. And the growth of inequality between and within nations makes the possibility of both international and internal conflict more likely. Second, wars are fought about differences in culture and ideology. In other words, they are about insults, prestige, and national pride as well as competition for territory and resources. You can't understand the regional wars of the 1980s—such as the conflicts in Central America, between Iran and Iraq, between Ethiopia and Somalia, between Israel and Palestine, or in Angola, or Afghanistan—without considering them as conflicts about both resources *and* national identity.

War is one type of conflict relationship between two or more parties whose spokespersons believe (1) that their goals are incompatible and (2) that they can each achieve their goals at the expense of the other party (adapted from Kriesberg, 1982:17). The key word here is *belief*: not only the belief that interests are incompatible but the belief that the conflict can be won.

But as a matter of fact modern warfare decreases the likelihood of a clearcut win, and even the *value* of winning, for several reasons. The costs of largescale mobilization for war, particularly with expensive technological instruments of destruction is very high on both sides of a conflict, even for those who can reasonably expect to win. Historically war was between soldiers for the spoils, resources, and territory of civilians. But increasingly the strategies of modern war involve the deliberate destruction of the social and economic infrastructure to reduce the opponent's ability to wage war. In modern wars there are few intact spoils to win. Even the conflict strategies of those most militarily disadvantaged, guerrilla warfare and terrorism, can result in prolonged costly conflicts with no clear cut winner at any given time. And the globalization of political and economic interests has meant that local wars have the possibility to escalate to larger conflagrations, a fact that increases the potential costliness of even a small war. Finally the encompassing destructive capacity of a global thermonuclear war makes the whole concept of winning nonsensical. Perhaps, as some argue, the balance of mutually assured destruction among the superpowers has prevented major wars. But this is certainly a potentially disastrous mechanism to maintain international peace, and one which has enormous costs for even the richest nations in the diversion of human economic resources and creativity.

Models of the Outbreak of Conflict   What kinds of tensions could provoke the outbreak of actual military conflict on a significant scale in the near future? I will describe three models of the structures that could provoke the outbreak of significant military conflict. They have different emphases on the outbreak of war, but they are not contradictory.

1. *East-West Tensions.* One model of the outbreak of war emphasizes tensions between the United States and the Soviet Union as global superpowers. That idea has long been deeply embedded in the popular American understanding of things. In this model the United States and its allies and the Soviet Union and its allies represent political-economic interest blocs and differing ideological worldviews that compete for world domination. I don't think either the United States or the Soviet Union wants to directly rule the entire world, but it is fair to say that they would both like to shape the global system so that it is compatible with their own systems. Superpower foreign aid is given not for neutral humanitarian purposes alone, but also to solicit the loyalties of nations in the East-West conflict. The East-West conflict is so pervasive that it becomes a part of significant domestic struggles in the third world, as various factions seek aid from either the Marxist East or the capitalist West. While the Americans and the Soviets have not directly waged war, since the 1950s the conflict has taken the form of protracted diplomatic and propaganda Cold War sustained by both parties in the arenas of global public opinion. There have been, however, direct military confrontations by proxies in, for instance, Vietnam, Angola, and Central America. But in the absence of actual war, both the East and West power blocs have built frightfully redundant systems of conventional and thermonuclear weapons, and the doctrine of mutually assured destruction has locked them into an escalating arms race that has no logical end. Restraint depends on the short-term rational maintenance of military balance, but in a larger human sense that system itself is irrational. Restraint also depends upon the economic stability and access to global raw materials of both the Western and Marxist industrial nations. "Until recently, their access to raw materials and markets seemed assured, reducing the threat that either superpower would use force for

economic reasons. This may change" (Bassis, Gelles, and Levine, 1982:127). Recent history may reassure us that the Americans and the Soviets are rational enough not to instigate a nuclear holocost. But in the context of the growing international economic and political stresses in the visions of the future mentioned above, the possibility must be taken seriously.

2. *North-South Tensions.* Another model of the outbreak of war focuses on the *North-South* hemispheric relations. The East and the West are divided by great power struggles for control, but the Northern and Southern hemispheres are divided by wealth. Most of the economic wealth and affluence is in the industrial nations of the North, and most of the poverty and hunger are in the nations of the South.[2] If Galtung's vision (above) of the future of this on- going North-South relationship is reasonable, there will increasingly be festering resentment and hostility in the third world, because of both (1) the frustrations of masses of displaced peasants being dominated and exploited by Westernized national elites and (2) the increasing frustration of among those elites seeking to maintain or improve their nation's economic and political status in the world system. It is important to remember that though the southern hemisphere is much poorer and composed of a multitude of smaller, less powerful nations, they collectively control vast resources (petroleum, mineral, and otherwise) and markets that the North depends upon for its economic health and survival. And if the Southern nations increasingly become the routine assemblers of goods in the global marketplace, their role in the system will become even more important.

Remember also the enormous burden of foreign debt that many Southern countries have accumulated in the last decades (see Chapter 11). While there are creative attempts to reschedule loans and stretch out payment, leaders of several third world nations (e.g., Peru in 1986, Brazil in 1978) have threatened to default. If this indeed were to become widespread the global system of banking and finance would be thrown into chaos. Remember also that there have emerged various of types of Southern coalitions to articulate their interests and grievances vis-à-vis the North. The South is not as helpless as it once seemed. The point is *not* that the Southern nations will collectively "declare war" on the North, which still has the balance of international power and military capability. The point is, rather, that given the growth of global interdependence and festering resentment, crises in the South have the potential to destabilize the global political system and result in the kinds of tensions that would lead to the outbreak of war. The future of North-South relations is likely to be disorderly, messy, and punctuated by periodic disasters. "As the world develops into a more tightly knit economic and political community, the causes of international war will increasingly come to resemble the causes of revolutionary wars" (Coleman and Cressy, 1987:575).

3. *Balkanization.* Both the East-West and the North-South models are bipolar, that is, they focus on a single axis of tension which defines the basis for the outbreak of military conflict. But another possible model is that war is likely to result from the many-sided (multi-polar) tensions among the nations of the

third world themselves. This model recognizes that at a concrete level many of the important political tensions are between the smaller nations of the world and that these are perhaps as important for understanding the potential for war as the overarching but more abstract tensions between the East and the West or between the North and the South. Examples of such local conflicts were not hard to find in the 1980s, such as the conflict between India and Pakistan, Iraq and Iran, Ethiopia and Somalia, Chad and Libya, as well as the "internal wars" in Angola, Afghanistan, and El Salvador. The world is in fact becoming full of small "over-militarized" states, many of them in the third world. Such nations have been customers and recipients of aid for elaborate weaponry from the industrial powers. Military budgets consume large parts of the GNPs of many third world nations.[3] While the world has avoided the outbreak of a major global conflict, the fact is that there have occurred dozens of small, regional bush wars among local rivals. These small wars (such as the war in Central America) have the potential to attract the interest of larger world powers and hence to escalate into wars of wider regional, and potentially global, significance. In a future in which global economic and political stress is anticipated, the volatility of such conflicts can be expected to increase.

These in sum are three models for understanding the stresses that make the outbreak of war possible in the near-term future. In a more abstract sense, you could say that in the future the world is likely to continue as an unstable political, economic, and military triad of relationships between the Western powers, the Soviet bloc, and the nations of the third world. Each leg of this triad is potentially explosive. And if the gloomy scenarios mentioned above come to pass, then the potential for wars of one sort or another, large or small, is amplified. *Will war really come?* No one knows, of course, and I remind you that the above scenarios are only possible courses for the future. Some of my colleagues think that the doctrine of mutually assured destruction guarantees rational restraint on the part of both the Americans and the Soviets. Some think that there are restraints that operate to keep local wars from becoming wider conflagrations. I hope they are right, but I must admit to you that I am frightened by the prospect of increasing global stresses in the presence of the diffusion of the instruments of mass destruction.

The Costs of Global Militarization   Even if such wars never come to pass the militarization of the world imposes an enormous burden on prospects for a positive near-term future of mankind. On a global basis military expenditures have increased steadily, going from about 4.7 percent of the world economic output in 1960 to over 6 percent in 1985. Stated otherwise, the global military expenditures in 1985 amounted to about 940 billion dollars, which exceeded the income of the poorest half of humanity (Brown, 1986b:196). The nations of the world spend three times as much for arms as for public health, and 40 percent more for arms than for education (Horton and Leslie, 1974:674). Of the world arms expenditures in 1980, 18 percent (over 81 billion dollars) was spent by third world nations that are not able to feed all their people (Coleman and Cressy, 1984:561). In short, military spending is a burden on *all* of the world's economies. High military budgets add significantly to government deficits in the United States and in the Soviet Union, where military spending soaks up about one-seventh of the economic resources; it prevents the development of a first-class economy despite the presence of considerable natural resources (Brown, 1986b:201). In the third world, where high military spending replaces scarce capital that could be used to invest in agriculture and food, economic development, or a better social infrastructure of roads, schools, and medical facilities, it is even more disastrous.

Put simply, the prospect of wars in a stressful future is disastrous, but high global military spending even in the absence of actual war imposes an enormous burden on the chances for a bright future for the nations of the world. The economic and political interests of nations are increasingly international, but loyalties remain extensively national. In a context where peace is maintained by various balances of power, extreme nationalism is increasingly dangerous. There is an even stronger need in the future for a more effective global structure for the management of conflict.

PROPHETIC VISIONS: SOME LONGER VIEWS

I shift the focus now away from these rather gloomy visions of the near- term future and the prospects of war to longer-range scenarios which attempt to envision the human future well beyond the year 2000. One of these is very optimistic and the other is more pessimistic but, as you will see, even it has a vision of a positive human future within it. Each provides some hope for a better human future, but in very different terms, and they form the parameters of much of the contemporary debate and speculation about the future.

Prophets of Boom

Since the 1960s, Herman Kahn (the late director of the Hudson Institute) and his colleagues have constantly articulated arguments in favor of a bright global future. In the words of Kahn and Phelps,

> We offer a generally optimistic view of the economic present and future, but with caution and qualifications. We believe that— barring serious bad luck or bad management—the prospects for achieving eventually a high level of broadly worldwide economic affluence and beneficent technology are bright, that this is a good and logical goal for mankind, and that our images of the economic future may substantially determine our progress toward that goal. (1979:202) [4]

How so? Kahn argues that, in a broad perspective, global change now and in the future is part of a *great transition* that began with industrialization in the 1700s. Kahn and his colleagues argue, "In much the same way that the agricultural revolution spread round the world, the Industrial Revolution has been spreading and causing a permanent change in the quality of human life. However, instead of lasting 10,000 years, this second diffusion process is likely to be largely completed with a total span of about 400 years or roughly by the late 22nd century" (Kahn, Brown, and Martel, 1976:20).

The great transition has three phases, encompassing (1) the Industrial Revolution and industrial societies of the early twentieth century, (2) the super-industrial economy—meaning the emerging global economy of high technologies, service industries, and multinational corporations, and (3) the future transition to a true postindustrial society. These phases overlap and complement each other in time in different parts of the world but, according to Kahn, the general patterns of evolution is clear. Kahn expects the general pattern of the great transition to follow an S-shaped curve. That is, from the 1800s there were exponential increases in world population, the "gross world product" (GWP),[5] and per capita incomes. Beginning in the mid 1970s there was, and will continue into the future, a leveling of world population growth and a decline in previously exponential rates of world economic growth, but a continuous spread of affluence so that world per capita incomes will continue to increase. Kahn and his colleagues are at pains to stress that the slowing of economic growth will occur because with the spread of affluence, there will be a reduction in the growth of *demand*, rather than shortages of *supply*.

There is in this transition a gap between the living standards of the poor and the rich nations, which Kahn argues is inevitable as industrialism spreads and living standards of some parts of the world relative to others are raised. But he argues that this is analogous to the misery of the working and living conditions of early industrialism, which eventually spread better living conditions to all classes in industrial societies. You can see Kahn's depiction of the great transition in terms of his estimates of changes in population growth, the GWP, and per capita incomes in Figure 13-1.

FIGURE 13-1 THE GREAT TRANSITION

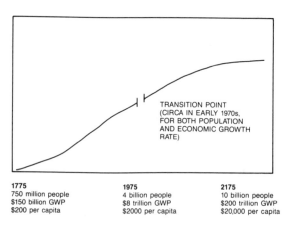

TRANSITION POINT
(CIRCA IN EARLY 1970s,
FOR BOTH POPULATION
AND ECONOMIC GROWTH
RATE)

1775	1975	2175
750 million people	4 billion people	10 billion people
$150 billion GWP	$8 trillion GWP	$200 trillion GWP
$200 per capita	$2000 per capita	$20,000 per capita

a GWP = Gross World Product. Dollars = 1979 dollars

Source: From Herman Kahn and John B. Phelps, 1979, "The Economic Present and Future," *The Futurist*, June: 202-222. Used with permission of the World Future Society.

Kahn envisions the future from now until about 2025 as a complex and "somewhat difficult" transition period. It will be a period of slowing down of percentage growth rates for the GWP, and a particular period of "malaise" for the rich countries. The spread of supraindustrial economies will present many problems (technological crises, pollution, labor problems, problems of coordination and control). Because many of the projects of superindustrial societies are so large scale, they are problem prone, and we do not (yet) know how to eliminate, control, or alleviate all these effects. There will be steps to colonize and to initiate economic activity in space, particularly regarding energy and minerals. As superindustrialism spreads among the developed countries, manufacturing industry will spread among the middle income nations and perhaps eventually to some of the poorer ones.[6] In sum, it will be a period fraught with many difficulties, but toward the end of the period the problems of superindustrialism will begin to be successfully managed. There will be the first signs of a worldwide maturing economy (Kahn and Phelps, 1979:204).

By 2175 Kahn and his colleagues expect superindustrial societies to be everywhere and true postindustrial ones to be rapidly emerging in many places. The colonization and economic utilization of space will be substantial. They predict after this date a slowing down of both population and economic growth rates, not only in percentages but in absolute numbers. But the slowdown of economic growth rates does not mean a decline in standards of living because of (1) the economies of scale, that acompany large-scale systems and (2) intensive technological progress that will provide energy savings and will substitute new resources for scarce ones. Thus in the context of growing economic efficiency, rapid advances in technology, and a stabilizing world population, unparalleled affluence can be sustained on a global basis.

What kind of social world does this vision of the future imply? Before the end of the twentieth century, Kahn and his colleagues expect to see

> the end of the post-World War II system politically, economically and financially, leading to a "unified but multipolar, partially competitive, mostly global and technological economy." This will exhibit "increasing worldwide unity in technology, private industry, commercial and financial institutions, but relatively little unity in international legal and political institutions. Despite much hostility [there will be] a continuing, even growing, importance of multinational corporations as innovators and diffusers of economic activity and rapid growth." (Kahn, Brown and Martel, 1976, cited in Freeman and Jahoda, 1978:48)

In other words, the future world envisioned by Kahn and colleagues would be a world of extremely large-scale, specialized, and complex economic and political systems with global interconnections. The process of technological change will be increasingly institutionalized. Technological developments may provide some basis for flexibility and decentralization, but the need for large-scale coordination and management will mean that political and economic power will still be significantly centralized. Since the societies of the future will be technology intensive, they will be, according to Kahn, increasingly dominated by specialists, technocratic elites and "the knowledge industry." The "problem of production" will progressively be "solved," and most people will work in service and/or information industries. Culturally, it will be a world dominated by values that are secular, pragmatic, utilitarian, manipulative, and hedonistic. Affluence will gradually diffuse on a global basis, so that there will be an end to the more absolute forms of poverty, but much more attention will be paid to the disruptive ecological effects of economic activity than at present. While they recognize problems and dangers and do not think that progress will come smoothly or painlessly, Kahn and his colleagues

> think that it is not very practical to adopt any deliberate alternative to growth, and it is probably safer to keep on growing than to try to stop. Attempting to change the historical trend would either have little effect or lead to disaster. (Kahn and Phelps, 1979:211)

In a nutshell, the "prophets of boom" accept the present trends in global change as basically benign. It is a *cornucopian* view of the future. With faith in human good will and inventiveness, they would counsel full steam ahead!

Prophets of Gloom

There are, as you might guess, more pessimistic visions of the future to provide counterpoints to the optimistic forecast of Kahn and his colleagues. The most influential view resulted from a 1960s futurist think tank called the Club of Rome, which was originally located in Italy and sponsored by a variety of industrialists and multinational corporations. Rather than rely on the mental and intuitive models of Kahn and his colleagues, the methodology of the Club of Rome used an elaborate computer simulation called a World System Dynamics (WSD) model developed by Massachusetts Institute of Technology scientists Jay Forrester, Donella Meadows, and their colleagues. This model started with what was known about current patterns and trends in population growth, economic growth, resource consumption, food supply, and pollution effects, each of which has been growing exponentially. The WSD model then developed an elaborate set of coefficients for how continued growth in each of these areas would impact the others, and attempted to project the sum of these interactions into the future for several hundred years (see Meadows et al., 1972).

The resulting projection by the WSD model was a classic *outbreak-crash model*, familiar to biological ecologists. It is what happens when populations of animals (say deer) grow at a such a rate that they strip the environment of available food supplies. After doing so, their population declines precipitously. The human outbreak-crash pattern predicted by the WSD model argues that current exponential growth in population, resource consumption, and food production will produce such enormous stress on the carrying capacity of the planet by 2100, that the resource and capital inputs to support such consumption levels will not be sustainable. So much investment of wealth is required to obtain dwindling supplies of natural gas, silver, petroleum, nickel, zinc, and other resources to maintain world industrial development that capital investments can no longer keep up with the growing needs. This prevents increases in fertilizer production, heath care, education, and other vital activities. Without food and necessary services, world population and living standards undergo a steady decline shortly after the beginning of the twenty-first century (Humphrey and Buttel, 1982:97-98). This is depicted in Figure 13-2, in what the M.I.T. analysts called their "standard run" reflecting current world conditions.

They produced a large variety of computer runs of the simulation to reflect more optimistic assumptions (e.g., doubling resource supply estimates, controlling population growth and pollution effects) but the result was the same: At some time after the turn of the century, growth would be unsustainable. The problem was not any single dimension but the cumulative effects of the way that they interact. And the underlying problem is growth itself. Hence the M.I.T. researchers emphasized the urgency of global efforts to dampen exponential economic growth itself (not just population growth and pollution side effects) and efforts to move toward a "steady state world." In this view, it is not enough to simply wait for markets to adjust to scarcity of food and nonrenewable resources: By that time irreversible declines in ecological equilibrium and resource availability may have already taken place, and a variety of points of no return may have been passed. Nor can technology save us. All that technological advances can do is delay the inevitable end, since dominant cultural patterns and

FIGURE 13-2 WORLD MODEL, STANDARD RUN

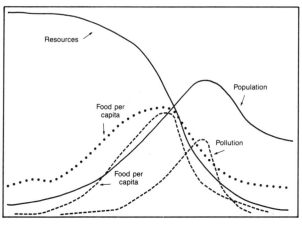

The "standard" world model run assumes no major change in the physical, economic, or social relationships that have historically governed the development of the world system. All variables plotted here follow historical values from 1900 to 1970. Food, industrial output, and population grow exponentially until the rapidly diminishing resource base forces a slowdown in industrial growth. Because of natural delays in the system, both population and pollution continue to increase for some time after the peak of industrialization. Population growth is finally halted by a rise in the death rate due to decreased food and medical services.

Source: The Limits to Growth: *A Report for the Club of Rome's Project on the Predicament of Mankind,* by Donella H. Meadows, Dennis L. Meadows, Jorgen Randers, William W. Behrens III. A Potomic Associates Book published by Universe Books, N.Y., 1972. Graphics by Potomic Associates.

institutional arrangements perpetuate conditions of profligate consumption and "problem-solving-by-growth" that are in the end self-defeating and environmentally destructive. The specter raised by this vision is that, if present trends continue, after 2100 a smaller human population will be eking out a more marginal existence on an exhausted and polluted planet.

This is indeed a sharp counterpoint to the cornucopian view of the future presented by Kahn and his colleagues. The views of the Club of Rome analysts have been forcefully stated in a variety of technical and popular publications (Meadows et al., 1974), and as you might imagine, they have provoked a blizzard of commentary and criticism (see Oltmans, 1974 for an interesting collection of these). The most common criticism questioned (1) the assumptions of resources estimates and/or (2) the interaction assumptions. It is the old bane of computer simulations—GIGO, garbage in, garbage out.[7] Another criticism was that efforts to dampen world economic growth would have the most dire consequences for the poor nations of the South, particularly in the absence of global political initiatives to promote a more equitable distribution of global resources. These kinds of political questions are not addressed by the M.I.T. researchers. Another criticism was that they used aggregated world averages for various projections, but different regions are likely to fare quite differently in the coming crash that they anticipate.

The Club of Rome analysts addressed *some* of these problems in subsequent reports that attempt to address the interactions between different regions (Mesarovic and Pestel, 1974; Tinbergen, 1976). The tone of these subsequent reports is also more moderate, offering several routes to global equilibrium, including (1) "the establishment of limits on population and economic growth, (2) an emphasis on development efforts tailored to the resource basis of each nation so that economic advances can be 'ecologically sustainable,' (3) increased national self-reliance rather than dependence on multinational corporations, and (4) emphasis on public rather than private control of economic organizations" (Shepard, 1984:571).[8] Still, concrete suggestions about how any of these "routes to global equilibrium" can be achieved are absent.

Appropriate Technology and the "Soft Path"   I said earlier that there is a positive vision of the future even in this more gloomy forecast, and the above illustrates some of it. But there is more. Many have argued that learning to live with limits is not just a nasty necessity, but the basis for a better social life, albeit one in which material consumption does not continue to grow exponentially. How so? In general the proponents of this view have argued for the adoption of *appropriate technologies*, defined as "technologies that are best able to match the needs of all people in a society in a sustainable relationship with the environment" (Humphrey and Buttell, 1982:187). This is a very different view than Kahn et al., who argued for the continued development of complex high technologies that require large-scale technocratic administration. Appropriate technology, by contrast, is often (1) "simpler" (and can be understood and repaired by the people who use it), (2) less prone to failures (as are more complex technological systems), and (3) have less severe ecological side effects. Proponents of appropriate technology would advocate, for example, the substitution of organic fertilizers for inorganic ones that have deleterious effects on soil and water, and the substitution of solar space heating for using electricity to heat homes. Heating homes with electricity (perhaps generated by nuclear power plants) when solar space heating is practical, cheaper, and less environmentally intrusive has been compared to cutting butter with a chain saw! The most articulate spokesperson for the use of appropriate technology was the late British economist E. F. Schumacher, whose book *Small Is Beautiful* has been widely influential (1973).

The shift to appropriate technologies would alleviate some of the problems of the growing consumption of nonrenewable resources implied in high-tech solutions and systems. But more than that, they tend to be *decentralized* strategies that would alleviate the problems of overcomplexity, alienation, and the powerlessness of people in large-scale, bureaucratic, and highly centralized economic and energy systems (see Dickson, 1974).

Physicist Amory Lovins (1976) has described two sharply divergent possible paths for human economic development. One is the *hard path* which is capital-intensive, large-scale, centralized, and bureaucratic and which uses energy-intensive technologies. The social world of the hard path would be one in which political power is technocratically based and also highly centralized. It would be a world in which structural unemployment is a chronic problem for those displaced by new technologies. It implies specialization and interdependency in massive structures, and a culture in which material consumption is in itself a measure of status and self-worth. It would also be, according to Lovins, a culture of alienation for the masses of people who live in systems that are too large and too technically complex for general comprehension. It is the epitome of the path advocated by Kahn and his colleagues. The *soft path*, on the other hand, envisions a world of decentralized or smaller-scale organizational structures, less complex and less resource-intensive technologies, and less-intensive capitalization required for production. It implies localism, bartering, and an emphasis on self-sufficiency.

The alternative technologies of the soft path would be more labor-intensive and would thus avoid the problem of structural unemployment inherent in the hard path. The soft path does not *necessarily* mean lower standards of living, although they would be gauged more in terms of quality rather than quantity. Frugality rather than consumption for its own sake would be highly valued. At the broadest policy levels, Lovins views the two paths as basically incompatible in that a persistent retreat to the prevailing hard path with its supply-expansion strategies will foreclose future options for a soft technology with a high standard of living (Lovins, 1977).

The Two Visions

Here are two strikingly different visions of the future. The prophets of boom argue that the good future is to be found in complex technological solutions to resource problems, and in economies of scale that come with the coordinated global management of large-scale, bureaucratic systems. They tend to gloss over the fact that such systems may increasingly become become unmanageable, less amenable to democratic control, and more vulnerable to catastrophic blunders, accidents, and disruptions. They take it as articles of faith that (1) resource limits and environmental decay can and will be overcome by "good management" and technological "fixes" and that (2) without any extraordinary measures, affluence will increasingly diffuse on a global basis. Both of these are at least arguable assumptions. By contrast, the prophets of gloom argue that continuing to seek high-tech solutions to sustain growth in a finite world is at best a Faustian bargain that will buy some time but will be ruinous in the end. They argue that the good future is to be found in a world of smaller-scale and more decentralized social units, appropriate technology, and self-sufficiency. Their vision is of a world where life is more comprehensible to ordinary persons, where there is "democratic restraint" in a culture of frugality, and where mistakes and blunders have less serious ecological consequences. If nothing else, this vision entails a reversal of the social trends of the last two hundred years. It involves a deliberate dampening of growth and resource consumption (at least in the industrial world) *before* the planet becomes exhausted and polluted. Doing so would require a coordinated effort on a global scale, and it is difficult to see how the political consensus to achieve such a fundamental redirection of recent trends would emerge. There are many powerful organizations and groups in contemporary industrial societies that have deeply embedded vested interests in perpetuating growth, and the culture of growth. And an anti-growth policy is of limited appeal to the poorest half of humanity, which has not been able to share in the culture of affluence.

There are some similarities between the two visions that you should not overlook. Both visions of the future take for granted that somehow an equitable distribution of the worlds, resources can emerge, but I don't think that either vision pays enough attention to political mechanisms by which this might (or might not!) come about. They both envision a global equilibrium emerging after the year 2000, with a stable population and lower rates of economic growth and resource consumption. And they both assume that a very good life— in fact, an affluent life by historic standards—is within the reach of most of humankind. How we will get there and exactly what the good society will look like is a matter of debate.

Which of these visions depicts the most probable future? No one knows, but that is not really the issue. They are, I think, extreme views that define the outer parameters of the contemporary debate about the future. I would argue that neither is likely, but whatever future emerges will be somewhere between these extreme. Exactly *where* in between makes a great deal of difference because the two views embody different hazards and risks, as well as different visions of the good life. And exactly where in between these views we arrive will be determined by some critical policy choices that are made, either deliberately or by default. Let me try to map out the terrain of some important choices.

DESIRABLE FUTURES: CHOICES, OPTIONS, AND VALUES

If the future is to be shaped by human choices rather than by default options, it requires that choices be made on the basis of some vision of a *desirable* future world. Surprisingly, at an abstract level it is not difficult to agree about what a desirable future would look like. There are, in other words, some broadly desirable characteristics of social systems with which few would disagree. Like what? First, few would argue against the desirability of an *ecologically sustainable society*. To argue in favor of living in a devastated environment is lunacy. Second, few would disagree with the goal of *system equity*, in other words that there are basic standards of justice that should govern interhuman relationships as well as the use and access to the worlds resources. To envision a *desirable* future world of opulent wealth juxtaposed with starvation and material misery is simply unconscionable. Third, few would argue against the goal of *system stability*, meaning not a frozen world of societies without change, but societies with enough stability to avoid ecological, economic, or political catastrophes. Fourth, few would argue against the desirability of developing societies that provide a *sense of dignity in the lifestyles of individuals*. This means societies that enable all persons to have (1) a basic sense of self-worth and (2) meet the minimal requirements for material security. While most would agree that these are desirable characteristics for societies to pursue, there is a great deal of disagreement about the degree to which these goals are practically realizable and particularly about the policies would move us in these directions. Let me invite you to engage in a mental exercise. Which of the above scenarios (the cornucopian model versus the small is beautiful model) of the future do you think would be most likely to produce a world order of societies with these desirable characteristics?

Before leaving the question of desirable futures, let me outline alternative futures in a different way with a model that is even more simplified than those mentioned above. Possible futures can be conceptualized as having two underlying dimensions: the likelihood of continuing *growth* of world productivity and consumption levels and the *distribution* of the fruits of productivity between the rich and the poor, both within and between nations (Gribben, 1981:17). Each dimension could develop in either of two directions in comparison to the present, so that there are four alternative futures to consider:

1. *High growth, high equality* (a big cake, fairly shared)
2. *High growth, low equality* (a big cake, hogged by the rich)
3. *Low growth, high equality* (a smaller cake, fairly shared)
4. *Low growth, low equality* (a smaller cake, hogged by the rich)

In the simplified terms of the model, there is no future that could not be fitted into one of these four scenarios.

Scenario 1 resembles the cornucopian future envisioned by Kahn and his colleagues. It is so inherently attractive that if achievable, one should not discount a serious effort to realize a world with its characteristics. *Scenario 2*, with the rich continuing to get richer while the poor are ground in the mire, is "so clearly a recipe for disaster in terms of global conflict that it can be ruled out of court" (Gribben, 1981:19). It is not only unconscionable by any ethical standards, but maximizes the likelihood of the outbreak of wars (as suggested in the above discussion), political disorders, and massive alienation among the world's poor. Indeed, part of the fears of the critics of Kahn et al. is that the efforts to produce a cornucopian world will not produce a world with the requisite equity to be stable. *Scenario 4* is an even better recipe for disaster, since with only modest riches to hold onto the rich would be even less likely to be able to hold the poor in subjection and would likely resort to brutal repressive measures. It represents the worst-case scenario of the limits of growth perspective, in which growth is not dampened and ecological and resource base points of no return are passed. It is, in fact, an exhausted world in which authoritarian elites struggle to hold on to privilege. In this scenario, wars of redistribution are likely to be pandemic (see Heilbroner, 1974, for an elaboration of such a scenario). *Senario 3*, with some belt-tightening among the rich and fairer shares for everyone represents the worldview of the soft path and small is beautiful evangelists. As with the cornucopian view, the political mechanisms by which this vision might be achieved are largely absent.

If, as I have argued, Scenarios 1 and 3 are the only desirable ones, and the others are situations to be avoided, how might one go about making a rational choice between them? Since it is not knowable (strictly speaking) which is most plausible, what is the best bet? There are those who argue that since the cornucopian model is so broadly appealing and not been proven wrong, there is no reason not to pursue this option with great vigor. That is the position not only of Kahn et al., but of the influential English SPRU futurist think tank led by Jahoda and Freeman. One could reason otherwise. One could ask the question, Which gamble has the least costs if it fails? If the cornucopian vision is pursued and indeed comes to pass, then all is well. If, on the other hand, there are limits to growth that are close at hand, and the cornucopian vision is unworkable, then the costs of failure—with the specter of an exhausted planet—are quite high, and perhaps devastating to *any* dignified human future. What if the soft path/small is beautiful vision is pursued? The costs of pursuing such a vision—even if the cornucopian vision is feasible—is that it entails giving up the dream of high mass consumption and limitless affluence, rather than irretrievably fouling the carrying capacity of the planet. For myself, I think that pursuing the soft path/small is beautiful vision is the best bet, if only because the costs of failure are not nearly so great. If we wait until we find out that the cornucopian future is unworkable, I fear that critical points of no return of global equilibrium will have been passed by the time we have clear signals that such is the case. In other words, in the face of uncertainty I think that moving in the direction of the small is beautiful world is the most prudent gamble.

Having said this let me hasten to add that I think the small is beautiful option is politically most difficult. In terms of its feasibility the great virtue of the cornucopian future is that we don't really have to do anything, except continue

to muddle through to a world of universal affluence (even though the likelihood and costs of technical and managerial blunders are quite high). Reversing the culture of affluence and opposing vested interests with stakes in high-growth policies would require, on the other hand, the emergence of a global consensus and a campaign strategy of worldwide scope. And it is difficult, to see how such a global initiative might emerge.

While I think that it is important to choose between these visions on the basis of desirability and best-bet criteria, it is certainly not an all or none choice. There are a series of less abstract, utilitarian policy choices that can be addressed piecemeal without opting for one total alternative or another. These include, for example, choices about the following: (1) *What should be planned and what should not?* It is not a matter of planning versus absence of planning because in a more crowded world with a systemic character muddling through in a completely laissez-faire socioeconomic system is no longer feasible. This is as true in the small is beautiful vision as it is in the cornucopian vision. Nor, I think, is it a choice between an increasingly irrelevant distinction between private domain or public domain. Planning can be—and is—both public and private. And the issue is certainly not anything so simplistic as the abolition of capitalism or the advent of socialism (those grand ideological catchphrases appropriate for the past). (2) *What should be centralized and what should be decentralized?* Where, in other words, is the efficient balance between the advantages of interdependency and economies of scale and the virtues of smallness and self-sufficiency? In the realm of politics, what issues should be decided at the highest global-systems levels, and what decisions should be left to nations and smaller-scale units? (3) *What should be in competitive arenas and what should be goals addressed through cooperative strategies?* There are those, such as Chirot (see above), who argue that all progress comes through competition, and others who argue that in closed systems such as the world is becoming cooperative strategies are imperative. (4) *How do we balance individual freedom with demands for global equity?* This, in another guise, is the old distribution question: Who has the right to do what, and who gets what?

Phrasing policy choices relative to the future in these ways suggests that while a vision of the future may be important, such choices really boil down to pragmatically making decisions about and "optimizing" certain less abstract (but contentious!) basic social dilemmas. I think that is only partly correct. Optimizing utilities in order to achieve efficient balances between goods is putting the question in technocratic language that disguises the fact that there are winners and losers with each solution, and that each option is inherently political. It leads one to consider needs—whether of individuals or social systems—as basic and uncontroversial. Yet, as anthropologist Dorothy Lee correctly notes,

It is value, not a series of needs, which is at the basis of human behavior. The main difference between the two lies in the conception of the good which underlies them. The premise that man acts so as to satisfy needs presupposes a negative conception of the good as amelioration or the correction of an undesirable state. According to this view, man acts to relieve tension; good is the removal of evil and welfare th

correction of ills; satisfaction is the meeting of a need; good functioning comes from adjustment, survival from adaptation; peace is the resolution of conflict; fear, of the supernatural or of adverse public opinion, is the incentive to good conduct; the happy individual is the well-adjusted individual. (Lee, 1959:72)

In conclusion, Lee writes "If there are needs, they are derivative and not basic....Accordingly, even physical survival cannot be demonstrated to be a universal human need....I know of no culture where human physical survival has been shown, rather than unquestioningly assumed...to be *the* ultimate goal [emphasis added]. The basic question is not: 'What are one's needs?' but rather, 'What are one's values, and what does one need to achieve them'" (Lee, 1959:72). The point I am making is that to envision the future in terms of human or social system needs is useful, but it puts the cart before the horse. Our visions and values about the future shape needs and possibilities. Looked at this way, the first question is, What kind of world future do we want?

NOTES

1. Given the perennial fascination of writing about the futurure, it is hard to historically locate the beginning of contemporary fututurism. I am talking about a social network of thinkers that emerged in the 1960s that included such widely popular writers as Alvin Toffler (*Future Shock*, 1970; *The Third Wave*, 1980) and John Naisbitt (*Megatrends*, 1982), as well as scholars from virtually all academic disciplines. I think the best broad surveys of the range of futurist thought and methods remain those of Toffler, 1972, and Tugwell, 1973. The most academically rigorous and balanced account of the contemporary debate about the future is undoubtedly that of Freeman and Jahoda (1978), though I have some serious reservations about the policy recommendations implicit in their work that I will mention briefly later in this chapter.
   Structurally, contemporary futurism has its own organizations (the largest of which is the World Future Society), conferences, and periodicals. Some futurists are free-floating intellectuals who have carved out for themselves unique careers as writers, speakers, and consultants. At the other end of the movement are the highly structured and more academic think tanks concerned wholly or partly about the future. These would include the Hudson Institute (Kahn et al.), The Worldwatch Institute (Lester Brown and his colleagues), The Club of Rome (Forrester, Meadows et al.), the Social Policy Research Unit at Sussex University in the United Kingdom (Freeman, Cole, and Jahoda), the Modrzhinskaya and Kosolapov groups in the Soviet Union, and the Bariloche Foundation in Argentina.

2. I have described this interdependent relationship between the developed North and the less developed South extensively in Chapters 10 and 11, so I won't repeat much of that here.

3. Military expenditures, for example, make up 13 percent of the GNP in Syria, 15 percent in Jordan, 8 percent in Egypt, 5 percent in Pakistan, 11 percent in Ethiopia, 4 percent in Venezuela, 25 percent in Saudi Arabia, and 17 percent in Libya (Brown, 1986a:198).

4. Kahn's writings are voluminous and I make no attempt to survey them here in any comprehensive way. The most elaborate early statement of his perspective is Kahn and

Weiner (1967). I have relied here mainly on the more recent short article by Kahn and Phelps (1974).

5. Kahn's term for all the the gross national products taken collectively.

6. At least there is an agreement on *this* between Kahn and Galtung's more pessimistic view (above).

7. In its defense, one could point out that estimates of some critical nonrenewable resources have been upwardly revised only marginally since the mid 1970s, and most energy analysts predict a very tight supply situation in the mid 1990s. See Chapter 12.

8. The last of these reports, entitled "Reshaping the International Order" advocated a virtual breakup of world market economy and the multinational trading system in order to produce national self-sufficiency. Not surprisingly, it was the last report sponsored by the multinational funding sources of the Club of Rome!

EPILOGUE: LIVING IN A RAPIDLY CHANGING WORLD

I began this book by describing some important changes in the lives of individuals in the "history" of my own family. But most of the book has been about large-scale structural and cultural change. I would like to end by returning briefly to the level of the changing lives of individuals. What are some lessons that can be drawn from our exploration of social change about how individuals cope with change? There are four major points that I would like to leave you with about living in a changing world, some drawn from the material of the book and some, admittedly, from my own personal philosophy.

1. *Expect change*. That may sound too obvious, but I think all of us have a longing for a world that is sheltered from the uncertainty of change. It is tempting to think that our lives will stop changing after we successfully conquer the next hurdle (whatever that may be—graduation, a new job, a new marriage). We want the world to settle down and stabilize. But alas, I think that is an illusion. Life is a continuous process of adapting to change. Life is not a safe harbor, but a hazardous journey on an open sea, and its final destination is alway uncertain—both individually and collectively. I think the important thing about expecting change is not only to attempt to understand its directions, but also to learn to live with a degree of ambiguity and uncertainty.

2. *Understand change.* While it is true that the outcomes of change are always uncertain there are, nonetheless, some major trends and dimensions of change that one can understand. The more you understand about these trends and the mechanisms by which they take place, the easier it will be for you to live in a changing world. This book is, I hope, a modest contribution to your understanding of change and change processes in the contemporary world. It has emphasized the importance of understanding the relationship between macro and micro change and the idea that changes in the personal and family lives of people are embedded in macroscopic change (in institutions and large-scale structures). Such macro change conditions and limits the possibilities we have as individuals, but seldom are we left without any maneuvering room or alternatives as to how we might adapt to such changes. Another major emphasis of this book has been the importance of what might be called *system thinking* about change: understanding how change in one unit or dimension is connected to changes in other elements of a larger system. In some ways *system thinking* is fundamentally at odds with how we are taught to think in the United States. We learn to isolate one aspect or dimension of life and focus on its development in a fragmented way without understanding its connections to other things or levels of change. Sometimes this is called tunnel vision. But we need to be able to think about change in a contextual way and understand how various dimensions and levels of social reality interact. That is admittedly not easy. Again, I hope that this book has contributed to your ability to see things in a systemic fashion.

In the introductory chapter I introduced some common distinctions about different kinds of change (linear versus cyclical, short term versus long term). There is another distinction I would like to leave you with one that I don't know how to describe very clearly but which, nonetheless, I think has some important consequences for how one copes with change. There are *changes driven by "deep" structural causes that, from the standpoint of the individual person, may be virtually irreversible.* Change driven by technology is of this sort, as is the increasing scale of social life, the growth of the human population, and the likelihood of ecological constraints on human economic activity. The emergence of a world system, as described in the last few chapters, is such a permanent change. Never again, I think, will the fate of individuals, communities, and nations be independent of what is happening on the other side of the globe. It seems virtually unthinkable, in the absence of a global catastrophe, that in the future you will live your life with a small human population, in small isolated communities, with resources so abundant that their use is not in question. Don't look for the disappearance of computers or the return of blacksmiths! But there is another kind of *social change that is driven not by these deeply imbedded technical, structural, and demographic factors but rather by alterations of the "rules of the game,"* that is, by changing political, policy, and legal arrangements. These arrangements are important because they define who benefits, who wins, and who loses. In relationship to individual adaptations to change, my point is simply this: Changes driven by deeply embedded technical, demographic, and structural causes are not likely to be altered suddenly or rapidly. You may as well learn to adapt to them. But to the extent that your life is supported, benefited (or for that matter disadvantaged) by existing laws and public policy, *watch out*, because those rules of the game can change suddenly and rapidly. Tax laws can be rewritten. New industries can be subsidized and old ones can lose their subsidies. Social welfare benefits—such as tuition scholarships, aid for dependent children, health insurance, social security, and the like—can change rapidly. Such public policy change, created by the actions of legislators and court decisions, can create new beneficiaries and new categories of losers.

3. *Changing yourself.* To the extent that the directions of change in the world are not subject to your control, you must be able to adapt to change. That means that if you can't modify you environment, you need to be able to modify youself. There are, for sure, limits to how much self-modification is possible; there are needs rooted in biology, and therefore the possibility of human characteristics not subject to self-modification. But beyond these biologically based requirements, other aspects of the human self and its needs are constructed by the socialization process and culture and are quite mutable. But since we learn many of these needs early in life, and often inherit them from an older generation, they are highly susceptible to being frustrated by the changing conditions of the social world. A great amount of human unhappiness and frustration results from becoming locked into a certain set of learned expectations that cannot be satisfied in a world of change. To believe that to be happy we must realize any particular set of learned expectations is to live with illusion. People can live and thrive under all kinds of conditions. Fortunately, the *self* is quite mutable.

Let me ilustrate this point by discussing what I think is a major impediment to happiness among contemporary Americans. We are, I believe, still quite bound by the American cultural dream of universal affluence. We would all like to be rich, and we believe that happiness is to be found in owning more things. This consumerist cultural ethic may have been appropriate in an expanding frontier society or in the post-World War II period of continuous expansion, but I think that today it is becoming a central problem in American culture. That many can realize the consumerist dream is increasingly unlikely in a crowded world of limits and tradeoffs, where there are no open frontiers (except those of the human spirit), and in which there are possibily absolute limits for growth in material consumption. The point is that the need for high levels of material consumption is a culturally programmed need that one can simply define away (if, of course, one learns to resist the seductive appeals of the consumerist ethic). You need not be unhappy because you are not rich and affluent. That is a self-imposed frustration. We need to learn to transcend the seemingly natural questions in the American scheme of things (such as, How can I get more?) to be able to ask other sorts of questions, such as, How much is enough? and whether or not more will be better. These are actually not natural questions in the American scheme of things. But they are, I argue, crucial questions to adapting positively to change in an age of seemingly stubborn limits to cornucopian material growth.

Self-change may demand breaking through the expectations others have for you, whether these are well intentioned or vicious. It may mean not accepting "your place" anymore. It may mean struggling to gain control of the self and to restore the unity of your mind and body. It certainly means putting aside cynicism and fatalism. The attitudes that people are basically rotten and that nothing can ever be changed are part of an ideology that encourages inaction and passivity (Ash Garner, 1977:412) and are the antithesis of creative self-mutation. If you cannot change the world, you can change yourself and redefine the expectations that make you unhappy.

4. *Changing society.* It is true that some things are, practically speaking, beyond our ability as individuals to control. In the short run, we must adapt to them to live. But in fact how people live as individuals and the choices they make do indeed shape the direction and pace of change. Although it is tempting to think of social change as some inexorable set of forces that proceeds willy-nilly, divorced from human action, in the final analysis is not true. To paraphrase Marx, men *do* make history, though they do not always do so on their own terms. I think it is important that while you are busy adapting and surviving in a changing world, you invest some time and energy working to bring about a better world for others. To live only for yourself is, I think, to live irresponsibly as a member of a human community. I think it is ethically irresponsible to profit from the misery of others or even to withdraw from any effort at social betterment and seek your own private salvation. That is my private opinion, but it is not only my own private opinion. It is also the ethical teaching of *all* of the great world religions, and of all of the purely secular ethical systems (such as secular humanism or Marxism). I think that being an ethically responsible person requires that you *be engaged* in some effort to shape social change in a positive direction.

It is true that most of us are not at the pinnacles of power in society, and it is tempting to throw up our hands and say, Well, what can I do? I'm just one person. My answer would be that it is important that you do *something*, however modest. Few of us are saints or martyrs, willing to devote our whole lives to the work of trying to create a better world for others. Most people do not want to be saints or martyrs; nor do the circumstances of their lives—their struggle to earn a living, to enjoy themselves a little, to live in peace with their family and friends—permit them to be (Ash Garner, 1977:412). But after satisfying such circumstances each of us has some measure of discretionary time, talent, energy, and resources that can be invested in efforts to shape the outcomes of the human journey in a positive way. Do you expend them all on yourself and self-gain? That, I think is ethically unconscionable.

How each of us pursues this ethical imperative to work for a better world will necessarily vary. It requires that you have some image of what a positive future would look like. And it requires that you have some knowledge about *how* to create change (I have devoted a whole chapter to this earlier, so I will not reiterate it here). One thing is certain. The task of creating a better world for others cannot be an individualistic effort; it must be a collective one. We cannot go it alone. We must unite in organizations that can help create a humane future or, to use Roberta Ash Garner's apt metaphor, "that can be the midwives for the birth of a new society. The birth pangs are inevitable. Our task is to ease the delivery, reduce the amount of suffering, and insure the life and health of the infant" (1977:412). You may not as yet have found an organization that is completely worthy of your efforts. But there are a large variety of organizations pursuing different goals and having different tactics. I urge you to learn more about them and to adopt a cause and a "tribe" that reflects your vision of the good society.

REFERENCES

Alexander, C.
　　1984　"Pulling the nuclear plug." Time magazine, Feb. 2.
Alinsky, Saul
　　1972　Rules for Radicals. New York: Vintage Press.
American Enterprise Institute
　　1981　"Public opinion roundup." Public Opinion, Sept./Aug. American Enterprise Institute for Policy Research.
Amin, Samir
　　1976　Unequal Development: An Essay on Social Formations of Peripheral Capitalism. New York: Monthly Review Press.
Andrade, R. de Castro
　　1982　"Brazil: the economics of savage capitalism," in Bienefeld and Godfrey (eds.), The Struggle for Development. Chichester, UK: John Wiley and Sons Ltd.
Applebaum, Richard P.
　　1970　Theories of Social Change. Chicago: Markham Publishing Co.
Aron, Raymond
　　1968　Progress and Disillusion. New York: Fredrick A. Praeger.
Ash Garner, Roberta
　　1977　Social Change. Chicago: Rand McNally Publishing Co.
Associated Press
　　1986　"Economic pie sliced 'thinner in heartland.'" Omaha World Herald, July 10:1.
Baran, Paul
　　1957　The Political Economy of Growth. New York: Monthly Review Press.
Barber, Bernard
　　1971　"Function, variability, and change in ideological systems." Pp. 244-65 in Barber and Inkles (eds.), Stability and Social Change. Boston: Little Brown.
Barnet, Richard J.
　　1980　The Lean Years: Politics in the Age of Scarcity. New York: Simon and Schuster.

Barnet, Richard J., and Ronald E. Muller
    1974   Global Reach: The Power of Multinational Corporations. New York: Simon and
            Schuster.
Barnett, Homer G.
    1953   Innovation: The Basis of Cultural Change. New York: McGraw Hill.
Bassis, Michael S., Richard J. Gelles and Ann Levine
    1982   Social Problems. New York: Harcourt Brace Jovanovich.
Beach, Stephen W.
    1977   "Social movement radicalization: the case of the People's Democracy in Northern
            Ireland." The Sociological Quarterly, 18, 3:305-18.
Beal, George M., and Everett Rogers
    1959   "The scientist as referent in the communication of new technology." Public Opinion
            Quarterly 22:555-63.
Beal, George M., et al.
    1964   "Social action in civil defense: strategy of public involvement in county civil defense
            education programs." Ames, IA: Agriculture and Home Economics Experimental Sta-
            tion.
Becker, Marshall H.
    1968   "Factors affecting the diffusion of innovation among health professionals." Paper read
            at the conference of the American Public Health Association, Detroit, MI.
Bell, Daniel
    1969   The Coming of Post-Industrial Society. New York: Basic Books.
Bennis, Warren G., Kenneth D. Benne, and Robert Chin
    1985   The Planning of Change. New York: Holt, Rinehart and Winston.
Berger, Peter, Brigitte Berger, and Hansfried Kellner
    1973   The Homeless Mind: Modernization and Consciousness. New York: Vintage Books.
Berger, Peter L., and Thomas Luckmann
    1967   The Social Construction of Reality. New York: Doubleday.
Berk, Richard A.
    1974   Collective Behavior. Dubuque, IA: Wm C. Brown Publishers.
Berle, Adolf, and Gardner Means
    1934   The Modern Corporation and Private Property. New York: Macmillan.
Birdsall, Nancy
    1980   "Population and poverty in the developing world." Population Bulletin 35:1-48.
Blake, Judith
    1979   "Structural differentiation and the family: a quiet revolution," in Hawley (ed.), Socie-
            tal Growth: Processes and Implications. New York: The Free Press.
Bluestone, Barry, and Bennett Harrison
    1982   The Deindustrialization of America. New York: Basic Books.
Blumer, Herbert
    1962   "The field of collective behavior," in Lee (ed.), Principles of Sociology. New York:
            Barnes and Noble Inc.
    1969   "Social movements," Pp. 8-29 in McLaughlin (ed.), Studies in Social Movements: A
            Social Psychological Perspective. New York: The Free Press.
Bondurant, Joan V.
    1972   "Satyagraha as applied socio-political action," in Zaltman, Kotler, and Kaufman (eds.),
            Creating Social Change. New York: Holt, Rinehart and Winston.
Boston Globe
    1986   "Ozone is simple gas that shields world from harmful radiation." Omaha World Herald,
            Nov 23:1K.
Boulding, Kenneth
    1970   A Primer on Social Dynamics. New York: The Free Press.
Braverman, Harry
    1974   Labor and Monopoly Capital: the Degredation of Work in the Twentieth Century. New
            York: Monthly Review Press.
Brinton, Crane
    1938/1965   The Anatomy of Revolution. Englewood Cliffs, NJ: Prentice-Hall.

Brown, Lester R.
  1976 World Population Trends. Washington, DC: Worldwatch Paper #8.
  1986a "A generation of deficits," in Brown et al. (eds), State of the World; 1986. A Worldwatch Institute Report. New York: W.W. Norton.
  1986b "Redefining national security," in Brown et al. (eds.), New York State of the World; 1986. A Worldwatch Institute Report. New York: W.W. Norton.
Brown, Lester R. et al.
  1986 State of the World, 1986. A Worldwatch Institute Report. New York: W.W. Norton.
Brown, Michael, and A. Goldin
  1973 Collective Behavior: A Review and Reinterpretation of the Literature. Pacific Palisades, CA: Goodyear.
Burnam, Walter
  1969 "The end of American party politics." In Etzkowitz (ed.), 1974, Is America Possible? Social Problems from Conservative, Liberal and Socialist Perspectives. St. Paul, MN: West Publishing Co.
Burns, Tom, and G. M. Stalker
  1961 The Management of Innovation. London: Tavistock.
Burton, Michael G.
  1984 "Elites and collective protest." The Sociological Quarterly 25:45-66.
Caplow, Theodore
  1964 Principles of Organization. New York: Harcourt Brace and World.
Caplow, Theodore, et al.
  1982 Middletown Families: Fifty Years of Change and Continuity. Minneapolis, MN: University of Minnesota Press.
Castells, Manuel
  1983 The City and the Grassroots: A Cross-Cultural Theory of Urban Social Movements. London: Edward Arnold.
Catton, William R., and Riley E. Dunlap
  1980 "A new ecological paradigm for post-exuberant sociology." American Behavioral Scientist 23 (Sept./Oct.): 15-47.
Chapin, F.S.
  1928 Cultural Change. New York: Century.
Chesshire, John, and Keith Pavitt
  1978 "Some energy futures," in Freeman and Jahoda (eds.), World Futures. London: Martin Robinson.
Chirot, Daniel
  1981 "Changing fashions in the study of the social causes of economic and political change," in Short (ed.), The State of Sociology. Beverly Hills, CA: Sage Publications, Inc.
  1986 Social Change in the Modern Era. New York: Harcourt Brace Jovanovich.
Chodak, Szymon
  1973 Societal Development. New York: Oxford University Press.
Clausen, A.W.
  1985 "Poverty in the developing countries—1985." The Hunger Project Papers, 3, March, The Hunger Project.
Coleman, James
  1982 The Asymmetric Society. Syracuse, New York: Syracuse University Press.
Coleman James W. and Donald R. Cressy
  1984 Social Problems, 2nd ed. New York: Harper and Row.
  1987 Social Problems, 3rd ed. New York: Harper and Row.
Coleman, James, et al.
  1957 "The diffusion of an innovation among physicians." Sociometry, 20: 253-70.
Collins, Randall
  1975 Conflict Sociology: Toward an Explanatory Science. New York: Academic Press.
Congressional Budget Office
  1983 Outlook for Economic Recovery, Part I. Washington, DC: Government Printing Office.
Cook, Earl
  1971 "The flow of energy in industrial society." Scientific American 224, 3:134-47.

Cooley, Charles H.
1902   (1964) Human Nature and the Social Order. New York: Scribners.
Coser, Lewis
1977   Masters of Sociological Thought. New York: Harcourt, Brace Jovanovich.
Couch, Lester, and J. P. R. French
1948   "Overcoming resistance to change." Human relations 1:512-32.
Cuca, Roberto
1980   "Family planning programs and fertility decline." Finance and Development 17, 4 (December):37-39.
Currie, Elliot, and Jerome Skolnick
1984   America's Problems: Social Issues and Public Policy. Boston, MA: Little Brown.
Cutler, M. Rupert
1986   cited in Associated Press, "Population mounts; concerns also grow." Omaha World Herald, Aug 7.
Cuzzort, Ray, and Edith King
1980   Humanity and Sociological Thought, 3rd ed. Hinsdale, IL: Dryden Press.
Dadzie, K. K. S.
1980   "Economic development." Scientific American 243, 3 (Sept.):1-7.
Dahrendorf, Ralph
1958   "Out of utopia: toward a reorientation of sociological analysis." American Journal of Sociology 64:115-27.
1959   Class and Class Conflict in Industrial Society. Stanford: Stanford University Press.
1968   Essays in the Theory of Society. Stanford: Stanford University Press.
Darmstadter J.
1971   Energy in the World Economy. Baltimore, MD: The Johns Hopkins Press.
Davies, James C.
1969   "The J-curve of rising and declining satisfactions as a cause of some great revolutions and a contained rebellion." Pp. 690-730 in Graham and Gurr (eds.), The History of Violence in America. New York: Praeger Publishers.
Davis, Burl E.
1968   "System variables and agricultural innovativeness in eastern nigeria." Ph.D. thesis, Michigan State University.
Davis, Richard H.
1965   "Personal and organizational variables related to the adoption of educational innovations in a liberal arts college." Ph.D. thesis, University of Chicago.
DeFleur, Melvin L., William V. D'Antonio, and Lois B. DeFleur
1984   Sociology: Human Society, 4th ed. New York: Random House.
Demerath, Nicholas J.
1984   "World politics and population," in Strange (ed.), Paths to International Political Economy. London: George Allen and Unwin.
Dennis, Wayne
1955   "Variations in productivity among creative workers." Scientific Monthly 80:277-78.
Dickson, David
1974   The Politics of Alternative Technology. New York: Universe.
Douglas, John H.
1976   "The slowing growth of world population." Science News 13 (November):316-17.
Durkheim, Emile
1947   The Division of Labor in Society. (Original publication date, 1893.) New York: The Free Press.
Duvall, Evelyn M., and Brent C. Miller
1985   Marriage and Family Development, 6th ed. New York: Harper and Row.
Edwards, Lyford P.
1927   The Natural History of Revolution. Chicago: University of Chicago Press.
Eibler, Herbert J.
1965   "A comparison of the relationship between certain aspects or characteristics of the structure of the high school faculty and the amount of curriculum innovation." Ph.D. thesis, University of Michigan.

Eitzen, Stanley
1974   In Conflict and Order: Understanding Society. Boston, MA: Allyn and Bacon.
Eldersveld, Samuel J.
1964   Political Parties: A Behavioral Analysis. Chicago, IL: Rand McNally.
Ellul, Jaques
1964   Technological Society. New York: Vintage.
Emerson, Richard M.
1962   "Power-dependence relations." American Sociological Review 27 (Feb) 31-41.
Etzioni, Amitai
1968a   "Shortcuts to social change?" Public Interest 12:40-51.
1968b   The Active Society. New York: The Free Press.
Fairweather, George W.
1972   Social Change: The Challenge to Survival. Morristown, NJ: General Learning Press.
Fanon, Franz
1967   Black Skins and White Masks. Charles Lam Markmann (trans.). New York: Grove Press.
1968   The Wretched of the Earth. Constance Farrington (trans). New York: Grove Press.
Ferguson, Thomas, and Joel Rogers
1986   "The myth of America's turn to the right." The Atlantic 257, 5 (May):43-53.
Firth, Raymond
1959   Social Change in Tikiopia: Re-study of a Polynesian Community after a Generation. London: Allen and Unwin.
Flavin, Christopher
1984   "Reassessing the economics of nuclear power," in Brown et al., State of the World, 1984. New York: W.W. Norton.
1986   "Moving beyond oil," in Brown et al., State of The World, 1986. A Worldwatch Institute Report. New York: W.W. Norton.
Fliegel, Fredrick C., and Joseph E. Kivlin
1966   "Attributes of innovations as factors in diffusion." American Journal of Sociology 72:235-48.
Food and Agriculture Organization
1977   FAO Production Yearbook, 1976. Rome.
Forrester, Jay W.
1985   "Economic conditions ahead: understanding the Kondratieff wave. The Futurist, June:16-20.
Frank, Andre Gunder
1969   Capitalism and Underdevelopment in Latin America: Historical Studies of Chile and Brazil. New York: Monthly Review Press.
1972   "Who is the immediate enemy?" in Crockcroft, Frank, and Johnson (eds.), Dependence and Underdevelopment: Latin America's Political Economy. Garden City, New York: Doubleday Anchor.
Freeman, Christopher, and Marie Jahoda
1978   World Futures: The Great Debate. London: Martin Robertson.
Freeman, David M.
1974   Technology and Society: Issues in Assessment, Conflict, and Choice. Chicago: Rand McNally.
Freeman, Jo
1979   Women: A Feminist Perspective, 2nd ed. Palo Alto, CA: Mayfield Publishing Co.
French, J. P. R., et al.
1960   "An experiment on participation in a Norwegian factory." Human Relations 3:3-19.
Furtado, Celso
1983   Accumulation and Development. New York: St. Martin's Press.
Fusfield, Daniel R.
1972   "The rise of the corporate state in America." Journal of Economic Issues 6, 1 (March).
Galbraith, John Kennan
1973   Economics and the Public Purpose. Boston, MA: Houghton Mifflin.

Galtung, Johan,
    1981   "Global processes and the world in the 1980s," in Hollis and Rosenau (eds.), World System Structure: Continuity and Change. Beverly Hills, CA: Sage Publications.

Gamson, William A.
    1968   "Rancorous conflict in community politics," in Clark (ed.), Community Structure and Decision-Making: A Comparative Analysis. San Francisco, CA: Chandler.
    1974   "Violence and political power: the meek don't make it." Psychology Today 8:35-41.
    1975   The Strategy of Social Protest. Homewood, IL: Dorsey Press.

Gannon, Thomas M.
    1981   "The New Cristian Right in America as a social and political force." Paper presented to the 1981 meeting of the Association for the Sociology of Religion, Chicago.

Gartner, Tim
    1981   "Bay area firms loaded with cash." San Francisco Chronicle, Jan. 16.

Garfinkel, Harold
    1967   Studies in Ethnomethodology. Englewood Cliffs, NJ: Prentice Hall.

Gerlach, Luther P., and Virginia H. Hine
    1970   People, Power, and Change: Movements of Social Transformation. New York: Bobbs-Merrill.

Getzels, Jacob W., and Phillip W. Jackson
    1962   Creativity and Intelligence: Explorations with Gifted Students. New York: John Wiley.

Giffin, Kim, and Larry Erlich
    1963   "The attitudinal effects of group discussion on a proposed change in company policy." Speech Monographs, 30:377-79.

Gilder, George
    1984   The Spirit of Enterprise. New York: Simon and Schuster.

Gillis, Malcolm, Dwight H. Perkins, Michael Roemer, and Donald R. Snodgrass
    1983   Economics of Development. New York: W.W. Norton.

Ginsberg, Eli
    1977   "The job problem." Scientific American (Nov.)

Ginsberg, Eli, and George Vojta
    1981   "The service sector of the U.S. economy." Scientific American (March).

Glenn, Norval, and J. L. Simmons
    1967   "Are regional and cultural differences diminishing?" Public Opinion Quarterly 31:176-93.

Goldstone, Jack A.(ed.)
    1986   Revolutions: Theoretical, Comparative, and Historical Studies. New York: Harcourt Brace Jovanovich.

Goode, William J.
    1982   The Family. Englewood Cliffs, NJ: Prentice-Hall.

Gorz, Andre
    1972   "Domestic contradictions of advanced capitalism," Pp. 478-491 in Edwards et al. (eds.), The Capitalist System. Englewood Cliffs, NJ: Prentice-Hall.

Gouldner, Alvin
    1954   Patterns of Industrial Bureaucracy. New York: The Free Press.

Granovetter, Mark S.
    1973   "The strength of weak ties." American Journal of Sociology 73:1360-80.

Gribben, John R.
    1981   Future Worlds. New York: Plenum Press.

Griffin, William B.
    1969   Culture Change and Shifting Populations in Central Northern Mexico. Tucson, AZ: University of Arizona Press.

Grimke, Sarah M.
    1848   Letters on the Equality of the Sexes and the Condition of Women. Boston MA: Isaac Knapp. Reprinted in 1970. New York: Source Book Press.

Gross, Neal, and Bryce Ryan
    1943   "Diffusion of hybrid seed corn in two Iowa communities." Rural Sociology 8, 1:15-24.

Gurin, Patricia
  1982   "Group consciousness." Newsletter of the Institute for Social Research (Spring/Summer), Pp. 4-5. Ann Arbor, MI: Institute for Social Research, University of Michigan.
Gurney, Joan N., and Kathleen J. Tierney
  1982   "Relative deprivation and social movements: a critical look at twenty years of theory and research." The Sociological Quarterly 23, 1:33-47.
Gurr, Ted
  1970   Why Men Rebel. Princeton, NJ: Princeton University Press.
Hadamard, Jaques
  1954   An Essay on the Psychology of Invention in the Mathematical Field. Princeton, NJ: Princeton University Press.
Hage, Jerald, and Michael Aiken
  1970   Social Change in Complex Organizations. New York: Random House.
Hannigan, John A.
  1985   "Alain Touraine, Manuel Castells, and Social Movement Theory: a critical appraisal" The Sociological Quarterly 26, 4:435-54.
Harper, Charles L.
  1974   "Spirit filled Catholics: Some biographical comparison." Social Compass XXI, 3:311-24.
  1981   "The Cult Controversy: Values in Conflict," proceedings of the Association for the Sociology of Religion-Southwest, pp. 65-72.
  1982   "Cults and communities: the community interfaces of three marginal religious movements," The Journal for the Scientific Study of Religion, 21,1:26-38.
Harper, Charles L., and Kevin Leicht
  1984   "Religious awakenings and status politics: sources of support for the New Religious Right." Sociological Analysis 45, 4:339-53.
Harrington, Michael
  1962   The Other America. New York: Macmillan.
Hawley, Amos H.
  1962   "Community power and urban renewal success." American Journal of Sociology 68:422-31.
Hays, Robert, and Robert Abernathy
  1980   "Managing our way into decline." Harvard Business Review (Sept./Oct.)
Heilbroner, Robert
  1974   An Inquiry into the Human Prospect. New York: W.W. Norton.
Herskovitz, Melville J.
  1947   Man and His Works. New York: Alfred Knopf.
Himmelstein, Jerome
  1986   "The social basis of antifeminism." Journal for the Scientific Study of Religion 25, 1:1-15.
Hoffer, Eric
  1951   The True Believer. New York: Mentor Books, New American Library.
Holdren, John
  1975   "Energy resources," in W.W. Murdock (ed.), Environment: Resources, Pollution, and Society. Sunderland, MA: Sinauer Associates.
Hoos, Ida
  1961   "When the computor takes over the office." Harvard Business Review 38:102-14.
Hopper, Rex
  1950   "The revolutionary process." Social Forces 28 (March):27-79.
Horowitz, Irving Louis
  1979   "Beyond democracy: interest groups and the patriotic gore." The Humanist (Sept./Oct.);4-10.
Horton, Paul, and Gerald Leslie
  1974   The Sociology of Social Problems. Englewood Cliffs, NJ: Prentice-Hall.
Howard, John R.
  1974   The Cutting Edge: Social Movements and Social Change in America. Philadelphia, PA: J.B. Lippincott.

Humphrey, Craig R., and Frederick R. Buttel
  1982   Environment, Energy, and Society. Belmont, CA: Wadsworth.
Huntington, Samuel P.
  1972   "Reform and political change," in Zaltman, Kotler, and Kaufman (eds.), Creating Social Change. New York: Holt, Rinehart, and Winston.
Hutter, Mark
  1981   The Changing Family: Comparative Perspectives. New York: John Wiley.
Inkeles, Alex
  1979   "Continuity and change in the American national character," in Lipset (ed.), The Third Century. Stanford, CA.: Hoover Institution Press.
Inkeles, Alex, and David H. Smith
  1974   Becoming Modern. Cambridge, MA: Harvard University Press.
Institute for Social Research Newsletter
  1979a   "Job satisfaction has decreased." Ann Arbor, MI: Institute for Social Research, University of Michigan.
  1979b   "Deepening distrust of political leaders is jarring public's faith in institutions." Ann Arbor, MI: Institute for Social Research, University of Michigan.
International Energy Agency
  1985   Annual Oil Market Report, 1984. Paris: Organization for Economic Cooperation and Development.
Janowitz, Morris
  1978   The Last Half Century. Chicago, IL: The University of Chicago Press.
Jenkins, Craig J.
  1983   "Resource mobilization theory and the study of social movements," Annual Review of Sociology, 9:527-53.
Johnson, Allan G.
  1986   Human Arrangements: An Introduction to Sociology. New York: Harcourt Brace Jovanovich.
Kahl, Joseph A.
  1968   The Measurement of Modernism. Austin, TX: University of Texas Press.
Kahn, Herman, W. Brown, and L. Martel
  1976   The Next 200 Years. New York: Morrow.
Kahn, Herman, and John B. Phelps
  1979   "The economic present and future." Futurist, June.
Kahn, Herman, and Anthony J. Weiner
  1967   The Year 2000: A Framework for Speculation on the Next Thirty-Three Years. New York: Macmillan Co.
Katz, Elihu
  1960   "Communication research and the image of society: Convergence of two traditions." American Journal of Sociology 65:435-40.
Katz, Elihu, and Paul Lazarsfeld
  1955   Personal Influence: The Part Played by People in the Flow of Mass Communication. New York: The Free Press.
Kelly, H. H., and E. H. Volkhart
  1952   "The resistance to change of group-anchored attitudes." American Sociological Review, 17:435-65.
Klapp, Orrin E.
  1969   Collective Search for Identity. New York: Holt, Rinehart and Winston.
Klapper, Joseph
  1960   The Effects of Mass Communication. New York: The Free Press.
Korhauser, Arthur
  1959   The Politics of Mass Society. New York: The Free Press.
Kriesberg, Louis
  1982   Social Conflicts. Englewood Cliffs, NJ: Prentice-Hall.
Kristof, Nicholas D.
  1985   "The third world: Back to the farm." New York Times, Sunday, July 28, Section 3:1,8.

Kroeber, A. L.
1937 "Diffusion," in Seligman and Johnson (eds.), The Encyclopedia of the Social Sciences II. New York: Macmillan.

Ladd, Everett C.
1979 "The American Political System Today," in Lipset (ed) The Third Century: America as a Postindustrial Society. 1979. Stanford, CA: The Hoover Institution Press.

Ladd, Everett C., and Charles D. Hadley
1975 Party Systems: Political Coalitions from the New Deal to the 1970s. New York: W. W. Norton.

Larsen, Otto
1964 "Social effects of mass communication," in Faris (ed.), Handbook of Modern Sociology. Chicago, IL: Rand McNally.

Lasch, Christopher
1979 The Culture of Narcissism: American Life in an Age of Diminishing Expectations. New York: The Free Press.

Law, Kim S., and Edward J. Walsh
1983 "The interaction of grievances and structures in social movement analysis." The Sociological Quarterly, 24, 1:123-36.

LeBon, Gustav
1896/1960 The Crowd. New York: Viking Press.

Lee, Dorothy
1959 "Are basic needs ultimate?" in Lee (ed.), Freedom and Culture: Essays. Englewood Cliffs, NJ: Prentice-Hall.

Lehman, Harvey C.
1953 Age and Achievement. Princeton, NJ: Princeton University Press.

Leighton, Alexander H.
1945 Governing Men. Princeton, NJ: Princeton University Press.

Leik, Robert J., and Anita Sue Kolmann
1977 "Isn't it more rational to be wasteful?" Paper presented at the University of Houston Energy Symposium, Houston, TX.

Lenski, Gerhard, and Jean Lenski
1982 Human Societies: An Introduction to Macrosociology. New York: McGraw-Hill.

Lerner, Daniel
1958 The Passing of Traditional Society: Modernizing the Middle East. New York: The Free Press.
1968 "Modernization, social aspects." International Encyclopedia of the Social Sciences 10:387. New York: The Free Press.

Levitan, Sar
1984 "The changing workplace." Society 21, 6 (Sept./Oct.):41-48.

Levy, Marion, Jr.
1966 Modernization and the Structure of Societies, vol 1. Princeton,NJ: Princeton University Press.

Lewy, Guenter
1974 Religion and Revolution. New York: Oxford University Press.

Linton, Ralph
1936 The Study of Man. New York: Appleton Century-Crofts.

Lipset, Seymour M., and Earl Raab
1970 The Politics of Unreason: Right-Wing Extremism in America. New York: Harper and Row.

Lipset, Seymour M., and William Schneider
1983 The Confidence Gap: Business, Labor, and Government in the Public Mind. New York: The Free Press.

Lofchie, Michael F., and Stephen K. Commins
1984 "Food deficits and agricultural politicies in sub-Saharan Africa," The Hunger Project Papers, 2, Sept. San Francisco, CA: The Hunger Project.

Lovins, Amory
   1976   "Energy strategy: The road not taken." Foreign Affairs (fall):65-96.
   1977   Soft Energy Paths. Cambridge, MA: Ballinger.
Lowenthal, Abraham F.
   1986   "Threat and Opportunity in the Americas." Cited in World Development Forum, 4, 6,
          March 31.
Mack, Raymond, and Calvin P. Bradford
   1979   Transforming America, 2nd ed. New York: Random House.
Magaziner, Ira C., and Robert B. Reich
   1982   Minding America's Business. New York: Harcourt Brace Jovanovich.
Makhijani, A.B., and A.J. Lichtenberg
   1972   "Energy and well being." Environment, 14:10-18.
Malbin, Michael
   1984   Money and Politics in the United States. Chatham, NJ: Chatham House Publishers.
Mamdani, Mahmood
   1972   The Myth of Population Control. London: Reeves and Turner.
Mannheim, Karl
   1950   Freedom Power and Democratic Planning. New York: Oxford University Press.
   1940   Man and Society in an Age of Reconstruction. New York: Harcourt Brace.
Marx, Karl
   1920   The Poverty of Philosophy. (H. Quelch, trans.) Chicago: Charles H. Kerr.
Maslow, Abraham H.
   1971   The Farther Reaches of Human Nature. New York: Viking Press.
Mastrand Pauline K., and Howard Rush
   1978   "Food and agriculture: When enough is not enough--the world food paradox." Chap-
          ter 4 in Freeman and Jahoda (eds.), World Futures. London: Martin Robertson and Co.
Mauss, Armand L.
   1975   Social Problems as Social Movements. Philadelphia, PA: J.B. Lippincott.
McCarthy, John D., and Mayer N. Zald
   1973   The Trends of Social Movements in America: Professionalization and Resource
          Mobilization. Morristown, NJ: General Learning Press.
McCleery, Richard H.
   1961   "The governmental process and informal social control," in Cressey (ed.), The Prisons:
          Studies in Institutional Organization and Change. New York: Holt, Rinehart and
          Winston.
McCormack, Thelma Herman
   1951   "The motivation of radicals." American Journal of Sociology.
McLaughlin, Barry
   1969   Studies in Social Movements: A Social Psychological Perspective. New York: The
          Free Press.
McPhail, Clark
   1971   "Civil disorder participation: A critical examination of recent research." American
          Sociological Review, 36, 6:1058-72.
Mead, George Herbert
   1934   Mind, Self, and Society: From the Standpoint of a Social Behaviorist. Chicago: Univer-
          sity of Chicago Press.
Meadows, Donella H., Dennis L. Meadows, Jorgen Randers, and William W. Behrens III
   1972   The Limits to Growth: A Report for the Club of Rome's Project on the Predicament
          of Mankind. New York: A Signet Book, New American Library, Inc.
Menzel, Herbert
   1960   "Innovation, integration, and marginality: a survey of physicians." American
          Sociological Review 25:704-13.
Menzel, Herbert, James Coleman, and Elihu Katz
   1957   "The diffusion of innovation among physicians." Sociometry 20:253-70.
Menzel, Herbert, and Elihu Katz
   1955   "Social relations and innovation in the medical profession: The epidemiology of a new
          drug." Public Opinion Quarterly 19:337-52.

Mesarovic, Mihajlo, and Eduard Pestel
    1974   Mankind at the Turning Point: The Second Report to the Club of Rome. New York: Signet Book, New American Library, Inc.

Michels, Robert
    1903/1949   Political Parties. New York: The Free Press.

Moore, Wilbert E.
    1974   Social Change, 2nd ed. Englewood Cliffs, NJ: Prentice-Hall.

Morse, Nancy C., and Everett Riemer
    1956   "The experimental change in a major organizational variable." Journal of Abnormal and Social Psychology 52:120-29.

Mott, Paul E.
    1965   The Organization of Society. Englewood Cliffs, NJ: Prentice Hall.

Murdoch, William W.
    1980   The Poverty of Nations. Baltimore, MD: Johns Hopkins University Press.

Murray, Charles
    1984   Losing Ground: American Social Policy, 1950-1980. New York: Basic Books.

Naisbitt, John
    1982   Megatrends. New York: Warner Books.

Newhouse News Service
    1986a   "The year is 2050; Earth warmer, more dangerous." Omaha World Herald, Nov 23:1K.
    1986b   "Stormier planet seen as ocean temps rise." Omaha World Herald, Nov 23:1K.

Nisbet, Robert A.
    1969   Social Change and History. London: Oxford University Press.

Nunn, Clyde Z., Harry J. Crockett, and J. Allen Williams
    1978   Tolerance for Non-conformity. San Francisco, CA: Jossey-Bass.

O'Neill, Gerald K.
    1977   The High Frontier. London; Cape.

O'Neill, William
    1969   Everyone Was Brave: The Rise and Fall of Feminism. Chicago: Quadrangle Books.

Oberschall, Anthony
    1973   Social Conflict and Social Movements. Englewood Cliffs, NJ: Prentice-Hall.

Ogburn, William F.
    1922   Social Change with Respect to Culture and Original Nature. New York: B.W. Huebsch.
    1927   Social Change with Respect to Culture and Original Nature. Revised edition. New York: Viking.
    1938   Social Change, 1950. New York: Viking Press.

Olsen, Marvin E.
    1978   The Process of Social Organization, 2nd ed. New York: Holt, Rinehart and Winston.

Oltmans, Willem L., (ed.)
    1974   On Growth: The Crisis of Exploding Population and Resource Depletion. New York: Capricorn Books, G.P. Putnam's Sons.

Oppenheimer, Martin
    1969   The Urban Guerrila. Chicago: Quadrangle Press. Organization for Economic Cooperation and Development,
    1982   Economic Outlook. Paris, December.

Osborne, David
    1984   "America's plentify energy resource." The Atlantic Monthly (March):85-102. 1986 "The origin of petroleum." The Atlantic Monthly (Feb.):39-54.

Page, Ann L., and Donald A. Clelland
    1978   "The Kanawha County textbook controversy: A study of the politics of life style concern." Social Forces 57, 1:265-81.

Palmore, Erdman
    1969   "Predicting longevity: A follow-up controlling for age." The Gerontologist 9 (winter):247-50.

Parsons, Talcott
    1951   The Social System. Glencoe, IL: The Free Press.
    1966   Societies. Englewood Cliffs, NJ: Prentice-Hall.
Parsons, Talcott, and Robert F. Bales
    1955   Family Socialization and Interaction Process. Glencoe, IL: The Free Press.
Payer, Cheryl
    1975   The Debt Trap: The IMF and The Third World. New York: Monthly Review Press.
Pelto, Pertti J., and Ludger Muller-Willie
    1972   "Snowmobiles: Technological revolution in the Arctic," in Bernard and Pelto (eds.), Technology and Cultural Change. New York: Macmillan.
Perrow, C.
    1979   "Three Mile Island: A normal accident." Unpublished Manuscript, cited in Bassis and Gelles, Social Problems, 1982:103. New York: Harcourt Brace Jovanovich.
Pettigrew, Thomas F.
    1964   A Profile of the Negro American. Princeton, NJ: Van Nostrand.
Pfohl, Stephen J.
    1985   Images of Deviance and Control: A Sociological History. New York: McGraw-Hill Book Co.
Phillips, Joe
    1984   "Economic pastoral and hunger-two perspectives." Covenant 4,8.
Pirages, Dennis
    1978   The New Context for International Relations: Global Ecopolitics. Belmont, CA: Duxbury Press.
    1984   "An ecological approach." Pp. 53-69 in Strange (ed.), Paths to International Political Economy. London: George Allen and Unwin.
Piven, Frances Fox, and Richard A. Cloward
    1982   The New Class War: Reagan's Attack on the Welfare State and Its Consequences. New York: Pantheon Books.
Pohl, Frederick
    1981   "Science fiction and science: a sometimes synergy." National Forum LXI, 3 (summer):6-7.
Polk, Barbara B.
    1974   "Male power and the women's movement." The Journal of Applied Behavioral Science 10, 3:415-31.
Pomper, Gerald
    1984a   "Party politics." Society 21,6:61-68.
    1984b   "The decline of the party in American elections." Political Science Quarterly 92:21-42.
Population Reference Bureau
    1985   World Population Data Sheet, cited in "Population Mounts; Concerns Also Grow," The Omaha World Herald, Aug 7, 1986.
Qadir, Abdul S.
    1966   "Change in the rural philippines: an analysis of compositional effects." Ph.D. thesis, Cornell University.
Queenley, Mary, and David Street
    1965   "The impact of the continuous development approach." Chicago: University of Chicago, Center for Social Organization Studies, Working Paper #45.
Redfield, Robert, Ralph Linton, and Melville Herskovitz
    1936   "Memorandum on the study of acculturation." American Anthropologist 38:149-52.
Reichstul, Henri-Philippe, and Goldenstein, Lidia
    1980   "Do complexo cafeiro a industgrializacao," Gazeta Mercantil, Edicao Especial, 19 January.
Reiss, Ira L.
    1980   Family Systems in America, 3rd ed., New York: Holt, Rinehart and Winston.
Reynolds, Lloyd G.
    1983   "The spread of economic growth to the third world: 1850-1980." Journal of Economic Literature 21 (Sept.):941-80.

Rhodes, Robert I.
1970　Imperialism and Underdevelopment: A Reader. New York: Monthly Review Press.
Richardson, James T, M. T. Stewart, and R. B. Simmonds
1979　Organized Miracles: A Study of a Contemporary Youth Communal Fundamentalist Organization. New Brunswick, NJ: Transaction Books.
Riesman, David, et al.
1961　The Lonely Crowd: A Study in the Changing American Character. New Haven, CT: Yale University Press.
Rigney, Bernice
1986　Personal communication.
Ritzer, George E.
1983　Sociological Theory. New York: Random House.
Robertson, Thomas S.
1976　"The determinants of innovative behavior." Paper read at the conference of the American Marketing Association, Washington, DC.
Rodgers, Roy H.
1973　Family Interaction and Transaction. Englewood Cliffs, NJ: Prentice-Hall.
Rogers, Everett M.
1962　Diffusion of Innovations. New York: The Free Press.
1973　"What are the opportunities and limitations in linking research with use? Presented at the International Conference on Making Population/Family Research useful. Honolulu, HI.
Rogers, Everett M., and Lawrence D. Kinkaid
1981　Communication Networks. New York: The Free Press.
Rogers, Everett M., and Floyd F. Shoemaker
1971　Communication of Innovations: A Cross Cultural Approach. New York: Free Press.
Rose, Stephen J.
1986　The American Profile Poster. New York: Pantheon Books.
Rosenthal, Donald B., and Robert L. Crain
1968　"Executive leadership and community innovation: The fluorodation experience." Urban Affairs Quarterly 1:39-57.
Rostow, W. W.
1962　The Process of Economic Growth. New York: W.W. Norton.
Rothman, Jack
1974　Planning and Organizing for Social Change: Action Principles from Social Science Research. New York: Columbia University Press.
Ryan, Bryce
1969　Social and Cultural Change. New York: Ronald Press.
Ryder, Norman
1965　"The cohort as a concept in the study of social change." American Sociological Review 30, 6:834-61.
Safilios-Rothschild, Constantina
1970　"Toward a cross-cultural conceptualization of family modernity" Journal of Comparative Family Studies 1:17-25.
Saxena, Anant P.
1968　"System effects on innovativeness among Indian farmers." Ph.D. thesis, Michigan State University.
Schaff, A.
1970　"The Marxist theory of social development," in Eisenstadt (ed.), Readings in Social Evolution and Development. Oxford: Pergamon Press.
Schattsneider, E. E.
1960　The Semi-Sovereign People. New York: Holt, Rinehart and Winston.
Schnaiberg, Allan
1980　The Environment: From Surplus to Scarcity. New York: Oxford University Press.
Schneider, Louis
1976　Classical Theories of Social Change. Morristown, NJ: General Learning Press.
Schneider, William
1986　"The new shape of American politics." Atlantic Monthly 259, 1 (Jan):39-60.

Schon, Donald
    1971   Beyond the Stable State. New York: W.W. Norton Co.

Schumacher, E. F.
    1973   Small Is Beautiful. New York: Perennial Library.

Schwartz, John E.
    1983   America's Hidden Success: A Reassessment of Twenty Years of Public Policy. New York: W.W. Norton.

Seashore, Stanley E., and David G. Bowers
    1963   "Changing the structure and functioning of an organization: Report of a field experiment." Ann Arbor, MI: University of Michigan, Insitute for Social Research, Survey Research Center, Monograph #33.

Seers, Dudley
    1963   "The stages of economic growth of a primary producer in the middle of the twentieth century." The Economic Bulletin (Ghana), 7, 4. Reprinted in Rhodes (ed.), 1970, Imperialism and Underdevelopment: A Reader. New York: Monthly Review Press.

Sharp, Lauriston
    1952   "Steel axes for stone age Australians." Human Organization, Vol 11, Number 1.

Shepard, Jon
    1981   Sociology. St. Paul, MN: West Publishing Co.
    1984   Sociology, 2nd ed. St. Paul, MN: West Publishing Co.

Shibutani, Tamotsu
    1955   "Reference groups as perspectives." American Journal of Sociology, 60:562-69. Chicago: University of Chicago Press.

Simmel, Georg
    1921   "The Conflict in modern culture," in Peter Etzkhorn (ed.), Georg Simmel: The Conflict in Modern Culture and Other Essays. New York: Teachers College, Columbia University, 1968.

Simpson, John H.
    1983   "Moral issues and status politics," in Liebman and Wuthnow (eds.), The New Christian Right. New York: Aldine.

Smelser, Neil J.
    1962   Theory of Collective Behavior. New York: The Free Press.
    1966   "The modernization of social relations." Pp. 110-21 in Wiener (ed.), Modernization: The Dynamics of Growth. New York: Basic Books.

Smith, James P., and Finis Welch
    1978   "Race differences in earnings: A survey and new evidence." Santa Monica, CA: Rand Corporation.

Sorokin, Pitrim
    1937-41   Social and Cultural Dynamics, 4 vols. New York: American Book Company.

Spector, Malcolm, and John Kitsuse
    1977   Constructing Social Problems. Menlo Park, CA: Cummings.

Spengler, Oswald
    1932   The Decline of the West. New York: Alfred A. Knopf.

Spindler, Louise S.
    1977   Cultural Change and Modernization. New York: Holt, Rinehart and Winston.

Stein, Morris I.
    1957   "Social and psychological factors affecting the creativity of industrial research chemists." Unpublished manuscript presented at the Industrial Research Institute. Pittsburg, PA (Oct.).

Stein, Morris I., and Shirley J. Heinze
    1960   Creativity and the Individual. New York: The Free Press.

Steward, Julian
    1955   "Evolution and progress," in Kroeber (ed.), Anthropology Today. Chicago: University of Chicago Press.

Stokes, Randall
    1975   "Afrikaner Calvinism and economic action: The Weberian thesis in South Africa." American Journal of Sociology 81:62-81.
    1984   Introduction to Sociology. Dubuque, IA: Wm C. Brown Publishers.

Swift, David W.
1971   Ideology and Change in the Public Schools. Columbus, OH: Charles E. Merrill Publishing Co.

Tausky, Curt
1984   Work and Society. Itasca, IL: F.E. Peacock, Publishers.

Tavris, Carol, and Carole Wade
1984   Sex Differences in Perspective, 2nd ed. New York: Harcourt Brace Jovanovich.

Thio, Alex O.
1971   "A reconsideration of the concept of adopter-innovator compatibility in diffusion research." Sociological Quarterly 12,1:56-68.

Thompson, W. Scott (ed.)
1978   The Third World: Premises of U.S. Policy. San Francisco, CA: Institute for Contemporary Studies.

Thurow, Lester
1980   The Zero Sum Society. New York: Penguin.
1984   "Building a world-class economy." Society 22, 1 (Nov./Dec.):16-29.

Tinbergen, Jan (coordinator)
1976   RIO: Reshaping the International Order. New York: Dutton.

Toch, Hans
1965   The Social Psychology of Social Movements. Indianapolis, IN: Bobbs-Merrill Co.

Toffler, Alvin
1970   Future Shock. New York: A Bantam Book, Random House.
1972   The Futurists. New York: Random House.
1980   The Third Wave. New York: William Morrow.

Touraine, Alain
1981   The Voice and the Eye: An Analysis of Social Movements. (Alan Duff, trans.). London: Cambridge University Press.

Toynbee, Arnold
1962   A Study of History. New York: Oxford University Press.

Tugwell, Franklin
1973   Search for Alternatives: Public Policy and the Study of the Future. Cambridge, MA: Winthrop.

Turnbull, Colin M.
1962   The Lonely African. New York: Simon and Schuster.

Turner, Jonathan
1986   The Structure of Sociological Theory. Fourth editon. Homewood, IL: Dorsey Press.

Turner, Jonathan, and Leonard Beeghley
1986   The Emergence of Sociological Theory. Homewood, IL: The Dorsey Press.

U.S. Bureau of Labor Statistics
1980   Cited in "The Typical Family is Hard to Find," in The Omaha World Herald. March 2, 1980:1-B.

U.S. Congress, Joint Economic Committee
1982   Economic Report to the President. Washington, DC: Government Printing Office.
1983   Economic Report to the President. Washington, DC: Government Printing Office.

U.S Department of Commerce, Bureau of the Census
1965   Statistical Abstract of the United States. Washington, DC: Government Printing Office.
1970   Historical Statistics of the United States, Colonial Times to 1970, Part I. Washington DC: Government Printing Office.
1980   Statistical Abstract of the United States. Washington, DC: Government Printing Office.
1981   "Concentration Ratios in Manufacturing, 1977," in Census of Manufacturers. Washington, DC: Government Printing Office.
1982   "Money Income of Households, Families, and Persons in the United States: 1980," Current Population Reports. Washington, DC: Government Printing Office.
1983a   Current Population Report, Series P-60, #137. Washington, DC: U.S. Government Printing Office.

1983b   Statistical Abstract of the United States. Washington, DC: Government Printing Office.

1984   Statistical Abstract of the United States. Washington, DC: Government Printing Office.

1985   World Population Data Sheet, Population Reference Bureau. Washington, DC: U.S. Government Printing Office.

1985   Statistical Abstract of the United States. Washington, DC: Government Printing Office.

1986   Statistical Abstract of the United States, Washington, DC: U.S. Government Printing Office.

1987   Statistical Abstract of the United States. Washington, DC: Government Printing Office.

Useem, Bert
1980   "Solidarity model, breakdown model, and the Boston antibusing movement" American Sociological Review 45:357-69.

Useem, Michael
1975   Protest Movements in America. Indianapolis, IN: Bobbs-Merrill.

Usher, Abbott P.
1954   A History of Mechanical Inventions. Cambridge, MA: Harvard University Press.

Vago, Steven
1980   Social Change. New York: Holt, Rinehart and Winston.

Van den Ban, Anne W.
1960   "Locality group differences in adoption of new farm practices." Rural Sociology 25:308-20.

VanderZanden, James W.
1986   Sociology: The Core. New York: Alfred A. Knopf.

Wallach, Michael A., and Nathan Kogan
1965   "Creativity and intelligence in children's thinking." Trans-Action (Jan.-Feb.):38-43

Wallerstein, Immanuel
1974   The Modern World System. New York: Academic Press.

Wallis, Roy
1977   The Road to Total Freedom. New York: Columbia University Press.

Walsh, Edward J.
1981   "Resource mobilization and citizen protest in communities around Three Mile Island." Social Problems 29:1-21.

Warren, Ronald
1976   Social Change and Human Purpose: Toward Understanding and Action. Chicago: Rand McNally.

Wattenberg, Ben J.
1976   The Real America. New York: Capricorn.

Weber, Max
1905   (1958) The Protestant Ethic and the Spirit of Capitalism. New YorK: Scribner's.
1921a   Economy and Society. Totowa, NJ: Bedminister Press.
1921b   The Protestant Ethic and the Spirit of Capitalism. New York: Scribner's.

Weinmann, Gabriel
1982   "On the importance of marginality: One more step into the two step flow of co munication." American Sociological Review 47:764-73.

Weinstein, E. A., and P. Deutschberger
1963   "Some dimensions of altercasting." Sociometry 26:454-66.

White, Gordon
1982   "North Korean juche: The political economy of self-reliance," in Bienefeld and Godfrey (eds.), The Struggle for Development: National Strategies in an International Context. Chichester, UK: John Wiley and Sons, Ltd.

White, Leslie
1949   The Science of Culture. New York: Farrar and Strauss.

White, Theodore
1985   "The danger from Japan." New York Times Magazine, July 28:18.

Wilkening, Eugene A.
    1960   "Why farmers quit doing things." Better Farming Methods 32:22-25.

Williams, Robin
    1970   American Society: A Sociological Interpretation, 3rd ed. New York: Alfred A. Knopf.

Wilson, John
    1973   Introduction to Social Movements. New York: Basic Books.

Wirth, Louis
    1957   "Urbanism as a Way of Life," in Hatt and Reiss, (eds.), Cities and Society. New York: The Free Press.

Wittfogel, Karl
    1957   Oriental Despotism. New Haven: Yale University Press.

Wood, James L, and Maurice Jackson
    1982   Social Movements: Development, Participation, and Dynamics. Belmont, CA: Wadsworth Publishing CompaNew York.

World Bank
    1982   World Development Report. New York: Oxford University Press.
    1984   World Development Report 1984. Washington, DC: The World Bank.
    1986   World Development Report. New York: Oxford University Press.

World Development Forum
    1986a   "India's new middle class," 4, 8 (April 30). Washington DC: World Hunger Project
    1986b   "Populations excess?" 4, 15 (Aug. 31). Washington, DC: World Hunger Project.
    1986c   "Mainstreet, U.S.A." 4, 17 (Sept. 30). Washington, DC: World Hunger Project.

Wriggins, W. H.
    1978   "Third world strategies for change," in Wriggins and Adler-Karlsson (eds.), Reducing Global Inequalities. Project of the Council on Foreign Relations. New York: McGraw-Hill.

Wunsch, James S.
    1977   "Traditional authorities, innovation, and development policy." Journal of Developing Areas 11, 3:357-72.

Yankelovich, Daniel
    1981   New Rules: Searching for Self-Fulfillment in A World Turned Upside Down. New York: Random House.

Yergin, Daniel, and M. Hillenbrand
    1982   Global Insecurity: A Strategy for Energy and Economic Renewal. Boston: Houghton Mifflin.

Yinger, Milton, and Steven Cutler
    1982   "The Moral Majority viewed sociologically" Sociological Focus 15, 4: 289-306.

Zald, Mayer M., and Roberta Asch
    1966   "Social movement organizations: growth, decay, and change." Social Forces 44:327-41.

Zaltman, Gerald
    1973   Processes and Phenomena of Social Change. New York: John Wiley.

Zaltman, Gerald, and Robert Duncan
    1977   Strategies for Planned Change. New York: Wiley Interscience.

Zaltman, Gerald, Robert Duncan, and Jon Holbeck
    1973   Innovations and Organizations. New York: Wiley Interscience.

Zaltman, Gerald, K. LeMasters, and M. Heffring
    1982   Theory Construction in Marketing: Some Thoughts on Thinking. New York: John Wiley.

Zimbardo, Phillip, Ebbe Ebbeson, and Christina Maslach
    1977   Influencing Attitudes and Changing Behavior. Reading, MA: Addison- Wesley Pub Co.

Zinmeister, Karl
    1985   "Snapshot of a changing America." Time Magazine. Sept. 2:16.

Zurcher, Louis A., and Russell L. Curtis
    1973   "A comparative analysis of propositions describing social movement organizations." The Sociological Quarterly 14, 2:175-88.

NAME INDEX

SUBJECT INDEX

Protestantism and capitalism, 59
public campaigns and innovation, 119

Q

quality of life and energy, 251-252

R

radicalization of social movements, 148-150
(*see also* revolutionary movements)
radical movements, 127, 146, 151
recession (global) in the 1970s and 1980s, 218,
224, 264-265
reeducative change strategy, 174 (*see also*
change strategies)
reference groups
and cross pressures, 186, 192
and interactionism, 91
reform movements, 127, 142, 152
relative deprivation
and feminism, 159
and social movements, 130
religion and popular revolts, 60
religious cults, 20
renewable energy resources, 250
reprivatization, 45
resistance
and innovation, 121
and reducing to change, 183
resource mobilization perspective and social
movements, 137
resources and development, 226 (*see also*
development; energy)
restratification (*see also* inequality, in
America; middle classes)
causes of, 50-51
regional and geographic, 51
and social class, 44, 49, 50
revolutionary movements, 142, 153, 165
right wing movements, 129, 132

S

scattered-site housing programs, 168-170
scientific methods, 9
secularization
and the future, 272

and innovation, 110
segmentation in social systems (vs. innovation), 106
self-change, 285
Seneca Falls Women's Rights Convention, 159
Senegal, 195
serendipitous learning and planning, 187
service economy, 29
significant events, 12
small-is-beautiful, 275, 278
social change
attitudes vs. behavior, 172-173, 176
basic conditions vs. short cuts, 191
and cross pressures, 186, 192
cyclical, 54, 68-70
definition of, 5
and definitions of situations, 91
dialectical, 54, 70-73
and individual adaption to, 4, 282-283
in institutions, populations, and structures,
12
and laws, 283
levels of, 6
linear, 63
and the mass media, 14, 114-116
and the "medical model," 191
and "muddling through," 187
and religion, 60
and social policy, 278, 282 (*see also* policy;
development; planning)
and sociology, 8-9
and stability, 5
top down vs. bottom up, 122
social conditions in third world countries, 196-
197
social construction of reality, 90 (*see also* interactionism)
social control
in America, 87
and conflict, 84
and the feminist movement, 162
and social movements, 135
social definition paradigm, 89 (*see also* interactionism)
social definitions of situations, 89 (*see also* interactionism)
social equilibrium, 78, 80 (*see also* homeos-
tasis; homeostatic system)
social inconsistencies and innovation, 104
social integration, 78 (*see also* consensus;
functionalism)
social justice in the U.S., 44, 82, 88, 95